Congress
against
Itself

Congress *against* Itself

ROGER H. DAVIDSON
and
WALTER J. OLESZEK

INDIANA UNIVERSITY PRESS
Bloomington & London

Published in Canada by Fitzhenry & Whiteside Limited, Don Mills, Ontario

Manufactured in the United States of America

Library of Congress Cataloging in Publication Data

Davidson, Roger H

Congress against itself.

Bibliography

Includes index.

1. United States.   Congress.   House—Committees.
I. Oleszek, Walter J., joint author.   II. Title.

JK1429.D38   1976   328.73'07'65   76-12378
ISBN 0-253-31405-4   1 2 3 4 5 81 80 79 78 77

To   Douglas and Christopher

R.H.D.

Janet

W.J.O.

CONTENTS

PREFACE

To say that Congress is held in low esteem by many citizens is no longer startling. So many commentators—journalists, editorialists, government specialists, and others—have embellished their careers by belittling our national legislature that its foibles are no longer newsworthy. There is, one must confess, much to belittle. The hoary precedents and creaky structures that serve to knit together the disparate purposes of 535 legislators sometimes border on the ludicrous, and in any event are on full public display. Behind the seeming majesty of presidential leadership or the solemnity of judicial decision making lie the same kinds of shortfalls and improvisations; but those institutions have been more successful than Congress at screening their inner machinations from public scrutiny. Yet nearly everyone seems intrigued by the workings of the Senate and the House of Representatives; indeed, the pace of the Nation's Capital perceptibly quickens whenever Congress returns to open a new session. Some scholars have professed to see in the structure of Congress a marvelously coordinated machine that mysteriously meshes to produce satisfactory if not brilliant results.

As close-hand observers of the congressional scene, we must confess that the truth lies somewhere in between these caricatures—more complex (as always) than conventional wisdom suggests. Many Capitol Hill traditions that form favorite targets for critics are in fact techniques that permit a conflict-laden institution like a legislature to maintain internal cohesion and stability. Too much ink has been spilled on trivial matters (how long must certain journalists continue to expose "congressional

junketing"?) and on issues (like seniority) that have lost much of their
urgency. Our own experience on Capitol Hill gives us a healthy respect
for our representatives who on the whole do a commendable job of serving their electorates' interests, insofar as those interests are articulated to
them. Considering the meager investment most people make in Congress' business—in terms of attention, information, and action—our national legislature provides leadership as enlightened as we deserve.

Yet Congress is seriously flawed as a policy-making instrument, so
much so that critical problems facing our society are not being addressed
as they should be. Two colleagues, Joseph Cooper of Rice University and
David Brady of the University of Houston, observe that at least since the
downfall of Speaker Cannon in 1910 the House of Representatives has
manifested a prolonged "crisis of adaptation," in which it has failed to
adjust its internal practices to cope with the rapidly changing national
and international environment. Lacking the strong centripetal force of
powerful leaders or disciplined parties, the House has become ever more
fractionalized and unmanageable. First the committees and now the subcommittees have become the nexus of activity; some aggressive and
some moribund, many of these self-contained work groups have taken
on the trappings of feudal domains whose leaders have adopted a policy
of mutual noninterference in the affairs of their peers. Thus vital, inter-
woven policy questions are confronted by a veritable phalanx of Capitol
Hill subcommittees, each striving for their own "piece of the action." The
result—in energy policy, environmental controls, health care, transportation, and many other questions—has often been chaos. Congressional
decision making sometimes resembles a meat slicer, reducing large public problems to a series of discrete, unrelated, and often contradictory
tidbits of policy.

Committee structure and procedures lie at the heart of Congress'
shortcomings because, as Woodrow Wilson pointed out nearly a century
ago, this is where the routine work of policy making takes place. To re-
cast jurisdictional lines, modernize procedures, consolidate supportive
services, and give leaders a true coordinating role—such steps would not
by themselves transform Congress into a more rational and equitable
policy-making body, but they would go a long way in that direction.
Creation of a House Select Committee on Committees in 1973—the first
concerted effort at committee reorganization in more than a generation—
was thus a hopeful occasion. The fact that it was instigated by the leadership augured well for its eventual success. The committee's struggle
for modernizing the House took place mainly outside the public's view
(the record was mostly public, but such things require more concentration than most citizens are willing to devote), but the public had a
large stake in its fate. Sometimes referred to as the "Bolling Committee"
after its chairman, the panel succeeded in producing a wide-ranging
plan for structural modification of the House—in one sense the most
comprehensive such design since the House began. What it failed to do
was to overcome inevitable objections to such changes voiced by committee and subcommittee barons. Its modest successes and its heart-
breaking failures speak volumes about the behavior and characteristics
of the House itself. As participants in the struggle, we believed that the
Select Committee's story should be told, not only to detail the practical

problems of reforming Congress but to illuminate essential features of its internal politics.

This book, then, focuses on the struggle for committee reform in the House of Representatives: how the reform plan was devised, what forces coalesced to oppose it, how the plan finally reached the House floor, and what happened there to facilitate adoption (on October 8, 1974) of a limited restructuring of House committees. Although we recount the events in some detail, we are interested in several more general questions. How and why do pressures for institutional change build up? Specifically, what developments led to creation of the Select Committee and today continue to plague the House? What factors facilitate or hinder the adoption of institutional changes? What happens when the legislators' immediate self-interest fails to harmonize with the institution's well-being? What are the unintended effects of change—sometimes so quixotic as to demand reforms of their own? What can the struggle over committee reform tell us about long-term prospects for maintaining the vitality of Congress? (The Senate suffers from the same problems as the House, though its smaller size mutes somewhat the problem of coordination. Accordingly, on March 31, 1976, the Senate created a select committee to study its committee system.) Definitive answers to those questions are elusive; but we will at least sketch some of the legislative terrain that reform proposals must circumnavigate.

Even at a narrative level, the Select Committee's history should hold considerable interest for informed citizens, not to mention professional observers of legislatures. The effort at restructuring committees—bastions of power and autonomy—proved even more arduous than we had first suspected. Some supporters of previous reforms became fierce opponents of committee reform. Cozy relations between congressional panels and outside interest groups often proved resistant to even the most innocent realignment schemes. Party caucuses, little used during much of the twentieth century, played a key role, especially for Democrats. Little-known House rules were invoked, though unsuccessfully, to bring the reform plan before the full House. The Select Committee's Republican vice chairman belatedly shifted support from his committee's reform plan to introduce a substitute of his own. Truly the Committee Reform Amendments of 1974 produced a legislative struggle.

Thanks to the idiosyncratic workings of congressional recruitment, we found ourselves working together as professional staff members of the Select Committee during its exciting and frustrating life. No professionals could ask for a more receptive setting for staff participation than we encountered while working with the committee. Much of our narrative in this book grew out of our personal observations of the events that took place. Incidents and quotations that appear without citation (especially in chapters 5 through 8) are derived from our personal observation and from the extensive notes which we accumulated. Occasionally, we have relied on the reports of trusted associates in writing our account.

Because the committee's report touched upon the whole range of congressional (and, hence, governmental) activity, staff preparation—through hearings, interviews, research, and informal fact-gathering—was no less than a crash course on the operations of our federal government. In pooling our ideas about congressional organization we were reminded again and again of the personal and professional self-effacement that is an inevitable part of any collective political enterprise. There is simply no "one best way" for organizing a legislative body. Political philosophy, policy preferences, even organizational habits dictate the type of structure that emerges, and the Select Committee's proposals, embodied in the original version of H. Res. 988, were no exception. At best, professional skills can merely help political actors to clarify their goals, identify structural alternatives, and illuminate likely consequences, intended or not, of various courses of action. They cannot conjure up a consensus when none exists or devise solutions that will realize everyone's goals.

While we have striven mightily for objectivity, we would be remiss if we did not confess our basic partisanship on behalf of what the committee was attempting to do. If a complex institution like Congress is to renew itself, someone must be authorized to step aside from day-to-day legislative activities and take a hard look at the way the institution is doing its work. And if meaningful changes are put forward, they are bound to provoke controversy. There is no way to make an omelet without breaking a few eggs, as they say; there is no way to reorganize without inconveniencing certain people, at least in the short run. In such a situation the best that proponents of change can do is to approach their task with discernment, fairness, and thick skins.

Chairman Richard Bolling not only proved a masterful presiding officer, but often turned committee sessions into post-graduate seminars because of his vast knowledge and insights about the ways of the House. Vice Chairman Dave Martin was no less dedicated to the cause of reform—a fact which eventually left him a disappointed man, estranged from the remainder of the committee. Two of the panel's junior members, Paul S. Sarbanes and William A. Steiger, embodied the highest traditions of the House; their combination of scholarship, wit, and common sense strikes us as a nearly ideal formula for enlightened public service. From our fellow staffers, too, we learned much. Linda H. Kamm, majority counsel, was a true legislative expert. Her knowledge of House procedures and precedents, the budgetary process, and Democratic party politics seemed inexhaustible. Moreover, she encouraged us throughout our study. Special Counsel Robert C. Ketcham's research into budgetary politics and energy policy benefited everyone with whom he worked. Melvin M. Miller, deputy chief of staff, shared his knowledge of House procedures and decision making in Republican inner circles. We were privileged to work with Gerald C. Grady and Terence T. Finn, whose comradeship and encouragement were invaluable. Without the learning experience we shared with our fellow staffers, we literally could not have written this book.

Many people assisted us in the specific task of writing the book. The entire manuscript was reviewed by Fred Pauls, deputy assistant chief of the Congressional Research Service's (CRS) Government Division. Louis Fisher and Clark Norton, two other CRS staff members, read portions of the study and made notable contributions. CRS Senior Specialist Walter Kravitz has given both of us valuable encouragement through the years. The CRS assumes no responsibility, however, for the facts and conclusions we report here. Nancy D. Davidson reviewed the manuscript and made many helpful editorial suggestions. At earlier states of the project, we tried out our ideas on friends and colleagues through lectures, conference papers, and articles in such journals as *The Annals, Policy Analysis,* and *Legislative Studies Quarterly.* To all those who tolerated our experimentations, and who did not hesitate to identify our errors, we express our gratitude. For whatever inaccuracies remain, alas, we have only ourselves to blame.

Friends often ask us whether reorganization makes any difference. For example, has the House benefited from the reform proposals that were approved? Had the Select Committee's plan not been weakened by the Democratic caucus, would today's Congress be a more effective policy-making body? We believe the answer to such queries is unquestionably in the affirmative, though we know full well that definitive judgments are hazardous. Congress' "crisis of adaptation" is a real and continuing phenomenon, to which structural anomalies contribute significantly. However, we are under no illusions that structural or procedural adjustments by themselves will solve all of Congress' problems, any more than the structural arrangements embodied in our Constitution solved the problem of nationhood. Americans have a tenacious and oftentimes touching faith in the ability of rules and structures to obliterate problems and liberate human nature for beneficial ends. No single reform of Congress can by itself achieve miraculous results. The central dilemma of the contemporary Congress is that individual legislators' careers are separated from the collective product of the institution. Performance is collective but accountability is individual. If we as citizens love our congressmen but ridicule Congress (as Richard Fenno has suggested), it is only because we have failed to realize that the two are ultimately and inextricably linked. And that brings us back to the central problem of political democracy: citizens ought to set high standards and hold elected officials to those standards; otherwise, we are bound to suffer in the long run. As the comic character Pogo once said, "We have met the enemy—and they is us!" Truer words were never uttered.

Santa Barbara, California   Roger H. Davidson
Washington, D.C.   and Walter J. Oleszek
April 1976

ONE

Reformism in Congress

INTEREST in congressional reform is one of the persistent themes in the literature on our national legislature. Academicians, journalists, and other close observers of the political scene have publicly worried over Congress during a good portion of the twentieth century. Their worries, which have magnified and sometimes distorted the genuine institutional problems of Congress, have produced a prodigious literature on congressional reform—its varieties, its imperatives, and even its politics.[1]

This fascination with reformism is not difficult to fathom. The amorphous body sometimes called the liberal intelligentsia, which is responsible for a large share of the commentaries on public life, has often displayed an aversion to the legislative style of decision making, especially toward specific congressional policies. If, as Thomas E. Cronin has compellingly argued, we have been beguiled by an awe-inspiring image of the omnipotent "textbook president," then it is equally true that the prevalent view of the "textbook Congress" has portrayed suspect qualities—inertia, disorderliness, and dispersion of responsibility. The spectacle of a conservative President confronting a liberal Congress, reinforced by the impact of such events as Vietnam and Watergate, has undermined much of the political basis for such criticisms. But if Congress falls short (as unquestionably it will) of the high expectations it has recently generated, the fires of reformism will certainly be rekindled, because American faith in the inherently optimistic liberal tradition tends to regard failure as an aberration, and structural reform as a means

1

of liberating the underlying progressive qualities of human nature.[2]

Reform is an attractive label for selling proposed innovations. From a political standpoint, it is important for proponents of change to label their proposals as reforms. That is true whether the issue is congressional reform, party reform, campaign financing reform, or tax reform. Journalists, legislators, scholars, or interest groups can more easily be wooed to the side of change if it is identified as reform. Girding themselves with rectitude, the reformers can then portray their opponents as protectors of nefarious and outmoded practices.

According to *Webster's Third New International Dictionary* (1961), reform means "to restore to a former good state." The word "reform," however, itself needs reforming. It is a loaded word. "Journalists and politicians," James Q. Wilson has written, believe that "any change that is broadly liberal or participatory in intent, and some changes that are libertarian in intent, are reforms."[3] He proposes that we rid ourselves of the word, or at least use it with great circumspection. "Reform" denotes change for the better; but whether change is reform depends on where you are standing. One person's reform is another's stumbling block. Nor is it possible to say with certainty whether a given innovation will resolve the problem for which it was designed, or even whether it will produce positive or negative results. Change usually brings in its wake costs as well as benefits. Moreover, the passage of time may render even the most useful innovations obsolete. History is strewn with examples of one generation's reforms that exacerbated the next generation's problems. Some innovations may require years or even decades before informed judgments can be reached about their total impact. As then Minority Leader Gerald Ford observed, " 'Reform' is a tricky word; change *per se* is not necessarily the same as progress. Each and every proposal for reform of Congress must be weighed against other suggested reforms, and all must be weighed in the balance of power between the branches of government."[4]

Yet the reformist tradition is strong and genuine. It reflects in its broadest sense the efforts of men and women to adjust their activities to changing patterns of reality. Legislative reforms, however, can be defined or categorized in several different ways. Sir Denis Brogan said that reform is a matter of making the "legislative department of the government of the United States adequate for the age of the H-bomb."[5] A lawyer put it this way, "Congressional reform in general means nothing less than the overall revitalization of the legislative branch of the United States Government, a reconstruction of the House and Senate through discard of anachronistic practices, and the adoption of twentieth-century procedures and utilization of contemporary techniques, to enable the Congress to effectively perform for modern-day America."[6] In 1910, during the floor fight to curb the immense power of Speaker Joseph Cannon, Champ Clark of Missouri said, "We are fighting to rehabilitate the House of Representatives and to restore it to its ancient place of honor and prestige in our system of government."[7] Ironically, the House under Speaker Cannon was clearly antireform, yet probably had more power in the political system than at any other time. All three definitions have a common theme: to restore Congress as a co-equal partner in the federal system.

A key problem in defining reform is contemporary uncertainty with respect to Congress' role in the polity. Without a clear notion of Congress' place in the larger political system, it is difficult to know whether the legislative branch is functioning as it should, or to evaluate reform proposals that might remedy its alleged deficiencies. Some legislators and scholars want to make Congress into the policy-making equivalent of a Brookings Institution. Others emphasize Congress' oversight responsibilities and urge deference to the President as chief legislator. A third group argues for disciplined national political parties that can take clearly defined policy positions; such a change would be implemented through cohesive majority party action in the House and Senate.

Congress' role varies as the demands on it change. As a dynamic institution, the legislative branch both reflects and responds to public sentiments. When Gerald Ford was the nation's first nonelective President, many citizens wanted Congress to fill a perceived leadership void. They expected Congress to develop a program of its own and to scrutinize critically the President's proposals. On the other hand, the American people wanted Congress to act quickly on President Franklin Roosevelt's New Deal and on President Lyndon Johnson's "Great Society."

What this underscores is that Congress has numerous and varying roles to perform: making laws, overseeing program implementation, representing group interests, serving constituents, educating citizens on public issues, and checking presidential authority. There might be disagreement as to the priority given them, but all are important legislative responsibilities. In view of the diversity of Congress' roles, it is no surprise that there is a large variety of reform proposals. Perhaps Congress will always have problems in meeting the obligations imposed by so many responsibilities. The result is a proliferation of both criticisms and reforms. It might be helpful, therefore, to analyze several typical criticisms of Congress and to examine Congress' reaction to some of them by briefly discussing the two most significant twentieth-century efforts to reform the House's committee system: the Legislative Reorganization Act of 1946 and the Committee Reform Amendments of 1974. Finally, after discussing legislative criticisms and these two major responses to them, some generalizations can be made about the politics of reform and the process of organizational change. Further, proposals for congressional reform will be categorized according to their subject matter, intent, or cause.

CRITICISMS OF CONGRESS

Historically, Congress has been a traditional whipping boy of the press and the public. Several considerations help to explain the poor public image of Congress. First, Congress' decision-making process is more open to public view than that of the executive branch or judiciary. Accordingly, if a representative or senator sounds ill-informed or advances an outrageous proposal during committee or floor debate, then representatives of the media are likely to stress that newsworthy event rather than the substance of the overall debate. While inanities also exist in the other branches of government, as witness the now famous White House tapes, reporters usually lack access to the early stages of executive or judicial planning.

A second consideration is the bad press received by Congress. No doubt part of this is Congress' fault. The President has learned to utilize the media to get his message across to the American people while Congress generally has not. Equally important, many important legislative events are simply ignored by broadcasters and reporters. Obviously covering the White House is both easier and more glamorous, but significant legislative events that go unreported have serious consequences, not the least of which is public ignorance about the roles and responsibilities of Congress. Moreover, the events that are sometimes reported border on the trivial or isolated rather than the significant. As Harvard Professor Arthur Maass noted:

> Congress suffers also from what appears to be a double standard for reporting the conduct of public servants. If an Assistant Secretary of State attends the Foliès Bergere while participating in a Paris international conference, this is not likely to be reported. If it is, it will be with understanding.
>
> If a member of Congress sees the same girlie show while on official committee business in Paris, this will be reported, and in a muckraking style.[8]

Third, there appears to be general public misunderstanding about the role of Congress. Public approbation is often high when Congress appears to agree with a popular President. During the first session of the 89th Congress, for example, 71 percent of the American people approved of Congress' performance. That can be partially explained by Congress' approval of many of President Johnson's "Great Society" programs. In our achievement-oriented society, the legislative record looked good to the public. But if Congress approves too many of the President's proposals, it is not long before detractors call it a rubber stamp. On the other hand, if Congress works its will in a deliberative fashion, and amends or proposes alternatives to presidential suggestions, then Congress may be labeled the obstructionist body.

Many citizens fail to appreciate that Congress is a co-equal branch of government with authority both to formulate public policies of its own and to ensure that the laws that it enacts are properly administered. Congress is not paid for piecework. Its productivity cannot be measured in terms of the number of public laws it enacts. By design and structure, Congress is a slow institution in comparison with the presidency and, perhaps, the judiciary. (On occasion, of course, it may act too quickly.) Congress is a consensus-building institution, which helps ensure that critical public policies will be accepted by the people. Hence, it may be unrealistic to criticize Congress for functioning as it was intended.

Fourth, Congress has often been criticized by its own members. This, too, helps to create a poor public image of the legislative branch. Legislators who attack the institution, but are unwilling to reform it, ought to be held accountable by the citizenry. In that regard, constituents might ask what their representatives are doing to improve the performance of the legislative branch, and then hold them accountable for the failures of Congress. Consequently, the performance of Congress as a whole might be strengthened.

Fifth, Congress is also criticized because it lacks sufficient modern technology to assist it in making informed policy judgments. Compared to the executive branch, Congress seems far behind in developing an independent automatic data-processing capability. If relevant and timely information is the key to informed decision making, then Congress should utilize every means possible to avail itself of the latest in computer and data-processing facilities. In this way, Congress' collective intelligence and capacity for making accurate and balanced judgments would be greatly strengthened.

Sixth, the various legislative party structures have failed to procure enough staff and other assistance to critique executive branch proposals, or to develop an independent party program. Numerous scholars have argued that disciplined political parties should formulate public policies, which could then be implemented through centralized congressional party structures. The goal of party government, so they hold, would facilitate national actions to meet national needs. However, party structures in Congress have traditionally been weak, although this may be changing in view of the revitalized party caucuses in both chambers.

The dilemma, however, is how to reconcile the presumed need for party discipline with a legislator's obligation to his constituents and his conscience.

Seventh, numerous jurisdictional overlaps among standing committees inhibit the formulation of coherent and coordinated national policies. As a *New York Times* editorial noted with regard to the 1975 energy issue, "This jurisdictional jumble undoubtedly is an important factor in the inability of the Congress to act comprehensively on one of the nation's most pressing problems."[9] While efforts have been made, through party task forces and ad hoc arrangements, to resolve some jurisdictional duplications in the committee system, much more could still be done to facilitate the development of comprehensive policies by standing committees.

Eighth, with its multiplicity of voices, Congress has no single spokesman to articulate the congressional viewpoint. What, indeed, is the congressional viewpoint, and who defines it? The Speaker, the majority or minority leaders, the party caucuses, the committee chairmen, or others? As a result, a serious communications imbalance has developed between the branches. While the President can communicate quickly to the American people concerning his goals and programs, Congress lacks such capabilities. A legitimate question is, "Who speaks for Congress?" Hence, the legislative viewpoint on public problems receives scant attention by the American people. To remedy this serious problem, Congress has been exploring various methods to improve its ability to communicate with the public.[10]

Ninth, Congress is often criticized because it lacks the ability to initiate policies. As the textbooks have so often stated, "The President initiates and Congress responds." However, where does the President often get many of his "innovations" before he initiates them? Often creative ideas are born and kept alive through the years and even decades within Congress by such devices as hearings and floor debate. The President, too, often tailors his proposals to meet anticipated congressional responses to them. Hence, Congress often sets the framework within which the President functions. Moreover, in numerous policy areas Congress has either taken the lead or reformulated and revised presidential proposals to make them its own.

Finally, some legislative procedures limit Congress' consideration of legislation in committee and on the floor. Some observers claim that such devices, practices, or entities as the filibuster, the House Rules Committee, or inadequate scheduling of committee and floor sessions all act to limit individual legislators' and the legislative branch's obligation to develop or enact legislation. However, numerous recent procedural changes (allowing the Speaker to nominate members to the Rules Committee, reducing the number of senators required to invoke cloture, and others) have underscored the legislative branch's willingness to reform its organization and procedures to meet new circumstances.

THE 1946 AND 1974 COMMITTEE REFORMS

For a traditional and consensus-prone institution, Congress has to a surprising degree sought wide-ranging, "radical" solutions to its organizational problem. The Legislative Reorganization Act of 1946 was an omnibus measure that contemplated far-reaching structural changes in the committees, the budgetary process, and staffing. Some of the alterations (notably in committee jurisdictions) were less comprehensive than they appeared, and large portions of the Act (notably the budgetary provisions) were never implemented. In the mid-1960s another comprehensive reorganization effort was mounted, but by the time the resulting Legislative Reorganization Act of 1970 was enacted, its impact had been diluted. Thus, the 93rd Congress (1973–1974) found the House of Representatives again groping for appropriate responses to its ever-more-complex external environment. The 1946 and 1974 reorganization efforts thus stand as major attempts at broad legislative reorganization.

There are many similarities and differences between the 1946 and 1974 reforms. Because both dealt with perhaps the most politically sensitive of all reform issues—jurisdictional realignment—it behooves us to compare the 1946 and 1974 changes. The 1946 reform provoked relatively little protest in comparison to that of 1974. Why? What principles of change guided both efforts? It is to questions of those sort that we now turn.

Members then as now believed the committee system to be the most important component of the legislative process. As workshops of Congress, committees performed such essential tasks as developing public policies, winnowing important proposals from the unimportant, modifying or presenting alternatives to execute branch measures, and reviewing agency implementation of public laws. Representative A. S. Mike Monroney, cochairman with Senator Robert M. La Follette, Jr. of the 1945 Joint Committee on the Organization of Congress, referred to committee reorganization as the keystone of reform.[11] Like members of the Select Committee on Committees of the 93rd Congress, the reformers of 1946 believed that strengthening the committee system strengthened Congress itself. This was necessary because congressmen were concerned about the growing power of the executive branch, and recognized the imperative of reestablishing Congress' role as a co-equal branch of government.

Both the 1946 and the 1974 reformers identified many of the same general defects in the committee structure. Three in particular are worth noting: jurisdictional overlaps, the burdens of multiple committee assignments, and imbalances in committee work load. Representative James Wadsworth, Jr., whose committee reorganization plan served as a model for the 1946 change, pointed out that the "subject matters of legislation are scattered far and wide over 47 [House] committees."[12] He recommended that committees be "charged with the performance of a function which extends over its related field completely. . . ."[13] Hence, jurisdictional consolidation was a key value and goal of the 1946 reformers.

Consolidation would help to eliminate the jurisdictional disputes that result from overlaps and facilitate comprehensive and coordinated analysis of public policy issues. The 1974 reformers also underscored the value of consolidation, as witnessed by their effort to aggregate in one committee each of five key policy areas: energy, environment, health, transportation, and trade. Clearly, Representative Richard Bolling, a leading proponent of reform in 1974, would have strongly endorsed this statement made by La Follette nearly three decades ago: "This diffusion of energy and responsibility among a large number of groups, many with overlapping jurisdiction, is not conducive to the formulation of coherent and continuous legislative policy."[14]

The reformers of 1946, like those in the 93rd Congress, were also concerned about members sitting on too many committees. Multiple assignments made it impossible for legislators to devote complete attention to each committee. As Representative Jerry Voorhis pointed out, "One of the worst experiences, and also one of the most common ones on Capitol Hill is that which confronts a Member of Congress when three or four committees of which he is a member hold meetings at precisely the same hour of the same day. In such instances, it is literally impossible for such a Member to discharge the duty which he owes to the people who elected him to office."[15] In 1974, the Select Committee on Committees recommended that the House of Representatives limit committee assignments. In its judgment, "Such a policy will concentrate Members' energies, encourage deliberation within committees, and facilitate scheduling. It hopes to eliminate the problems Members frequently face when they are scheduled to be in several different meetings at the same time."[16]

The cochairman of the 1945 Joint Committee on the Organization of Congress, Representative Monroney, also declared that too many committee assignments inhibited the development of legislative specialization:

> We have now 970 committee seats filled by Members of this House. That is 2.2 seats per Member on an average. Many men have five, six, and seven committees. It is impossible for them to specialize and do the kind of a job that is necessary.[17]

The 1946 reforms halved committee seats down to 484, slightly more than one for each member. There were relatively few subcommittees. Yet by the 93rd Congress, each congressman served on an average of six committees and subcommittees.

Finally, imbalances in committee work load concerned both the 1946 and 1974 reformers. In 1946 some committees rarely met, others were completely inactive, and still others had little to do. As one congressman said, "I belong to three committees now that seldom meet. They could be combined."[18] Reform leader Voorhis noted that "Consideration must be given to the fact that there are some committees that have too much to do. For example, I believe the Ways and Means Committee has its hands completely full with taxation. . . ."[19] A major goal of the Select Committee on Committees was to equalize the work loads of committees, and the Ways and Means Committee was of particular concern to committee members. Select Committee member John Culver, for example, pointed out that the jurisdiction of Ways and Means is "vast in public policy areas which are both highly complex and numerous."[20] In the judgment of the Select Committee, balanced committee work loads would "promote not only equity but also efficiency in House deliberations."

While there were broad similarities in the two reform efforts, there were several key differences as well. First, unlike the 1946 Act, the Committee Reform Amendments of 1974 involved only one legislative chamber. In effect, this meant there would be no second chance for reformers through a conference committee to correct defects, make other changes, or consider the views of another chamber. The 1974 effort was a one-shot affair involving the House alone. Of course, when both chambers are involved one or the other might allow a measure to languish, as occurred when the Senate enacted the Legislative Reorganization Act of 1967 while the House took no action on it during the 90th Congress.

Second, the 1946 reformers believed that committee reorganization would promote better legislative-executive relations. As Representative Earl Michener said during floor debate on the 1946 Act, the correlation of House and Senate jurisdictions would "avoid duplication, conserve the time of the Members, as well as the time of innumerable executive and agency representatives, who spend weeks appearing before different House and Senate committees dealing with the same subject, and are compelled to tell their stories and make their cases over and over again." Some of the 1946 reformers even favored increased use of joint committees and hearings as a means to reduce the number of times a federal official would be called to testify on the same subject before several different committees.

The Select Committee, though not adverse to promoting better legislative-executive relations, never gave the matter high priority. The

Select Committee did reject, however, the necessity of developing parallel committee structures between the House and Senate. As the Constitution states, each chamber may determine the rules of its proceedings. Thus, committee members believed it important to recommend a reform plan that suited the needs of the House rather than the Senate. Nevertheless, the committee reform plan adopted by the House in 1974 directed the "House members of the Joint Committee on Congressional Operations . . . to work with the Senate members of such joint committee in an effort to rationalize the committee jurisdiction between the Houses." The members of the Select Committee also made a decision early in its deliberations not to develop a committee structure imitating executive branch organization.

Third, party caucuses in 1946 functioned mainly to elect party leaders and committees. Otherwise, perhaps because party leaders preferred not to call them, their role was limited. Speaker Sam Rayburn, for example, "never made much use of the Democratic caucus or other institutional leadership devices, preferring to handle leadership problems in his own way."[21] By 1974, however, the Democratic caucus had been revitalized and could not be ignored as a forum for the discussion of committee reform. In fact, it was incumbent that House Resolution 988, the Committee Reform Amendments of 1974, be considered in the Democratic caucus, so majority party members would have the opportunity to discuss key provisions, suggest modifications, and eventually endorse it. This process, as we shall see, did not work out quite as it was planned.

Finally, opposition to the 1946 Act was mild compared to that which developed against the 1974 committee changes. In fact, much of the floor debate on the 1946 Act concerned the proposed Congressional Personnel Office rather than jurisdictional changes. The 1946 Act, of course, was confined principally to consolidating or abolishing generally minor committees rather than shifting jurisdiction from one committee to another. Moreover, there was wide agreement among members in 1946, unlike 1974, that numerous committees should be abolished or consolidated. As one scholar concluded, the "recommendations to reduce the number of committees was accepted with little dissension because the majority of Congress had seen the need for it for a long time."[22]

Varieties of Reform

Like any complex structural change, congressional reorganization is not easily compartmentalized. Our categories, therefore, should not be viewed as mutually exclusive. Nevertheless, there are several values to categorization: it imposes order; it both clarifies and facilitates analysis by identifying several elements that impinge upon the reform process; and it facilitates our understanding of the interrelationships among proposals within and between reform categories.

One simple way to categorize reforms is according to the *subject* of change. In 1965, for example, Congress established a Joint Committee on the Organization of the Congress, which received extensive recommendations for reform from representatives, senators, political scientists, government officials, and others. Fifteen volumes of testimony totalling 2,322 pages were presented. All of the proposals for change were organized by committee staff into more than a dozen major categories, including, among others, ethics, scheduling, staffing and work load, oversight, electronic aids and television, committee jurisdiction, research services, floor procedures, and fiscal controls. An important advantage of this classification is that it makes no judgments regarding the merits or faults of the reforms. At the same time, little is revealed about the goals of the proponents. Nevertheless, the types of procedural or structural changes that might be required of Congress are both suggested and clarified by the discrete recommendations listed under each category.

Congressional reforms can also be evaluated according to their *intent*. Several themes are suggested: efficiency, power redistribution, institutional prerogatives, public accountability, and policy outcomes. Because Americans place a high value on efficiency, it should be no surprise that frequent efforts are made by legislators to improve the operation and organization of Congress. In fact, the first omnibus legislative reform measure adopted in 1946 was entitled, "An Act to Provide for Increased Efficiency in the Legislative Branch of the Government." Among efficiency reforms commonly advocated are those that would improve the scheduling of the congressional workweek, reduce duplication in committee hearings, divest Congress of nonessential functions, and provide adequate office space for professional and clerical staff. Of course, various reforms can be justified on the grounds of efficiency when their real purpose is to shift power from those who wield it to those who want it.

Changes designed to redistribute power seem to be the most difficult to enact. Those who gain from institutional arrangements are unlikely to yield power voluntarily and will probably try to thwart such efforts. Examples of reforms of this type include modifying the seniority system, reducing the number of votes required to invoke cloture, and strengthening party institutions or leaders at the expense of committee leaders. In the judgment of Representative Bolling, significant institutional change cannot be achieved "while leaving untouched the substance of the internal 'power structure'—that is, the internal organization and those influential seniors who man it."[23] For example, those who profit from a decentralized legislative system, particularly committee and subcommittee chairmen, generally will not favor reforms that centralize decision-making authority in party caucuses.

Reforms involving institutional prerogatives usually seek to strengthen Congress as a co-equal branch of government. These might involve both a restructuring of Congress' organization and procedures, and the redistribution of authority within the chambers. They are designed to enable Congress to assert or to reassert control over governmental activities and constitutional responsibilities. In recent years, for example, Congress has sought through legislation ways to reestablish its influence in the making of foreign policy. Under provisions of a 1972 statute, the secretary of state is required to submit to Congress within sixty days the final text of international agreements made by the executive branch. Likewise, a war powers resolution passed in 1973 curbed the President's ability to commit American troops abroad without congressional consent. In 1975, Congress utilized the "legislative veto" as a device to enable it to block by concurrent resolution proposed arms sales of $25 million or more. All this underscores the persistent drive for legislative participation in foreign policy making. Other examples of less direct institutional prerogative reforms can be discerned in efforts to improve Congress' decision-making process through new support services, to provide the legislative branch with a long-range planning capability, and to develop mechanisms for better coordination of the work of congressional committees. Such changes should enable Congress and its committees to assess more accurately the future implications of legislative enactments, to develop alternative choices and priorities, and to anticipate problems before they become crises.

Another reform grouping is comprised of actions to increase the visibility of Congress' decision-making processes. Such changes are designed to open up the legislative process so members can be held more accountable for their actions and to increase popular trust in Congress. Efforts to reduce the number of closed committee sessions, to permit radio and television broadcasts of House and Senate floor sessions, and to require the recording and publication of members' votes in committees are examples of reforms to remove the cloak of secrecy from congressional proceedings. A related group of proposals aims to improve Congress' representative capacities by creating an office of congressional ombudsman to deal with citizen complaints, by utilizing various methods to determine constituent opinion on public issues, and by developing better ways to handle "casework" requests.

A major category of intentional reforms are those designed to influence policy. Legislative reforms are basically related to public policy. There are several components to this concept. First, legislators often propose procedural reforms in order to effect certain policy outcomes. In fact, calls for legislative reform are often linked to Congress' failure to pass certain legislation deemed important to various legislators and groups. Perhaps the seniority system, the filibuster, or an outmoded committee structure will be blamed for frustrating policy initiatives, which in turn will lead to a temporary public outcry for congressional reform. Once the issue is resolved or public interest subsides, the effort to win adoption of legislative reforms likewise often disappears.

This linkage between policy and procedure has been noted by Senator Edward Kennedy, who stated in 1975 that the "development and passage of progressive, comprehensive Federal health legislation has been seriously impaired by the outmoded and anachronistic committee structure."[24] A different viewpoint has been expressed by Gary Orfield: "It is a delusion for liberals to think that there is a hidden majority for basic social reform somewhere inside Congress that could be liberated by a few institutional reforms." In this view, consensus for change will arise when there is "clear majority support for major policies" among the citizenry.[25] These divergent opinions underscore our imperfect knowledge about the processes and politics of organizational change. Precisely, what is the relationship between institutional organization and policy output? Procedural and structural features unquestionably affect policy development, but the size of the effect is open to question.

There are, finally, reforms that can be classified according to their *internal or external causes*. Attempts to change the internal processes and procedures of the House or Senate often antagonize powerful members who prefer established ways of conducting business. To overcome such opposition requires the support of outside groups who can arouse and mobilize popular support for change. Conversely, an effective "inside-outside" coalition can bring about a proposed reform's modification or defeat.

Until recently, no outside interest groups consistently followed and lobbied for legislative reorganization. Traditional lobbying groups devote most of their energies to substantive issues: unions lobby mainly for labor measures, farmers for agricultural measures, or business groups for laws to strengthen enterprise. However, several of the newer "public interest" organizations, such as Common Cause, Ralph Nader's Congress Watch, and the National Committee for an Effective Congress, monitor the legislative process and lobby for structural changes that would open legislative activities to public view and ultimately benefit policies they espouse. The example set by such groups has sensitized external groups to the issue of structural change.

Of all the external stimuli to reorganization, however, the growth of executive power is undoubtedly the strongest. By 1946 this phenomenon

—triggered by the Great Depression and augmented by the Second World War—led reformers to view a reorganized Congress as a way to redress the imbalance of power that had developed between the branches. Scholars, particularly those on the 1941 Committee on Congress of the American Political Science Association (APSA), functioned as catalysts for change, pointing out congressional defects and recommending ways of legislative self-improvement. In addition, popular support for change was mobilized through media and journalistic reports. As George B. Galloway, chairman of the APSA's Committee on Congress, stated, "We have also sought to arouse and inform public opinion on legislative problems and practice by stimulating radio debates, forum discussions, newspaper editorials, magazine articles, and reports on the subject."[26]

It is generally recognized that since Franklin Roosevelt's presidency the powers of the White House have grown at the expense of legislative prerogatives. Perhaps as a repercussion, the recent decade has been marked by an increase in confrontations between the executive and legislature over such issues as Vietnam, Watergate, war powers, dismantling of federal programs without congressional consent, executive privilege, the power of the purse, and even abuses of the pocket veto. Particularly under President Nixon did there seem to be a breakdown of comity between the branches, and the extensive use of the veto by President Ford has not reduced this friction.

Our political system depends heavily on what might be called gentlemen's agreements between the two branches. While often not written, these tacit understandings define the outer limits of acceptable behavior between the branches. One of these is the expectation that neither branch will push its formidable powers beyond constitutional requirements for a sustained period of time. When one of the actors breaches that understanding, it provokes an inevitable reaction by the other. For example, passage of the Congressional Budget and Impoundment Control Act of 1974, a landmark reform measure, resulted in large part because of President Nixon's aggressive use of impoundments for unwarranted policy purposes.

Power struggles between the chambers or among members also provoke legislative changes. The Legislative Reorganization Act of 1970, for example, strengthened the House's posture of opposition to the addition of nongermane amendments to bills at the conference committee stage. Under House rules, as altered by the act, amendments cannot usually be added in conference unless directly related to the parent measure, that is, the amendments must be germane. Senate rules, however, are more flexible. As a result, nongermane Senate amendments are not infrequently added to House-passed bills. Thus, a senator might offer an amendment to a minor House bill on hobby protection that would require the President to institute a program of gasoline rationing. This type of action often infuriates congressmen, as illustrated in former House Rules Committee Chairman William Colmer's remark: "I have chafed for years about the other body violating the rules of this House by placing entirely foreign, extraneous, and nongermane matter in House-passed bills."[27]

Sometimes outrageous or questionable behavior of members may also stimulate legislative reform. For example, in 1967 the House created an ethics committee (the Committee on Standards of Official Conduct) in part because Adam Clayton Powell had abused his authority as chairman of the Education and Labor Committee. In 1968, the Standards Committee recommended, and the House adopted, an official Code of Conduct for members. Until that time, the House operated to a large degree without written rules to guide the conduct of its members.

Some changes might be perceived as idiosyncratic, or perhaps status quo, reforms, because they are adopted to accommodate the wishes of specific members. During floor debate on the Committee Reform Amendments of 1974, the Committee on Interstate and Foreign Commerce was allowed to retain jurisdiction over railroads because its chairman, Representative Harley Staggers, wanted to retain control, and the railroad unions supported him in his request. The House recognized Staggers's interest, and voted to keep railroads in the Commerce Committee even though a new Public Works and Transportation Committee had just been created.

Finally, numerous legislative changes simply evolve informally through the initiative and agreement of members and party leaders and because of the pressure of events. For such reforms neither formal rules changes are required nor is approval by the respective party caucuses necessary. Of course, members must be willing to abide by these changes. As an example, the Senate is often called the world's greatest deliberative body, mainly because it permits extended debate (the "filibuster"). That characterization, however, needs to be modified. At least since the days of Senate Majority Leader Lyndon Johnson and particularly under Majority Leader Mike Mansfield and Assistant Majority Leader Robert C. Byrd, unlimited debate has been voluntarily curtailed, often through the use of unanimous consent agreements. These agreements, negotiated among the various leaders and other senators interested in the legislation, place limits on the time devoted to debating the bill, including amendments and other subsidiary motions. Practically all noncontroversial legislation is called up by unanimous consent and enacted without debate; major legislation, too, is typically governed by such agreements. "Unanimous consent agreements play a very important part in the legislative process in the Senate," Senator Byrd has explained. "Without such agreements, and with the Senate rules allowing free and quite unlimited debate, much more time would be consumed in the passage of major legislation than is often the case."[28]

While some senators have complained about their increased use, it appears unlikely that unanimous consent agreements will be curtailed. The growing legislative work load and the pressures and circumstances of contemporary issues almost demand their use if the Senate is expected to meet its responsibilities. In this instance, senators agreed to change former practices regarding floor debate in order to accommodate their work load.

CONCLUSIONS

When President Harry Truman signed the Legislative Reorganization Act of 1946, he declared that it was "one of the most significant advances in the organization of Congress since 1789." While that was perhaps an overstatement, it was nevertheless true that the 1946 Act signaled Congress' willingness to reform its procedures and organization to meet new circumstances. Unfortunately, twenty-eight years had to pass before the House of Representatives undertook a comparable study of its committee system. The Senate meanwhile underwent no similar committee realignment, perhaps because as a smaller body it could better accommodate organizational inadequacies as they developed. The impulses for change, however, were compelling, as witness the several resolutions introduced in both the 93rd and the 94th Congresses calling for a study of Senate committee jurisdictions.

Structural and procedural reforms represent important legislative changes, but they do not guarantee the improved performance of Congress. Arcane procedures might temporarily inhibit effective legislators, but efficient procedures are unlikely to propel inept legislators into wise decisions. Improving committee efficiency, eliminating jurisdictional overlaps, facilitating integrated consideration of public policies, developing mechanisms of committee coordination, and similar changes create necessary conditions for raising the standing and competence of the legislative branch. But they are not sufficient by themselves. Without the will and commitment to make the reforms work or to correct deficiencies that might develop, Congress can expect few beneficial results regarding its capacity to formulate and oversee independent policy initiatives or restrain executive power.

The searching examination of 1974 confronted the House with a complex reality combining its historic traditions, its contemporary political realities, and its future capacities. In order to understand the proposals for change, it is necessary to understand the historical process by which the present-day House of Representatives evolved into its present decentralized but institutionalized state.

No fewer than seventy-seven standing committees have existed in the House at one time or another, corresponding to the growing diversity of public business and, consequently, the rising work load of the House. The list of committees may be viewed, George B. Galloway pointed out, as reflecting American history, for the creation (and, in rare instances, the abolition) of each committee paralleled important historical events and shifting perceptions of public problems.[4]

The legislative duties of the House were for much of our history anything but burdensome—limited in scope, small in volume, and simple in content. "It was a pretty nice job that a member of Congress had in those days," recalled Representative Robert Ramspeck, who came to Washington in 1911 as a staff member.[5] At that time a member's mail was devoted mainly to rural mail routes, Spanish-American War pensions, free seed, and very occasionally a legislative matter. Floor debate was lively but sessions were short and issues few in number.

Today's legislative duties, in contrast, have grown to staggering proportions. When the first House convened (1789–1790), only 142 bills were introduced and 85 reports filed from committees (mainly select committees). In the 93rd Congress (1973–1974) no fewer than 6,901 House bills were introduced and 899 committee reports prepared. Legislative business now keeps the House and its committees in virtually continuous session.

Legislative work load has broadened in scope and complexity as well as sheer volume. With heavy demands generated by a larger population, more complex technology, and broader governmental involvement, today's House must cope with a variety of issues that in the past were left to state and local governments, or deemed altogether beyond the scope of government activity. A glance at the range of committee hearings (on topics from "abortion" to "zoos") indicates the pressures toward division of labor, specialization, and technical expertise.

The rise of committee specialization, so crucial to the processing of business, has profoundly altered the House as a deliberative and representative body. In its early days, the House maintained close supervision over its committees' work. Bill introduction and referral were strictly controlled by the House. Legislative subjects were usually referred to a Committee of the Whole in order to develop the broad outlines, then sent to select committees for specific drafting of bills. These ad hoc bodies were required to report back to the House, whether favorably or unfavorably, and were dissolved when they completed their assignment. When standing committees were created, they received their rights and powers from the parent body. Committees were regarded as creatures of the House, subject to its direction.

As the standing committees proliferated, their influence and prestige grew. Increasingly, they became autonomous in their operations. By 1885 Woodrow Wilson, then a graduate student at the Johns Hopkins University, wrote of government by the standing committees of Congress. At the turn of the century Mary Parker Follett, one of the most incisive students of Congress, observed that "Congress no longer exercises its lawful function of lawmaking; that has gone to the committees as completely as in England it has passed to the Cabinet."[6]

At brief intervals during the House's history, strong central leadership has appeared to neutralize the centrifugal tendencies inherent in the committee system. It appeared for a while, in fact, that this leadership would be institutionalized in the speakership—that is, regularized so that it became a matter of duty and expectation, and not dependent on the personality of the person who happened to hold that office.

The first of the strong Speakers who demonstrated the potentialities of the office was the charming and magnetic Henry Clay. In 1811 he was elected Speaker on his very first day as a member of the House—in striking contrast to modern practice, in which members serve two decades or more before ascending to the post. Twice Clay left the House for other pursuits, and twice when he returned he was promptly reelected Speaker (1815–1820 and 1823–1824). While Clay admittedly had unique skills, external circumstances were favorable to strong House leadership. With President Jefferson's retirement, strong personal legislative direction no longer emanated from the White House, and legislators, especially the "War Hawks," who advocated conflict with England, were restless for action. Internally, too, the House needed direction: the admission of new states brought the House its first great surge in members, from sixty-five in 1790 to twice as many only three decades later.

Clay established the speakership as a political post, using his eloquence and persuasive powers to guide his colleagues. As MacNeil sums it up, "he claimed and freely used his right to debate in the House and his right to vote at any time a vote was put to the House."[7] In addition, Clay employed his power of appointment to stack committees with members favorable to his views. Cooper writes that he "organized the committees to serve the interests of the highly nationalistic and war-minded coalition that he represented."[8] Though more sparingly used today, these powers mark the Speaker as a political leader, not merely a presiding officer—thus distinguishing the post from its counterpart in the British House of Commons.

Clay's leadership was not bequeathed to his successor, and, for more than thirty years, the office went into eclipse. In one respect, in fact, Clay established precedents that could enfeeble less persuasive leaders. Clay had demonstrated that command of the House's rudimentary rules was a useful resource. In doing so he established the practice of assigning bills automatically to the committee with jurisdiction—a practice that over the years helped to institutionalize the standing committees as autonomous bodies.

The post–Civil War era witnessed the reappearance of a vigorous speakership. The trend was not continuous, and decentralizing forces were still powerful; but the movement toward centralized control was unmistakable.[9] Reviving Clay's political interpretation of the post, several subsequent Speakers seized potential powers of the office and enlarged its domain. Even when the Speaker himself was not the true power in the House, centralized influence could be discerned at work. During the speakership of the popular Schuyler Colfax, for example, actual direction came from the intense, vengeful Thaddeus Stevens, who masterminded the first presidential impeachment.

The next of the strong Speakers was James G. Blaine, the celebrated "plumed knight," who later was nominated for President and served briefly as secretary of state. Eloquent and dignified, Blaine echoed the political conception of his office first expressed by Clay. "Chosen by the party representing the political majority in this House," he told his colleagues, "the Speaker owes a faithful allegiance to the principles and policy of that party."[10]

Blaine gained leverage primarily by exploiting the Speaker's long-standing power of appointing committees. After an initial experiment with elected committees, the House had agreed in 1790 that "all committees shall be appointed by the Speaker unless otherwise specially directed by the House." Most Speakers viewed this as a routine function, frequently following seniority in making the appointments. Blaine, in contrast, calculated his legislative priorities and composed committees accordingly. This newly discovered source of influence was bequeathed to his successors, who broadened it. Blaine also revived the party caucus, using it to gain advance agreement on the party's candidate for Speaker and, more importantly, to enforce party discipline.

During the 1880s the House was often a chaotic place, but Speaker John G. Carlisle added one significant power to the Speaker's arsenal: the discretionary use of the power of recognition. The House rules formulated in 1789 stated that "when two or more members rise at once the Speaker shall name who is first to speak"; this wording suggests that the Speaker simply determines the order of speaking. However, Carlisle construed the rule more expansively, asserting the power to refuse recognition if he so chose. A perceptive student of parliamentary procedures, the suave Carlisle devised a simple query by which he and successive Speakers have been able to avoid recognizing someone who might intend to delay or offer unwanted motions. "For what purpose does the gentleman rise?" Carlisle would ask. If the member's explanation was unsatisfactory, the Speaker would simply turn to someone else, leaving the member speechless. Custom delimits this power, but it remains an influential tool for controlling floor debate.

Despite growth in the Speaker's prerogatives, centrifugal forces in the House remained strong, even dominant. In the 1880s legislative output was small and insignificant, and the House became the object of ridicule. The most serious defects centered on floor procedures, where in full public view small minorities were able to bring the House to a grinding halt by interposing dilatory tactics. During debate on one bill —to refund the states for taxes collected by the Federal government during the Civil War—no fewer than eighty-six roll calls were taken, each consuming about half an hour. In January 1889, James B. Weaver of Iowa led a well-publicized filibuster against a bill organizing the territory of Oklahoma. Newspapers began to call for changes in the rules. *The New York Tribune,* for example, ran a series of editorials condemning the House rules as "legislative lunacy" and calling for amendments.[11] Woodrow Wilson, in his celebrated doctoral thesis, wrote that "outside of Congress the organization of the national parties is exceedingly well-defined and tangible ... but within Congress it is obscure and intangible."[12] Henry Cabot Lodge, later to become Wilson's antagonist in the Senate, was more blunt: "The American House of Representatives today is a complete travesty upon representative government, upon popular government, and upon government by the majority."[13]

In today's House of Representatives, with its elaborate rules of floor procedure and tightly controlled debates, filibusters are exceedingly rare. Occasionally dilatory tactics may be imposed; but they are short-lived and feasible mainly under extraordinary circumstances—for example, at the end of a session, when unanimous consent is needed to speed up business. The nineteenth-century House however, witnessed repeated delaying maneuvers. The rules, shaped during the argumentative pre–Civil War times, were powerless to stop them. Two tactics were the *disappearing quorum* and the *dilatory motion.*

The *disappearing quorum* appears to have originated with John Quincy Adams, the "old man eloquent," who served with distinction in the House after leaving the White House. Prior to Adams, it had been customary for every member who was present to vote. In 1832, when a proslavery measure was being considered, Adams broke precedent by sitting silently in his seat as the roll was called during voting; enough members joined him so that fewer than a quorum voted on the measure. Without a quorum (a majority of all members), the House could only adjourn or order a call of the House to muster a quorum. Armed with this precedent, obstructionist minorities for more than fifty years could bring the work of the House to a halt. *Dilatory motions* are simply delaying motions, including quorum calls, interposed by obstructionists to slow the deliberations and wear down the opposition.

These practices were curtailed when Thomas Brackett Reed of Maine became Speaker at the opening of the 51st Congress in December 1889. A gigantic man, Reed had entered the House in 1876 (taking Blaine's seat) and quickly became a walking compendium of parliamentary knowledge. Intelligent and forthright, he also possessed a ready and sometimes bitter wit—a quality that perhaps kept him from the White House. Joseph G. Cannon of Illinois, who as a rising figure in the House became one of Reed's lieutenants, recalled that "in half a dozen words [he] could annihilate an opponent or, what was worse, make him appear ridiculous."[14] Even while Republican minority leader, Reed wrote biting criticisms of House procedures for such journals as *The Saturday Evening Post* and *North American Review* and called for efforts "to establish rules which will facilitate the public business—rules unlike those of the present House, which only delay and frustrate action."[15]

As Speaker, Reed moved quickly on two fronts, delivering tough rulings from the chair and instituting systematic rules changes. The day after he was elected Speaker by a margin of two votes, Reed blocked adoption of the rules of the preceding House, arranging instead to have them referred to the Rules Committee. As Speaker he chaired this committee and controlled a three to two majority on it. For ten weeks, while the House labored under general parliamentary rules of debate, the Rules Committee worked on a new code, written primarily by Reed. After protracted discussion in the Republican caucus, the rules were reported to the floor, debated heatedly for four days, and finally adopted, 161 to 144.

The "Reed rules" revolutionized House procedure by completely revising the order of business, outlawing dilatory motions, reducing the quorum in Committee of the Whole to 100, authorizing that committee to close debate on any section or paragraph of a bill under consideration, and permitting every member present in the chamber to be counted in determining whether a quorum was present. Most of these changes proved durable, even after the Democrats became the majority party.

Even before the Reed rules were adopted, the Speaker provoked national controversy by quashing the disappearing quorum. With a narrow 170 to 160 voting edge, Republican leaders had their hands full keeping a quorum (then 165) on the floor at all times. At best, the GOP could count on only three more than the quorum. The dam broke on January 29, 1890. A West Virginia election case had been called up, only to be challenged by the Democratic leader, Charles Crisp of Georgia. On an ensuing roll call the Democrats declined to vote, dissolving the quorum. Reed calmly intervened: "The Chair directs the Clerk to record the fol-

lowing names of members present and refusing to vote." He then proceeded to call out the names of 38 members he spied on the floor.[16] Pan-
demonium broke loose, and for three days the House debated the ruling.
The Democrats, led by Crisp and ex-Speaker Carlisle, defended the traditional House practices, stressing the minority's need for protection
from arbitrary majority rule. The chief Republican spokesmen, Joseph
Cannon of Illinois and William McKinley of Ohio, argued that the majority must be given the power to govern. Reed's ruling was finally upheld by a party-line vote.

During the parliamentary battle Reed made another controversial
ruling that he would deny recognition to members rising to make dilatory motions. "The object of a parliamentary body is action, and not
stoppage of action," he observed. "Hence, if any Member or set of Members undertakes to oppose the orderly progress of business, even by the
use of the ordinarily recognized parliamentary motions, it is the right of
the majority to refuse to have those motions entertained, and to cause
the public business to proceed...."[17]

Reed ruled with a strong hand for six years. He greatly expanded the
powers of his office, and the precedents he established were generally
continued by his successors, Crisp and later Cannon. (Crisp, in fact, developed a weapon of his own by using the Rules Committee to set items
on the agenda and determine how each was to be handled.) Reed himself had an expansive view of his achievement. He wrote to his constituents:

> If we have broken the precedents of a hundred years, we have set the
> precedents of another hundred years nobler than the last, wherein the
> people, with full knowledge that their servants can act, will choose those
> who will worthily carry out their will.[18]

It was not to be. Considered on its own merits, however, Reed left the
House a more polished instrument than he had found it, and he deserves
recognition as perhaps the most able parliamentary leader Congress has
produced.

If these Speakers added piecemeal to the prerogatives of the office,
Joseph Gurley Cannon of Illinois (1903 to 1911) exploited them all at
once. "If no Speaker has yet seized upon the sum of all the gains of his
predecessors, nearly every one since the Civil War has continued by
some device to assert his mastery," wrote Mary Parker Follett in 1896.
This proved a prophetic observation; Cannon proceeded after 1903 to
stretch the powers of the speakership to their outer limits, and beyond.
By 1909 the Speaker was considered a virtual dictator, even though the
conditions supporting the strong speakership were rapidly deteriorating.

Joseph Gurley Cannon, from Danville, Illinois, was a hard-shell Republican who adhered to the principles that underlay the founding of the Grand Old Party—the Union cause, low-cost western lands, high tariffs, and minimal governmental involvement in social programs. His failure to bend these principles to the winds of changing times, in fact, was one reason he failed to preserve the powers he had inherited.

When elevated to the speakership in 1903, Cannon appeared nearly invincible. As beneficiary of the Reed rules, he enjoyed such powers as appointing committees, designating chairmen, referring bills to committees, sitting as chairman of Rules, and determining who would speak on the floor. Cannon quickly proceeded to exploit the full range of these powers to further the traditional Republican cause. He had been one of Reed's lieutenants when the rules were adopted, and he championed the concept of party responsibility that underpinned them. In his early years as Speaker, his position, though sometimes shaky, was by no means in jeopardy. A genial, homey man, Cannon was as shrewd as Reed but lacked Reed's glacial manner and rapier-like wit. Even his enemies liked "Uncle Joe."

Nor did Cannon at first seize every opportunity to frustrate his opponents. Although inheriting the power to appoint members to all the committees, he initially used this power selectively. About two-thirds of all members in a given Congress would be reappointed to the committees on which they served. A majority of shifts were caused by vacancies from resignations, deaths, or defeats. During his eight years as Speaker, Cannon transferred forty-one members from one committee to another. Some of these were clearly politically motivated; in other cases, however, they accorded with the legislator's wishes. Occasionally, he deposed committee chairmen who disagreed with his viewpoints.[19] And although his power extended to the minority Democrats, Cannon reached an informal agreement with Minority Leader John Sharp Williams of Mississippi to follow the latter's wishes in assigning Democrats to committees.

Cannon's powers were nonetheless extensive, and he eventually exploited all of them. He used the party caucus to bind Republicans to vote with their party on the floor. By dominating the Rules Committee, he was able occasionally to modify House rules to his purposes of the moment by reporting out "special rules," which could shape debate by prohibiting unwanted amendments. Sometimes Cannon even used "special rules" to alter the rules of the House. Once, when Democrats refused to honor a unanimous consent request, Cannon brought out a "special rule" permitting the rules to be suspended by a simple majority rather than the normal two-thirds vote. The Rules Committee was not only chaired by the Speaker but was dominated by him as well: it was convened at his pleasure and met in his chambers.

As the years went by, grumbling over Cannon's tactics became increasingly audible. Taken individually his powers were little different than Reed's; but when taken together and exercised in tandem and to their limits, they bordered on the dictatorial. His behavior became more erratic; and he moved swiftly to punish those identified as dissidents. In 1909, following the initial challenge to his authority, Cannon moved ten legislators from their committee posts, stripping them of their seniority without offering them an attractive assignment in exchange.[20] Historically, this was not an unusually high figure; but it conspicuously reversed the trend toward greater deference to seniority, and was widely resented.

In every human group there exists a gap between a leader's *formal* power and the amount of power he can realistically exert on a day-to-day basis. Cannon breached this gap, stretching his powers beyond their tolerable limits.[21]

Unrest was not merely a function of Cannon's personal treatment of members. In an era of changing party issues, Cannon steadfastly refused to deviate from the orthodox Republicanism of the "stand-patters" whom he led. Reform was in the air, the muckrakers were exposing corruption in politics and industry, and in the White House Theodore Roosevelt proposed vigorous remedies. The winds of change however, had little impact on the gentleman from Danville, Illinois. His reaction to Upton Sinclair's *The Jungle,* which painted a lurid picture of working and sanitary conditions in the meatpacking industry, was typical. Cannon simply responded with memories of his boyhood. "We had no trouble about pure food laws or canned goods," he noted, "for the meat came from the hog pen or the pasture where the cattle and sheep grew fat, the butter came from the family churn, and the canned berries were homemade."[22] Making a virtue of consistency, Cannon adamantly opposed such heresies as food and drug laws, income and inheritance taxes, federal investigation of labor disputes, licensing of corporations, and child labor laws.

The increasingly vocal anti-Cannonites included not only the minority Democrats but also a small group of Insurgents on the Republican side of the aisle. Representing reform-minded constituencies, especially in farming areas of the upper Midwest, they urged federal action far more extensive than that condoned by the orthodox businessmen who controlled the GOP in the North and East. Only by aligning themselves with the minority Democrats could the Insurgents hope to break the Speaker's procedural stranglehold. Deposing the Speaker was not the answer, however.

When the 61st Congress convened for a special session in March 1909, the Insurgents mustered only 12 votes against the Speaker, who won handily against the Democratic candidate, Champ Clark of Missouri. The hopes of the reformers were frustrated because the Cannon forces had converted the new President, William Howard Taft, to their side along with a faction of the Democratic party. Hence, major changes in the rules were impossible to achieve.[23]

On procedural issues, however, the Democrats and Insurgents began to chip away at Cannon's prerogatives. The first warning signal flashed in 1909 when the usual motion to adopt the rules of the previous Congress failed, opening the door for floor amendments. Although a direct assault on the Rules Committee was beaten back, several minor changes were approved—including provision for a unanimous consent calendar. This was designed to routinize scheduling of noncontroversial bills, freeing members from the odious burden of appealing to the Speaker on such matters. Later that same year, the "Calendar Wednesday" device was instituted. Under this procedure, the names of committees are called alphabetically each Wednesday (except for the last two weeks of the session), and the committee chairman may call up nonprivileged legislation reported by his committee. This procedure, though cumbersome in practice, gave the committees a channel for bypassing the Rules Committee. Although Cannon tried to thwart its effect by arranging to have Calendar Wednesday set aside every week (a practice that is customary to this day), Calendar Wednesday provided the vehicle for the ultimate assault on Cannonism.

It was Wednesday, March 16, 1910. As usual, Cannon set about postponing Calendar Wednesday, this time by supplanting it with privileged business. As arranged, one of his cronies, Edgar Dean Crumpacker of Indiana, moved that the House take up a matter pertaining to the thirteenth decennial census, scheduled for that year. Also as arranged, Cannon ruled the proposal privileged because it dealt with a function—the census—required by the Constitution. The census resolution would thus take precedence over Calendar Wednesday. This ruling drew a point of order, on which Cannon promptly ruled negatively. Seeing their chance, Cannon's foes appealed the ruling on the grounds that the regular two-thirds vote was required to set aside Calendar Wednesday. The debate was on.

The arguments raged back and forth as both sides explored the procedural issues and mustered their forces. The Democratic spokesmen, Clark and Oscar Underwood of Alabama, led the debate. Underwood shrewdly pointed to the slippery nature of constitutional privilege: much of the House's work, after all, flows from mandates of the Constitution. The Speaker's ruling, he argued, had the effect of nullifying Calendar Wednesday, which was supposed to permit the House to retain control of its business without the Speaker's interference. He challenged the members to declare through their vote "whether they stand for the House to attend to the business that the House thinks should be considered, or whether they intend to go back to the old system and allow the Rules Committee to say to you what business shall be transacted in this House."[24] Perhaps sensing impending defeat, Cannon assumed an air of unconcern:

> So far as the Chair is personally concerned, whatever might perhaps be in the mind of one or more Members, seemingly to rebuke the Chair, through pique or otherwise, the Chair cares nothing about a proposition of that kind. If the House sees proper to overrule the precedents and to make this precedent that may come to plague the House in the future, well and good.[25]

If the House should decide to reverse his ruling, he concluded, it would simply "make it plain that he has no more and no less authority than any Speaker who has preceded him."

Cannon suffered a stunning setback: his decision was overruled by a 163 to 112 vote, with 113 abstaining or voting "present." The liberal dissidents had strengthened their hold on the Calendar Wednesday device. Cannon's devious circumvention of the procedure had drawn enough votes or abstentions from his own ranks to make the defeat unequivocal.

But more was to come. On the next day, March 17, Crumpacker again called up the census measure. At that point George W. Norris of Nebraska, a Republican Insurgent, rose on the floor of the House and finally obtained recognition for what he claimed was a motion privileged under the Constitution.[26] Norris's resolution—introduced two years earlier but pigeonholed in the Rules Committee—would have replaced the five-man Rules Committee with a fifteen-member body independent of the Speaker (indeed, he would be barred from membership), elected by the full House, and apportioned geographically. The elected members would select their own chairman, and then would in turn appoint all other standing committees. The resolution would have toppled one of the pillars of the Speaker's power: his control of the Rules Committee.

Norris claimed privilege for his resolution on the grounds that the Constitution specifies that each house "may determine the rules of its proceedings." To protect his prerogatives, Cannon would have to rule against Norris—seemingly contradicting his ill-fated ruling of the day before. Cannon's friends argued that, unlike the census, adoption of internal rules was a discretionary function; but no one denied that the Speaker was in an awkward position.

Inconsistency was a minor irritation compared to the political peril Cannon faced. The real danger of Norris' challenge was that it exposed the Speaker's authority to a direct challenge in the wake of the defeat of the day before. Whichever way Cannon ruled on the Norris motion, he would be subject to a floor vote on his powers. The referendum on "Cannonism" was at hand.

Once John Dalzell of Pennsylvania, a Cannon ally, raised a point of order against Norris's resolution, the debate was unleashed. For four days the debate dragged on, often animatedly and sometimes boisterously, both on and off the floor. Closeted in his chambers, Cannon sought through his lieutenants to strike a bargain with Democratic leaders. The Rules Committee could be reconstituted if the Speaker were not barred from being a member. On this point, however, neither Democratic leaders nor Insurgent Republicans would budge.

In defending the Speaker's prerogatives, Cannon and his friends argued that party responsibility was essential if popular will were to prevail in the House. As Cannon eloquently put it following the vote:

> This is a government by the people acting through the representatives of a majority of the people. Results cannot be had except by a majority, and in the House of Representatives a majority, being responsible, should have full power and should exercise that power; otherwise the majority is inefficient and does not perform its function.[27]

Cannon's fidelity to this principle, however, is open to question. Cannon was in fact working not through the party caucus but on his own, thus stretching the limited mandate conferred by his election as Speaker. His statements hint at a direct responsibility to the populace as a whole, over the heads of his House colleagues. This personalized view of his role is buttressed by his choosing not to resign after his defeat but to declare vacant the office of Speaker. As one scholar has concluded, Cannon's position actually rested upon "strong, personal party leadership with limited accountability to party members, much less the nation as a whole."[28]

Although the timing of Norris's resolution took everyone by surprise, the basic pact between Democrats and Insurgents had been forged some time earlier. The minority Democrats were grasping for fractional leverage—the ability to construct bipartisan alliances that could prevail against the Speaker. As long as the Speaker controlled access to the floor through the Rules Committee, this was impossible. "I violate no secret when I tell you," Clark declared, "that the Committee is made up of three very distinguished Republicans and two ornamental Democrats. . . . There never would be a rule reported out of that committee that the Speaker and his two Republican colleagues do not want reported."[29] The Insurgents, defying party loyalty, spoke loftily of "fighting a system." As John Nelson of Wisconsin eloquently stated, "We are fighting with our

Democratic brethren for the common right of equal representation in this House, and for the right of progressive legislation in Congress."[30]

Late Friday afternoon, after twenty-six hours of continuous session, the House finally adjourned to await the Speaker's ruling, promised for the next day. Before a crowded chamber and packed galleries, Cannon ruled, as expected, to sustain the point of order raised against the Norris resolution. Long and loud applause from the GOP side greeted his ruling. Following some procedural skirmishes, however, the House voted to overturn the Speaker's ruling. The vote was 182 to 162, with 37 not voting and 7 recorded as "present."[31] The procedural correctness of Cannon's ruling was not the primary issue and, in fact, was later upheld by the House itself; but, by that time, the procedural question was beside the point.

Norris's resolution now became the pending business. According to a compromise worked out by the anti-Cannon forces, Norris introduced on March 19 a simpler substitute calling for a ten-person Rules Committee, six from the majority party and four from the minority. As in the earlier version, however, the Speaker would be prohibited from being a member of the committee. The substitute was passed by a 191 to 156 vote. The winning coalition included 149 Democrats and 42 Republicans.

Cannon did not suffer defeat without performing his own act of defiance. Gaining recognition after the vote, he observed that the action revealed "no coherent Republican majority in the House."[32] Declining to resign his post, he declared to a loud Republican applause that "the Speaker is not conscious of having done any political wrong." Instead he stated that he was ready to entertain a motion declaring vacant the office of Speaker. A Texas lawmaker obliged by making the motion, but the resolution was defeated by a 155 to 192 vote. Cannon's enemies split over whether to seek to depose him, found they did not have the necessary votes and decided "not to undertake the proposed action." Realizing the situation, Cannon exploited their indecision. Thus, he retained his speakership even though the office was a shambles.

Nevertheless, the Insurgents' victory marked the demise of Cannonism and, with it, the strong speakership. The new rule diluted the Speaker's power by removing him from the Committee on Rules and depriving him of his power to appoint that committee's members. Appointment of committee members was a party issue and thus not amenable to bipartisan action on the floor. The matter had not escaped the anti-Cannonites' attention, however, and the next year saw a change in the formal procedures for selecting committee personnel. During the 1910 campaign the Democrats renewed the call, first made in their 1908 platform, for reform of Congress. The Democrats favored using their members of the Ways and Means Committee as a committee on committees, and this method was adopted and retained until 1974. On the other side of the aisle, Minority Leader James Mann continued to appoint party members to committees until 1917, when a separate Committee on Committees was established.[33]

The erosion of the Speaker's role in making committee assignments had been under way long before the fight over Cannonism, however. Seniority commonly guaranteed reappointment to one's committee even before the era of the strong speakership; and even Cannon reappointed the vast majority of members holding seats on major committees. In filling committee vacancies, the guiding principles—seniority, party loyalty, geographic balance, and constituency needs—apparently changed little over the years. After 1911, the seniority principle in selecting committee chairmen became virtually inviolable. The revolt of 1910–1911 therefore represented the climactic, though not necessarily the decisive, episode in the long-term "institutionalization" of committee selection procedures.[34] Nor did the anti-Cannon revolt divest the Speaker of all his appointment powers: Cannon's successors retained the privilege of appointing House conferees, select committees, and chairmen of the Committee of the Whole.

Yet taken together, these changes thwarted the development of strong centralized leadership in the House of Representatives. The years 1870 to 1910 represent a fascinating watershed era in the history of the House, for it was filled with possibilities, paradoxes, and reversals. The events of those years still cast a shadow over the House of Representatives. The legacy of the "revolt" was a weakening of central party leadership and an expansion of the role of the committee chairmen. In effect, the House turned from hierarchy to bargaining. As a result, the majority party was unable to develop cohesive and coordinated legislative programs under the Speaker's direction. One result of the House's incapacity for adaptive responses, in the form of unified approaches to public problems, was an increased delegation of policy responsibility to the executive. With so many chieftains, moreover, the House became an enigma to the general public, who could never be quite sure who was responsible for what legislative actions.

THE TRIUMPH OF SUBCOMMITTEE GOVERNMENT

The immediate objectives of the anti-Cannonites (interestingly enough, they were seldom called "reformers") were realized. Returned with a hefty majority by the 1910 congressional elections, the Democrats proceeded to shape the rules ratifying the 1910 revolution. Incorporated into the rules was the Norris resolution, as was the requirement that standing committees be "elected by the House, at the commencement of each Congress." The two 1909 innovations, Calendar Wednesday and the unanimous consent calendar, were retained and strengthened.

As happens with so many "reforms," however, the 1910–1911 revolution produced problems of its own—or rather, placed the dilemma of House organization in a different light. The most important single result was, of course, to reinforce the particularistic tendencies of the body. True, neither Reed nor Cannon had ruled alone, preferring rather to rely upon a small coterie of lieutenants; nor, for that matter were post-Cannon Speakers barred from exerting a leadership role. Nonetheless the circle of leadership was perceptibly widened to include such people as the floor leader, the chairmen of key committees like Rules, Ways and Means, and Appropriations, and, during the 1920s, members of the Republican Steering Committee. To the extent that influence shifted to seniority leaders rather than elective ones, power was not only dispersed but autonomous as well. "Nowadays," wrote Robert Luce in 1926, "the leadership of the House is in commission, with the membership of the commission more or less fluctuating and shadowy."[35]

Norris's resolution, for example, severed the Rules Committee from the Speaker, but failed to make that committee responsible to the House as a whole. As House business burgeoned and the calendars bulged with bills awaiting for action, Rules became more crucial than ever in regulating the flow of business to the floor. Its chairmen wielded even more power than in the days of Reed and Cannon, including the power to "pocket veto" bills approved by their own committee, or to defy the caucus for whom they were presumably agents. Though subject to pressure from the Speaker and other party leaders, Rules Committee chairmen were beholden to neither. One student stated matter-of-factly that "the power of the chairman of the committee seems to have no limit." Rules, he concluded, was guilty of more abuses after the 1910 revolt than before—"abuses at which even the Czar Cannon would look with disfavor."[36]

The zenith of Rules Committee independence occurred during the 1937–1961 period, when it came to be dominated by a bipartisan conservative coalition. Prior to 1937 the committee, though often independent and sometimes capricious, had not been unresponsive to the party leadership of the day. Cooperation was encouraged by the practice of maintaining a two-to-one majority advantage in the committee's membership. After 1937, however, the committee became the scourge of moderate to liberal policy makers of both parties. For many years the committee was led by Howard W. Smith of Virginia, a wily and skilled legislative tactician whose aim was to allow the fewest possible liberal measures to filter through his committee. In the 80th and the 83rd Congresses the chairman was Leo Allen of Illinois, another unwavering conservative. When supported by a bipartisan majority, these chairmen had an array of powers to delay, revise, or kill legislation, especially near the end of congressional sessions, when time was of the essence.[37]

Liberals tried a variety of methods, none satisfactory, to circumvent the Rules Committee in the post–Second World War period. With the advent of an activist Democratic administration in 1961, however, Speaker Sam Rayburn and President John F. Kennedy realized they would need greater leverage with the committee and succeeded in packing it—increasing its size and adding loyalists to the majority-party seats. This triumph was, as one liberal Congressman prophesied, "the end of the beginning."[38] But the unrepresentativeness of the committee continued for several years, and it was not until 1971 that membership changes enabled the Speaker to deal with the committee from a position of strength. Accordingly it was not procedural devices but the slow and steady infusion of "national" Democrats that finally brought the committee into line. In 1974, the Speaker was granted authority to nominate all the committee's majority members, subject to ratification by the caucus. Thus, the House reverted to something approaching the pre-Cannon state of affairs.

The party caucuses remained powerful during the decade that followed the anti-Cannon revolt. Like Reed before him, Cannon claimed (not always accurately) that he acted as an agent of the caucus; when he demoted the Insurgents in 1909, for example, it was because they "refused to respect the will of the Republican caucus."[39] When the Democrats assumed majority status in 1911, their caucus was so active that it was called "the second House." In effect, "caucus rule" was substituted for "czar rule." The shift was aided by a Democratic caucus rule that permitted two-thirds of the party to bind all Democrats to support a measure once it reached the House floor. Power flowed also into the hands of Oscar Underwood of Alabama, who was chairman of the Ways and Means Committee (his party's committee on committees) as well as floor leader. Underwood worked closely with President Woodrow Wilson and Senate Majority Leader John Worth Kern in developing Democratic party policy. Wilson in turn relied on caucuses in both chambers to line up partisan support for his programs. This period was one of the rare times when party government characterized the political system.

As the dominant figure in the House, Underwood frequently resolved differences over legislation within the caucus, then bringing those matters to the floor for passage. Many bills were thus shaped by the caucus, which functioned as an instrument of party unity and responsibility. Ironically, Insurgent Republicans were no happier with the Democrats' "King Caucus" than they had been under czar rule—although Cannon too had used the caucus to bind partisans to his positions.

Democrats' use of the caucus gradually waned, however, until by the early 1920s it was used only intermittently. One reason for its decline was the "strong feeling" that developed in the House against binding caucuses, which made party leaders hesitant to call on it.[40] Further, the unwieldy size of the caucus reduced its effectiveness as a policy-making or even a discussion-oriented body. Turnover in party leadership also altered the influence of the caucus. For example, following Underwood's election to the Senate in 1914, Claude Kitchin of North Carolina became floor leader. Kitchin's relationship with President Wilson was cool, in part because of his vigorous opposition to the President's war policies. In any event Wilson became increasingly absorbed in foreign policy during his second administration, and neither he nor Kitchin exerted their influence to shape domestic legislation in the caucus.

Perhaps most significantly, the caucuses withered because the parties themselves were rent with factionalism. Because stable partisan majorities no longer confronted one another on most issues of the day, the caucuses were unable to achieve party cohesion within their ranks. When the Republicans regained control of the House in 1919, they utilized a steering committee instead of their caucus (renamed "conference" to underscore its advisory role) to develop and to coordinate party policies.

The decline of first the Speaker and then the caucuses reflected a profound change in Congress: heightened independence of members and diminished party loyalty. "Freedom from party control," one writer observed, "[meant] . . . freedom from assuming responsibility for a national program."[41] Henceforth, party leaders functioned less as generals commanding loyal troops, and more as brokers or mediators building coalitions from bits and pieces. The leadership's loss of power was, of course, relative, for their influence was still manifested in both committee and floor activities. And, since the Second World War, there has been some revival of the caucus (or conference, as the Republicans term it), especially among liberal Democrats, who saw it as a lever for factional advantage.

The role of the Speaker, everyone agrees, has never regained the lofty place it enjoyed in the Reed-Cannon period. Cannon himself (not an impartial observer, to be sure) looked upon the reformed speakership with scorn:

How times have changed! Nowadays a Speaker is expected to be nothing more than a Sunday School teacher, to pat all the good little boys on the head and turn the other cheek when the bad boys use him as a target for their bean shooter.[42]

Dispassionate observers agreed. "Of this small number of directors [of the House] the Speaker is merely one of the most important," wrote one leading scholar.[43] Some modern Speakers, to be sure, have exhibited leadership skills that equal those of Reed and Cannon. Nicholas Longworth of Ohio (1925 to 1931) and Sam Rayburn of Texas (1941 to 1947, 1949 to 1953, 1955 to 1961) come most readily to mind. From a base of power far more restricted than that commanded by Reed or Cannon, they were able to construct working coalitions by dint of compelling personality, parliamentary skill, and capable advisors. Their leadership, in short, rested less upon formal prerogatives than upon informal influence. However, because their resources did not inhere in the office, they could not bequeath their gains to their successors. Consequently, performance in the office of Speaker has been quite varied.

Of all the decentralizing forces in the House, the most significant has surely been the growing importance of the standing committees, supported by rigid application of the seniority principle and the rise of careerism among House members. In spite of periodic attempts at consolidation and reorganization, committee and even subcommittee autonomy has become more pronounced with each passing decade. "The role of the House is now largely limited to ratifying decisions made by its committees," observed George B. Galloway in 1959.[44] A few years later Nelson W. Polsby concluded that:

> Committees nowadays have developed an independent sovereignty of their own, subject only to very infrequent reversals and modifications of their powers by House party leaders backed by large and insistent majorities.[45]

The advent of congressional careerism was one of the most momentous developments in the institutional life of Congress. Tenure in office has risen more or less steadily as the political system has matured. In the nineteenth century, the average tenure of congressmen usually ranged from 2 to 2.5 terms. Turnover was high, often approaching half of the entire membership. As new states were admitted, their delegates swelled the ranks of the newcomers. Once elected, members tended to consider Washington as a "hardship post," often quitting the House for other pursuits.

The twentieth-century House is a vastly different institution. At the turn of the century the average tenure of members reached three terms; by the 93rd Congress it had peaked at 5.6 terms, or more than eleven years.[46] Turnover is lower (normally ranging between 15 and 20 percent), and lateral mobility to or from other prestigious careers is relatively rare. Probably as a consequence, House members are older than their nineteenth-century predecessors. The professionalization of the House has been accompanied by a proliferation of career opportunities within the House, and by longer apprenticeship for House leadership posts. In the 93rd Congress, for example, the average committee chairman had served on Capitol Hill for 14.3 terms; the average subcommittee chairman, 8.7 terms.

Congressional careerism has increased the number of veteran legislators with whom the elective leadership must contend in exercising influence. As they move up the seniority ladder, such legislators owe little or nothing to the elected leaders. Though formally accountable to their party caucus, they understand only too well that their real bases of power lie far away in their home constituencies.

Future historians may well remember the years 1937 to 1971 as the "era of the committee chairman." It was the product of long evolution. Committee autonomy was associated with the rising congressional work load and the careerism of members as individuals. It was reinforced by the enfeeblement of centralized leadership—the anti-Cannon revolt of 1910, followed by the decline of caucus control after 1919. And after 1890, the seniority rule was more rigidly adhered to with each passing decade.

Reformers have attacked "the seniority system" so vociferously that the casual observer might conclude it was an inevitable and unvarying feature of Capitol Hill life. Nothing could be farther from the truth. A wide variety of social institutions, of course, exhibit some form of seniority in dealing with their members, as witness academic tenure and industry's rule of "last hired, first fired." But the systematic use of seniority to select committee leaders did not develop overnight. The available evidence indicates that seniority was practiced only sporadically before the 1880s.[47] It was one of several criteria of selection, and was circumscribed by partisan and factional considerations. And, it must be recalled, seniority was less meaningful in an institution with as high a turnover rate as the nineteenth-century House of Representatives.

Ironically, the use of seniority for selecting committee leaders seems to have received its first major push during the era of the strong speakership; and Speaker Cannon's capricious departures from seniority fed discontent over his speakership. After the anti-Cannon revolt, the seniority rule became virtually inviolable, and for thirty years following the Second World War, it was almost never breached.

The seniority system was not always controversial. Indeed, the reformers of 1910 saw in the automatic workings of seniority a palliative for the arbitrary decisions of party leaders. Succeeding generations of legislators found seniority convenient because it avoided divisive controversies over leadership posts; this was especially important for a body lacking strong central leadership. Even if it could be shown that senior-ity wasted talent at the low- and middle-seniority levels, the principle had the virtue of rewarding experience and strengthening Congress' hand in dealing with the executive branch.

During the zenith of seniority rule, which may be located between the years 1937 and 1971, both houses of Congress were marked by a larger number of strong committee chairmen. These leaders, of course, varied in their level of skills and in the degree to which their policy ob-jectives synchronized with those of their committees. The most success-ful of them were able, vivid personalities, dedicated to Congress and its work, and operating with the tolerance if not support of a majority of their committee. In the case of conservative southern chairmen, this working majority was often a bipartisan one, which they used to over-ride the objectives of liberal Democrats. The personalities of these chair-men placed an indelible stamp on the work of the House: Clarence Can-non of Appropriations, "Uncle Carl" Vinson of Armed Services, "Judge" Howard W. Smith of Rules; Wayne Aspinall of Interior, and Wilbur Mills of Ways and Means, the last of the breed. Oftentimes a keystone of their power was a close working relationship with their minority counterpart, the most notable examples being the bond between Cannon and John Taber of New York, and between Mills and John Byrnes of Wisconsin.

It should not be supposed that the age of the strong chairmen yielded solely a series of crotchety, obstructive, and autocratic barons. Some of them, to be sure, were all of those things, but the best of them were a unique breed of public servant. Who would not be flattered by this de-scription of Aspinall, given by a liberal Democrat on his committee?

> Aspinall's a marvelous chairman. He knows more about that jurisdic-
> tion than any other person in the country, bar none. He's in at 8 a.m.,
> works all day, no social life. He dominates those subcommittee chairmen;
> they have no autonomy at all. He's with them every step of the way. And
> everything's by the numbers, according to good parliamentary procedure.
> When we wanted rules [for the Post Office Committee], we followed As-
> pinall's rules. He lets everybody talk, he's fair. He'll say if a freshman has
> anything to say, let's hear it. Aspinall's the best chairman anyone could
> have. It's time consuming, time consuming as hell; but it's run perfectly.[48]

Like Aspinall, the successful chairmen were those whose forceful intel-lect or personality earned them the respect of their committees and of the House. Beyond these personal traits, the model chairman was one who facilitated the political goals of a majority of his committee members, and who represented major clientele groups served by the committee.

There was no guarantee, however, that the seniority system would yield such happy results. Occasionally, committee chairmen would approximate the caricature invented by the editorial writers and cartoonists—feeble, senile, and intractably opposed to any and all governmental programs since the Morrill Act of 1862. The chairmen's powers were formidable. By controlling the flow of legislation, hiring staff, dominating the paperwork, and manipulating subcommittee work loads, canny chairmen could make it difficult for their critics to mobilize against them. Ruthless utilization of these prerogatives was the "other face of power" for even the most lauded chairmen, like Aspinall, Vinson, or Mills. Nor did such chairmen lack powerful allies. Backed by bipartisan coalitions within their committees, buttressed by their close ties to clientele groups, many chairmen were politically invulnerable even though they failed to represent majority sentiment within their party.

Why did the seniority system become such a popular target of criticism? Like all political controversies, this one had political origins. While seniority was an obvious target for editorialists, conflicts over the practice were primarily motivated by factional struggles on Capitol Hill—and between Capitol Hill and the White House.[49] These factional conflicts, especially marked between 1937 and 1965, were centered in the Democratic party and formed an essential part of the background against which the 1973–1974 Select Committee functioned.

The Republicans' problems with seniority were on a smaller scale. The GOP, after all, controlled the House for only four out of the 40 years following 1937. In one Congress (1953–1954), conflicts between seniority leaders and moderate Republicans were severe. No doubt seniority would have been a larger issue within the GOP had the party won more congressional elections. Greater electoral success, moreover, would have bred longer congressional careers. As it happened, many senior Republicans were defeated in the Democratic landslides (1958, 1964, 1974); and many more, discouraged over the prospect of continued minority status, simply retired.

The major political attribute of the seniority system is that it tends to overrepresent certain factions at the expense of others. Southern conservatives were the most notable beneficiaries of the seniority system in Democratic Congresses during the period in question. The figures compiled by Barbara Hinckley, who successfully deflated some of the criticisms of seniority, nonetheless confirm that southerners have been overrepresented in committee chairmanships during periods of Democratic control, at least since 1921.[50] Prior to the second Roosevelt administration, this overrepresentation apparently failed to produce serious policy conflicts. Roosevelt received crucial support from the South, and southern committee chairmen from one-party districts helped pass the flood of early New Deal legislation.[51] The divisive struggles over social welfare legislation and civil rights had not yet rent the party.

After 1936, however, the rift became greater and at times threatened to destroy the party. Most historians date the birth of the modern conservative coalition at the second Roosevelt administration, with such explosive issues as antilynching, tax reform, farm policies, and the disastrous Court-packing scheme. "Deadlock on the Potomac" was the way one historian described relations between the White House and Congress in the late 1930s.[52] Following the political hiatus of the Second World War, fissures within the Democratic party became even deeper. From the Dixiecrat revolt of 1948 to the Wallace movement of the 1960s, the southern wing of the party served notice that the "national" Democrats had abandoned them. On Capitol Hill, there flourished what some liberals called the "unholy alliance" between southern Democrats and conservative Republicans. Unholy or not, the alliance was real, and its fortunes were assiduously followed by journalists and commentators, including *Congressional Quarterly* with its "conservative coalition index."

In this quarrelsome atmosphere, the committee chairmen became a focal point for liberal discontent. The chairmen's power to obstruct liberal legislation was emphasized. Attention was directed to such autocratic chairmen as crotchety old Cannon of Appropriations, wily and courtly Smith of Rules, and even Smith's less effective successor, William Colmer of Mississippi, whom Richard Bolling once characterized as being "slightly to the left of Ivan the Terrible." Southern overrepresentation at the higher seniority levels made Congress a veritable minefield for liberal legislation.

Nor was the liberals' paranoia merely self-induced: as late as the 90th Congress (1967–1969), the Democratic Study Group (DSG) found that committee leaders were frequently at loggerheads with the national party's policies. The DSG study issued in March 1969 reviewed the voting records of the 114 House committee or subcommittee chairmen. Of these committee leaders, 42 had voted more frequently in opposition to party policies than in support of them. Their votes had provided the margin of defeat on nine, or better than half, of the losses sustained by the Democratic majority. "On many of the most crucial votes of the 90th Congress," the study concluded, "one-third of Democratic committee chairmen voted against the Democratic administration, Democratic party principles, and the majority of their Democratic colleagues—and were responsible for the defeat of many Democratic programs."[53] Among the apostate barons were such chairmen as Colmer, Mills, Mendel Rivers, John McMillan, George Mahon, and W. R. Poage.

Conservative southern dominance persisted even as the Democratic party, nationally and eventually in the House itself, shifted its center of gravity. Historically, the South and the Democratic party have been inextricably linked. Prior to the Roosevelt administration, southerners constituted nearly two-thirds of the Democratic ranks in the House (see table 1). Although the Roosevelt coalition broadened the party's base, the South remained the largest faction within the House Democratic caucus, its strength ranging up to 50 percent or more—a fact often overlooked by critics of seniority. Starting out with this advantage, southern and rural districts were aided by one of the most direct attributes of the seniority system: its tendency to favor areas of a party's most consistent voting strength.[54] Southerners were naturally on the receiving end of this "bonus" after 1930, when the Democrats came to power on Capitol Hill.

TABLE 1   *The Southern Share of House Democratic Seniority Leadership Positions, 1921–1976*

Period	Percent of All Democratic Members	Percent of Democratic Seniority Leaders
1921–1932	63	83
1933–1946	44	72
1947–1956	51	60
1957–1966	41	62
1967–1976	32	46
93rd Congress	30	43

SOURCE: Barbara Hinckley, *The Seniority System in Congress* (Bloomington: Indiana University Press, 1971), table 9, p. 41. Calculations for 1967 to 1976 and for the 93rd Congress by the authors.

Ever since the "Roosevelt revolution," however, the southerners' share in the Democratic caucus has shown a long-term decline though the trend has been uneven. In the 93rd Congress, southerners accounted for 74 of the 243 Democratic seats, or 30 percent, the lowest proportion in some years. The once-solid South, long alienated by Democratic presidential politics, was slowly losing grasp of its last bastion of power, Congress. When massive partisan victories at the polls in 1958, 1964, and finally 1974 swelled liberal ranks in the House, enough of these members were able to survive reelection to shift the center of gravity in the caucus. As centers of Democratic strength multiplied in other parts of the country, the southerners' own ranks were dwindling. Slowly the Republicans gained a foothold in the not-so-solid South: in the 93rd Congress there were 34 southern Republicans, whereas in 1950 there were only two.

Factional strengths among House Democrats shifted more rapidly than factional strengths in the committee leadership. This phenomenon reflects yet another attribute of the seniority system: inevitably it records party triumphs of a *past generation,* favoring the party's centers of strength as they existed 25, 30, or more years earlier. If the party's coalitional structure remains stable, the seniority principle will not distort the leadership ranks. But if the factions are shifting, fissures between the leaders and the backbenchers can appear. Such a gap—in region, district type, and ideology—lay at the heart of the controversies over seniority in the 1940s, 1950s, and 1960s. Despite the ready target that a few aged committee chairmen presented to outside critics, age alone could not have generated the intense attacks on seniority that marked this period.

These inherent characteristics of the seniority system—its overrepresentation of strong party areas, and its lag in reflecting party factional shifts—probably account for most of the controversy over seniority. Some observers argue, however, that southerners had other factors working for them. Why, they ask, was the other major long-term Democratic stronghold—core-city districts in the North—less heavily represented in committee leadership posts than the South? Such districts are fully as "safe" for Democratic incumbents as those in the South, but their share of committee chairmanships has been proportionately smaller. One answer is that northern Democrats have been less likely to make careers out of their House service, preferring to transfer to promising opportunities in municipal and state government and even private enterprise.[55] In contrast, the southerners' dedication to House careerism is legendary. Even if they stayed in Congress, the non-southerners had a greater tendency to committee-hop (perhaps because their initial assignments were less attractive), thus reducing their chances of attaining committee leadership.[56] Southern dominance was especially marked in the three "top" committees: Appropriations, Rules, and Ways and Means. Of the seven chairmen of these three committees between 1947 and 1966, five were southerners.[57] Some students further contend that northern Democrats were more vulnerable to defeat in Republican landslide elections, such as that of 1946. Other writers counter that this vulnerability did not extend to safe, core-city districts, whose representatives would be the prime candidates for committee leadership posts.[58]

In addition to the seniority system's factional bias, it imposed serious human costs. Once elected to the House, members found themselves queued up awaiting leadership responsibilities. As they passed the peak of their productive lives, often they were still years away from a committee chairmanship. In industry and the professions, people in their age bracket would be performing leadership roles. By the same token, mature men and women who have distinguished themselves in their jobs or professions have little incentive to enter Congress, because the promise of leadership posts has already passed. The average committee chairman in the 93rd Congress was sixty-six years old and had been in Congress for 14.3 terms (almost thirty years). Not only does such a system waste talent in the middle seniority ranks, but it generates frustration and resentment. One man, elected to the 88th Congress (1963–1964) while in his sixties, declined to run two years later because, as he stated, "These old men [the committee chairmen and seniority leaders] have got everything so tied down you can't do anything."[59]

Reform politics in the 1960s and early 1970s were mainly efforts to give more legislators a "piece of the action." Little by little, the reformers chipped away at the power of the seniority leaders. The attack on seniority came on three fronts. In several committees, revolts against errant chairmen resulted in new committee rules limiting the chairman's authority. Meanwhile the caucus reasserted its right to approve all committee assignments, including chairmanships, and subcommittees grew in number and autonomy, adding to the number of leadership posts and further circumscribing the committee chairman's power. When reformers achieved their final victory early in 1975, the seniority principle was in disarray.

The Committee Revolts. The first assaults on the prerogatives of chairmanship occurred within the committees themselves. Chairmen became vulnerable to redefinition of their powers when they failed to facilitate the political or career goals of a majority on their committee—either through incompetence, laziness, or obstreperousness. A series of "committee revolts" against errant chairmen actually took place. In each case new rules were adopted and the chairman's powers constricted.

The Education and Labor Committee, whose subject matter and clientele made it the House's most liberal committee in the 1960s, experienced two such revolts—one in 1959 against Graham Barden of North Carolina, another in 1966 against Adam Clayton Powell of New York. Barden was an archconservative who, in cooperation with sympathetic committee Republicans, blunted the objectives of programmatic liberals and kept the committee relatively inactive for six years.[60] A flamboyant Black from Harlem, Powell was generally in harmony with the goals of his committee's liberal contingent; but his quixotic temperament, his inattentiveness to committee business, and his erratic behavior placed liberal legislation in jeopardy. Finally, as one liberal put it, "we decided to write some rules that would make it possible for the Committee to function without a chairman."[61] Indeed, it is hard to imagine a chairman functioning dictatorially under the committee's present rules.

Over in the Post Office Committee, Chairman Tom Murray's torpor

proved his undoing in a 1965 revolt. Conservative in ideology and phleg-
matic in temperament, he obstructed his committee through sheer inertia. The 1965 changes were aimed at instituting binding rules of procedure and decentralizing power to the subcommittees. When the rules
were approved, in the words of one observer, Murray "just sat there."[62]

Similar decentralization of decision making took place in other committees, including Interior and Banking and Currency. And in Ways and
Means, Chairman Mills's illness and prolonged absences from Washington during the 93rd Congress threw the mantle of leadership on Acting
Chairman Al Ullman of Oregon, who opened up procedures somewhat
and instituted an informal subcommittee system. Later, these innovations were institutionalized when Mills withdrew as chairman. Ironically, the committee revolts were as often the outgrowth of weak re-
gimes as of strong ones. Authoritarianism was disciplined, but so was
indecision, incapacity, or lack of interest—in other words, failure to serve
the interests dominant within the committee.

The Caucus Shows its Muscle. Liberal critics of seniority launched
their major assault within the Democratic caucus. Their reasons for
selecting this arena were factional as well as ideological. As the liberals'
ranks swelled, they saw that they stood a better chance of achieving
gains in the caucus than in the committees or on the House floor, where
bipartisan conservative votes could defeat them. As national Democrats,
moreover, they believed that the party ought to count for more—in short,
that there ought to be more party responsibility.[63]

The liberals' major objective was to underscore that committee assignment and seniority within committees were not automatic rights,
but rather privileges granted by the caucus. While no one openly disputed the principle of caucus control, responsibility for such decisions
had in reality been delegated to the Committee on Committees, that is,
the Democratic members of the Committee on Ways and Means. From
1951 to 1965, in fact, the caucus had not bothered to meet in order to
ratify the assignments recommended by its Committee on Committees.
In the latter year the liberal Democratic Study Group (DSG), its ranks
swollen by the previous fall's elections, persuaded Speaker John Mc-
Cormack of Massachusetts to call a second caucus to ratify the committee assignment list. No rules change was required—only a determination to apply the rules.

Thus the caucus reasserted its role in making committee assignments
—timidly at first, because there were no established procedures for challenging such appointments. Still, liberal reformers struggled to establish
precedents for caucus review of seniority privileges.[64] In 1965 the caucus
removed the seniority of two southerners who had supported GOP

presidential nominee Barry Goldwater in the 1964 election. Two years later, Adam Clayton Powell was stripped of his seniority. (The House went further, however, by denying him his seat because of a series of unethical actions, including misuse of House funds.) Another legislator was disciplined in 1969 for disloyalty. Two years later, a pair of challenges—to the entire five-man Mississippi delegation, and to John McMillan of South Carolina, chairman for twenty-two years of the District of Columbia Committee—were turned back by caucus votes. With the lone exception of Powell (who was under investigation for various improprieties), all these cases involved charges that the members had defied the national Democratic party. Each time, party discipline was urged primarily to establish precedents that would make legislators more responsible to the caucus.

The frontal assault on seniority was launched by a DSG initiative early in 1970: a proposal for a caucus-selected committee to study the question.[65] Led by Donald Fraser of Minnesota, DSG's chairman for the 91st Congress (1969–1970), the DSG leadership drafted a resolution calling for such a committee and placed it on the agenda for the March 1970 Democratic caucus meeting. The committee, to be appointed by the chairman of the caucus, would:

> ... review, consider and recommend ways in which the caucus may assure itself that those it selects as chairmen of standing committees will, in such capacity, be responsive to the caucus and to the Democratic leadership, and ways in which chairmen can be assured of working majorities on their committees who will support Democratic programs and policies.

The idea was quickly adopted, with the committee directed to report back to the caucus by January 1971. The eleven-person committee, named a week later by caucus Chairman Daniel Rostenkowski of Illinois, was headed by Julia Butler Hansen of Washington, a respected five-termer who chaired an Appropriations subcommittee. Though officially named the "Committee on Organization, Study, and Review," the group was normally called the Hansen Committee.

As an instrument of the caucus, the Hansen Committee avoided much of the instinctive antipathy with which many conservative and moderate Democrats viewed proposals emanating from the DSG leadership. As Richard Conlon, DSG staff director and an originator of the concept, put it, a caucus committee was "an inoffensive way to maneuver for change in the seniority system."[66] Membership in the Hansen committee, moreover, was carefully apportioned among the various factions. It included liberals, moderates, and southern conservatives; it embraced persons of varying seniority, from freshmen to committee chairmen; and its members had lines of communication to virtually every segment of the caucus.[67] It was an unlikely combination—"a real circus," one member called it—but it became an effective instrument for altering the seniority principle.

The Hansen Committee's recommendations, rendered unanimous by a series of informal bargains within the group, clarified procedures for selecting committee chairmen. Adopted by the caucus in January 1971, the procedures served to ratify and extend the precedents begun in 1965 for asserting caucus supervision over committee assignments. (The Hansen group rejected such direct assaults on the seniority principle as scrapping the principle altogether, setting age limits for chairmen, or shifting the committee assignment function to a caucus committee.) According to the Hansen Committee proposal, recommendations of the Committee on Committees would be presented to the caucus one committee at a time. Assignments "need not follow seniority." Any ten members could demand a separate caucus vote on any portion of the recommendations, with forty minutes of debate for each challenge. If the challenge succeeded, the committee list would be recommitted to the Committee on Committees. An individual member could be nominated for a committee assignment by submitting a letter signed by a majority of his state's Democratic members. Committee ratios had to ensure "firm working majorities" on each committee.

Challenges to committee chairmen were soon mounted. In 1971 the liberals decided to test the new rules by selecting as their target John McMillan of South Carolina, whose leadership of the District of Columbia Committee had been singularly arbitrary and antagonistic to the District's residents, a majority of whom were Black. McMillan retained his chairmanship by only twenty-nine votes—a margin that could probably be attributed to the intervention of Speaker Carl Albert and Ways and Means Chairman Wilbur Mills. Fearing further inroads on the seniority principle, the two leaders met privately with McMillan the day before the caucus vote and extracted a promise that he would curb his arbitrary practices. McMillan's continued intransigence made him a likely target for caucus challenge in 1973. However, the target was removed (much to the dismay of some liberals) when McMillan suffered defeat for reelection in his state primary. Thus the precedent for removing a chairman was delayed two years.

In 1973 another important gain was recorded. Realizing that a way would have to be found to protect those who cast votes against their chairmen, the liberals pressed to assure secret ballots in the caucus. After lengthy debate, a compromise was adopted that provided for secret ballots if requested by one-fifth of the Democrats present. As it happened, all the chairmen were subjected to pro forma challenges, and all received some negative votes—ranging from only two (in the case of Melvin Price) to forty-eight votes (against Chet Holifield, chairman of the Government Operations Committee). The only serious challenge was to Holifield, who was obliged to deliver a defense of his committee stewardship in response to a memorandum circulated by Benjamin Rosenthal, his most vocal critic in the committee. Although all chairmen retained their posts, Common Cause and other proreform lobby groups hailed the new procedure as "a tremendous victory in the efforts to eliminate the evils of the seniority system."

Seniority leadership was decisively altered in the 94th Congress. It was not that seniority was abandoned as a principle of leadership selection (indeed, it was expanded to apply to subcommittee chairmen); but its influence had been tamed. In a series of actions in organizational sessions of December 1974 and January 1975, the caucus completed the process begun by liberal reformers ten years before. Three major actions were taken. First, the functions of the Committee on Committees were taken away from the Democratic members of Ways and Means and placed in the hands of the Steering and Policy Committee. Second, caucus voting procedures were streamlined to assure secret ballots on all chairmen (and Appropriations subcommittee chairmen) and permit freer consideration of other nominees. Finally, after considerable maneuvering, chairmen of three committees—Agriculture, Armed Services, and Banking, Currency and Housing—were actually removed from their posts by votes of the caucus. The erosion of seniority rule was well under way long before these climactic developments and formed an important element of the House as confronted by the Select Committee on Committees.

The Advent of Subcommittee Government. A third method of circumscribing the power of committee chairmen was the institutionalization of subcommittees. Though not unknown in earlier times, subcommittees received a major impetus when the Legislative Reorganization Act of 1946 reduced the number of standing committees from forty-three to nineteen. Many of the abolished committees simply continued as subunits of the newer, larger committees. The fourteen Congresses following implementation of the 1946 Act boasted an average of 128 House subcommittees apiece.[68]

The power of committee chairmen was inversely related to the vigor and autonomy of subcommittees. Some committees were little more than holding companies for activist subcommittees; and revolts against chairmen usually resulted in a blossoming of subcommittees. Strong chairmen, however, tended to downgrade subcommittees—either by abolishing them altogether (as Mills did when he became chairman of Ways and Means); by maintaining them as ad hoc bodies and manipulating their jurisdictions (as did Carl Vinson in Armed Services and Brent Spence in Banking and Currency); or by retaining control over major legislation, either in full committee or a subcommittee led by the chairman. These tactics were eradicated by a series of reforms approved by the Democratic caucus between 1971 and 1974.

The relatively unpublicized 1971 recommendations of the Hansen Committee were aimed at institutionalizing the subcommittees and protecting their autonomy.[69] One provision was designed to spread subcommittee chairmanships more widely and limit the number of subcommittees that a committee chairmen could head. Specifically, no legislator could be a member of more than two legislative committees, no member could head more than a single legislative subcommittee, and no chairman could head more than one subcommittee within his own committee. Another provision permitted each subcommittee chairman to hire one professional staff member—though such appointments were to be approved by the full committee caucus.

In a real sense, these subcommittee reforms were "sleepers." True, a few subcommittee chairmen, especially liberals like John Moss and John Dingell, protested hotly over the prospect of limiting themselves to a single chairmanship. In the caucus, however, the subcommittee reforms were secondary issues. Most of the attention, in both the caucus and the press, centered on the selection of committee chairmen.

Two years later, the caucus further strengthened subcommittees by enacting what came to be known as the "subcommittee bill of rights." Again, the innovation originated with DSG's liberal activists and was eventually approved by the Hansen Committee and finally the caucus. By this time the Hansen Committee had considerable legitimacy on the strength of its adroit handling of the seniority issue two years before; and esprit within the committee, as well as respect for it from other caucus members, served to smooth the way for the new reforms.[70] The reforms specified that all subcommittees have fixed jurisdictions; that legislation be referred promptly to the relevant subcommittee; that subcommittees were authorized to meet, hold hearings, receive evidence, and report to the full committee; and that party ratios "shall be no less favorable to the Democratic Party than the ratio for the full committee." The innovations also established committee seniority as the basis for allocating subcommittee chairmanships and memberships.

Immediate advantages flowed to the liberal faction in the House from the subcommittee reforms. Most obviously, the new limitations on chairmanships served to spread leadership posts more broadly. Of the twenty-nine new subcommittee chairmen in 1971, a scholar calculated, sixteen got their posts solely because of the reforms. A majority of the sixteen were liberal nonsoutherners.[71] Liberals captured no fewer than seven subcommittee chairmanships on three important committees—Banking and Currency, Judiciary, and Foreign Affairs. The Foreign Affairs Committee was especially changed: four new chairmen (three of whom were beneficiaries of the Hansen reform) took over and revitalized their subcommittees, holding more hearings than their predecessors, initiating legislation, and promoting an activist role for the committee. "A young challenging minority on the House Foreign Affairs Committee," commented a *National Journal* reporter, "is demanding, and getting, a more critical appraisal of U.S. foreign policy from the House side than anyone on Capitol Hill can recall."[72] In sum, the reform helped to counteract the conservative and southern overrepresentation in the ranks of committee chairmen.

The subcommittee reforms of 1971 and 1973 had the broader effect of reducing the committee chairmen's powers. No longer was it feasible for chairmen to strong-arm their committees, manipulating subcommittee assignments, jurisdictions, and chairmanships to hoard power and to pigeonhole legislation. Indeed, observers noticed that subcommittee chairmen, rather than full-committee chairmen, seemed to be wielding more authority and handling more legislation on the House floor. If liberals were prevented from controlling the chairmanships, they could at least democratize the committees and force the chairmen to adopt a more consultative style of leadership. Compliance with the new reforms was not universal, but in the end there were no chairmen strong enough to swim against the current of these reforms. In the wake of the reforms two years later, in 1974, none of the old-style autocratic chairmen remained.

Several features of the 1965–1975 reforms are notable. First, they were caucus reforms, not alterations of the House rules. The reason for this was transparently simple. The liberals, as an emergent but underrepresented faction, could in theory seek redress either by changing the House rules or by changing the Democratic caucus. But the "rules reformers" met scant success, simply because they could commandeer liberal majorities for such changes in the House only in extraordinary situations. It was the "Goldwater Congress," the 89th, that reinstated the 21-day rule to permit challenges to the House Rules Committee; but the rule was dropped two years later. The next landslide Congress, the 94th, did not even bother to consider the rule, for by then it was superfluous. The caucus, on the other hand, was a more favorable arena for liberals in the years following the 1964 election. With the exception of the divisiveness that racked the caucus and even the DSG over the Vietnam

tee jurisdictions was codified and embodied in the House rules. The entire legislative domain, as it was then understood, was set forth and divided into categories, each assigned to a separate standing committee. In the process obsolete committees were eliminated or consolidated, responsibility for programs was focused, and many potential jurisdictional conflicts were avoided. The Act also laid the groundwork for a modern staff system to support committee operations—probably its most lasting achievement.

Few of the objectives of the 1946 Act were achieved, however. The most conspicuous failure was the inability to coordinate the congressional budgetary process. Even its apparent accomplishment—"streamlining" the committees by reducing their number from forty-eight to nineteen—was mainly cosmetic. Though the number of committees was reduced, many of the old jurisdictional lines survived within the new committees; subcommittee proliferation was especially acute in the years following 1946. Most of the jurisdictional provisions of the Act were borrowed verbatim from *Hinds' and Cannon's Precedents,* perpetuating all of the ambiguities of the earlier language. Finally, by reducing the number of standing committees and hardening their jurisdictional lines, the Act tended to strengthen the seniority system, reinforce committee autonomy, and inhibit the ability of the House to adapt to new configurations of public problems.

Twenty years later (in the 89th Congress) a second Joint Committee on the Organization of the Congress reexamined the state of Congress and its committees. A number of its recommendations eventually found their way into the Legislative Reorganization Act of 1970. Although covering many of the same topics as the earlier measure, the 1970 Act was more modest in scope. In the important area of committee jurisdictions, the Joint Committee proposed a limited number of refinements rather than wholesale alterations. In light of its prohibition against recommending direct changes in the rules of either house, the Joint Committee decided against making an extensive survey of jurisdictional problems; and its proposals (only two of which were directed at House committee jurisdictions) were hardly earthshaking.[75] Of these proposals, few were adopted. The Senate accepted only two jurisdictional alterations and the House none at all.

In the twenty-five years following passage of the 1946 Reorganization Act, there were only fourteen House rules changes relating to the standing committees' jurisdictional responsibilities—including the creation of two new committees (Science and Astronautics; Standards of Official Conduct) and reorganization of another (Internal Security).[76] In addition, there were innumerable de facto and statutory jurisdictional shifts through referral decisions. Neither formal nor de facto changes were made with any consideration of their overall rationale or their work load implications.

Until the Select Committee's creation, therefore, it is fair to say that there had been no comprehensive review of jurisdictional lines or committee work loads. The 1965 Joint Committee had recommended that the rules be revised to "include areas over which the committees are currently exercising jurisdiction without clear authority in the rules."[77] This would have simply ratified de facto jurisdictional alterations since 1946.

By the 1970s, jurisdictional entanglements seriously impaired the ability of Congress to respond in a timely and coherent fashion to public problems. Studies initiated by the Select Committee showed unmistakably the disarray into which the House's policy-making structure had fallen. Jurisdictional conflict was endemic, and hundreds of such cases, involving virtually every committee, were detailed in the staff-prepared monographs. Following the imperatives of bill referral politics, alert legislators had historically shaped the structure by drafting bills designed for reference to their own committees. Likewise, interest groups or governmental agencies preferred to have legislation written so that it would be handled by friendly rather than hostile committees. Once handled by a given committee, a law remained there by precedent. The result was a vast de facto structure of responsibilities that often bore only the vaguest resemblance to the House rules. As a report on energy jurisdiction stated:

> The present operational structure in Congress for energy jurisdiction is fragmented among numerous committees. It is now as much a product of legislation initiated by a particular committee or assigned to it by the Parliamentarian as it is the result of carefully circumscribed rules and procedures.[78]

The short-term results may have been beneficial or not, depending on one's perspective; but the long-term result for the House as a whole was conflict and confusion, a triumph of politics over logic.

Overlapping responsibilities were no doubt inevitable in view of the scope of government's activities, but the Select Committee's research uncovered far more overlap than anyone had suspected. Most committee aides who were interviewed had their own examples to add to the committee's long list of anomalous jurisdictions. Two committees (Agriculture and Interior), for example, claimed jurisdiction over national forests, the line of demarcation being fixed approximately at the Mississippi River.[79] The origin of this delineation, now virtually forgotten, had a historical logic: most western preserves were created out of public lands, while in the East the federal government had to purchase private lands, mainly agricultural, for this purpose. International fishing agreements were overseen by two committees (Merchant Marine and Foreign Affairs), depending on which species of fish was involved. Automobile and highway safety were divided between the committees dealing with consumers and roads.

Jurisdictional confusion was especially prevalent in broad-gauged issues that had emerged since 1946. Mass-transit legislation, for example, had somehow wound up in the Banking Committee. Apparently the logic was: monetary policy directly affects housing, housing affects urban areas, and mass transit serves urban areas—hence, the Banking Committee was entrusted with mass transit. To complicate matters, two other committees held sway over related programs: Public Works controlled mass-transit funds pried loose from the highway trust fund; Commerce handled rail transit as well as transportation research and development sponsored by the Department of Transportation. In the pressing energy question, no fewer than fourteen House committees had a major or minor role in processing legislation, not including the Joint Atomic Energy Committee. Even this count understated the problem, however, for five Appropriations subcommittees handled funding bills relating to energy programs. In the first ten months of 1973, a dozen House committees held a total of 180 separate hearings on energy matters.[80]

The casual observer might well laud such evidence of congressional diligence; and indeed it would be praiseworthy if some instrument existed to coordinate the activity and mold it into coherent policy directives. Historically, however, the House had long since rejected the principle of strong centralized leadership. The testimony of Speaker Albert and Minority Leader Ford concerning their inability to orchestrate the work of committees and subcommittees was only the last in a long line of similar laments by party leaders. Nor did the Select Committee's inquiries disclose much informal coordination among committees (or even subcommittees) dealing with the same or parallel matters. Indeed, the evidence pointed in the opposite direction.[81] Most staff aides reported little or no communication with their counterparts on other committees, and exhibited fragmentary knowledge of what was going on in those bodies. The standard for cooperation, in the eyes of some staffers, seemed to be whether documents requested from other committees were promptly provided. Of all the hearings or meetings held by committees in 1973, only sixty-three, or 2.1 percent, were joint sessions involving two or more subcommittees of the same or different committees. Four out of five of those joint meetings involved two committees, Foreign Affairs and Interior.[82] Occasionally jurisdictional conflicts flared into the open, resulting in a negotiated agreement or a "race to the Rules Committee" between two or more rival panels.[83] More commonly, the committees elected to tend to their own responsibilities, enlarging upon them gradually without either coordination or open warfare.

Within the committees, too, all was not well. Committee specialization and expertise, so praised by academic observers, seemed by the 1970s to be considerably diluted. In terms of sheer activity, the committee system could boast impressive performance. With the advent of "subcommittee government" in the 1970s, there were more working units than ever, more leadership posts, and more hearings and meetings. During 1973 House standing committees held a total of 3,037 hearings and business sessions.[84] The effectiveness of this activity, however, was open to question. As a result of insistent pressure upon party leaders to create new committee slots for members, the average size of House standing committees had risen from twenty-five in 1947 to thirty-three a quarter-century later. Multiple assignments were the norm rather than the exception. The average member of the 93rd Congress held seats on two committees and three to four subcommittees, a total of 5.56 assignments. One could only speculate whether members' levels of information and expertise had suffered proportionately. But there was no denying the physical impossibility of carrying out the responsibilities accompanying these assignments: on an average weekday morning while the 93rd Congress was in session, from one-fifth to one-fourth of all House members had two or more committee sessions to attend at the same time.[85] Absenteeism and meeting-hopping were widespread. One of the most common complaints, from committee leaders and staff aides alike, was the difficulty of obtaining quorums for the conduct of business. The Select Committee's investigations suggested that the House committee system had dangerously overextended itself.

It is not decentralization itself that impairs congressional policy making, but rather decentralization that is rigid, obsolete, and lacking in coordinating mechanisms. To overcome the debilitating aspects of this type of decentralization, leaders need more institutional resources for orchestrating legislative consideration of problems as they arise, especially when—as is frequently the case—two or more committees lay claim to the issue at hand. Needless to say, more recent Capitol Hill leaders lack prerogatives of the type exercised by Reed and Cannon, and now exercised as a matter of course by many statehouse leaders across the nation.

Critics of the House committee system did not overlook the importance of committees, or even the advantages that can flow from decentralized initiation of policies. Nor was there any support for a rigid system of central leadership. As we have seen, however, a growing number of members, including younger legislators and the party leaders, had come to recognize that restructuring of the committees was long overdue.

Conclusions

This, then, was the House of Representatives as the Select Committee on Committees began its work. The developments that had shaped the House since the overthrow of Speaker Cannon in 1910 had produced an institution that was baffling in its complexity and frustrating in its decentralization.

The House was very different from the body that turned its back on centralized leadership in 1910. Its work load had risen dramatically, its impact now reaching into virtually every nook and cranny of life in the United States. However, if Congress was more influential in absolute terms, it was less autonomous than its predecessors. With the advent of big government and the rise of a mammoth bureaucracy to implement governmental programs, Congress had become more dependent on information and initiatives from the executive branch than ever before. Its place was larger, but its prerogatives were shared.

Internally, the most important aspect of the post-Cannon House was its stability of membership, with the resulting rise in the average tenure of members. This seems to have been the major force behind the crystallization of the seniority principle—which created a cadre of key leaders with tenuous ties to the elected party leadership and the party caucuses. The party leadership, while more formalized, was less autonomous and less influential than in the days of Reed and Cannon. More than ever, decentralization pervaded Capitol Hill.

The parties themselves were less clearly differentiated than in the era of the strong speakership. If there ever existed in America an era of party government, the two decades immediately preceding the downfall of Cannon—along with the first two years of Woodrow Wilson's presidency—most closely approached that definition. From his study of the House in the McKinley period, Brady concluded that "the two major parties were spatially more distinct on the urban-rural and industrial-agricultural continuum than are the two parties today."[86] At the grass roots the parties were differentiated to a degree unheard of today, and party organizations were militant by American standards.

It was no accident that theories of party responsibility flourished in that era (though commentators differed as to the degree of actual party control). Even some scholars who lamented the meaninglessness of American political parties—in particular, A. Lawrence Lowell—acknowledged the common habit of denouncing parties for the "despotic" control of legislators and legislation.[87] Moisei Ostrogorski, who dissented from the contention of Lowell, Woodrow Wilson, and others that parties were meaningless, lamented the power of the caucus. "Cowardly and servile to the behests of the party chieftains," he declared, "these legislators may defy public opinion, which has itself conferred on them the power to do so by acquiescing in the false assumption of the sacredness of the Caucus decision."[88] Nor, as we have seen, was such sentiment merely the product of academic thinking. Speaker Cannon, and Speaker Reed before him, were echoing widespread sentiment when they asserted the paramount responsibility of the majority party to govern in the House.

This backdrop is essential for understanding the contemporary House: the era of the committee chairman (1937 to 1965) as well as the liberal reformist reaction from 1965 to 1975. These conflicts paralleled factional fissures within the Democratic caucus, between the seniority leadership and the caucus rank and file. As the latter took on a more liberal coloration, the committee leaders, representing party strengths of an earlier period, became unrepresentative. The collective thrust of the 1965–1975 reforms was to reduce the committee chairmen's prerogatives, to something approaching life size. By enacting committee procedures, the reformers made the committee chairmen behave in a more consultative fashion. By building up the subcommittees, they made the committee chairmen share their powers.

If, however, the caucus reformers succeeded in taming the committee leadership, they did little to resolve the problems caused by the underlying fragmentation of the committee system itself. To the extent that the reforms helped institutionalize the subcommittees, in fact, they actually increased their autonomy. Any efforts to reorganize the committee system in the House would have to cope with that fact. The question even arose whether such a decentralized legislative body could successfully complete a major reorganization. The Speaker and the Minority Leader were convinced of the need to restructure the committee system, but with so many members having a stake in the system, would significant changes be possible? This was the situation that the Select Committee on Committees confronted as it undertook its assignment.

THREE

Creation of the
Select Committee

COMMITTEES are the heart of the legislative process. Although early Congresses functioned mainly with ad hoc committees that ordinarily expired after their specific mission was completed, by about 1816 both chambers had developed a system of permanent standing committees. That basic structural pattern has persisted to this day, with few legislators, scholars, or journalists suggesting a return to the earlier system. Representative Bella Abzug did propose in 1973 that all House standing committees be abolished and replaced by a system of ad hoc committees.[1] Needless to say, no one rushed to take up her suggestion.

Committees have enabled Congress to respond to the problems and complexities of the twentieth century. If they perform their tasks successfully, through a rational division of labor, the committees sustain the vitality of Congress as an equal partner in national policy making. Public policy is, of course, the outgrowth of many individuals, opinions, and influences. Often, Presidents and other individuals are given credit for policy innovations that are in fact the product of many people working over a period of months or even years. A common question is, "Where do policies originate?" To a greater extent than most observers realize, the answer lies in the committee and subcommittee rooms of Congress.

Committees serve the formation of legislative policy in a variety of ways. Most obviously, they enable a large number of measures, many of them extraordinarily complex and technical, to be developed through expert study. By dividing its membership into a number of work groups,

Congress is able to consider simultaneously dozens of proposed laws. Through the committee, Congress winnows the important from the unimportant, the workable from the unworkable. The committee system is, therefore, a technique for effectively utilizing time and energy in the development of quality legislation.

Committees serve also as arenas for expressing the multitude of viewpoints that are found in our society. By serving as channels for national concerns, committees help to resolve tensions as well as to solve problems. Maintaining themselves as "listening posts" for citizens' concerns, especially by use of hearings, the committees form a vital link in the representative process.

Finally, committees perform an oversight function. They help to ensure that legislative programs are properly and efficiently administered by executive officials. This is done through such oversight techniques as investigations, field hearings, or staff studies. As a result, committees develop refinements and alternatives to existing public policies, and they assure that executive policies reflect the public interest.

On the other hand, there are several arguments against the utility of congressional committees. At times, they are dysfunctional to the national interest and to the legislative process because they can block or delay the consideration of needed programs. Moreover, committees can serve to dilute the effectiveness of our democracy by preventing most voters from knowing whom to blame for delays, if not the burial, of legislative policies.

Another weakness associated with congressional committees is their inability, as they are presently organized, to develop comprehensive and coordinated programs for the nation. Fragmentation and diffusion, rather than unity and consistency, keynote the internal decision making of Congress. Woodrow Wilson recognized long ago that the existence of independent, and often conflicting, committees affects substantive policies and programs:

> For the chairmen of the Standing Committees do not constitute a cooperative body like a ministry. They do not consult and concur in the adoption of homogeneous and mutually helpful measures; there is no thought of acting in concert. Each Committee goes its own way at its own pace. It is impossible to discover any unity or method in the disconnected and therefore unsystematic, confused and desultory action of the House, or any common purpose in the measures which its Committees from time to time recommend.[2]

The lack of coordination among committees and the lack of central direction over them prompted one scholar to state that committees in Congress are so isolated from one another that to refer to them as a committee "system" is inaccurate.[3]

In view of their important policy-making, oversight, and representative functions, it is essential that committees keep pace with contemporary developments. Senator La Follette noted in 1946 that, "As the 'workshop of Congress,' the committee structure, more than any other arm of the legislative branch, needs frequent modernization to bring its efficiency up to the requirements of the day."[4] Subsequent to the enactment of the Legislative Reorganization Act of 1946, twenty-seven years elapsed before a climate for significant change had developed in the House. Finally, by 1973, a majority of legislators, Democrats and Republicans, conservatives and liberals, agreed at least in principle that the time was ripe for a significant study of the House committee system. How and why that consensus for change occurred is a complex story.

The Climate for Change

Inadequacies of the Committee System. The committee reorganization of 1946 both consolidated jurisdictions and reduced the number of standing committees in the House from forty-eight to nineteen. What resulted, however, was a proliferation of subcommittees (from 91 in 1947 to more than 125 in 1973). Of equal importance, by reducing the number of standing committees and defining their jurisdictions, the 1946 Act tended to reinforce committee autonomy and inhibit the ability of the House to respond to new configurations of public problems.

Many members were concerned about the obsolescence of the committee system. John Culver, later appointed to the Select Committee, summed up the thoughts of many congressmen in 1972:

> Some of our committees are already catch-basins for miscellaneous or tenuously related subjects; others have acquired an unmanageable breadth of subject matter greater even than those which would be incorporated in each of the new executive departments proposed by the President; still other standing committees have jurisdictions too archaic or too narrowly conceived when viewed against modern public policy issues. And there are other policies—legislative and investigative—such as urban affairs, health services, the environment, economic conversion, energy, national population distribution and growth which fit at best uncomfortably and sometimes not at all into the committee structure within which we now operate.[5]

Moreover, Representative Mike McCormack noted during the 1973 hearings on committee reorganization, "Just when the need for decisive legislative action in the energy field is so critical and the necessity for acting wisely is the greatest, we find that the existing committee structure in the House actually precludes effective action in the energy area."[6]

Energy provided an example of why the House could not develop a comprehensive or coordinated approach to that serious problem. More than a dozen committees and subcommittees—each usually going its own way—exercised some control over a part of the energy area. Oil depletion allowances are considered by the Committee on Ways and Means; atomic energy is handled by the Joint Committee on Atomic Energy; energy regulation is within the purview of the Interstate and Foreign Commerce Committee; naval petroleum reserves are the responsibility of the Armed Services Committee; mining is in the Interior and Insular Affairs Committee; energy power administrations (Bonneville Power Administration in Oregon, for example) are under the Public Works Committee; and proposed federal energy agencies are within the jurisdiction of the Committee on Government Operations. Further, several subcommittees of the Committee on Appropriations consider energy program expenditures. All of this jurisdictional overlap and rivalry in energy produced an unseemly scramble when the energy crisis arose late in 1973. "It was a mess," wrote Representative Tom Rees in a constituent newsletter. "Committee chairmen wouldn't speak to each other, and the gasoline lines got longer and longer."[7]

Such "scatteration" of responsibility is not unique. Transportation provides another example. In 1973, mass transit matters were handled by the Banking and Currency Committee; highway construction by Public Works, although automobile safety was in another committee; railway and aviation matters were in Interstate and Foreign Commerce; and merchant marine and most barge matters were in the Merchant Marine and Fisheries Committee. Those committees competed with each other to protect their own "turf" from real or perceived attempts at jurisdictional encroachment and to obtain a larger "piece of the action." For example, on July 30, 1974, the House defeated a measure reported from the Banking and Currency Committee to grant federal subsidies to urban mass transit systems partially because Public Works Committee members urged that their committee would soon produce a more rational approach to the problem.

This fragmented consideration of policies by numerous committees and subcommittees, with little or no consultation or cooperation among them on matters of mutual concern, has several negative consequences. First, the House rarely has the opportunity to consider comprehensive approaches to national problems. Measures that directly affect particular policy areas are usually considered on the floor in piecemeal, thus inhibiting comprehensive policy development. Mass transit matters might be scheduled early in a session, highway construction and railroads at midpoint, or aviation at the end of a legislative session. Efforts to relate one to the other—either by the concerned committees or on the House floor—are minimal at best, with the result that there is no effective national transportation policy. Certain components of the transportation system have been allowed to decline (railroads) while others (highways) have flourished. As the final report of the Select Committee notes, jurisdictional "overlaps which are tolerable and even desirable if kept at moderate levels, have in certain fields reached the point where coherent policy formation is inhibited."[8]

Few question the value and necessity of some overlap in the committee system, which may promote multiple points of access for citizens and groups; encourage members to develop expertise in several policy areas; inhibit executive agencies or interest groups from overly dominating a specific public issue; and allow the insights and contributions of several committees in problem solving. Moreover, jurisdictional overlap may promote healthy competition among the committees. Some of these alleged advantages are more theoretical than real. For example, jurisdictional overlaps have not prevented several committees and subcommittees from being dominated by clientele groups or executive agencies.

There are also disadvantages associated with too much overlap, duplication, and tangled, outmoded jurisdictions. Not only is timely legislative action sometimes prevented by the fierce jurisdictional scrambles on Capitol Hill, but also the development of quality legislation is hindered when broad policy issues are fragmented into bits and pieces among rival committees who fail to talk to one another about mutual and interdependent concerns.

Another negative consequence of outmoded jurisdictional lines is the resulting imbalance in committee work load. Some committees have too much to do while others lack sufficient responsibilities to keep them busy. When Minority Leader Gerald Ford testified before the Select Committee in 1973, he used the Committee on Interstate and Foreign Commerce to illustrate the point. When Commerce was established in 1946, Ford said, its work load "was significantly less and its interests far more restricted," but as Congress has moved into new areas, Commerce "has had a tremendous increase in its burden and responsibility." Ford recommended that the Select Committee "seek to equalize some responsibility in work load so that one committee is not overburdened and one or more other committees do not have a sufficient amount of responsibility."[9]

Finally, public understanding of the House as an institution might be facilitated if committees were more rationally structured. Most citizens, ill-informed about how Congress operates and what tasks its committees perform, view the House only as a nameless collection of public servants. Citizen understanding is further inhibited by the maze of jurisdictional overlaps that even baffles many members. Moreover, because of its complexity, the House usually receives inadequate press and television news exposure. As a result, those easier-to-cover institutions—the White House and Senate—receive a disproportionate amount of public attention in comparison to the House. As Judiciary Chairman Peter Rodino observed, "overlapping jurisdictions should be resolved where this is possible," for that would "enable the public and the Congress to better perceive what in fact is being done with regard to a given issue."[10]

The Challenge From the White House. Modern Presidents have both challenged and usurped the prerogatives of Congress. In several different areas—impoundment, executive privilege, or the war powers— the Chief Executive has been asserting his powers at the expense of Congress. Members are concerned about the imbalance of power that has developed between the two branches, and have, in recent years, sought ways to strengthen their internal organization so that Congress could function as the first branch of government, as the Framers intended. In several different areas, the House has responded to the challenge, as indicated by congressional passage of war powers and budgetary reform measures.

The Congressional Budget and Impoundment Control Act of 1974 was enacted in large measure because President Nixon blamed the $49.1 billion deficits of 1970 to 1972 on a Democratic Congress, and repeatedly accused it of "reckless spending" and "fiscal irresponsibility." Moreover, the President impounded large sums of money, not only to economize and combat inflation, but also because he disagreed with some of the programs Congress had enacted and funded. Provided this impetus by President Nixon, as well as its own jurisdictional problems, Congress enacted a new congressional budgetary process that will enable it to relate expenditures to revenues, choose appropriate budget surpluses or deficits, set spending targets for broad policy areas, and, in general, evaluate and control expenditures better.

Congress' dissatisfaction with its loss of power in foreign affairs and long period of acquiescence to the President's war-making power led to enactment in 1973 of a War Powers Act that limited presidential power to commit armed forces to hostilities without congressional approval. That law, which was enacted after Congress overrode a presidential veto, established a consultative process between the legislative and executive branches on the critical question of whether the United States should go to war. It also made clear that the war-making power is a shared responsibility between the President and Congress.

Creation of the Select Committee was another manifestation of member concern with improving the functioning of the House. Unless committees are reformed, one congressman stated, the House "will have little choice but to be preempted and ignored by the executive branch."[11] The report of the Select Committee recognized the disparity of power between the legislative and executive branches:

> Congress must put its House in order if the balance of powers is to be combatted. Imbalances frequently occur not because one branch usurps another's powers, but because one branch moves into a vacuum caused by another's ineffectiveness. To the extent that congressional powers have ebbed as a result of failure to develop timely and coherent responses to public problems, Congress has itself to blame for the predicament. And to the extent that better organization will strengthen the ability of Congress to fulfill its constitutional duties, periodic changes are justified to help preserve congressional powers from further decline.[12]

Abetting this concern about the need to strengthen the House has been the turnabout by many scholars and journalists who until the Vietnam war were natural allies of the presidency against the "parochial" Congress. Scholars like Arthur Schlesinger, Jr., and journalists like James Reston have urged that Congress be strengthened as a countervailing center of authority. Moreover, those spokesmen have urged both public support for legislative prerogatives and changes in the internal structure and procedures of the Congress so that it can exercise leadership in policy making.

Public Disenchantment with Congress. Although Congress has been a perennial topic of criticism, public disenchantment with it has grown in recent years. In 1971 a national survey by noted pollster Louis Harris revealed that only about a third of the American populace thought the Congress was doing its job well. Three years later Harris found seven out of every ten Americans held the Congress in low esteem.

Such survey results are somewhat confusing, for researchers have also found that citizens tend to "love" their congressmen but still remain critical of the House as an institution. This paradox may be explained in several ways. Members of Congress are fairly well insulated from general public criticism of the legislative branch, provided they perform well such local dimensions of their jobs as constituent service and communication with the district. Members spend a great deal of time cultivating reelection, and this means they are careful to assist as many individuals as possible. In communicating with their constituents, moreover, congressmen frequently cater to popular distrust of Congress by denigrating the institution and differentiating their own stewardship from its collective product. "Running against Congress" is a familiar theme in grass roots campaigning. For their part, citizens often distinguish between electing an able representative and evaluating an institution that in their estimation fails to resolve public problems with dispatch. And it must be conceded that, while there is no consensus on standards for evaluating Congress, constituents can and do judge legislators from such concrete criteria as service to the district.

Legislators, however, are mindful that many people lack faith in Congress as a institution, and they recognize the importance of restoring public confidence in the House. A lack of faith in Congress contributes to frustration and causes the public to look to other institutions, usually the White House, for the resolution of its problems. As one congressman said, "The message is clear: either we act to reform our own procedures and [make the House] responsive and responsible, or we will no longer enjoy the privilege of representing the people."[13]

Party leaders, too, recognize the need to reestablish public confidence in the House. Two months after passage of the resolution creating the Select Committee, Speaker Albert stressed the importance of restoring to the House a "public image that it responds as quickly as it can . . . to the changing moods and methods of the country."[14] And Select Committee Vice Chairman Dave Martin stated that Congress' low public standing facilitated creation of the Committee, for congressmen recognized that something was needed to demonstrate that the House could put itself in order.

Internal and External Pressures on the House. For the past several years, a number of groups and individuals in and out of the House have taken a renewed and sustained interest in the House of Representatives —its structure, procedure, and other institutional arrangements. Such interest groups as Common Cause, Americans for Democratic Action, the United Auto Workers, the League of Women Voters, Ralph Nader's groups, the National Committee for an Effective Congress, and church groups have become keenly interested in strengthening Congress. At least since the passage of the Legislative Reorganization Act of 1970, reform-minded outside groups have cooperated with inside groups, such as the Democratic Study Group and the Republican Wednesday Club, to win adoption of both party and legislative reforms. For example, in 1973 an ad hoc coalition of approximately fifty groups interested in committee reform worked with members of the Democratic Study Group to win adoption of seniority and subcommittee changes in the Democratic caucus.

Committee reform was viewed as a logical correlative of the effort to strengthen the House, but it was also the reform that many realized would be the most difficult to achieve. Any major jurisdictional realignment involves redistributing power, something most power-holding members resist. Members, too, become familiar with things as they are. While they may sense that all is not what it should be, legislators have learned to adjust to the House's outmoded and deficient ways of doing business and are reluctant to change. Not only have they learned to adjust, but the present system serves many of their interests and careers. For many, the risks of change are not worth the potential costs. Moreover, just as groups can ally with congressmen to seek change, "inside-outside" combinations develop in support of the status quo. Hence, committee reform is truly a difficult issue that requires a sustained and coordinated effort.

Without the presence of two other factors, the effort to change the committee system would probably have been stillborn. First, there was the influx of new members. Since the election of 1968, 163 of the 435 House members have been replaced.[15] Not since the end of the Second World War has there been such a large turnover. The result: juniority has become a key factor in efforts to change the House. Members with one to three terms of service have little stake in the status quo and are, therefore, more likely to initiate or support procedural and legislative change. The election of 1972 brought sixty-nine new members to the House. Two years later, seventy-five new Democrats were elected to the House, a fact that helps to explain why three incumbent chairmen were deposed prior to the start of the 94th Congress. "Like those entering other trades and professions," journalist David S. Broder explained, "the House newcomers tend to be men and women impatient with the old ways of doing business; less willing to 'move up the chairs,' waiting silently for years for their turn at a subcommittee chairmanship; less deferential to their elders; and more insistent on grabbing a piece of the action now."[16] Hence, newcomers in both parties generally viewed institutional change in a positive light, for they had little to lose and often something to gain.

Second, and perhaps most important, the principal leaders of each party were solidly behind the formation of the Select Committee on Committees. Both Speaker Albert and Minority Leader Ford thought committee reform was long overdue. Party leaders had long faced difficulty persuading various committees to expedite their work so that measures could be scheduled for timely floor consideration. As veteran member Frank Thompson, Jr., observed, "For years Congress tolerated a system wherein legislative business was conducted at the whim of committee chairmen who occasionally deigned to consult with House leaders as to how and when major legislation would be handled."[17] The Speaker perceived reform as a way to undercut the power of certain committee leaders while simultaneously strengthening his ability to establish legislative priorities. Speaker Albert had complained that the leadership was "at the mercy of the committees in planning floor schedules and in disposing of the critical business of the House."[18] That situation could change, however, in light of the adoption of certain committee reforms.

Party leaders, too, were under pressure to expedite House business and establish a legislative program. Yet they generally lacked the tools to do much about either. Both Albert and Ford realized that committee reform would better enable the House to meet its policy-making responsibilities, regardless of which party controlled the White House. As Ford stated:

> I am a partisan in the strongest sense for the role and responsibility of the legislative branch. I am even more emphatic in that regard as far as the House of Representatives is concerned. Any downgrading of that [policy-making] responsibility or role I would vigorously oppose.[19]

Of course, GOP leaders also viewed committee reform as a way to gain benefits for their party in such areas as additional minority staffing, abolishing proxy voting in committee, and splitting the Education and Labor Committee (long a goal of Republicans). Certainly the minority party's opposition role could have been enhanced by the adoption of these institutional changes. Moreover, some thought that reforms might even brighten GOP prospects for becoming the majority party. In some respects, then, committee reform involved the "haves" against the "have nots"—party leaders against chairmen, junior versus senior legislators, and the minority seeking benefits from the majority party.

THE DETAILS OF CREATION

Two members were principally responsible for developing the select committee reform proposal: Speaker Albert and Richard Bolling. Minority Leader Ford also had an important role, for as leader of the Republicans his influence was considerable. In the fall of 1972, Speaker Albert began discussing the need for committee reform with Bolling, a longtime advocate of congressional reform. In Albert's judgment, the time seemed propitious for a reevaluation of the committee system. Bolling agreed. Other congressmen, including Ford and John Culver, were also talking with Albert about the need for committee reform and urged action during the 93rd Congress. They argued that while individual committees might be performing adequately, the system was not working as an integrated unit. Committees would often spend more time fighting among themselves for jurisdictional control of measures than working together to develop the best substantive solutions to problems.

Disturbed by this, Culver wrote a "Dear Colleague" letter to all congressmen on December 29, 1972. That letter was drafted with the encouragement of Bolling and served to focus member attention on the ills of the committee system and to precipitate a discussion among members of both parties on the need for committee reform. Peter Rodino later praised Culver for "highlighting to us all our need to have a new and fresh look at the basic structure under which our committee system operates."[20] Another member said, "That letter, in my judgment, more than any other single factor, moved the House to the action we are now taking to do something about this most important problem [committee reform]."[21]

After his fall meetings with Albert on committee reform, Bolling asked House Parliamentarian Lewis Deschler to draft a resolution on committee reform. Bolling's plan called for a ten-member select committee, equally divided between the majority and minority with staff and funds similarly shared. In Bolling's judgment, such a group would be just the right size for developing good working relationships among members and staff. Under the rules of the House, the chairman and members of the proposed select committee would be appointed by the Speaker rather than by the party caucuses.

In essence, the select committee approach to reform was developed by Albert and Bolling in consultation with Ford. As Bolling said, "The decisions were made in consultation with the minority leader, not in every detail . . . but on almost every detail. We [Albert, Bolling, and Ford] came to a sort of a meeting of the minds on how this might conceivably be done. . . . "[22] Of course, the bipartisan nature of the proposed committee, which was Bolling's idea, was certainly a key factor in gaining strong GOP support for the Albert-Bolling proposal.

The 93rd Congress Convenes. On January 15, 1973, Bolling and Martin jointly introduced House Resolution 132. Proposed at the request of Speaker Albert, the resolution called for a ten-member bipartisan select committee to study the committee system. The proposal was referred to the Rules Committee, where both Bolling and Martin sat as high-ranking members.

The Rules Committee considered the resolution and voted on January 30, 1973, to report it to the floor, but not without some opposition from Republican John Anderson. Anderson would have authorized the Joint Committee on Congressional Operations to study the House committee system. He argued that the Joint Committee was the "cheaper and sounder approach" and would facilitate coordination between the committees of each house. An attempt to have his plan substituted for the Bolling-Martin resolution was defeated on January 30 by majority vote of the Rules Committee.

The Select Committee Is Approved. The next day the Bolling-

Martin resolution was debated on the House floor. Customarily, before the House examines the substance of an important measure, it first adopts the "rule" from the Rules Committee. A "rule" enables measures to reach the floor for priority consideration and establishes the framework within which those measures are debated. For example, a "closed" rule prohibits amendments to bills while an "open" rule permits them. The first order of business on January 31, therefore, was consideration of the proposed "closed" rule, which would make the Bolling-Martin resolution in order for floor consideration.

After Rules Chairman Ray Madden announced that the committee reform resolution would be considered under a "closed" rule, H. R. Gross immediately voiced objection on the ground that adoption of the "gag rule," as he labeled it, would preclude the House "from considering the Committee on House Administration as a vehicle for this [committee reform] study or the Joint Committee on Congressional Operations from being constituted, or any other presently constituted committee of the House."[23] Known as the fiscal watchdog of the House, Gross also opposed funding a new select committee at a cost of $1.5 million when there were other committees that could do the job. Bolling countered by arguing that if reform were approached on a partisan basis without equal and meaningful participation by the minority party, then the probabilities of adopting lasting reforms would be severely diminished. As Bolling said, "It [the closed rule] is the only way that we [Albert and Bolling] can figure out to protect the resolution from what I would consider to be a perversion [partisan reform]." He went on to add that "we [Albert and Bolling] were eliminating or hoping to eliminate all partisanship at the very outset" so that it would be clear to all congressmen that committee reform was designed to improve the House and not advantage partisan or other interests.[24]

Given the importance of the bipartisan concept to Albert and Bolling, it was almost inevitable that a select committee would be proposed. All standing committees in the House (except one) and all other select and joint committees are controlled by the majority party. Party ratios on committees usually reflect the division between the parties in the full House. A select committee, however, is a flexible entity: it can be of any size; its membership can be divided equally between Democrats and Republicans; the Speaker appoints all members, including the chairman; its jurisdiction can be specifically defined; and it automatically expires after two years unless reestablished by the next Congress. Moreover, select committees have the added potential advantage—a real one in this case—of having the strong backing of the Speaker and other party leaders.

In addition to the need to preserve bipartisanship, several other considerations led Bolling to demand the closed rule as a way to preserve the integrity of his plan. First, all standing and joint committees have ongoing responsibilities that would limit their ability to make reform a priority matter for a sustained period of time. The press of new legislation, oversight activities, investigations, and other work would prevent those entities from devoting full attention to committee reform. A select committee, however, would have one principal task, and the members assigned to it would be expected to work diligently at that task. Some members even suggested that a standing committee "might very well be destroyed by an attempt to deal with this subject," given its political explosiveness.

Members like John Anderson, however, continued to argue that the Joint Committee on Congressional Operations was the logical choice for the job. His arguments were not successful. "Why," some members asked, "take on the added complexity of the other body?" Many representatives opposed the idea of having the five Senators on the Joint Committee play any role in deciding the jurisdictions of House committees. More specifically, Minority Leader Ford reminded his party colleagues that the Select Committee option gave the GOP leverage:

> I am speaking very parochially to my Republican friends. This resolution gives us five Members for Members on that side of the aisle. If you turn it over to the Joint Committee, the majority party has three Members on that side and we have two in the other body and the majority party has three Members in this body and we have two. Now, how silly can you be? You do not know what a break you are getting from a Republican point of view.[25]

Bolling promised his colleagues on the floor of the House that the select committee would be broadly based and representative of various viewpoints and interests. No single standing committee would dominate its membership. As a result, the varying experiences and perspectives of members from different standing committees would aid the select committee in the conduct of its work.

Finally, the Bolling-Martin proposal granted the proposed select committee budgetary independence from the Committee on House Administration. This was done, Bolling said, to "be sure that [the select committee] would be as little influenced as possible by anybody in the institution who might wish to influence us in behalf of his particular jurisdiction." Normally, committee budgets and expenditures require approval by the Committee on House Administration. To avoid or prevent any hint of untoward pressure on the select committee, the Bolling-Martin proposal would allow it to draw funds directly from the House contingency fund—subject to the direction of the chairman and the approval of the Speaker. Its proposed $1.5 million budget was to be equally divided between the majority and minority party, with each party exercising control over its share of the funds.

All these features Bolling considered essential for success. "If any of the significant elements of the [select] committee were changed," Bolling said, "I would not be prepared to be involved in it."[26] He went on to state that if "it is not desired to do it this way, then vote this [the closed rule] down and somebody else can come in with a proposition." Faced with this prospect, members of the House voted 205 to 167 to accept the closed rule, which indicated that a majority of the House would support the Bolling-Martin committee reform resolution.

Upon the adoption of the closed rule, the Bolling-Martin resolution then became in order as the official business of the House. The House had moved technically from a debate on procedure to one which involved substance. Members, of course, continued to discuss committee reform, and asked several questions: "Why was $1.5 million required for the select committee?" "Should committees parallel federal agencies?" "Would new standing committees on Transportation and Environment be created?" After these and other points were discussed the House voted 282 to 91 to adopt the select committee approach to reform. There were 168 Democrats and 114 Republicans who voted in favor of the Bolling-Martin resolution; and 33 Democrats and 58 Republicans who were opposed. The vote against the proposal might have been larger had legislators been forewarned that committee reform was in the wind. Few realized that the matter was under serious consideration. Hence, when the plan came to the floor soon after the new Congress convened, many members realized that it was impolitic to vote against congressional reform, an issue akin to motherhood.

Immediately upon the adoption of the resolution, Speaker Albert appointed the ten members of the new panel, which was soon named the Select Committee on Committees: Democrats Richard Bolling, chairman; Robert Stephens; John Culver; Lloyd Meeds; Paul Sarbanes; and Republicans Dave Martin, who became vice chairman; Peter Frelinghuysen; Charles Wiggins; William Steiger; and C. W. Bill Young.

SELECTING THE MEMBERS

Although the Speaker appoints the membership of select committees, he usually consults with key congressmen. In this case, Bolling and Albert selected the Democratic members and Ford chose the Republicans. Bolling consulted with Ford about certain prospective GOP nominees, but exercised minimal veto power over those appointments. Vice Chairman Martin had no hand in selecting the other Republicans, and even opposed the appointment of at least one of them.

Committee assignment is a significant event in the life of a congressman. First, the type of assignment a member receives may affect his reelection. Second, committees tend to attract people who are concerned about the subject matter and also possess the background to make a contribution; hence, committees are important for career advancement. Third, certain committees tend to maximize a member's influence among his House colleagues, while others do not. Fourth, most members prefer assignments that offer a meaningful challenge to their interests and intellect. Finally, some committees confer personal benefits—such as foreign travel, a chance to associate with prestigious or glamorous activities (diplomacy and the space program, for example).

These factors relate specifically to membership on standing committees. A select reform committee is rather different, however. Albert, Bolling, and Ford were determined to name congressmen who had the interest, intellect, and capacity to take the "heat" from colleagues and groups who would be distressed by jurisdictional changes. Prospective nominees had to ask themselves: "Would service on the Select Committee alienate groups in my constituency? How would colleagues on my other committee(s) react to changes that I had a hand in recommending? Is committee reform really an issue I should take on in addition to my other responsibilities?" Of course, any member could have refused to serve and concentrated his energies elsewhere; at least one did so.

Great care was taken to ensure that the Select Committee was balanced ideologically and geographically and that junior as well as senior members were represented. All major regions of the country were represented: East—Sarbanes and Frelinghuysen; West—Meeds and Wiggins; South—Stephens and Young; Midwest—Martin, Culver, and Steiger; and Border—Bolling. There were conservatives (Martin, Stephens, Young, and Wiggins), liberals (Culver, Meeds, and Sarbanes), and moderates (Bolling, Frelinghuysen, and Steiger) on the committee. The individual "liberalism" scores of the members were as follows (listed by seniority):[27]

Bolling	78	Martin	5
Stephens	15	Frelinghuysen	30
Culver	93	Wiggins	15
Meeds	96	Steiger	38
Sarbanes	90	Young	12

Put another way, the ten-member Select Committee reflected relatively accurately the "constituency" that would have to vote on their recommendations.

For Democrats, the most junior member (Sarbanes) had 2 terms of service, while the most senior member (Bolling) had been elected to 13 terms; the range for Republicans was 2 terms (Young) for the most junior to 11 for the most senior (Frelinghuysen). It was a foregone conclusion, of course, that Bolling would be the chairman: he was a principal proponent of committee reform and had close personal and political relationships with Speaker Albert.

Other factors, too, were important in the selection process. In general, a member had to be perceived as above average in intelligence, hardworking, able to withstand political heat, and committed to strengthening the House. For Democrats, another criterion was important: membership in "the Group." Launched originally by Bolling to help elect Carl Albert to the speakership in 1971, "the Group" is made up of about twenty Democrats who meet informally every Wednesday morning in a member's office to talk over party and legislative matters. Meeds and Culver were early members, while Stephens and Sarbanes had been invited to join "the Group" just before the select committee was established. Through this forum Bolling became better acquainted with the four Democrats named to the Select Committee and was successful in urging their appointment on Speaker Albert.

The appointment of Democrat Lloyd Meeds will highlight some of the factors involved in the selection process. In late 1972, Bolling informed Meeds that committee reform was in the works for the 93rd Congress and asked whether he would be interested in serving on a select reform committee. Bolling made clear that there was no guarantee that Meeds would be selected in the event a committee was created, but that he simply wanted to determine Meeds's willingness to work on committee reform. Surprisingly, Meeds was not informed beforehand that he would be selected and learned officially of his appointment at the time the Speaker announced who the members of the Select Committee would be. Of course, Meeds did receive clear signals from Bolling that it was highly likely that he would be appointed to the select reform committee. So Meeds's appointment did not catch him completely unaware.

Several factors help to account for Meeds's appointment. First, he could take the heat from members and special interests that would surely result from any attempt to change the jurisdictional alignments of the committees. Second, Meeds had been active in previous committee reform efforts. For example, in 1965 he helped to modernize the rules of the Interior and Insular Affairs Committee, and in 1967 he was one of several who reformed the Education and Labor Committee. Moreover, Meeds supported the 1971 and 1973 Democratic caucus reform efforts of the Democratic Study Group, which liberalized the custom of seniority and democratized committee procedures. Third, he was a member of "the Group."

The members of the Select Committee reflected the variety and strength of the House of Representatives.

RICHARD BOLLING—A Democrat from Kansas City, Missouri, Bolling was first elected to the House in 1948 and has been reelected ever since. Early recognized by Speaker Sam Rayburn as a very able, intelligent, and perceptive legislator, Bolling became one of the Speaker's trusted lieutenants and a junior member of the House power structure. In fact, many members thought he was destined to be Speaker himself, but his fortunes changed when Rayburn died. Bolling ran for the majority leadership in 1962, opposing Carl Albert, but withdrew his candidacy a week before the Democratic caucus selected a majority leader. Bolling expressed his criticism of House organization and procedure, and of the leadership of Speaker John McCormack in his books: *House Out of Order* (1965) and *Power in the House* (1968). With Albert's election as Speaker, Bolling became his close advisor.

Third-ranking member on the Rules Committee, Bolling was generally considered the House's leading expert on congressional organization and procedure. He chaired a Rules subcommittee that led to the creation of the Committee on Standards of Official Conduct and the House's first code of ethics, was a member of the Rules subcommittee that drafted the Legislative Reorganization Act of 1970, and was floor manager of the 1974 congressional budget reform bill after his appointment to the Select Committee on Committees. With a reputation as a master of the rules of the House, Bolling is considered one of the best parliamentary tacticians and strategists in Congress.

ROBERT G. STEPHENS, JR.—He was a warm, friendly, witty sixty-year-old Democrat from Georgia, first elected to the House in 1960. A staunch defender of small businessmen, Stephens was chairman of the Subcommittee on Small Business of the Banking and Currency Committee; and he was a member of his party's Steering and Policy Committee. A great-nephew of the vice president of the Confederacy, he was highly influential with his southern colleagues.

JOHN C. CULVER—A member of the Foreign Affairs (renamed International Relations in 1975) and Government Operations Committees, Culver was elected to the House in 1964 after serving as legislative assistant to Senator Edward Kennedy. Active in the DSG—aside from the caucuses the largest organization in the House—Culver was elected to head the DSG in 1973. Long interested in committee reform, Culver had written several "Dear Colleague" letters that sparked debate on the need for committee reform. A star football player at Harvard, Culver had a sharp, boisterous sense of humor that frequently left his committee colleagues and staff members limp with laughter. In 1972 Culver declined to make a tough Senate race in his home state of Iowa, only to see his former administrative assistant, Dick Clark, run and win. In 1974 Culver followed his former aide to the Senate.

LLOYD MEEDS—Elected in 1964 from the state of Washington, Meeds served on the Education and Labor Committee and is chairman of the Indian Subcommittee of the Interior and Insular Affairs Committee. One of the busiest members of the House, Meeds had over the years impressed Albert and Bolling by his industriousness. In fact, a study conducted by the Select Committee revealed that Meeds had more scheduled committee meetings than any other member of the House. Meeds has played a pivotal role on the Education Committee and was the architect of numerous compromises that brought competing factions together on education measures.

PAUL S. SARBANES—A two-term member from Baltimore, Sarbanes was a Rhodes scholar whose intellectual and political skills had impressed his colleagues. Sarbanes made his own contribution to reforming the seniority system by being responsible for the defeat or retirement of two committee chairmen. When he first ran for the House in 1970, he defeated the chairman of the Public Works Committee in the Democratic primary. Two years later, as a result of redistricting, Sarbanes again was pitted against a committee chairman, Edward Garmatz of the Merchant Marine and Fisheries Committee. Garmatz resigned rather than face Sarbanes in the primary.

A member of the Judiciary Committee, Sarbanes was a key member during the impeachment proceedings against President Nixon and sponsor of the first article of impeachment on obstruction of justice. He was also a member of the Merchant Marine and Fisheries Committee. Speaker Albert, also a former Rhodes scholar, was very receptive to naming Sarbanes to the Select Committee.

DAVID T. MARTIN—A conservative Republican from Nebraska, Martin was elected to the House in 1960. As ranking minority member of the House Rules Committee, Martin was the logical choice to cosponsor, with Bolling, the select committee proposal. From the vantage of the Rules Committee, Martin had observed numerous jurisdictional squabbles among committees and talked with Bolling about the need for committee reform. A retail lumber firm owner who sometimes did his bookwork in his Capitol Hill office, Martin was stubborn and often had to be handled with kid gloves.

PETER H. B. FRELINGHUYSEN—The representative from New Jersey was the most senior Republican on the Select Committee and a ranking member of the Committee on Foreign Affairs. He was also on the GOP

Policy Committee. A strong supporter of Gerald Ford during his successful deposing of Charles Halleck as minority leader in 1965, Frelinghuysen was selected at the last minute by Ford as a replacement for Clarence Brown of Ohio. A scion of a wealthy and distinguished family, Frelinghuysen was noted for his quick mind and sharp tongue.

CHARLES E. WIGGINS—An able, conservative legislator, who represented much of former President Nixon's old House district in California, Wiggins ranked sixth on the Judiciary Committee and served on House Administration during the 93rd Congress. Wiggins had prior experience on a select committee, having been a member of the Select Crime Committee during the 91st and 92nd Congresses. A member of the GOP Policy Committee, he was considered by his colleagues an authority on constitutional matters. During the impeachment proceedings against President Nixon, Wiggins was a leading defender of the President until the release of additional tapes subsequent to U.S. v. Nixon (94 S. Ct. 3090).

WILLIAM A. STEIGER—Active in party reform efforts, Steiger was a member of a bipartisan group that helped to gain passage of reform amendments to the Legislative Reorganization Act of 1970. Steiger also headed a GOP National Committee group studying presidential convention reforms. Steiger wrote to Ford and asked that he be appointed to the select reform committee because of his long interest in strengthening the House. He and Culver were apparently the only ones who really volunteered for the job. A moderate Republican from Wisconsin, Steiger as a member of the Education and Labor Committee had become a leading expert on federal manpower training programs and coauthored the Occupational Safety and Health Act.

C. W. BILL YOUNG—Elected to the House in 1970, Young soon became allied with Minority Leader Ford. Several times he had remarked to Ford that his Armed Services assignment was not enough to keep him busy, and that he would welcome an additional committee position. Ford heeded Young's request. Later, when John Rhodes was named minority leader after Ford became Vice President, Young was selected to fill Rhodes's seat on the Appropriations Committee, an important assignment for a junior member. Ideologically compatible with the right wing of his party, Young was an advocate of reforms ("sunshine" laws) to open legislative proceedings to public view.

GETTING ORGANIZED

Committee staff perform important tasks. Some have even called them the "third house" of Congress. Committee staff members help write legislation and draft reports that can influence public policy; they organize hearings and panel sessions and schedule witnesses to testify;

they research proposals and suggest innovative approaches to problems; they analyze information; they maintain contacts with executive agencies, interest groups, other committee and member staffs, and the Senate; and they anticipate the needs of the chairman and other committee members.

A good staff can influence the overall performance of a committee and facilitate enactment of committee measures reported to the full House. Surprisingly, Congress was very slow in providing itself with professional staff. It was not until 1946 that Congress authorized permanent professional staff for each standing committee. As of March 31, 1973, there were 848 professional and clerical staff members working for standing and select committees of the House. In 1947 the corresponding figure was 182.

The day the Select Committee was established, Chairman Bolling called a brief meeting of the members and introduced his nominee for staff director—Charles S. Sheldon, head of the Science Policy Division of the Congressional Research Service. Sheldon had worked with Bolling on the Joint Economic Committee and impressed Bolling with his industriousness. Although Sheldon had been asked by Bolling to serve as staff director several weeks before the Select Committee was formally established, his appointment was formally ratified by the committee's other members at the initial meeting.

Sheldon was then authorized by Bolling to hire the rest of the Democrats' staff, professional as well as clerical. Martin personally hired all GOP staff. Bolling and Martin had agreed that each party should have five professional staff members and a sufficient number of clerical assistants. This, of course, was in the spirit of bipartisanship that surrounded the creation of the Select Committee. On few other committees does the minority receive anything approaching an equal staff.

During the next several weeks, the full complement of professional and clerical staff was hired by both parties. The professional staff was a mix of those with practical and theoretical experience in legislative affairs, and all had either a law or Ph.D. degree. While several were primarily academicians, most were professional congressional staff members and all had close contacts with Capitol Hill. Professional competence rather than partisan consideration was the major criterion for most staff appointments, and, in fact, not all staff members found themselves working on the side of the aisle that corresponded to their party affiliation. The Select Committee also hired several temporary consultants to draft alternative committee reform plans and to assist in planning for hearings and panel sessions. The Select Committee was assigned office space in an annex, the former Congressional Hotel, and arrangements were made for telephones, typewriters, and other necessities.

During the first two months, the Select Committee held five meetings. These meetings had several purposes: to allow the members to become acquainted with one another and the staff; to approve the hiring of professional and clerical staff; to authorize Chairman Bolling's wife, a professional filmmaker, to record hearings and meetings of the committee; to adopt rules for the committee; and to plan for hearings and panel sessions (see chapter 4). The members of the committee also agreed to conduct personal interviews with other congressmen in order to elicit their views of committee reform. Bolling had underscored the importance of the member-to-member interviews during floor debate on the creation of the select committee. In response to an inquiry from John Ashbrook, who suggested that only a very few people would be making the decisions about committee reform, Bolling had remarked:

> That is as far from the case as it can possibly be, because the reason why we have agreed, among us, that we need 10 working members instead of perhaps three or four is that we do not think there is any possibility of succeeding with a product that will be accepted by the institution unless we involve every member of the institution.

> I have made up a list of the people I expect to see and have conversations at length with on this select committee, and it is 100 people.[28]

Not all members were as enthusiastic as Bolling about the value of interviewing their colleagues, but others cited their potential values. First, they served to educate the members of the Select Committee about the complexities and intricacies of the committee system. Even though many had served in Congress for years, there was still much they could learn about how various committees functioned. Second, the interviews demonstrated that the Select Committee was not aloof but interested in the real problems that members faced. Finally, the interviews helped to parry criticism that rank-and-file members were not asked their opinions on committee reform. Steiger, too, thought the member-to-member interviews valuable, for they allowed legislators to talk off-the-record about members, committees, and staff.

On the other hand, several members thought the interviews ineffectual: interviewing was unsystematic; the members were not encouraged enough to do them; and the results were not recorded or analyzed properly. In short, the interviews did not adequately assess member opinion on reform nor was much learned from them that could be integrated in the work of the Select Committee.

The professional staff, meanwhile, began organizing their own interviews with their counterparts on the standing committees. A questionnaire was developed, pilot interviews were held, and then each staff member was assigned one or more standing committees as his principal responsibility. Each staff member was expected to conduct as many interviews as possible with the majority and minority staff on each of his assigned committees, and, whenever possible, to have another staff member accompanying him during these sessions.

Staff-to-staff interviews were valuable. Copies of all interviews were circulated among the staff, and then a composite perspective of each committee was developed, covering such areas as jurisdictional conflicts among committees, committee work load, and subcommittee organization. As a result, certain staff became the in-house experts on certain committees and could assist the members in understanding why some committees functioned well and others did not. Various staff also became subject-matter specialists in such areas as energy, tax expenditures, scientific research and development, and committee staffing patterns.

In addition, plans were being developed for hearings or panel sessions with members, legislative experts, and representatives of special interest groups. Certain staff had principal responsibility for this function, although each staff member had ample opportunity to make recommendations and suggestions about prospective witnesses. Throughout, staff decision making tended to be collegial rather than the result of individuals functioning in isolation.

CONCLUSIONS

To the extent that structural deficiencies have contributed to the perceived imbalance between the legislative and executive branches—and structural factors are by no means the only causes, or perhaps even the most important ones—then committee reform might help to restore the health of the policy-making partnership that the Framers had intended.

Nevertheless, reforms do not develop by themselves, nor are they neutral in their effect on legislators or outside groups. For example, an ardent opponent of the Select Committee's reform plan, John Dingell, who was adversely affected by the proposed changes, charged that "it seems to be a fact that reformers try to profit at the expense of their colleagues."[29] Proposals for institutional change require serious and sustained public attention before Congress will consider altering its established ways of conducting the people's business. Moreover, it is almost unheard of to create a select committee for just that purpose. Why the House took that step was the result of a complex configuration of internal and external factors. Many legislators, however, came to perceive that something needed to be done or the House would find itself in the uncomfortable position of having to abdicate further responsibilities to the executive branch. The House, some feared, was being perceived as a debating society where members talk only among themselves with few in the citizenry paying them any heed.

The select reform committee would have a life of only two years, so it was clear that a reform plan needed to be developed and then adopted in a relatively short period of time. In beginning its task, the Select Committee employed several techniques to assess the "reform market" in the House. Members of the committee solicited the opinions and recommendations of their House colleagues by means of informal interviews. Meanwhile, Select Committee staff were interviewing more than 150 staff personnel from the other committees, following a loosely structured questionnaire aimed at pinpointing problems in jurisdiction, staffing, oversight, scheduling, and committee rules and procedures. Staff and consultant studies were undertaken on specific topics. Members and staff were also planning a round of hearings and panel sessions, which is the focus of the next chapter.

FOUR

Committee Work:
The Public Phase

THERE IS a rhythm to congressional committee work that is familiar to close observers of Capitol Hill life. A subject is first identified, either because legislation has been introduced or because committee leaders have decided (or have been pressured into deciding) that it is a fruitful area of inquiry. Formal hearings are then held. These hearings may last an hour or they may drag on for months; they may attract national attention or, as is more likely, they may be ignored by all but the most dedicated *cognoscenti,* playing themselves out before tiny audiences in one of the Hill's numerous hearing rooms. If they have not already done so, the committee staff will usually prepare a document that can form the basis for a report on the subject. If committee leaders want to report legislation to the parent house, they will then schedule working meetings—appropriately called "mark-up" sessions—to labor over the provisions. When a majority has reached agreement, the bill is printed and a report is prepared. The committee then presents its handiwork to the full house for consideration.

Although the Select Committee's assignment was hardly routine, most of its activities fell easily into those work patterns common to congressional committees. In part this occurred because members' schedules were constrained by their standing committee responsibilities and time was short. The members, moreover, seemed comfortable with proceedings that did not challenge the habits developed in their years of committee experience. In a real sense, therefore, the Select Committee's work closely resembled the typical work patterns of standing congressional committees and subcommittees. In recounting the committee's story, therefore, we are describing many of the workings of other committees as well.

Nevertheless, the Select Committee was unique in certain notable respects. It was, of course, an ad hoc body created for the duration of the 93rd Congress. Despite occasional suggestions that the life of the committee be extended, Chairman Bolling insisted that the group should be dissolved at the end of its allotted time period, whether or not it had succeeded in its mission. Unlike other congressional bodies, the Select Committee did not begin with those habits of cooperation that can develop when members work together year after year. Its members had to learn to work together as a group and master their subject matter, all within the span of a single Congress. Their assignment, moreover, was a complex and delicate one, demanding a working knowledge of every one of the House's standing committees. The task had not been undertaken in twenty-eight years, nor had any of the members ever served on a reorganization committee. The methods the committee chose for approaching its assignment, therefore, assumed special significance.

The Many Uses of Hearings

As a procedure designed purely to impart information, the congressional hearing would probably receive low marks. Witnesses commonly read their testimony from prepared texts—an uninspiring prospect, to say the least. While the testimony drones on, committee members quickly leaf through the prepared text or, just as frequently, use the opportunity to sign their mail or review files from their offices. Attendance is often haphazard, with members coming and going, often taking time out to greet constituents or consult with staff aides. When the witness has finished the testimony, the questioning begins, with committee members asking questions serially. Very rarely does there occur a genuine interchange between the legislators and the witness; more frequently, while one member asks questions his colleagues assume an attitude of benign noninterference. There is typically only one witness at a time (though sometimes a witness will be buttressed by assistants), and thus there is no opportunity for interaction among witnesses of varying views.

The somnolent pace and somewhat ritualized structure of the hearings, however, suggests that gathering information is only one function served by the proceedings, and probably not the most important one. Hearings are public events and serve public purposes. Even though hearings may be poorly attended, they will be studied carefully by interested publics and specialized journalists. Hence, the participants—

legislators no less than witnesses—must pay attention to the impact their words will have. Their purposes include personal advertisement, seeking publicity for their views, reminding influential constituents that they are on the job, and building a public record in support of a given course of action. A freewheeling, open-ended exchange would not serve these purposes as fully as does a more structured performance; moreover, it would pose added difficulties if it took an unanticipated turn or otherwise got out of control. A certain amount of predictability and inflexibility, then, serves the interests of the participants.

The Select Committee's hearings were no exception to these generalizations. Perhaps because of their unique assignment, members relied heavily upon the hearings to gain information and to orient themselves to the problems of the various House committees. The hearings served several other purposes as well. Chairman Bolling and the committee's staff devoted much thought to the hearings and weighed alternatives to the traditional format. The multiplicity of functions performed by hearings were well understood, and the hearings themselves were planned with those objectives in mind.

GETTING PEOPLE'S ATTENTION

The Select Committee, most realized, would need every scrap of support it could glean from members of the House. Indeed, its first task would be to gain recognition for itself as a serious-minded body that intended to recommend changes in the House's modes of operation. The House had reorganized so rarely that it would be difficult for veteran legislators to take the committee seriously, and awareness of the committee's hearings would help establish its credibility.

The lead-off witnesses, Speaker Carl Albert and Minority Leader Gerald Ford, drew attention to the Select Committee and lent the leadership's support to the reorganization effort. His feet barely touching the floor from the witness chair, the diminutive Speaker explained:

> ... I am always reluctant to appear before committees, but this committee was set up as a result of the recommendations of the leadership, and I felt it my obligation to appear.

> I appreciate the fact that you have invited me to be your first witness. I consider it an honor. I think it is fitting because ... this committee was created because of my own conviction that this kind of study was due.[1]

Chairman Bolling and Vice Chairman Dave Martin drew attention to the event. The latter termed the Speaker's and minority leader's appearances "a clear signal that the leadership of the House is dedicated to accomplish the task of analyzing the workings of our own institution in order to improve the legislative process."[2] Bolling, a professed admirer of the Speaker, pronounced Albert's testimony "very penetrating" and "wise," and noted that it was the first appearance of a Speaker before a committee in approximately a hundred years.[3]

Albert and Ford both stressed the scheduling problem, an irritant for the two men but perhaps not the key reason they advocated reorganization. With little direct influence over the pace of committee operations, the leaders had found themselves hard pressed to induce committees to report legislation early enough to permit orderly floor consideration of measures. "So long as I can remember," Albert explained,

> the leadership has been confronted with the difficulty of inducing committees to conclude their work on major legislation early enough in the session to allow their bills to be scheduled for action by the House. This is especially true of important authorization bills. . . .
>
> To a degree at least, the leadership is at the mercy of the committees in planning floor schedules and in disposing of the critical business of the House.[4]

During the early months of a new Congress, leaders rarely find enough business to keep a respectable agenda; in the closing months, however, a flood of bills pours from the committees and cannot be given adequate time for debate. "I remember the closing days of the last session as a nightmare," Albert said ruefully. Echoing this concern, Ford blamed the proliferation of authorizations for preventing timely action by the Appropriations Committee. He suggested cutoff dates and longer-term authorizations as possible solutions.[5]

In their concern over scheduling, both leaders mentioned the desirability of an early organizational session to be held following the congressional elections. Following the precedent of the transition period provided Presidents, Congress would provide funds so that newly elected members could travel to Washington and set up their offices, and the parties could caucus to select the committee memberships. "Some committees wait an unconscionable length of time to get organized," Albert observed.[6] Ford endorsed the proposal. Actually, the two had discussed the idea privately (Albert termed it "a little personal idea") and were on the verge of introducing it themselves but decided to delegate it to the Select Committee.

Beyond these items, the Speaker had no specific suggestions to offer; he did not, for example, voice his concern over circumscribing the Ways and Means Committee's power—perhaps his main reason for urging creation of the Select Committee. He stressed the broad mandate of the committee, its responsibility to survey the committees and suggest changes in the number and jurisdiction of the committees. But he would not dictate.

> . . . While I think you have the opportunity to make important contributions to the operations of the House, I am not going to undertake to prescribe the areas within which you work, or to influence your decisions. . . .

> I will be glad to discuss with your chairman or members, any important point on which you might desire my opinion. I will not, however, dictate: I will try to cooperate. If I had the answers, I would not have recommended the creation of this select committee.[7]

Albert's lack of specificity drew a mild reproach from Representative William Steiger, who professed himself disappointed at what the Speaker excluded from his remarks. However, questioning failed to elicit from the Speaker anything more specific.

The minority leader, however, was not so reticent about revealing his views about jurisdictional shifts. If Albert's major premise was to curb Ways and Means, Ford's was to curb the liberal-leaning Education and Labor Committee. He proposed partitioning the committee into two components, citing the phenomenal growth of educational programs and the absence of close linkage between these matters and traditional labor-management issues.[8] Another overburdened committee, he noted, was Interstate and Foreign Commerce, whose attractiveness had grown with its work load. As examples of committees that could handle added responsibilities, he cited Science and Astronautics and Foreign Affairs.

GIVING EVERYONE A DAY IN COURT

The appearances of Albert and Ford drew attention to the Select Committee, garnered considerable press coverage, and, to skeptical members of Congress, served notice that the committee was open for business. Thus intense interest among legislators in testifying before the Select Committee was anticipated. No less than 199 representatives and senators had testified or submitted statements for the Joint Committee on the Organization of the Congress (1965), and eighty-eight had testified or submitted statements in 1969 to the Subcommittee on Legislative Reorganization of the Rules Committee. Considering the relevance of the committee's mandate to the career interests of members, the number of House witnesses was somewhat below expectations. In two sets of member hearings, fifty-two representatives ultimately appeared to testify and sixteen others submitted written statements for the record.

Great efforts were expended to accommodate all members wishing to testify. Letters of invitation were sent to every member of the House before the first series of hearings opened on May 2, 1973. Later, a second round of invitations was issued for the final member hearings in September, when because of time constraints, each witness was limited to half an hour. Witnesses' crowded schedules needed to be taken into account. At Bolling's direction, complete records were kept of the detailed negotiations with the witnesses' staffs over scheduling the testimony. He did not want disgruntled colleagues to fault the committee for lack of cooperation. Further, several legislators indicated an interest in testifying but did not do so, either because they had schedule conflicts or because they changed their minds about appearing.

Once they appeared before the committee, witnesses were given a free rein in making their presentations. In initial planning for the hearings, the committee's staff had suggested that nontraditional formats might be tried: encouraging witnesses to focus their remarks on specific problems, and perhaps even grouping witnesses by committee or subject-matter expertise.[9] It also urged that a room be found that would facilitate informal interchange—for example, utilizing a large table around which both committee members and witnesses could sit. Neither of those proposals were implemented. Although a number of the public witnesses were grouped into panels, House members, it was decided, might resent such a format; and so they were heard in the traditional fashion. Scarcity of space and the inflexibility of House facilities killed the other suggestion. The hearings were held in the elegant but cavernous Caucus Room on the third floor of the Cannon Building across from the Capitol. The chamber featured lovely decorations, including vintage chandeliers, but its dimensions were huge and its acoustics poor. The only concession to informal interchange was that Select Committee members, by mutual consent, occupied only the lower tier of seats on the dais, thus placing themselves a bit closer to the witness table.

Congressmen in the witness chair were treated with studied courtesy, and the congratulatory rhetoric that politicians utilize in speaking publicly with one another was much in evidence. Witnesses were welcomed profusely, encouraged to proceed however they wished, and usually thanked effusively for their "provocative," "thoughtful," or "wise" contributions. Chairman Bolling, considered by some a difficult man to deal with, was a model of graciousness and restraint.

Witnesses were assured that the Select Committee welcomed all suggestions, and that it labored under no preconceived conclusions. During the later set of hearings, for example, Bolling sought to pacify an incensed Leonor K. Sullivan, chairwoman of the Merchant Marine and Fisheries Committee. Learning of proposals to abolish her committee,

Chairwoman Sullivan appeared before the committee to deliver a sting-
ing statement threatening "vigorous opposition" to any such plan. "I
gather from your statement and from other things that I have heard that
there are a great many rumors around," Bolling observed mildly. He then
stated:

> The committee as a committee and the staff as staff has come to abso-
> lutely not one single conclusion. I have some views as a person. Other
> members of the committee no doubt have, but where the notion got
> around that we had arrived at conclusions fascinates me. Of course, hav-
> ing been around a long time, I find that Congress is probably more full of
> rumors and alarm excursions than any place I have ever been, including
> all the fraternity clubs, and so forth.

Sullivan shot back:

> Mr. Chairman, if I might say, I think it is foolish to think that you and
> the other select committee members would have come to any conclusions
> in this short time.[10]

Although Sullivan's statement bristled with challenges to anyone who
might have the temerity to break up her committee, neither Bolling nor
Paul Sarbanes—the other Select Committee member on hand, and a
member of Sullivan's committee as well—elected to engage her in a
dialogue. She was thanked effusively for her contribution and the hearing was adjourned.

Occasionally Select Committee members forgot the need to cultivate
their colleagues and allowed animosities to jar the proceedings. The first
tense exchange occurred during the appearance of Carl Perkins, chairman of the controversial Education and Labor Committee. Probably the
most liberal committee in the House, Education and Labor had long
aroused the ire of conservatives, and its bills were frequently altered on
the House floor.[11] Unquestionably Education and Labor was a target for
reorganization: the Monroney-Madden Committee (1966) had proposed splitting it into two committees, a proposal reiterated by Minority
Leader Ford. Two of the Select Committee's Republicans, Martin and
Frelinghuysen, harbored grim memories of the apprenticeships they had
served on Education and Labor under Perkins's predecessors, Graham
Barden and Adam Clayton Powell.

Following Perkins's plea that his committee should be left intact
("It is entirely possible that jurisdictional niceties have nothing at all to
do with the problem," he observed[12]), Martin subjected him to a lengthy
cross-examination. As Perkins fumbled for the answers, Martin prodded
more boldly.

MARTIN: There isn't too much work then actually in the legislative field for this [Special Subcommittee on Education] subcommittee to pursue at the present time; is that correct? Just give me a yes or no, if you can, please.

PERKINS: The answer is that there is plenty of work . . . .

MARTIN: Well, you say in your statement that you want additional staff and additional money and additional rooms and so forth, in order to do more work on oversight and involve the junior members. Why don't you bring the junior members in now?

PERKINS: What I am stating, Mr. Chairman—I mean Mr. Martin—

MARTIN: I am vice chairman, not chairman.

PERKINS: Excuse me, Mr. Vice Chairman, what I am stating, Mr. Martin, is that we are doing presently as good a job as anyone else is doing in the area of oversight, but we could still do a better job if all of the committees were properly equipped and staffed to conduct oversight to the extent that it should be conducted in the Congress.

MARTIN: That isn't getting to the point which I raised. But I have had difficulty in this area before, Mr. Perkins.[13]

The barrage was continued by Charles Wiggins, and Perkins was asked for large amounts of data on his committee's operations—material that was not forthcoming for several months. Lloyd Meeds, usually a defender of Education and Labor, where he had served since 1965, arrived late and did not participate in the exchange.

The shoe was on the other foot when Representative William L. Dickinson came before the committee in early June. He outlined the need for more staff for the minority, bitterly recalling that a minority staffing provision had been included in the 1970 Legislative Reorganization Act, only to be rescinded the following year as a result of action by the Democratic caucus. Not only was this a sore spot with Republicans, but it remained an embarrassment for Democrats interested in bipartisan reorganization efforts. The vehemence of Dickinson's attack on the caucus, however, irritated the committee's Democrats. When called upon, Meeds answered the witness sharply:

Mr. Dickinson, I regret that it is necessary, but I feel it is necessary, not to inform you in this hearing, but to invite you to come to my office some time, or we can get together some time, and spend about an hour talking about the Democratic Caucus. You admit that you know very little about it, and it is very clear that you do know very little about it. . . .[14]

With that statement, Meeds ended his questioning.

Perhaps the most acrimonious exchange occurred during a later hearing in which Banking and Currency Chairman Wright Patman appeared with several of his colleagues. During the first round of hearings, Thomas Morgan, chairman of the Foreign Affairs Committee, had alluded to a long-standing jurisdictional dispute over international financial and monetary organizations (assigned to Foreign Affairs by House Rule XI, but actually handled as an extension of the banking jurisdiction of Banking and Currency).[15] Patman sought to rebut this recommendation. It was a familiar dilemma: did international financial institutions fall under foreign policy or banking? Said Patman:

> All of us are aware of the fact that in our interrelated economic world, most every important action taken in the United States, be it an increase in the prime rate, money supply, domestic tax policy, and so forth, all have international implications.

> Carrying this observation to its logical extreme would clearly indicate that there should be no committee in the House other than the Committee on Foreign Affairs. This, I am sure, should strike everyone as being absurd.[16]

Such organizations as the World Bank, he argued, had always been considered banking institutions; and multilateral lending operations were carefully maintained as nonpolitical. He also noted that Foreign Affairs members had been invited to join hearings held by his committee concerning the various international financial institutions.[17]

When the period for questioning began, Peter Frelinghuysen, ranking Republican on Foreign Affairs, lashed out at the trio. In his thirteen years on Foreign Affairs, he said, he had never been aware of an invitation to join any session of Patman's committee.

> The invitations couldn't have had stamps or perhaps were misaddressed if they were sent to individual members of the committee, because I had no knowledge that we were invited to share in listening to testimony.[18]

Nor was Frelinghuysen mollified when Patman explained that the invitation had probably been relayed to Chairman Morgan but for some reason not passed on to the members of Morgan's committee. Frelinghuysen had acid comments for the witnesses' implication that Foreign Affairs might treat international financial institutions as political playthings. "Do you think if there is going to be any trembling in the world markets there might be trembling because the House Foreign Affairs Committee assumed jurisdiction over this area?" he queried. Though conceding that Banking and Currency had a strong claim to the jurisdiction, he labeled as "absurd" the "clear insinuation that if the Foreign Affairs Committee got its hand on the jurisdiction of this area it would treat these situations as political instruments."[19] Frelinghuysen's outburst, while not unprovoked, was embarrassing to the Select Committee; and Bolling had to ask the witnesses, who were chafing to escape the cross fire and get to another meeting, to remain long enough to receive friendly questioning from Robert Stephens, a senior member of Banking and Currency.

These incidents were rare interludes in the seventeen days of hearings involving House colleagues. In general, the sessions were marked by polite but probing treatment of witnesses. Moreover, the Select Committee benefited from unusually faithful attendance by its members; at a typical session, most of the committee's ten members would be on hand at one time or another. About the only open profession of doubt concerning the committee's seriousness of purpose came from Representative Robert Leggett, who concluded his testimony with a blunt challenge:

> I do not mean to be flippant, but I don't expect that the committee is going to consider seriously these recommendations, but you did set aside the time. I wanted to express myself frankly as to some of the things I think should be done in the Congress of the United States. I don't have the slightest hope that you are going to do anything, but I have made my remarks in the hope that you are conscientious in this job.[20]

Bolling thanked the witness for "your contribution up to the last three sentences."

It later became evident that many congressmen shared Leggett's doubts about whether the committee could live up to its assignment. The very difficulty of the task, not to mention the infrequency with which it had been undertaken, no doubt lulled many, reformers and standpatters alike, into assuming that the committee was simply another futile exercise. Bolling himself rated the chances of producing a meaningful report as no more than fifty-fifty. The hearings had succeeded in arousing the dedicated reformers, as well as a few members with special interests to defend; but for the majority of House members, stronger signals would have to be sent.

HEARING THE ADVOCATES

An important group of witnesses wished to push House organization in a particular direction, or sensed that their formal powers would be in jeopardy in any reorganization deliberations. On several jurisdictional disputes, the committee was lobbied by one or more inside participants. In addition, several outside groups had proposals to advertise before the committee. Thus, the committee quickly assumed one of the key functions of congressional hearings: to provide a platform for advocates of various positions.

The most vocal advocates appeared in the field of energy jurisdiction. With Congress' belated discovery of the urgency of "the energy crisis," there ensued an unseemly scramble for jurisdictional advantage among a number of committees and subcommittees. During the course of the committee's deliberations the energy issue intensified, and it was generally assumed that its report would attempt to resolve the jurisdictional scramble. Various claimants for the jurisdiction thus used the committee's hearings to advertise their wares.

Some legislators advocated a new joint energy committee, and several bills to that effect had already been introduced. Others favored a new standing or select committee in the House to deal with the problems. One of those urging a new committee was J. J. Pickle, who added that he certainly was not speaking for his committee chairman, Harley Staggers.[21] When queried about the Commerce Committee, Pickle declined to make any concrete recommendations, though his proposed energy body would have embraced large segments of Commerce jurisdiction. One of the busiest committees in the House, Commerce was heavily involved in energy policy making through its responsibilities in transportation and in the regulatory agencies. Indirect efforts to induce Chairman Staggers or other ranking members of Commerce to appear were unsuccessful (Pickle, eighth-ranking Democrat, was the most senior member to testify); for the moment, Staggers as a major claimant for energy seemed to be preoccupied with other matters.

A strong case on behalf of the Science and Astronautics Committee was advanced by Mike McCormack, a young nuclear physicist who had been designated chairman of its Energy Subcommittee. Accompanied by Committee Chairman Olin Teague, McCormack presented a knowledgeable brief, filled with statistics and accompanied by voluminous documents. His case for the Science and Astronautics Committee rested on expertise, technical staff, access to outside information, and a systematic and scientific approach to problems.

> I believe that these responsibilities logically fall to the Committee on Science and Astronautics. This committee has established a tradition of dealing with technological problems, and of doing so in a scientific manner. Solving the energy problems facing our nation is not something which a committee can do as a sideline; nor can any committee, with or without a competent technical staff, treat energy-related problems intelligently except in the context of an overall energy policy. The scientific method, a systems approach, and high technical competence are essential to success in this area.[22]

The combination of McCormack's expertise and his thorough presentation impressed the Select Committee, as its subsequent recommendations were to demonstrate.

Still another claimant was the Joint Committee on Atomic Energy, long noted for its championship of the cause of nuclear power. The Joint Committee's précis on the energy crisis, a narrated slide show on the importance of nuclear power, was aired early in the Select Committee's hearings. Although Joint Committee Chairman Melvin Price was one of the witnesses, the chief instigator was the former chairman, Chet Holifield. His presentation was a bit puzzling because it avoided the question of what precise committee structure should be adopted; but the general thrust was transparent. "I think we get the message," Bolling acknowledged. "I think we need a committee on energy." "Mr. Chairman, I think that is inevitable," Holifield replied.[23]

Other legislators had their own organizational strategies for dealing with the energy problem. Several advocated creation of a select or joint committee to handle the subject. Among these was Representative Paul W. Cronin who testified in support of his bill calling for a joint committee modeled after the Joint Atomic Energy Committee.[24] No doubt the witnesses who raised the energy problem harbored a variety of motives. Some, as we have noted, were spokesmen for their own committees; others were disinterested observers; still others seized upon the topic as a way of demonstrating their awareness of a pressing public problem.

As the various claimants intensified their lobbying, Select Committee members became uneasy about mediating the dispute, and, more than once, Bolling tried to nudge the legislators into helping solve the dilemma. Promising to give consideration to the views of the Joint Atomic Energy Committee, he urged Holifield and his colleagues to develop a jurisdictional proposal:

> I think I can state dogmatically that this select committee is not going to ignore the legitimate interests in how your committee decides to recommend on where and what the energy committee should be. I think I can guarantee that given some sort of rule of reason, if you can come back to us with the recommendation by at worst early fall . . . we could then be in a position to give full consideration to your views and those of the people with whom you work.

> You are aware I know—and I suppose the rest of the committee is—that there are other committees that have set their caps for this jurisdiction, and that there are all kinds of political problems.[25]

Later, after listening to the Science and Astronautics Committee's case, Bolling suggested that the various claimants negotiate among themselves.

It seems to me it would be unwise if we [the Select Committee] began to
settle such matters unilaterally—if of course at some point we are going
to bite the bullet, because of the charge to the select committee. It seems
to me that we need some preliminary discussion on a very informal basis
to see whether we can approach it in a noncontroversial way to begin it. I
know that is what everybody wants.[26]

Like the earlier witnesses, Teague and McCormack acknowledged that
the suggestion had merit. But if anything came of the proposal, the
Select Committee was not aware of it.

Congressmen from other committees came to plead their causes. One
of the most delicate matters before the group concerned the Education
and Labor Committee. As noted, a proposal to split its jurisdiction had
been around for some time; and, rightly or wrongly, it was widely presumed that the Select Committee would be a vehicle for accomplishing
the change. At the same time, because Education and Labor was generally liberal, splitting it was considered a Republican, or conservative,
objective. This gave the issue a partisan cast that the Select Committee
was unable to dispel.

The partisan element was dramatized by juxtaposing the testimony
of Chairman Perkins and the ranking GOP member, Albert H. Quie. Quie
urged dividing Education and Labor, buttressing his case with statistics on the growing work load, especially in education. He argued that
there were too many subcommittees, that committee members were
overextending themselves, and that legislative business was lagging because quorums were difficult to obtain. Though his contentions were
based on experience with Education and Labor, he observed that the
problems were widespread in the House and could be alleviated by limiting members' assignments.[27] A respected veteran legislator, reform-
minded yet close to the leadership, Quie commanded the Select Committee's attention and, as we will see, was questioned about many of his
views. Although separation of Education and Labor was not the only
thrust of Quie's remarks, his views on that question were bound to be
influential.

Perkins, in contrast, defended his committee's current jurisdiction
and questioned what difference the matter really made to the House as
a whole. "It may make sense to consolidate or split from a purely ab-
stract or rational point of view," he said, "but it seems to me that the
question you should be asking is whether the legislation is being handled
efficiently, effectively, and responsibly under the current setup."[28] Beyond Perkins, however, no one appeared to defend Education and Labor's existing domain.

Several other committee chairmen sought to protect their committees against possible incursions. Notable among these were Richard Ichord of Internal Security, Leonor Sullivan of Merchant Marine and Fisheries, and Wright Patman of Banking and Currency. The latter two appeared in order to counteract previous testimony or rumors (incorrect, as it happened) of tentative decisions reached by the Select Committee. Other congressmen came forward to promote their proposals for new committees highlighting current problems—most notably, aging, urban affairs, and transportation.

In contrast to members of the House, the public witnesses gingerly approached matters of committee jurisdiction. The seven individuals or organizations who appeared were handpicked by Bolling, who wanted to limit the scope of controversy and discourage outside groups from developing inflexible positions on reorganization questions. However, several witnesses, including Ralph Nader and John Gardner, noted that Ways and Means was vastly overextended and should be relieved of some of its responsibilities.[29] Further, spokesmen for the National Association for the Advancement of Colored People (NAACP), Clarence Mitchell and Joseph Rauh, advocated abolishing the Rules Committee. Answering the contention that Rules, a liberal nemesis of the past, was no longer a threat, Rauh argued that "the time to fix the roof of the building is when the sun is shining, not when it is at its worst, when it is raining out."[30] This struck a responsive chord with Select Committee member C. W. Bill Young, who had tried unsuccessfully to persuade his colleagues to adopt curbs upon Rules' power; but it provoked an animated response from Martin, Rules' ranking GOP member, who countered that the panel had declined to report only a very few bills.[31]

In matters other than committee jurisdiction, House members displayed less intense interest. However, the panelists and public witnesses ranged widely into organizational and procedural issues. One proposal that received important support from spokesmen for outside groups was rotation of committee members. The scheme would simply place a limit of six to eight years on the time a legislator could serve on a single committee. At the end of that period the member would have to seek another assignment. While the proposal was mentioned by several reform-minded legislators, including Don Fraser and Bill Frenzel, its greatest push came from Ralph Nader, John Gardner of Common Cause, and Lucy Wilson Benson, president of the League of Women Voters of the United States.[32] Several advantages were claimed for the rotation proposal. For one thing, it would give legislators broader exposure to a variety of issues and problems. As Nader put it:

> The issue of rotation combats quite effectively the getting into a rut, an intellectual rut or a subject matter rut, which occurs to people in all walks

of life. Rotation, I think permits a fresh perspective and the questioning
of provincial assumptions that are now just never questioned.[33]

Both Nader and Gardner drew analogies from private business to demonstrate the effectiveness of lateral transfers in preserving organizational
vitality and flexibility.

The underlying appeal of rotation, however, was undoubtedly political. On the one hand, rotation would single-handedly "solve" the seniority problem, effectively minimizing seniority within committees. Groups
long disadvantaged by the seniority principle therefore saw rotation as a
means of achieving final victory. A more subtle justification for rotation
lay in its presumed effect upon what Gardner called the "unholy trinity"
—alliances among committees, middle-level bureaucrats, and clientele
interest groups.[34] Rotation of committee personnel, it was claimed,
would help break up those cozy relationships.

The rotation idea, despite vigorous support from the citizens' lobbies, had virtually no chance of serious consideration. The only proponent of the notion on the Select Committee was John Culver. When
present at the hearings, Culver often queried witnesses about the feasibility of the plan; privately he argued in vain that the idea be included
in the committee's report. Although several other members sympa-
thized with the plan, only Culver urged the Select Committee to endorse it. Bolling, for example, seemed to feel that the solution was too
mechanical, that it would simply replace one inflexible system, seniority,
with another, rotation. More importantly, the idea would have created a
political furor, impinging upon the parties' prerogatives in making
committee assignments and vastly complicating the Select Committee's
already difficult task. William Steiger, no foe of the principle embodied
in the suggestion, seized on a minor incident in the committee chambers
during his colloquy with Lucy Benson to emphasize the political problems.

> STEIGER: I couldn't help but notice that the lights in this hall began to
>   flicker at the suggestion that we have rotating committees and commit-
>   tee chairmen. That proposal strikes at the very roots of this institution.
> BENSON: It was with fear and trepidation we put it forward.
> STEIGER: It is an interesting idea. It will, unfortunately, never get any-
>   where.
> BENSON: I suspect you are right.[35]

Steiger, of course, was an accurate prophet.

No doubt some of the advocates' views were aired before the Select
Committee for the sake of publicity, but others were motivated by a
commitment to reform. Certainly the proposals were received with

varying degrees of interest. Some, like rotation, were politically unfeasible; others, like the proposed Urban Affairs Committee, were politically attractive but were judged to be conceptually flawed. In at least one instance—the panel hearing on the budget process—the testimony was directed not toward the Select Committee but toward Rules, where Bolling and Martin were negotiating a budgetary reform bill. Whatever the cause, the Select Committee had to give its sponsors a full and fair hearing. The concept of procedural justice, of the importance of a "fair hearing," is revered in Congress, and the knowledge that the committee had listened carefully to all views would enhance the credibility of its recommendations.

"Making a Record"

If it is imperative to convey to interested parties at least the impression of a fair hearing, it is equally important for a committee to lay the groundwork for the actions its members anticipate or advocate taking. This is commonly known as "making a record" preparatory to the committee's report. Hearings provide a useful forum to publicize the committee members' objectives and elicit supportive testimony. If legislators have already committed themselves to a policy, they can legitimize their positions by selecting friendly witnesses, mobilizing supportive lobby groups, and posing questions designed to buttress their case. To exploit this function of a hearing, of course, the committee members must have reached prior conclusions about their objectives. Most experienced legislators harbor many such prior commitments, at least in general outlines, to particular policies. Thus, few legislative hearings are purely open-ended fishing expeditions, entirely devoid of prior understandings as to their direction and probable results. In fact, it is probably fair to say that hearings are more frequently convened to advertise and buttress the legislators' concerns than to elicit information for the legislators' edification.

The ten members of the Select Committee were, however, experienced observers of the House of Representatives. They had been selected, as we have seen, not only for ideological balance but also for their commitment to structural and procedural reorganization. Some had volunteered. Their service on the committee offered, in view of the tough choices that would be made, little promise of political benefit. It is little wonder, then, that these members brought to the committee explicit notions of how the House was functioning and what should be done. The hearings gave them ample opportunities to pursue these themes.

Oversight of the executive branch was probably the strongest leitmotif of the hearings—mainly because two of the committee's members repeatedly played upon the theme. Ever since the 1946 Legislative Reorganization Act enjoined congressional committees to exercise "continuous watchfulness" over the federal agencies under their scrutiny, oversight had been conceded one of the central responsibilities of Congress. (The 1970 Legislative Reorganization Act dropped the problematic word "oversight" in favor of "legislative review." However, the Select Committee's hearings suggested that the older term had embedded itself into legislative terminology. Therefore it was favored, with the term "review" reserved for certain special jurisdictions.) Most observers, however, conceded that the record of congressional committees was spotty at best, and the hearings provided ample evidence for this conclusion. As Morris S. Ogul, one student of the subject, concluded, "There is a large gap between the oversight the law calls for and the oversight actually performed."[36]

The hearings cast considerable light on the oversight problem. Witnesses frequently complained that they lacked the time and the staff assistance to maintain surveillance over executive agencies. Indeed, the goal of "continuous watchfulness" may simply be unattainable, considering the size and complexity of the federal establishment. There is also the matter of political incentives. As with most people outside the legislature, members of Congress tend to think of the legislative process as largely a matter of passing laws—a process that is completed when the President signs a bill and passes out presidential pens to the measure's authors. While exposing defects in the legislation might yield some publicity, it also carries the risk of making legislators *persona non grata* with the bill's sponsors, administrators, and beneficiaries. Oversight is most likely to take place when legislators are willing to incur these political costs—when, for example, they are adamantly opposed to the legislation that has been enacted, or when they support the legislation but feel administrators, perhaps of the opposition party, are sabotaging its purposes.

Occasionally these ingredients are present, and vigorous investigations are launched. More frequently, however, the norms of the congressional committee are hostile to inquiries that might tend to cast disrepute on legislation the committee has championed. As Representative Wiggins observed,

> It has generally been regarded . . . that the members of the committees should almost be partisans for the legislation that goes through the committee and for the interest groups that are affected by it.[37]

These norms are often influenced by unrepresentative committee memberships.[38] Considering the membership and disposition of many committees, asking them to maintain watchfulness is setting the fox to guard the henhouse. If the Agriculture Committee were to engage in a thoroughgoing review of the Department of Agriculture, Chairman W. R. Poage said:

> About all we would accomplish, as I see it, is to create hard feeling, a loss of confidence on the part of our farmers that the Department of Agriculture could render them a service, because we can be so critical of the Department . . . that there won't be any farmer in the nation that will have any confidence.[39]

Commenting later on the constituency problem, Wiggins observed that it would be "idle to think that the Agriculture Committee is going to take a critical look at the effectiveness of agricultural programs in doling out the public purse to the farmers."[40] No doubt Agriculture is an extreme example of committee clientelism, but the phenomenon is found in varying degrees within other committees.

Select Committee members were undaunted in the efforts to highlight the oversight problem and to find solutions. The most vocal champions of oversight were Martin and Culver, who on most other issues were found at the extremes of the ideological spectrum. Martin argued, with some force, that constituency interests should not limit a legislator's choice of committees. He noted that although he represented a district almost totally devoted to farming, he had no intention of serving on the Agriculture Committee:

> I think it [the Agriculture Committee] should be spread out among people from metropolitan areas as well as agricultural districts, but all members from agricultural areas are not interested in going on the Agriculture Committee . . . .[41]

When a panel of political scientists cautioned the committee not to expect consistent attention to oversight until it held adequate incentives for legislators, Culver launched into an animated appeal for scholarly advice on how to solve the problem:

> I am really at a loss to follow you when you say there is not adequate political incentive. I think there should be. What we need from you are suggestions as to how to strengthen the organizational design and shape and activities of the Congress and its members so that we can build into our system a far more effective program of congressional oversight. . . .
>
> I hope we can get something more from you gentlemen than the idea that there is not enough political incentive.[42]

When the scholars confessed they had few concrete suggestions, Culver continued to badger them for proposals. It was a curious reversal of traditional relations between scholars and practitioners: the scholars urging caution and citing practical political pitfalls, the legislators insisting on bolder structural solutions.

Few witnesses were as sanguine as the political scientists about the failure of Congress to engage in oversight. A parade of legislators, including committee chairmen, were queried and admitted that their committees were not doing an adequate job, citing a variety of reasons—time, staff, money, and so forth. If the witnesses agreed on the importance of the problem, it was no doubt partly because Select Committee members—Martin and Culver particularly, but the others as well—would not let them leave the witness table before commenting. Thus, the impression grew that oversight was a leading theme of the hearings, even though relatively few witnesses brought the matter up voluntarily. The "oversight matter," Chairman Bolling declared, "has come up persistently in different ways in the hearings."

> I doubt that there is a single subject that more witnesses have talked about and more members of Congress have complained about than the failure in one way or another of the structure as a whole really to engage itself in anything like the beginning of an adequate oversight function.[43]

Martin, who described oversight as a "knotty problem," noted that it was "a thread [that] has run through the testimony of the members of Congress who have appeared before us."[44] Although there was little agreement on what should be done to stimulate effective oversight, it was obvious that the Select Committee would direct some of its more important proposals in that direction. Nevertheless, the committee successfully "made a record" substantiating their concern about oversight.

While oversight was virtually the only topic in which the committee's members persistently attempted to build a public record, individual members had certain issues that they eagerly pursued. Sometimes they stemmed from a committee assignment or subject-matter expertise; sometimes from a long-standing advocacy or antipathy of one kind or another. For example, the second-ranking Democrat, Robert Stephens, several times raised the issue of what he considered unfair criticism of congressmen's travel. "I think we ought to point out to everybody," he said, "that travel is a duty of a member of a committee and irresponsible criticisms which have caused people to be gunshy have been because we have not said it is a duty of members."[45] It so happened that, a few years earlier, Stephens had traveled to Europe on an international banking mission and had been criticized by a home-state paper for spending taxpayers' dollars to make the trip. Thus chastised, he sought to air his views about the need for congressional travel. "But how can that oversight meaning [of travel] be emphasized so that it doesn't become a weapon against the member of Congress who is running for reelection?" he asked."[46]

Steiger used the hearings to criticize House Parliamentarian Lewis Deschler's slowness in completing the long-awaited updating of *Hinds' and Cannon's Precedents*, mandated by the 1970 Legislative Reorganization Act.[47] Other Steiger concerns centered around jurisdictional matters. As one of the House's leading experts on federal job training programs, he was concerned about House jurisdiction over these programs, and especially the overlapping responsibilities of the Education and Labor and Ways and Means Committees. Furthermore, he vented his feelings about the Internal Security Committee in a series of pointed questions to Chairman Ichord designed to demonstrate overlaps between Security's tiny jurisdiction and that of Judiciary.[48]

Culver had a variety of concerns to publicize, including oversight and rotation of committee members, already mentioned, and a stronger speakership. Another was his attraction to the study of futurism, stimulated by exposure to the popular writings of Alvin Toffler and others. At the Iowan's suggestion a panel discussion on futurism was scheduled, with witnesses urged to forecast the future needs of the House. Culver took an active role in the discussion and was delighted with the session, pronouncing it "the most provocative and challenging presentations that the committee has received to date or is likely to receive."[49]

The committee's junior Republican, C. W. Bill Young, participated less frequently than his colleagues; but even he had identifiable issues that he pursued upon occasion. In private sessions of the committee he had tried, without much success, to persuade his colleagues to reduce the role of the Rules Committee. When he encountered witnesses from the NAACP who advocated abolishing the body altogether, he seized the chance to air his views, though making it clear he would not go so far as to do away with the committee altogether.[50] Like many Florida legislators, moreover, he was proud of his state's so-called sunshine law assuring public access to committee deliberations, and he indicated that he would apply such standards to Congress.[51]

GLEANING INFORMATION

The ostensible rationale of all congressional inquiries is gathering information. Many observers, in fact, have written as if this were the *only* function of such inquiries. "A legislative body," wrote Telford Taylor in the stormy McCarthy period, "is endowed with the investigative power *in order to obtain information,* so that its legislative functions may be discharged on an enlightened rather than a benighted basis."[52]

In his celebrated study, Woodrow Wilson referred to congressional inquiries as performing "the informing function."[53]

As we have seen, the process of conducting an inquiry has in fact a variety of purposes—personal, factional, institutional, political—that loom large in the committee's (or individual members') definition of the task at hand. This is even more true of committee hearings, the most common form of inquiry but not necessarily the most efficacious one. Our stress on the variety of functions performed by hearings, however, must not obscure the importance members attach to hearings as means of gleaning information on the subject at hand. Thus the hearings were often employed to orient members to their demanding assignment; and witnesses were informally judged on their ability to assist the committee.

The hearings served as a singularly fascinating advanced seminar in congressional politics and procedure. Witnesses were questioned at length and encouraged to impart their views on how the House should be organized. Though concrete issues received the most attention, broad philosophical questions were not ignored. Several members—Sarbanes especially but others as well—showed keen interest in such questions. What, the members inquired, was the optimal size for a committee? How many committee assignments should legislators be permitted? Should committee jurisdictions be broad or narrow, disparate or focused? Should jurisdictions be designed to parallel executive agencies or Senate committees? The eagerness with which Select Committee members tackled such questions betokened a commitment to regard reorganization as a method by which the House could adapt more effectively to its external environment.

The informational component of the Select Committee's hearings was especially evident in the panel discussions organized by the committee's staff for June 13 through July 13, 1973. We played a leading role in designing these sessions because of our contacts with the academic community, the source for many of the expert witnesses. Other staff members participated in the planning, and were assigned to work on specific panels. The prospectus for the panel sessions was then referred to Chairman Bolling, who approved it with one exception (vetoing a proposed panel composed of congressional journalists). The panel format was chosen to facilitate interchange and maximize the number of witnesses that could be heard. Staff members were assigned to each panel to brief the witnesses, outline the anticipated lines of inquiry, and join the witnesses in the discussion before the committee. In addition, most of the witnesses produced brief working papers that were edited, printed, and circulated to committee members prior to the hearing in question.[54]

Considerable thought was given to the subjects of the panel discussions, with the objective of informing committee members on key aspects of the House committee system. An introductory pair of hearings was scheduled on the general topics of committee structure and dynamics. The staff's assumption was that each House committee would have to be considered in light of its special problems of jurisdiction and political environment—that reorganization strategy would, in Richard F. Fenno's phrase, be necessarily based on a retail rather than a wholesale logic.[55] Nonetheless, it was thought that scholars and other observers could assist by identifying the critical variables that cause committee differences and that presumably should influence reorganization decisions. Later panels dealt with staffing, oversight, and information facilities and services. Because of the complex linkages between congressional committee organization and the structure of the executive branch, two panels were scheduled on that subject, featuring administrators as well as scholars. Two experts on state legislatures were brought in to outline innovations in the states. Although no single state legislature enjoys facilities and resources equal to those of Congress, many of them have pioneered in specific innovations, one of which—the Office of Law Revision Counsel—was included in the Select Committee's report. Finally, at the urging of Representative Culver, a panel of futurists was held to conclude the panel phase of the hearings.

An especially significant informational benefit, though it turned out to be indirect, came from a pair of panel hearings concerning the budgetary process.[56] During the committee's deliberations in 1973, budgetary reform was definitely in the air. Challenged by the unprecedented number of impoundments of funds made by the Nixon Administration, the 93rd Congress had created the Joint Study Committee on Budget Control (the Ullman-Whitten Committee), which in late spring published a report calling for a revised budgetary process. For a time it was unclear whether this proposal would be handled by the Select Committee or turned over directly to the Rules Committee—both of which had jurisdiction over the subject. Eventually Rules took over the negotiations, which led to the Budget and Impoundment Control Act of 1974. Although some Select Committee members and staff urged that budgetary recommendations be included in the Select Committee's report on committee jurisdictions, Bolling concluded that the two subjects—both necessitating careful and delicate negotiations—could better be handled separately. However, the staff decided that members would profit from an intensive briefing on the complexities of the budgetary process. The two panels were carefully designed and prepared by staff members Linda H. Kamm and Robert C. Ketcham, who took their assignment so seriously that they became two of the most knowledgeable experts on the Hill outside the taxing and spending committees themselves.

Harvard Law professor Stanley Surrey added a new dimension to the members' understanding of this critical aspect of legislative politics with an exposition of the novel concept of "tax expenditures"—provisions of the tax code, amounting to an estimated $60 billion annually, whose major purpose is not raising revenue but aiding groups and serving social goals. Once a decision has been made to assist a given group or activity:

> We can then ask the question: Is it more efficient, better, fairer, to use a direct grant or to use a special exclusion from taxes, a deduction or a credit? That is a rational question to ask. In the past it was never asked. The tax expenditures system just grew up.[57]

Surrey's point was that tax expenditures were policy questions that should be weighed not just by Ways and Means, but by the authorizing committees as well. Previously Ways and Means had devoted no systematic attention to this question. The insight raised the possibility of dividing functions that had been handled exclusively by Ways and Means —for example, assigning trade policy to Foreign Affairs while retaining the actual drafting of tariff provisions in Ways and Means. This concept would reappear in the Select Committee's deliberations.

The remainder of the hearings—involving House members and public witnesses—could not be systematically directed toward informational objectives. In the case of House members, the hearings were, as previously noted, open to all comers; outside witnesses were invited selectively with an eye to achieving political balance among the major lobbying groups. Yet virtually all those who came before the Select Committee were sources of information pertinent to the job of committee reorganization. Every member of Congress, for example, is an expert of sorts on the work of his or her committee—its responsibilities, procedures, staff, and jurisdictional peculiarities. Of course, for committees on which Select Committee members had served—Education and Labor, Foreign Affairs, Banking and Currency, and Rules, for instance—strong, informed (though not always accurate) views already existed. Less was known about other committees, however, and witnesses from these committees were especially valued. Such committees were Appropriations, Ways and Means, Public Works, Armed Services, and Select Small Business.

Some members, because of their expertise, were given detailed questions during their appearances. For example, at the conclusion of Representative Quie's detailed presentation, Bolling departed from his usual procedure to ask him a series of involved queries concerning oversight, committee jurisdictions, and joint referrals of bills. "I am not trying to shut you off," Bolling explained, "I am just not interested in forcing you to make a quick answer."[58] Quie's responses were forwarded to the committee several weeks later.

A variety of methods were available to elicit desired information, even though the selection of witnesses was largely beyond the committee's control. Often, witnesses or their assistants contacted the committee's staff to ascertain what lines of inquiry most interested the committee. Some witnesses thus presented material that had been "coached" by the staff of the very committee to which the testimony had been given. Once on the stand, moreover, witnesses could be queried along lines of interest to the committee; suggested questions were occasionally provided by the staff (especially for the panel discussions) at the request of members. More commonly, members evolved lines of questioning that they repeated with many witnesses. Sarbanes, for example, was intrigued by theoretical problems surrounding the committee system and repeatedly asked witnesses their views concerning the size, number, representativeness, and breadth of committees, as well as their relation to executive-branch structure. Other members developed their own lines of questioning, trying them out with variations on a variety of witnesses.

Testing the Political Waters

A special kind of information gathering, especially well suited to the mechanism of the committee hearing, is the gathering of political data, probing the attitudes of individuals and the groups they represent, and gaining clues as to the policies they can "live with." Such information is often as important to a congressional committee as the facts and figures that delineate the substance of a problem. Moreover, while facts and figures are most efficiently compiled and analyzed outside the formal hearing, political information is effectively transmitted in such a format. This is true because, as we have already explained, the various actors—interrogators and witnesses alike—view the hearing as an essentially political arena, ideally suited to "making a record" for the benefit of their constituents and others to whom they wish to convey their messages.

In view of the political delicacy of the Select Committee's assignment, political data gathering was potentially a prime function of its hearings. In fact, however, this function was somewhat muted. To test the political waters, one must know what is to be tested. Many committees debate issues repeatedly over the years, spending much of their public deliberations plowing over familiar ground and reciting well-rehearsed positions. The Select Committee had no such familiarity with the issue at hand.

Possible reorganization schemes were by no means self-evident. Members were using the hearings to orient themselves and sometimes advertise their own views; on most issues they kept open minds. In few instances, therefore, were the committee members able to take accurate political readings on the proposals, because the proposals themselves were unformed. Had the committee scheduled hearings after floating its trial balloon in December, the political exchanges would have been much sharper and more informative.

In several cases, of course, alternative reorganization plans were known to the committee even before the hearings began. Probing these alternatives was usually tactful but nonetheless directed toward eliciting clues as to what the interested parties would tolerate.

The Ways and Means Committee was an obvious target for jurisdictional reshuffling. A small, exclusive committee, it had over the years aggregated enormous responsibilities in such diverse fields as health care, welfare, unemployment compensation, intergovernmental relations, and resource regulation—all ostensibly extensions of the taxing power. Its prerogatives touched those of many other committees; yet its small size and its refusal under Chairman Wilbur Mills to operate through subcommittees meant that if it was considering one major issue, other pending issues would hang in suspension. If welfare reform was on the agenda in a certain year, other matters like tax reform or tariff revisions would have to wait until the next year. Resentment from other committees of the House would have spilled over had it not been for the high reputation of the committee and the uncritical adulation accorded Mills in the press.[59] Inability to bring Ways and Means into line was unquestionably one of Speaker Albert's motivations for creating the Select Committee. In one way or another, therefore, the committee would have to deal with Ways and Means.

With the Ways and Means problem looming ahead, members of the Select Committee groped for clues about what certain members of that committee might accept. The problem of communication was complicated by personal factors. Mills and Bolling had never been close; and, in any event, Mills was absent from Washington much of the session, undergoing treatment for a back ailment. Moreover, the picture varied depending on which legislator or staff aide one queried. The intertwining of member and staff specialties confused many of the jurisdictional problems considered by the Select Committee.

Only three members of Ways and Means appeared before the Select Committee. Although none of them broached their committee's jurisdictional problems in their prepared testimony, all three were questioned in some detail about them—as they must have known would happen. Acting Chairman Al Ullman of Oregon came to talk about his budgetary reform proposals ("If the people really understood how irresponsible our procedures were, I think there would be a political go-around in the country"). Nevertheless, Martin led him to the subject of his own committee and its vast responsibilities. After discussing Ways and Means' failure to create subcommittees to distribute the work load, Martin asked pointedly:

> Do you feel that if the jurisdiction were reduced somewhat that perhaps you would be able to do a little better job? Maybe you have too much jurisdiction.[60]

Ullman responded that he favored "restructuring responsibility" but expressed the committee's standard defense that economic matters were too closely intertwined to be separated. "Remember," he said later, "all of these taxes are interrelated, and I think it is important that they be held together."[61] The suggestion, advanced by such Foreign Affairs specialists as Representative Dante Fascell, that tariffs and trade be shifted from Ways and Means to that committee, was politely but firmly turned aside. Then Steiger, an expert in income maintenance programs, asked about welfare funds, which accrued to Ways and Means through the Social Security Act of 1935 but which are not generated by the Social Security tax. Ullman's reply suggested compromise.

> Without committing myself, I would say that would make a lot more sense than something like trade which is really a gut economic issue that needs to be held, I think, much more tightly with other economic policies. . . .
>
> I repeat, I see a valid reason for keeping jurisdictions over trust fund operations in the committee. . . . I am trying to think whether the field of health might also be mentioned here. . . . I presume you are thinking in terms of putting welfare and health together.
>
> MARTIN: Yes. I think you could conceivably go into that kind of arrangement.
>
> ULLMAN: The gentleman is thinking of a new committee altogether.
>
> MARTIN: Yes.
>
> ULLMAN: Here again, I would have to see the package before I could make any real comment on it.[62]

"As to welfare," Ullman said in closing, "certainly you can make a far better case of transferring welfare to a new committee. I am not recommending it."[63]

Much the same tone was struck by the two other senior Ways and Means members who testified. Phil Landrum had come to talk about splitting Education and Labor (where he had once served), but the discussion inevitably got around to Ways and Means. Martin wondered whether some jurisdictional changes might not also raise Ways and Means' efficiency.

> LANDRUM: Well, at the risk of incurring the wrath of some of my senior members on the committee, at the risk of suggesting to them that some of our wings should be clipped, I would say that there is no real justification for the Ways and Means Committee having jurisdiction over welfare legislation, for example. It is there because it is a part of our social security statute. And for that reason only, a tax matter.[64]

Incensed that Landrum had singled out Education and Labor for partitioning, Meeds turned the tables by suggesting that what was good for Education and Labor would also be good for Ways and Means:

> LANDRUM: I just used welfare and social security as an example. There are other examples.
> MEEDS: Indeed.
> LANDRUM: And the gentleman states it well.
> MEEDS: The gentleman is being very consistent when he brought it out about his own committee, about the lack of commonality between trade and child care, which comes under welfare. So it may be necessary in deliberations and suggestions of this committee to split jurisdictions in a number of committees, might it not, in addition to the Education and Labor Committee?
> LANDRUM: I hope the gentleman will not think that I was being evasive . . . . We could very well take some of the present jurisdiction of Ways and Means. As a matter of fact, I would support the removing of some of that jurisdiction. I think it would be well for the Congress. I am not opposed to that at all.[65]

Outside of welfare, a high-conflict issue whichever committee it was assigned, Landrum refused to be specific in recommending jurisdictional changes in Ways and Means. Nor was the story much different from Florida's Representative Sam Gibbons, a reform-minded middle-seniority Democrat. Though admitting that Ways and Means ought to create subcommittees, he too nominated welfare for transfer to another body:

> I don't believe that the Ways and Means Committee ought to give up much of its jurisdiction. We could, however, well give up welfare functions. . . . I think we have plenty to do with taxes and trade, frankly. They cover enough heavy work to keep us busy all the time.[66]

These responses, cautious and conditional though they were, indicated some support for divesting Ways and Means of its controversial and somewhat unpleasant welfare responsibilities. As it turned out, however, that course of action did not appeal to the Select Committee.

A similar dilemma surrounded the fate of the Internal Security Committee (HISC). Known as the House Un-American Activities Committee (HUAC) before its name was changed in 1969, it had for more than a generation been a target of liberal critics. Though its witch-hunting days were apparently over, Internal Security had survived numerous concerted efforts to abolish it; and in 1973 it was still expending more than $800,000 annually on its investigatory activities, largely to maintain its voluminous files and publish reports on various left-wing or radical activities. Its only legislative jurisdiction was the Internal Security Act of 1950 and proposed amendments; the topics covered by this law—treason, sedition, and subversion, among others—normally fell to the Judiciary Committee. Indeed, Judiciary was the logical home for all of HISC's responsibilities.

HISC Chairman Richard Ichord forcefully rejected this alternative. In a tactic reminiscent of HISC's past reputation, Ichord rested his objection primarily on the ground that the proposal was being advanced by the National Committee against Repressive Legislation (formerly the National Committee to Abolish HUAC), which he charged was a communist-front organization. Additionally, he stated, it would be unwise to add further to the scope of Judiciary, whose jurisdiction is "so vast . . . that it is obvious that it cannot cope with it effectively."[67] Rather, the chairman suggested, why not add to HISC's jurisdiction or create a new committee with a broader assignment in the internal security field, including the work of the Federal Bureau of Investigation, Secret Service, and other agencies. No doubt HISC's real fear was that Judiciary, heavily weighted by liberals, would simply dismantle the committee's extensive files and investigatory activities.[68]

When he appeared to state his case, Ichord was pressed for his reaction to several types of change. On the question of whether HISC needed to remain a separate entity, Ichord indicated flexibility:

MARTIN: Do you think you could function as a subcommittee out of some other legislative committee in an efficient manner?
ICHORD: I think yes. I think I made it clear that there are many ways that this work [of HISC] can be done. My position is that we be sure that it is done. I think you have definitely got to write into the mandate of the particular committee or subcommittee . . . the authority to have the jurisdiction over this area.[69]

When pressed first by Frelinghuysen and then by Steiger on the possibility of aligning with Judiciary, however, he was unalterably opposed. Steiger bore down on the issue:

STEIGER: Are you saying there is no way in your judgment that it would be appropriate for the Committee on the Judiciary to deal with internal security matters if the mandate — — —

ICHORD: No, I can't say that to the gentleman from Wisconsin because the work is done in the Senate as a subcommittee of the . . . Senate Committee on the Judiciary.

I think, though, that if the committee should choose to do that the preferable way, as I indicated, would be to bestow jurisdiction upon a new committee. The House Committee on the Judiciary hasn't asked for this jurisdiction, to my knowledge—I am extremely concerned that the work would not be done if the House Committee on the Judiciary is called upon to do the work.[70]

A different line of reasoning was used by Lloyd Meeds, who suggested that as an investigatory body HISC was more like an oversight committee than a legislative one. In light of the Select Committee's ultimate proposal, the exchange was significant:

MEEDS: Do you consider your committee to be primarily an investigative committee?
ICHORD: That is right.
MEEDS: Rather than an oversight or legislative committee.
ICHORD: Yes, sir.
MEEDS: Then you investigate for a purpose. What is the purpose?
ICHORD: I went over the investigative authority. . . . When we investigate we have to have some legislative connection. . . .
MEEDS: This is all for the purpose of legislating?
ICHORD: Yes. There would have to be a legislative connection of any investigation of any committee.
MEEDS: Which is really also the same purpose the Government Operations Committee has in oversight in providing the information so that legislation can be enacted to improve the operation of government agencies and things like that.[71]

The committee's exchange with Ichord was inconclusive. As it happened, no one on the Select Committee was enthusiastic about continuing HISC; but conservative members at least wanted to assure that its functions would continue. The political problem of accomplishing this dual goal was the theme of Ichord's appearance. His responses indicated deep opposition to a merger with Judiciary; but they also revealed he was open to other alternatives, and Meeds had opened a promising approach to the dilemma.

The fate of the Education and Labor Committee was the subject of another key political probe during the hearings. Chairman Perkins and ranking minority member Quie, the only Education and Labor members to appear in the hearings, vigorously articulated their views about the committee, Perkins opposing a split of Education and Labor and Quie arguing for it. With lines fairly clearly drawn on Capitol Hill, a large question mark surrounded the reaction of the committee's main external lobby, the American Federation of Labor and Congress of Industrial Organizations (AFL-CIO). While organized labor lobbies on a wide variety of issues, issues falling under the control of Education and Labor are of particular concern. These include such matters as labor-management relations, labor standards, workmen's compensation, manpower, and occupational safety and health standards. As one AFL-CIO official told Richard F. Fenno,

> We watch the Education and Labor Committee very carefully, but it's the only one we're interested in. Otherwise, you would spread yourself too thin. We have to control the labor committee. It's our lifeblood.[72]

Understandably, then, the giant coalition of unions enjoys privileged access to the committee and normally clears prospective Democratic members of the committee.[73] It was unlikely, therefore, that any attempt to alter the committee's responsibilities could succeed without at least the tacit consent of AFL-CIO.

Bolling acted quickly to gain organized labor's acquiescence. In a series of meetings at Bolling's home, he and AFL-CIO chief lobbyist Andrew J. Biemiller and deputy Kenneth Young negotiated an informal agreement concerning the projected labor panel. Biemiller was a former representative (Democrat-Wisconsin, 1945–47, 1949–51) and long-time friend of Bolling. Later in the hearings he and Young appeared to unveil the terms of their agreement. "The AFL-CIO does not believe that any committee's jurisdiction is sacred," Biemiller declared.

> For example, there has been considerable testimony before this committee that there should be separate Education and Labor Committees. We do not oppose changing the jurisdiction of the Education and Labor Committee; however, we want to make it clear that just changing the jurisdiction of one or two committees will not accomplish the necessary job of reform.[74]

To listeners, Biemiller's pronouncement forecast the end of the integrated Education and Labor Committee; but there was a *quid pro quo*:

> If the proposal to split the Education and Labor Committee is to merit consideration, the jurisdiction of the Labor Committee must not be too narrow and the jurisdiction of the Education Committee too broad in terms of work load and cohesiveness of issues. . . .

> To us, if there is to be a separate Labor Committee, its jurisdiction must include: full employment, pensions, unemployment insurance, workmen's compensation, job discrimination, manpower, job training, voca-

tional training, job safety and health, service contracts, railway labor, civil service, fair labor standards, Walsh-Healy, Davis-Bacon, and labor-management relations.[75]

Labor was clearly driving a hard bargain. Biemiller's lengthy list of categories included not only the labor items from the existing committee (including some, like manpower and vocational education, that lay in the gray area between education and labor), but also a number of items, like civil service and unemployment insurance, that were key responsibilities of other House committees.

Biemiller's testimony appeared to have settled the issue of the Education and Labor Committee; but subsequent developments were to alter the situation drastically. Although the Select Committee subsequently acceded to most of the labor spokesman's conditions, the AFL-CIO's position itself became unstuck—as we shall see later.[76] For the time being, however, Select Committee members assumed that labor opposition could be contained and relied on the Biemiller formula in their deliberations.

These public exchanges were not, of course, the committee's sole means of obtaining information. On the Education and Labor jurisdiction, for example, the Select Committee was hardly in the dark: four of its members and one staff aide had served with Education and Labor, and there were numerous informal staff and member contacts. Bolling and the AFL-CIO's Biemiller were old friends, veterans of countless collaborations in steering labor-supported bills through the sometimes balky Rules Committee. Nevertheless, there is a special emphasis given to public testimony: because it is "on the record," it can be employed to bolster subsequent actions. In the case of the AFL-CIO, Biemiller's testimony provided a point of departure for subsequent deliberations on the delicate matter of Education and Labor jurisdiction. In the end, Biemiller's position proved to be misleading; but it was probably accurate as of the date he stated it, and it unquestionably emboldened the Select Committee to take action.

These examples indicate both the utility and the limitations of testimony as an indication of the political marketplace for policy initiatives. Because legislators are interested in public responses, they are prone to rely a great deal on testimony given in hearings; but because of the very public nature of the commitments, both witnesses and legislators are inclined to view them with caution.

. . . And a Few Real Ideas

Occasionally hearings will disclose genuine innovations—proposals that simply have not surfaced previously. Unfortunately, this is a relatively rare occurrence. More commonly, public testimony simply serves to reiterate familiar viewpoints or, occasionally, lend visibility to proposals that might otherwise be passed over. Once in awhile, however, a new idea is articulated by a witness, either in prepared remarks or in unprepared exchanges with committee members. When they are articulated, such ideas sometimes produce a flurry of interest as legislators and slightly bored staff members sit up, join in the discussion, explore possibilities, and in general seek to analyze a familiar problem from a new perspective.

The most conspicious example of an innovation that was presented during the Select Committee's hearings was the plan for using the Rules Committee as a jurisdictional review mechanism. The idea did not initially appear in a mature form, but took shape as it was alluded to by several witnesses. Even before the hearings began, Armed Services Chairman F. Edward Hébert proposed that Rules identify any jurisdictional conflicts as it cleared bills for floor action. In a letter, Hébert suggested that Rules:

> . . . adopt a procedure to determine in each instance whether there is any jurisdictional conflict in bills before it and, if so, to afford each committee involved an opportunity to be heard on the matter. We suggested that if such a recommendation was adopted it would tend to induce more timely committee liaison on jurisdictional problems.[77]

Such a practice would flow naturally from Rules' traditional review of legislation before sending it to the floor. Something broader was suggested by Representative Quie who, in a supplemental statement submitted at Bolling's request, stated that Rules be given "increased authority over committee jurisdictions."

> I think the Rules Committee should decide which committee should be given jurisdiction over issues that are not clearly defined in the Rules. We should not allow just any committee or subcommittee that has the desire to get involved in national problems because they become the "in" issue. The recent experience of many committees passing legislation dealing with the environment is an example of what should be controlled by the Rules Committee in the future.[78]

Although the Rules Committee unquestionably has authority to recommend jurisdictional shifts through changes in the rules, it would clearly be exercising a new type of authority under the Quie proposal. The details of the plan still had to be developed. Meanwhile, other witnesses were mentioning such concepts—new to the House—as multiple referral of bills and deployment of new combinations of members in ad hoc bodies.

It was left to Representative Jonathan Bingham to outline in detailed fashion the proposed role of the Rules Committee. Bingham's testimony came relatively late in the hearings; his legislative assistant had read the previous witnesses' testimony, and Bingham himself had pondered the jurisdictional problem. (An author of the resolution creating the revised Democratic Steering and Policy Committee, he had perhaps applied portions of the concept to Rules.) The result was a lucid, detailed strategy for coordinating and monitoring committee jurisdictions:

> My recommendation is that the Rules Committee be given the mandate and authority to hear and rule upon committee jurisdictional questions and provide for appropriate handling of each such case and that the rules of the House be amended to (1) define this authority with respect to the Rules Committee, and (2) to establish a procedure by which such jurisdictional questions could be referred to the Rules Committee.[79]

The Bingham plan would have authorized a jurisdictional appeal by a committee chairman whenever another committee announced hearings on a disputed issue. The Rules Committee's decision would be binding, although any of the parties involved could appeal the decision to the House floor. Bingham had not exhausted the possibilities inherent in the idea, but he had proposed the basic ingredients, and he had given added impetus to staff work already under way. The result was the jurisdictional review mechanism eventually recommended by the Select Committee.

Several witnesses impressed the Select Committee not because of any specific proposals, but because of the overall quality of their remarks and of the way in which they were able to present a comprehensive reassessment of the committee system. Notable among these witnesses were Democratic Representatives Bob Bergland, George E. Brown, and Fortney H. Stark, and former Republican Representative Thomas P. Curtis.[80] With perhaps one exception, those witnesses had been encouraged by Bolling to present testimony; in each case the invitation had paid off. Without exception, they construed broadly their role in appearing before the Select Committee, proposing reorganization plans so bold they could not politically be followed. Nevertheless, their testimony served to expand the thinking of members and staff. Moreover, it was refreshing to see individuals capable of thinking institutionally without regard to their personal spheres of influence.

SERVING POSTERITY

Both members and staff were aware of the historical importance of their hearings, studies, and reports. Bolling insisted that the committee's public record be as complete and accessible as possible. Staff members familiar with the record of previous reorganization attempts were equally convinced that the committee's published product be regarded as an historical legacy.

The concern for posterity, therefore, was reflected in the content and format of the committee's documents. Of course, the committee exercised no control over the content of their fellow legislators' statements—except as individuals were informally urged to testify, or guided by colloquies into questions of interest to the committee. The panel sessions, however, were carefully structured to highlight key topics and to give exposure to leading experts. Further, the interest-group hearings were limited to a few representatives of organizations having broad legislative interests. Papers authored by panel members were required, and in most cases received, in advance. They were published both individually and as part of the hearing record, along with an extensive bibliography.[81] A large number of historical and statistical compilations, most of them containing new data, appeared as appendices to the committee's final report.[82] Even alternative committee reorganization plans, written by staff task forces and outside consultants, were printed in their entirety.[83] Although this wealth of material might have provided ammunition for the committee's opponents—because it evidenced alternative methods of organizing the House—it was never used in that way. Perhaps that was because staff and consultant plans called for far more sweeping changes than did the Select Committee's final report.

Concern for accessibility of the committee's public record led also to a decision to index the hearings. The result was one of the rare indexed committee hearings in history. The difficulties scholars had encountered in using earlier congressional documents were significantly reduced by this simple decision.

To assure that scholars and other interested citizens would have access to the committee's documents, it was important to disseminate them to libraries throughout the country. Because of the controversiality of the committee's report, this proved to be a thorny task. The first printing of the hearings and related documents amounted to fewer than 1500 copies, which were soon exhausted by members (copies going to every member of the House), staff aides, and the committee's unsystematic mailing list of scholars and libraries. The solution was to designate the hearings as a House document, therefore making available a larger number of copies and automatically supplying copies to government repository libraries throughout the country. By the time the request was made, however, the committee's report had been released and had angered key members on the House Administration Committee who had to approve the request.

An effort was also made to assure that committee documents appeared in a timely fashion. The Government Printing Office (GPO), which
produces all congressional documents, is the world's largest publishing
house. Each day when Congress is in session, it performs the herculean
task of printing the *Congressional Record,* often hundreds of pages long,
in the space of a few hours. Committee hearings and reports are given
lower priority, but like most things on Capitol Hill the schedules can be
pushed forward by the application of political influence. Day-to-day
printing decisions were handled by a GPO printer assigned to the committee. He collected the raw transcripts from the hearings, distributed
them to committee members and witnesses, supervised the editing, and
designed the printing format. Using his contacts, he prodded GPO to
meet printing deadlines. When his efforts failed to yield results, the influence of Chairman Bolling and occasionally Speaker Albert brought
results.

Conclusions

There are some who denigrate the importance of the public record
left by governmental agencies. The really critical decisions, so that thinking runs, are made behind closed doors, as powerful individuals work
out among themselves what they would not dare articulate in public. A
veneer of cynical validity surrounds this bit of political lore. No doubt
public records are deficient, and all too many important meetings are
closed to observers. Politicians do not always reveal their motivations,
preferring to deal in nuances and indirections. They are, after all, public
men and women, and their political positions are fashioned for public
consumption. Thus, those interested in learning about the workings of
government are advised to begin with the transcripts of public deliberations—hearings, meetings, and floor debates. These deliberations appear,
often with startling clarity, in the record. Even where the true purposes
are cloaked in rhetoric, they can usually be inferred with reasonable
precision by the careful analyst.

The public face of a congressional committee is manifested in its
hearings and public meetings, bound for posterity in the volumes of its
publications. People who do business with a committee, whose liveli-
hoods are perhaps dependent upon what the committee does, attach
great importance to the record made in those hearings. Members, too,
place great stock in the hearings. While the manifest function of hearings is the gathering of information, there are a variety of other purposes, often more important to the participants. We have detailed some
of these purposes: gaining the attention of affected individuals and
groups; giving everyone their opportunity to advertise their positions;

laying the groundwork for the committee's subsequent actions; testing the political marketability and various proposals; serving the interests of scholars and historians; and—one should not forget—gaining information and even new ideas. Not all the topics eventually covered by the Select Committee were aired in the hearings and public discussions, but the public discussions of the hearings set the boundaries for what later transpired.

Public hearings, of course, are far from ideal mechanisms. Not all the topics eventually covered by the Select Committee, for example, were aired in the hearings and public discussions. More importantly, many of the House members who were later to surface as the committee's most vocal opponents failed to appear to state their views in public. Some were perhaps philosophically opposed to what the committee was doing (so they claimed later); others simply failed to take the process seriously until forced by the committee's report; still others, perhaps as a tactical maneuver, were silent. Whatever the reason, the hearings failed to attract some of the most crucial figures in the House. Nevertheless, the public hearings and panels set the boundaries for what later took place, and were a powerful influence on the subsequent behavior of the committee.

When the gavel fell on the last hearing on October 11, 1973, the public phase of the committee's work was in a sense ended. By this time staff investigations and member deliberations were well under way. They intensified in the fall of 1973, peaked before the preliminary report was issued in December and again during last-minute negotiations and mark-ups leading to the committee's final report of March 21, 1974. Many of these sessions were public; transcripts of some of them were even published in committee prints—another innovation in committee proceedings. However, an intimate knowledge of the committee's internal workings is necessary to unravel the tangled skeins of these deliberations. Thus, we turn in the following two chapters to the "private" face of the Select Committee on Committees—its deliberations and negotiations.

FIVE

Committee Work:
The Deliberative Phase

Public hearings tend to obscure a congressional committee's inner life. Behind the committee's every public action lies an inner history, sometimes fleeting and transparent, sometimes extended and complicated. At least two aspects of inner committee life bear careful examination: first, the work of the staff, including not only research but also what might be termed "staff politics"; and second, the committee members' deliberations, with their interplay of personalities and interests.

Such aspects of committee work are rarely documented, and even more rarely understood by the public. Until the 1970s, in fact, most committee meetings were closed to reporters and to the public. Even when the sessions were open, attendance was limited to a few interested observers, a scattering of journalists from specialized publications, and perhaps some tourists who wandered into the committee rooms. An understanding of staff and member relationships, of course, requires a deeper acquaintance of the situation.

The Select Committee's work pace was episodic, dependent upon the members' other responsibilities and geared to formal deadlines either imposed on the committee or set by Chairman Bolling. Staff efforts fluctuated to meet these demands. The protracted public hearings and panel sessions, for example, tended to impede the committee's progress. As long as the hearings transpired, it was very difficult to schedule working sessions with committee members; it was hard enough to turn them out day after day for the hearings themselves. Whenever administrative matters demanded committee action, Bolling would insert the business item between witnesses' appearances. For the staff, the hearings were often a distraction. Admittedly, some useful information was gleaned from the hearings and panels, especially by preparing advance memoranda for the members and consulting with prospective witnesses or their aides. Long stretches of testimony were, however, barren of productive material and, in any event, could be more efficiently perused in printed form. Nevertheless, day after day virtually all of the staff's dozen professionals, not to mention some of the clericals, trooped into the committee chamber to follow the proceedings. In truth, staff members were reluctant to miss any of the action, which incidentally presented the best opportunities for hurried consultations with committee members. But as long as the hearings were in session, only half of each day was available to the staff for research and investigation.

The staff nonetheless planned their projects and worked to conclude them. The hearings supplied useful leads and helped to refine the assignments, as committee members' questions or comments suggested avenues of inquiry. Once the hearings were concluded, the committee would have to fulfill its mandate, transforming itself into a deliberative body in the process. No one knew exactly how, or even whether, this could be accomplished; but it must be done, and staff work could pave the way.

COMMITTEE RESEARCH

Aside from its hearings, the Select Committee employed several techniques to learn about the House committee system and assay the "reform market." One method—member interviews with House colleagues—yielded mixed results. At the urging of Bolling and other members, each Select Committee member was assigned a list of colleagues to interview, so that virtually every member of the House would be contacted. The major purpose was to solicit opinions and recommendations, although a subsidiary objective was to gain the attention of the House and demonstrate the committee's desire to respond to members' wishes. Most of the conversations were held in the interviewees' offices, to encourage candor and underscore the committee's responsiveness. However, interviews lagged as the session proceeded and schedules became more crowded; neither Bolling nor the staff were willing to prod committee members into fulfilling their quotas. No effort was made to standardize questions or transcribe replies, nor were staff members invited to sit in— the idea being to encourage candor. Several committee members claimed that their conversations provided them insights that could not have been gleaned any other way, but most were skeptical.

More successful was a staff project designed to collect data on each committee of the House. Each professional staff member was charged with gaining expertise on one or more House committees. Documents and records were scrutinized, and committee sessions were observed. The heart of the project was a series of interviews with more than 150 staff members from the twenty-one House standing committees. The interviews followed a loosely structured format covering such problems as jurisdiction, staffing, oversight, scheduling, rules, and procedures. Based on these materials, reports were prepared on each House committee and eventually published.[1] During committee deliberations those staff members were looked to for expert information and advice. As we have already observed, the picture drawn of a given committee depended greatly on who was being interviewed because staff aides tended to transmit the views of their principals, who in turn stressed those subjects that interested them most. Thus, Select Committee staff members had to fit pieces of the puzzle together in order to gain a balanced picture of the committee's internal dynamics. It was hard for the researchers to be totally neutral observers. In the course of their research, they naturally came to serve as liaisons with the respective committees, sometimes assuming an advocacy role in behalf of "their" committees.

A variety of specialized projects were also undertaken, either by the staff or by Capitol Hill experts or agencies such as the Congressional Research Service. Such studies, most of which were included as appendices to the Select Committee's report, covered diverse topics: historical information on committee and subcommittee formation; committee work loads; numbers of bills by legislative category; jurisdiction over energy issues; and jurisdictional coordination among Appropriations subcommittees.[2] Because of difficulties in compiling the information, many hours were expended merely to generate a single number in a table. Far more original research could perhaps have been undertaken; but the data that were collected represented a treasure trove for students of the House.

Although staff research was considered extremely important, it was often denied sustained attention because of the committee's immediate needs. Work loads were profoundly influenced by the episodic pace of the committee's work—hearings, mark-up sessions, reports, and the like. These were the high points of the committee's life, establishing deadlines toward which staff assignments were pointed. Reporting deadlines set with little notice by the committee chairman were equally important in defining the staff's work load. Frenzied activity and hours of overtime preceded each of these deadlines. Once the deadline was met, a lull would follow as the staff resumed its longer-range research. In Capitol Hill offices, as elsewhere, immediate demands tend to crowd out long-range tasks. One staff project, however, is remarkable enough to deserve special elaboration. Occurring late in the summer of 1973, it came to be known as "the August Study."

THE AUGUST STUDY

Early in June, Bolling directed the Select Committee staff to prepare its own plan for reorganizing the House committee system. The product, he said, should be a comprehensive package deemed "acceptable to Vice Chairman Martin and me." It was to be ready by September, when the last of the hearings was slated to end, and the committee's deliberative work would commence. In essence, the staff was asked to simulate the Select Committee's decision-making process. While the staff members were not asked to play the roles of individual committee members, it was clear that they were expected to take account of the members' concerns and formulate a report that would have some chance of being adopted.

The staff implemented the project after the first round of hearings ended in mid-July. For the next several weeks it consumed virtually all of the staff's time. A demanding and tiring exercise, it nonetheless gratified staff egos, for it gave them an opportunity to grapple directly with the Select Committee's assignment and, in the process, to play at being legislators.

Because revamping the House committee system was not an everyday occurrence, the staff devoted a good deal of thought to procedures and approaches. A flurry of memoranda was circulated, and eventually a basic strategy emerged. First, it was agreed, there would need to be broad agreement on certain "organizing principles," such as the number and size of committees, bases for allocating jurisdiction, oversight, the budgetary process, and so on. Although not necessarily binding on subsequent decisions, these principles were noteworthy because many of them were eventually applied by the Select Committee itself. The staff decided to deal not only with committee jurisdictions but also with oversight and budgeting; such collateral matters as staffing, information resources, administrative support, and the role of party leaders were rejected as outside the scope of the immediate assignment. It was decided to equalize work loads and eliminate the distinction between major and minor committees, ignoring the jurisdictional lines of Senate committees or executive agencies. Subcommittees would not be dealt with directly. Jurisdictional overlaps were to be minimized with a procedure to accomplish coordination among committees and periodic updating of jurisdictions.[3] No agreement could be reached about the optimal size of committees, nor about the number of assignments to be allowed each member. Nor was there consensus on whether committee jurisdictions should be broad or narrow in scope. With but a couple of exceptions, these principles were to be embodied in the Select Committee's final recommendations to the House.

After some preliminary discussions, the staff group met almost continuously during late July and early August, using the committee's room in the Cannon House Office Building. Task forces were appointed to draft portions of the report dealing with budgeting, oversight, and committee coordination. Complex jurisdictional questions were approached cautiously, first by brief reports on each existing committee by the staff member who had done the interviewing, then by canvassing the group for general comments. At one point each staff member prepared an optimal jurisdictional plan. Gradually the discussions focused on specific issues, the comments turning into straw votes and eventually into final votes. For the most part deliberations were professional and bipartisan, but assumptions about desirable policy outputs naturally came into play. The experience was exhilarating but physically and mentally wearing. In comparison with the committee members who eventually would face the same challenge, the staff members were less burdened by collateral responsibilities. Thus the gaming exercise suggested that the decision-making process would be more demanding than anyone had expected, and might even fall beyond the collective capacity of a group of busy legislators. Either a method of structuring a concentrated deliberation would have to be devised, or a subgroup of the committee would have to bear the brunt of the task.

Another lesson vividly demonstrated by the exercise was that no "right" or "logical" committee plan could be conceived that would win everyone's wholehearted acceptance. Every participant had the bitter experience of being voted down on an issue he or she deemed critical. Thus, the resulting "staff plan" was a patchwork product of compromises, entirely acceptable to no one. Although the plan turned out to be far more ambitious than the Select Committee's ultimate report, its political salability was kept in mind.

Nevertheless the staff plan was an intriguing document developed by a group of people who at that moment were as knowledgeable as anyone about the workings of the House. The plan was full of improvisations but contained a number of promising ideas. A total of twenty or twenty-one committees were contemplated. No less than nine House committees would have been abolished (the staff were unsure about the District of Columbia Committee), including the fifty-five-member Appropriations Committee. The plan revived the notion, actually implemented between 1876 and 1921, that authorizing committees should also recommend appropriations; unlike the earlier practice, however, a powerful Budget

Committee would coordinate and reconcile the various appropriations bills. The Ways and Means Committee would be radically reduced in powers; Education and Labor would be split, as would Interior. New education, labor, energy, natural resources and environment, transportation, social services, health, and communications committees would be created. The staff plan pointed toward greater clarity of committee jurisdictions, but occasionally placed countervailing interests in a single committee. A strong mechanism for monitoring committee work loads and effecting cooperation among various committees was recommended, under the auspices of a Rules and Jurisdiction Committee. Oversight was to be encouraged by a variety of techniques. A powerful Government Review Committee would have broad investigative powers and privileged status for oversight-related floor amendments to bills. All legislative committees would be required to establish oversight subcommittees and devote more attention to oversight matters in drafting bills and reports. The staff declined to make recommendations about House administrative services. While a majority felt that most of the matters handled by the House Administration Committee could be delegated to administrative personnel, they were unwilling to eliminate that body outright without further exploring the alternatives.[4]

Once the staff exercise was finished, it was unclear what function it would serve other than upgrading the staff's own understanding of the committee's task. The staff plan was a provocative document, bound to be a target for criticism outside the Select Committee. Bolling, who has a scholar's tolerance for provocative ideas, laughingly commented that the plan would "mess things up in the House." The committee and subcommittee barons, however, would not see it in such a perspective.

Bolling, however, had further objectives in mind. At the committee's first meeting following the August recess, staff members described the project and outlined the plan they had evolved. Staff Director Charles S. Sheldon stressed that the plan did not constitute a staff recommendation *per se*. "It's the report of a very interesting experiment," he said. The plan's linkage of authorizing and appropriating functions, however, attracted Lloyd Meeds of Washington, who pointed out that the budget question, although under consideration in the Rules Committee, was within the Select Committee's mandate. In this and the next meeting Meeds suggested that the group take a position on the matter. Bolling, who had assumed leadership on the budget bill, promised early action by Rules and would not hear of involving the Select Committee. "As a member of both committees," he stated, "I don't want to mix the two."

The staff document received sharper attention at the next meeting, when Bolling offhandedly sought to include it as part of the committee's final hearing record to be published shortly. The suggestion provoked immediate controversy. Already rumors were circulating on Capitol Hill. It was being said, for example, that the Appropriations Committee was about to be scuttled. Some chairpersons like Leonor Sullivan were asking to appear at the second round of member hearings to attack such rumors and defend their committee domains. Some members, like Meeds, observed that the best way to stifle such rumors would be to publish the full document and let everyone know its status. Others, including Vice Chairman Martin and John Culver, thought publication would be impolitic or premature. "The average Representative won't discriminate between this document and a staff recommendation," Culver contended. "If this is the only report put out," Paul Sarbanes added, "it will be assumed that it's the only premise for our deliberations." Bolling looked stymied. "Let's forget it," he said. "Perhaps I shouldn't raise this." The next day Bolling confided that his proposal was only a ploy to goad his colleagues into reading the staff document, and that they had reacted "just as I had predicted." At the time, however, his discomfort seemed genuine. The proposal was rescued when Bolling took up Sarbanes's suggestion that the staff prepare two or three alternative committee plans, building from a variety of premises, to put the August plan in perspective.

As a result, the staff split into subcommittees to produce a series of reorganization plans. One plan contemplated a limited number (twelve) of "multi-interest" committees that would "embrace a variety of interests and viewpoints in an effort to institutionalize 'checks and balances' within each committee"—a notion given an added boost when Representative Donald Fraser mentioned it during the hearings.[5] This plan featured single committee assignments for congressmen, strong central leadership (with agenda-setting and administrative powers), and oversight performed by authorizing committees and Appropriations. Another scheme, the "many-committees" plan, featured no less than thirty-six standing committees and six select committees, not to mention numerous ad hoc panels.[6] The large number was designed to maximize leadership opportunities as well as outside groups' access to committee influence. Committees were divided into "A" and "B" categories to facilitate scheduling, each member being assigned to two committees. Memberships would be rotated periodically for flexibility. A third scheme, the "minimal-change" plan, was designed to "achieve a workable realignment of the committees' structure with a minimum of change in the existing system."[7] Stress was laid on procedural changes pertaining to bill referral, oversight, and budgeting; realignment was to be achieved in a two-step process, through creating new committees rather than shaking up old ones. Yet, even this version would have immediately abolished the Internal Security and Post Office committees and split Education and

Labor; and in the final stage, Merchant Marine and Veterans Affairs would have been eliminated.

These plans were presented to the committee members two weeks later. Although patently intellectual exercises, the schemes were useful in spelling out alternatives. Members expressed genuine interest in such features as the multiple-interest concept and the categorization of "A" and "B" committees, both of which surfaced in subsequent discussions and in the committee's final report. Once several schemes had been aired, the members' objections to publication evaporated, and all the plans were printed as appendices to the hearings. As Robert Stephens remarked puckishly, "It will show we did consider them and had the wisdom to reject them."

Staff Politics

"Staff politics is as complex as committee politics," Holbert Carroll has written.[8] Time has underscored this judgment as congressional staffs have grown both in size and influence. Since 1946, when the La Follette-Monroney Committee uncovered the need for better committee staffing, the number of committee employees has risen steadily; in 1973 approximately 850 people were on House committee payrolls.[9] At the same time, staffs have come to play a more central role in legislative decision making. Historically, congressmen prided themselves on "doing their own homework" and expressed resentment at having to negotiate with Senate staff members in conferences with "the other body," whose members had long since delegated the bulk of substantive policy deliberation. The House has been generally slower than the Senate to equip itself with additional staff, and more reluctant than senators to relinquish the work of legislating.[10] Yet House ways are changing. The combined pressures of more numerous and more vocal constituencies, excessive numbers of committee and subcommittee assignments, and the exponential growth of complex public policy problems are slowly but surely forcing congressmen to reassess their schedules. More than ever, staff relationships are crucial to legislating.

The Select Committee on Committees was no exception. Although emphatically a working body, its members had heavy outside commitments and relied upon the staff for research, briefings, drafting, and sometimes solutions to nagging questions. For its size, the committee had a relatively large staff: approximately twelve professionals and five clericals (the number fluctuated), split equally between the two parties until late in the committee's life, when bipartisanship broke down. Bolling and Martin seemed to favor a "nonpolitical" staff. The chief of staff, Sheldon, was a Congressional Research Service (CRS) economist who, though previously associated with Bolling and familiar with the Hill, was known primarily as a science-policy expert. Initially it was thought the deputy chief of staff job might go to Spencer M. Beresford, a friend and former CRS and Space Committee colleague of Sheldon's. However, Martin was persuaded by Republican colleagues outside the committee to give the post to Melvin M. Miller, a long-time Hill staff member then serving as minority counsel for the House Administration Committee. Beresford joined the staff as assistant minority counsel. The other staff members were appointed primarily on a nonpartisan basis (at least two of Martin's appointees were in fact Democrats) and for the most part performed accordingly. A few had political backgrounds on Capitol Hill and later, when lobbying became an important part of the committee's tasks, were pressed into service as lobbyists and vote counters.

In approaching the committee's mission, staff members tended to group themselves into several identifiable groups, though the lines were oftentimes blurred. The "scientists," especially Sheldon and Beresford, saw committee reorganization primarily as an intellectual problem and were receptive to ambitious conceptualizations grounded in systems analysis. Sheldon's initial committee plan, prepared at CRS and inserted anonymously into the hearing record, was entitled a "planning exercise" and proposed a sophisticated matrix of subject issues and committees.[11] As the staff member responsible for the futurists' panel, Beresford became the principal staff advocate of long-range forecasting, complementing Representative Culver's strong interest in that topic and authoring a memorandum on the subject.[12] However, in questions impinging upon their backgrounds and concerns—foreign intelligence and committee handling of classified materials, for instance—the "scientists" demonstrated their capacity for reacting politically. The "politicos" on the staff, especially Miller, Democratic associate counsel Linda H. Kamm, and professional staff aide Gerald J. Grady, tended to stress the saleability of proposed changes. Miller expounded the views of the most conservative segment of the GOP, often finding himself alone arguing for a status quo solution against other staff members and even committee members. Kamm had an encyclopedic knowledge of House rules and precedents combined with political and intellectual adroitness. Closely associated with the Democratic Study Group, she might have saved the Select Committee some of its conflicts with liberals had she been more extensively employed by Bolling. Grady, onetime intern in Bolling's office and later a Democratic congressional candidate, had Bolling's ear and did what he could to assist the chairman. In between those two was a third group that might be labeled the "scholars," which included several political scientists and at least one lawyer. If their views can be summarized, they would comprise a blend of the conceptual and the political. They were intrigued by the prospect of devising procedural mechanisms for achieving substantive results. Two of them, the authors of this book, gravitated to such topics as oversight and the proposed mechanism for adjudicating jurisdictional disputes.[13] Another, special counsel Robert Ketcham, was an expert in federal energy policies.

These observations simplify what were actually complex and volatile staff relationships. Every staff aide had opportunities to make contributions in all aspects of the committee's work. Politically oriented staff members spent much of their time wrestling with substantive problems; the "scientists" and "scholars" often had sensitive political chores to perform. Because of their recruitment and tasks, the staff probably worked more closely as a team than most committee staffs. Without exception, however, they were strong-willed individuals with their own ideas about committee reorganization. During one committee session, in fact, Chairman Bolling warned the staff against too much independence. As the committee reached majority positions, he quipped, the staff's freedom would narrow as "a little tiny bit of democratic centralism comes into view." As it happened, most everyone on the staff developed firm loyalties to the Select Committee and its members, and in many cases to each other; but they were too experienced to be relegated to a subservient status. Especially during the committee's early discussions, staff members were accepted as active participants; and the staff impact on the committee's report was substantial.

The October Seminar

When the hearings were nearly concluded, the Select Committee began a series of meetings aimed at easing into their deliberative assignment. As the various staff reports were presented and discussed, the committee seemed unable to focus its discussions. The hearings, fascinating though they were, had not fully prepared the members for the task of shaping a reorganization package. Unlike the staff, they had not undergone the concentrated experience of hammering out a complete scheme. After briefing one of the more active committee members, one staff aide estimated that the legislator was at least two months behind the staff in thinking about the task looming ahead. Somehow the committee members would have to bridge that gap—though on a few matters the members were far ahead of the staff.

Meanwhile, Bolling was fretting about the committee's timetable. Originally he assumed that the report would need to reach the House floor by early summer 1974 to ensure action before the 93rd Congress adjourned. At a September 12 meeting, however, he unveiled a much tighter schedule. The committee's report, he announced, should be finished by Easter and floor debate scheduled no later than May 1. Politics in Washington had become unusually acrimonious that year, as the Watergate affair gathered momentum. The elections, more than a year away, would in Bolling's judgment be "bitter and ugly" for both parties. The Select Committee's report, promising plenty of controversy of its own, should be scheduled early to avoid as much of the partisan wrangling as possible. Several weeks later, one of the committee's meetings was interrupted by a new complicating factor: announcement of the sudden resignation of Vice President Spiro Agnew. In spite of these uncertainties, Bolling urged his committee on. "We'll have to work hard and present our report clearly," he said. He would insist on "a genuine product," and would even be willing to report that the committee had failed to reach any conclusions. Above all, he stated repeatedly, he wanted to avoid the fate of the 1946 La Follette-Monroney report, which he termed "a cosmetic, award-winning fake." Bolling was impressed with the contrast between the 1946 Reorganization Act's favorable publicity and its failure to achieve reform, and he tended to ignore its modest though genuine achievements.

Beyond the problem of developing a committee report, there was the matter of dealing with party leaders. "We can't pass our product without the leadership," Bolling stated bluntly. He explained that Speaker Albert wanted the report sent through the Rules Committee, not for new hearings but for "justification and a 'rule' for floor debate." Martin, meanwhile, would consult with the leaders on the Republican side of the aisle. There was a slight problem. Gerald Ford, who with Albert had conceived the Select Committee idea, was no longer minority leader, having been nominated to replace Agnew as vice president and at that moment undergoing confirmation hearings. The new GOP leader, Arizona's John Rhodes, had voted against creation of the Select Committee. Martin was sanguine about Rhodes's support, however, and intimated that Ford might still take a beneficial interest in the project. Shortly after Rhodes's elevation, moreover, a committee staff member, Dennis Taylor, joined the new minority leader's staff, and subsequently helped assure his support. But for the moment, the GOP situation was a question mark.

At the committee's September 12 session, Representative Culver suggested a weekend meeting for uninterrupted discussion. Vice Chairman Martin eagerly seconded the suggestion, even though Georgia's Robert Stephens had a scheduling problem: "Don't pick the weekend Georgia plays Tech," he warned, not quite tongue-in-cheek. Though Bolling seemed to accept the idea reluctantly, he immediately instructed the staff to explore possible dates and to begin preparing such a session. Soon Bolling and Martin asked their committee colleagues to draw up their own jurisdictional plans and ponder such related issues as scheduling and limiting committee assignments.[14]

Discussions during the next several meetings were exploratory and unfocused—plagued by absences and recesses for answering roll-call votes on the House floor. With the prospect of an intensive weekend session in the near future, the members seemed reluctant to consider specifics. Bolling explained later that he was deliberately trying to ease his colleagues into their assignment and prevent them from taking inflexible, final positions. No doubt the members' reluctance stemmed also from a growing realization of the political stakes involved. "They have suddenly realized," Bolling explained privately, "that this rather honorific, pleasant task has turned on them. . . . They started looking around at all their colleagues, and all of a sudden it begins to look like a disagreeable job."

Bolling brought his colleagues along cautiously, in the process revealing some of his own preferences. During a session on October 16, he outlined a series of general propositions noteworthy because they embodied many of the principles that eventually found their way into the committee's report. On jurisdictional matters, Bolling's goals were modest. "I don't think we'll have a model rewrite of jurisdictions," he said, "and I suggest we don't even pretend to do that." Yet he suggested a new energy committee to sidestep the clashing aspirations of the Science and Astronautics and Joint Atomic Energy committees. He argued for an adjustment of work load from Ways and Means to Foreign Affairs, retaining international financial institutions for Banking and Currency. "It's not very clean, but it's realistic," Bolling commented. Procedurally, Bolling wanted to institutionalize the Speaker's power to refer bills, perhaps in tandem with some body like the Rules Committee. Whatever the mechanism, there should be constant review and renewal of work loads and jurisdictions. "I believe more in process than in plan," he said, significantly.

Lively discussions were produced by the matter of the ideal number of committees and assignments. Peter Frelinghuysen, whose Foreign Affairs Committee had in 1971 decentralized to its subcommittees, voiced concern over weakening the full committees and suggested that subcommittees ought to be controlled. This proposition surfaced several times, but it was fraught with danger. As Frelinghuysen himself observed, subcommittees had been "a salvation" for Democrats. Bolling agreed. "The seniority system on the Democratic side has a deadly effect," he explained. "We've ended it by setting up an infinite number of subcommittees, and many of these younger leaders have influence." Equally controversial was the matter of committee assignments. Several members, notably Frelinghuysen, were interested in limiting assignments to one per member—to focus members' efforts and facilitate scheduling. "There's a fine theoretical argument for a single-track system," Bolling responded, "but many members have geared their life style to two committees. They don't want to give up their assignments." He noted that some committees, like Government Operations and House Administration, were valued because they broadened members' intra-House contacts and influence. Sarbanes suggested a larger number of committees, with scheduling handled by dividing committees into A or B categories. Bolling proposed computerized scheduling of meetings along with an appeal to the party caucuses to move toward single assignments.

Other matters rose in desultory fashion. Seniority was conceded a problem, but member rotation attracted little support. Bolling had concluded that the questions of information and administrative support were too complex for the committee to handle. His solution, a pair of blue-ribbon commissions, was floated.

By the eve of the weekend meeting, therefore, members' views were beginning to form. Seven of the members—Bolling, Martin, Frelinghuysen, Meeds, Culver, Steiger, and Sarbanes—had faithfully followed the hearings and discussions. Of them all, Sarbanes had probably devoted the most attention to the committee's mission. Blessed with a powerful intellect, Sarbanes was intrigued by the intellectual challenge and for the time being (later he was to be enmeshed with the Nixon impeachment in the Judiciary Committee) had the time to indulge his fascination. Bolling and Martin had been thinking about many of the problems for a long time; Martin was formulating a comprehensive plan to present to the group. Steiger, whose mind was as supple as Sarbanes's, was rapidly mastering details and shaping a committee plan of his own. Frelinghuysen and Meeds, though expressing relatively clear philosophic positions, were not far advanced on specifics. Although launched into a Senate race, Culver had vigorous views on various matters, especially oversight and long-range planning. The remaining three committee members lagged behind the others in their thinking. Wiggins, incisive and persuasive, was already emerging as Nixon's most able defender in the Judiciary Committee, and the burgeoning Watergate scandal was consuming his energies. If Stephens harbored concrete preferences, he was communicating them privately to Bolling. Young, although he had a few strong notions, never was fully engaged by the committee's assignment. Thus the committee members were at varying stages in their thinking, and Bolling regarded the weekend seminar as a means of focusing members' attention and congealing their views.

The long-awaited seminar took place October 27-28 (the weekend of the Georgia-Georgia Tech game), at Bolling's home in suburban Maryland. For the lengthy sessions, members and staff crowded into a

narrow book-lined basement study where a large table had been set up.
As in the committee's other informal sessions, minutes were kept by the
staff; our own account here is based on our more extensive notes. The
staff had prepared thick loose-leaf notebooks, informally labeled "the
Sunday plan" and filled with memoranda on every topic the group was
likely to take up. The materials were designed mainly for reference purposes, but if the discussion lagged they could be used as an agenda. To
launch the session and stimulate discussion, Bolling was relying on a
plan prepared by Vice Chairman Martin.

To most of his casual acquaintances, Dave Martin was the personi-
fication of rock-ribbed Republicanism that had typified much of the
party's heartland since the days of Uncle Joe Cannon. It was true that
Martin was often taciturn, sometimes blunt, and possessor of one of the
House's most conservative voting records. As senior Republican on
Rules, moreover, it was his duty to champion minority procedural rights,
sometimes cooperating with the majority but often in vigorous opposition. Perhaps it was his very conservatism that led him to be a critic of
the way the House operated; but with his ideology there was also an
inquiring mind and a studious disposition. Though his style differed
sharply from Bolling's, his institutional commitment was no less strong.
And, like Bolling's, Martin's constituency allowed him the luxury of time
to study the House, its procedures and practices. Martin's plan, a product of assiduous study and faithful attendance at committee sessions,
was an original and wide-ranging design that testified to his reformism.
Although it contained some partisan features (such as eliminating proxy
voting in committees and splitting Education and Labor), it cut deeply
into House structure and procedures. There would be twenty-two standing committees, all of which would be exclusive (except for Standards
of Official Conduct) and averaging twenty or twenty-one members. Except for Appropriations, committees would be limited to six subcommittees, one of which would deal exclusively with oversight. Additional
subcommittees could be created only by House resolution. Three committees would be eliminated—Merchant Marine and Fisheries, Post
Office and Civil Service, and that darling of conservatives, Internal Security. Ways and Means would lose jurisdiction over Medicare, Medicaid, and public assistance to a new health and welfare committee, obviously conceived as a liberal domain. A bill referral procedure would
be centered in the Rules Committee, along with an ongoing monitoring
of jurisdictions. A three-year cycle was proposed for authorization, budgeting, and fiscal projections. An early organizational session would be
held by each new Congress. Oversight would be stressed through a series of changes, including a muscular Government Operations Committee, a majority of whose members would be drawn from the party not

controlling the White House. Several procedural alterations were also proposed.

Martin's plan proved to be an excellent icebreaker. Several items were approved with little discussion. The early organizational session, originally proposed by House leaders, was endorsed as a "sweetener" for the committee report, with discussion centering on details. Such an innovation, however, would not resolve the larger problem of scheduling. Institutionalization of bill referral procedures—discussed in the hearings, refined in staff documents, and included in the Martin plan—was discussed only briefly, but it was decided to develop "a complete approach to the problem of reference." There was also agreement on the need for an ongoing review of committee jurisdictions. Bolling proposed that the assignment be given to the Joint Committee on Congressional Operations. Bolling wanted to buy support from that body's House members, one of the few organized centers of opposition to forming the Select Committee. But no one came to Bolling's aid: members were wary of the body's status as a joint committee, feeling that it lacked identity and lacked Rules' close association with jurisdictional problems.

The oversight proposals—labeled by one member "a helluva platter-full"—triggered a stimulating, favorable discussion. The notion of putting Government Operations in the hands of the non-White House party failed to generate support, though it was conceded that some method had to be found to bolster the committee, termed "a eunuch" by one participant. The advantage of Government Operations was its independence from executive agencies and their supportive clienteles; but that very quality diluted the committee's influence. The goal, asserted Government Operations member Culver, should be to:

> . . . encourage increased aggressiveness of Government Operations. Their mandate is now "economy and efficiency." This tends to produce exposés, but obscures broad evaluations of programs.

Martin's suggestion that the committee be authorized to investigate any matter, regardless of whether other committees were handling it, met with unanimous approval; but his suggestion that the committee be allowed privileged floor amendments based on oversight findings was disputed. No one belittled oversight, but some were pessimistic about the chances for improvement. "The interest of members is the key," said Steiger. "It's not a matter of rules or structure; it's a human problem."

Less successful was Culver's attempt to persuade the group to support ways of strengthening the party leadership. There was general agreement that party leaders required additional resources for developing policy positions and coordinating committee activities. Nevertheless, debate over means of achieving this goal was lengthy and, like earlier staff discussions on the same question, inconclusive. The Democrats' Steering and Policy Committee, though it functioned effectively in certain respects, did not live up to its name. As one liberal said, "All we have to go on is whip notices, DSG notices, and the morning paper." The GOP's Policy Committee was more active; but a member of that body spoke caustically of its limitations. "It can't shape policy," he stated. "When they come to a divisive issue, they avoid it. They articulate mainly typical Republican positions." Some members favored authorizing House funds so that party committees could equip themselves with more extensive staffs and eventually play a larger role. Others were doubtful. As one discussant put it, "Is the Policy Committee partisan or nonpartisan? If it's institutional, then it will have to be bipartisan." A majority argued that these were partisan rather than institutional matters. Bolling argued forcefully that leadership could be revived indirectly through new, and ultimately centralizing, procedures for bill referral, scheduling, informational and housekeeping matters, and planning. The discussion of party problems was unusually candid, but it was impossible for a bipartisan group to deal directly with the question and propose partisan recommendations.

Scheduling was directly addressed. The goal was to minimize meeting conflicts and maximize members' attendance. Staff studies showed that members experienced frequent meeting conflicts, which provided excuses for not attending. Steiger, as usual, saw the problem in human rather than mechanical terms. "This is a people problem—even if you were to go so far as to publish committee attendance records. You have the freshmen and the 'Tuesday-Thursday clubbers.' In my first year, for example, I went home every weekend." Most seemed to side with Sarbanes, who observed that "the schedule is simply not used imaginatively. It's more important to let interested members meet their responsibilities than to force them to be there." Later, Bolling announced his intention to write the House Administration Committee to have its House Information Systems (HIS) test a computerized scheduling system. Because the request would go to Wayne Hays, the committee's crusty and controversial chairman, Culver drew a laugh when he quipped, "You don't need all of us to sign the letter, do you? Just don't say please!" "It's agreed," deadpanned Bolling.

Hays' controversial committee came up again during discussion of Martin's proposed Capitol Hill Planning Commission. Bolling was thinking along similar lines, although he believed the commission ought to be controlled by the parties' leaders. He was not yet ready to take on House Administration, but a study commission would presumably recommend a "rational" housekeeping system under some sort of office responsive to the leadership. One or two wanted to attack the matter directly: "Eliminating House Administration would be part of any modernization of the committee system. Members' time shouldn't be dissipated with such petty matters." Bolling, while sharing that sentiment, preferred the two-step approach. Besides, he argued, we do not know enough about the details to create an administrative office.

The issue of proxy voting within committees was briefly considered. Martin had proposed a ban on proxies. He recalled that the late Chairman Adam Clayton Powell of Education and Labor would simply announce that he had so many proxies and his statement would go unchallenged. Meeds responded that he would agree to limit proxies if committee assignments could be limited. The committee members favored abolishing proxies, subject to adoption of a specific jurisdictional plan.

On two key matters the committee members in effect decided not to act. The proposal to combine authorizations and appropriations, which figured prominently in the staff's August plan, was raised by Culver, who favored the idea. Practical objections were immediately raised. The fifty-five members of the Appropriations Committee were bound to oppose the reform, in spite of promises that they could continue to play key budgetary roles within the authorizing committees. Immersed in Rules Committee negotiations over proposed new budgetary procedures, Bolling and Martin were unwilling to cloud the picture. "I don't think it's a good idea," Frelinghuysen said of the plan for phasing out the Appropriations Committee. "I'd like to see the idea shot down quickly so we can deal with other items." And so it was.

Also shunted aside was the proposal for mandatory rotation of committee members in order to reduce clientelism and blunt the effects of the seniority system. Only Culver was seriously interested in the idea, most of the members finding it "completely unrealistic." Entrenchment of committee members was a genuine problem, but most of the proposed solutions raised as many objections as the seniority system itself. However, some legislators were intrigued by a compromise suggestion for encouraging voluntary rotation. If House-wide seniority were applied to committees, then members could change their assignments without forfeiting all of their seniority. Members might carry to their new committee all or part of their House seniority, which would ease their ascension to leadership roles. The staff was directed to study the impact of alternative rotation plans.

More central was the issue of whether to propose controls on subcommittees. Historically, House business had been conducted in full committees; but the burgeoning volume of business and the factional struggle over seniority among Democrats had yielded a rapid flow of power into the subcommittees and their leaders. In some cases—Interior and Education and Labor, for example—the full committee had been weakened by "revolts" against chairmen; in others, like Foreign Affairs, the decentralization had occurred peacefully in line with the Democratic caucus' "subcommittee bill of rights" of 1973. Although its ramifications were imperfectly perceived at the moment, the problem was clear: "If we don't control the subcommittees, we may lose the whole ballgame," Culver said. As a DSG leader and a subcommittee chairman by virtue of the caucus rules passed in 1971, he no doubt sensed the problem more keenly than many of his colleagues. The others drew back from that bold assertion. Most seemed to prefer indirect controls on subcommittees, leaving jurisdictional questions to be resolved within the committees. They agreed with Martin that limiting the number of committees, along with House controls on formation of additional subcommittees beyond a certain number, would suffice. Someone suggested tackling the problem by limiting members' subcommittee assignments. "We ought to put committees under pressure to do their job," Sarbanes said. Several others agreed. Bolling cited the difficulty of dealing directly with the subcommittees. "Going down to the subcommittees would mean a radical new plan," he commented. Direct confrontation with subcommittee chairmen, many of whom had recently attained their posts, was not a pleasant prospect. Thus, the group put aside the matter of subcommittees. It was a momentous decision in light of changing House committee structure.

The debate warmed up when members began to unveil their tentative jurisdictional plans. Martin's plan, which appeared to have generalized support, was already on the table. Meeds's plan, introduced as a "first shot" at the problem, was not dissimilar, although it would have cut more heavily into Ways and Means' powers. Steiger, who by this time had given the matter his concentrated attention, wanted to go even farther. His preliminary plan called for sixteen committees "of more or less equal standing, and . . . generally composed of multi-interest subject matter so as to attract a full range of members interested in committee service." The plan envisioned exclusive committees, although there were two nonexclusive secondary committees and one joint body. Frelinghuysen, who had no formal plan of his own, expressed attraction to Steiger's formulation, as did the absent Charles Wiggins, who conveyed his reactions through a staff aide. "If you want to wean people away from two committees," Frelinghuysen elaborated, "you must have committees that at least sound good. The problem is that members want assignments for constituency reasons and then don't keep up their interest in the committee's work."

Sarbanes proposed an opposite approach—a larger number of committees, narrower in scope and divided into two tiers. His "rough" plan called for twenty-five committees. There would be twelve primary committees, with every member assigned to one. A secondary list of thirteen nonexclusive committees would provide members at least one secondary assignment, if they desired it. Major committees would be relatively equal in size (averaging thirty-eight members) while secondary committees could vary greatly in size. Sarbanes explained that he had come to his conclusions in a round-about way. Initially inclined toward a limited number of broad committees, he now favored a larger number of committees. His reasons were frankly tactical:

> I wrestled with exclusive assignments, and it just can't be done. Two-thirds of the members are now on two committees, and these assignments are important to them. But it's not necessarily bad— *if* you can schedule so as to avoid conflicts. This plan opens up a range of alternatives for members. Their personal, political goals can be served while business is being taken care of.

Sarbanes's approach was for the moment a minority view, but it was a persuasive and politically attractive solution. It sought to make a virtue out of members' attachments to their multiple assignments.

Those advocating the two approaches clashed the next day when the agenda turned to the energy problem. Two congressional bodies—Olin Teague's Science and Astronautics Committee and Chet Holifield's House contingent of the Joint Atomic Energy Committee—were out to capture the energy jurisdiction. Bolling's solution was characteristically indirect and procedural: set up a special energy committee with legislative powers and a mandate to make recommendations concerning its own future role. Personnel would be chosen by the party caucuses. "It would hurt all the present committees in the field," he explained, "but it would deal none a death blow." This solution did not satisfy the advocates of multi-interest committees. As one of them stated, "How do you make the trade-offs necessary in multi-interest committees if you have a special energy committee?" Energy policy, they contended, should embrace not only production, but also resource management and conservation, because any narrowly constituted energy body, dominated by oil and gas interests, would emphasize production and neglect conservation. Although Bolling's special panel was intended to minimize opposition, some questioned whether it would have that effect. "We'll outfinesse ourselves," Steiger speculated. "The Holifields and Teagues won't be fooled; so why not take on the fight?"

A basic cleavage thus appeared between advocates of one-track and two-track approaches. The conflict was more over tactics than basic goals, for by this time the committee was in basic harmony on objectives. The one-trackers (Steiger, Frelinghuysen, Martin, and Wiggins) wanted to move toward a limited number of exclusive committees to ease scheduling conflicts and engage members' undivided attention. To make the committees equally attractive and to encourage policy trade-offs within the committees, the one-trackers advanced the "multi-interest" concept, outlined earlier in hearings and staff documents. The two-trackers (Sarbanes and Meeds) would solve the problem by consolidating committees into two lists and instituting stringent scheduling controls. Members would be unwilling to give up the publicity or electoral support accruing from multiple assignments, they argued, and thus the best strategy was simply to rationalize the system. Besides, a large number of committees made it feasible to create special new committees in such pressing problem areas as energy and transportation. Culver wavered between the two camps, but he encouraged his colleagues to think boldly:

> We've got to raise our sights and stake out the high ground. Otherwise, you'll nickel and dime yourself with political barnacles—to mix a metaphor. There are always reasons for not doing a thing. Let's think big, at least at the outset.

A report too modest, he argued, would be as politically naive as one that was too idealistic. A timid product would be denounced on the floor by reformers "to a standing ovation by everybody."

In contrast Sarbanes, speaking from a similar ideological stance, counseled caution:

> There is no "super-duper" plan. Most changes are incremental. And my ideas about what is "super-duper" may not be agreed upon.

In the middle was Bolling, whose objectives were bold but whose experience told him to steer a moderate course. He had no committee plan per se, but rather an overall strategy and a patchwork of personal preferences and reactions to others' preferences. Out of this patchwork he hoped to fashion a blend of reformism and shrewdness. Balancing appeals to outside interest groups, including reformers, and the House insiders, he hoped to produce a viable report. "I've concluded," he said, "that you don't make changes by a totally new approach. We could agree on minor changes and *a few* major changes."

Most major topics had been aired at this brief but useful "seminar." Before it closed, however, Bolling announced that he had appointed Sarbanes and Steiger as a drafting subcommittee to work with the staff in giving concrete form to the group's sentiments. They were asked to report back within three weeks. Such a step was imperative, for the larger group could not handle the job efficiently. Steiger and Sarbanes were obvious choices, because they had studied the subject minutely and because they both possessed the needed stamina and concentration. (Martin was, however, offended at the choice; he had not been consulted and no doubt would have preferred someone less flexible than Steiger.) Other members, including Bolling and Martin, either had schedule conflicts or were less advanced in their thinking about the problems. Besides, Sarbanes and Steiger would effectively articulate the opposing one-track and two-track committee concepts.

THE DRAFTING TASK FORCE

Over the next two weeks, Sarbanes and Steiger met with the staff in a series of eight intensive sessions, usually lasting three hours or more, to hammer out a draft document for the committee. Though representing opposite parties and different backgrounds, the two young legislators (Sarbanes was forty, Steiger thirty-five) were veteran politicians, keen observers of the House, and concerned about the institutional future of Congress. On behalf of their fellow committee members, they were to review minutely the Sunday Plan and staff memoranda, reaching tentative decisions or pinpointing alternative choices for their colleagues. No other members sat in on the sessions—though Vice Chairman Martin, wanting to keep the subcommittee on a short tether, sent a Rules Committee staff aide to represent his interests and keep him informed.

Some matters were noncontroversial and required little attention. In this category was the proposal for early organizational sessions, although the question of timing was debated (the earlier the session, the greater advantage to incumbent party leaders seeking reelection). The committee's mandate on the jurisdictional dispute mechanism was also unmistakable, although Sarbanes and Steiger worried about delegating this function to the Rules Committee, in view of Bolling's and Martin's roles on that body.

Several issues were as puzzling to Sarbanes and Steiger as they had been to the full committee. One was House-sponsored staffing for the Democratic Steering and Policy Committee and the GOP Policy Committee. Minority committee staffing, a heated partisan issue, was in the same category. Nor was much progress made on the subcommittee problem, which had such a thorough airing at the weekend seminar. Finally, the two negotiators resolved to present the full committee with several alternatives: limiting members to two committee and four subcommittee assignments—a course that would threaten one-third of all House members; requiring each standing committee (except Appropriations) to set up no more than six subcommittees; limiting each committee to six subcommittees (as above), but providing a procedure for a committee to create additional subcommittees; and requiring each committee to establish an oversight subcommittee.

On the question of oversight, there was less leeway because the committee had already indicated the direction it wished to take. Attention was focused on coordinating Government Operations' activities with those of authorizing committees, and several proposals were outlined. One staff member was also developing ideas for an "oversight agenda" proposed and coordinated by the leadership—a solution addressed not only to oversight, but also to the goal of bolstering the Speaker's powers.

The opposing approaches to committee jurisdiction assumed concrete form as Sarbanes and Steiger attempted to outline a plan. As the discussion became more specific, it became more protracted. The full committee had as yet devoted little time to the question; of all the thorny jurisdictional dilemmas, only energy had been discussed in any detail, and that had proved inconclusive. Thus, Sarbanes and Steiger plunged into the labyrinth of committee jurisdictions, first listening to the staff's committee-by-committee briefings and then haltingly launching the process of arranging the pieces for themselves. Something like a domino effect was involved, as the staff already realized: the disposition of one piece of jurisdiction affected the disposition of the next piece and so on down the line. And in completing this intricate task, the two men were tacitly expected to reconcile their opposing approaches: the one-track versus the two-track system, multi-interest versus single-interest committees.

The would-be reformers started with radically different designs. Sarbanes's plan called for multiple assignments and a large number of committees organized for scheduling purposes into "A" and "B" tiers. Admittedly, the plan was not symmetrical and that bothered Steiger. "This plan doesn't come out for any principle," he observed, "and in fact it disrupts present committees quite a bit." He proposed instead a plan of exclusive committees representing broad congeries of interests and disrupting current practices as little as possible. While Sarbanes seemed philosophically attracted to this position, he sensed that the politics were wrong. "The one-tier system will flounder on the numbers issue," he said, citing the many members who would have to relinquish seats on major committees. He continued:

Junior members won't see smaller committees (under the one-tier system) as a plus if they get knocked off one of their committees. The Speaker has made an extraordinary effort in placements during the past two Congresses, to accommodate the wishes of newly elected members. Along with the need to introduce new blood into certain committees, this has resulted in larger committees.

Staff compilations showed that the impact of a one-tier plan would be widespread. Under the one-track plan, no less than 113 members or delegates, or about 26 percent, would be forced to yield one or more of their major committee assignments (though about a third of these choices would be necessitated by splitting Education and Labor); and this assumed that members would be permitted to remain on their favorite committee. If some form of coercion were needed to attain similar-sized committees, more members would be affected.

The committee membership problem was complicated because in theory committee assignments are an action of the House but in practice they are the domain of the parties. Indeed, making committee assignments and protecting committee tenure is perhaps the most potent function performed by the parties. For assignment purposes, the parties distinguish among three types of standing committees: exclusive, major (or semiexclusive), and minor (or nonexclusive).[15] The three exclusive committees—Appropriations, Rules, and Ways and Means—are eagerly sought after, and party leaders carefully screen the candidates. Members of these bodies serve on no other standing committees. Major committees, as formally designated by the Democrats in 1973, were: Agriculture, Armed Services, Banking and Currency, Education and Labor, Foreign Affairs, Interstate and Foreign Commerce, Judiciary, and Public Works. Members of both parties are assured membership on either an exclusive or a major committee. Interestingly, the Interior Committee was still classed as a minor committee, though its mandate in energy and environmental affairs had in recent years diluted its earlier regional coloration and broadened its attractiveness. Both parties had taken steps to limit members to one major committee, but many members retained multiple assignments because they were "grandfathered"—that is, exempt because their assignments predated the rule (Democrats adopted it only in 1973). Of course, minor committees—often with demanding responsibilities—add to legislators' burdens. Under pressure from individual members and factions desiring representation on committees, leaders have allowed committee sizes to increase.[16] In 1947, after passage of the Reorganization Act, the nineteen House standing committees averaged twenty-five members; in 1973 those same committees averaged thirty-three members. Counting the two additional committees created in the interim, the 93rd Congress offered 681 House standing committee positions, compared with only 484 in 1947.

As the discussion between Steiger and Sarbanes proceeded, they moved closer in their views. Steiger had the better theoretical argument, but in practice the one-track plan was virtually impossible to implement. The result was an amalgam of the two approaches. The one-track approach was applied to the major committees, using such guidelines as subject-matter coherence, equality of work load, and balance of interests. At the same time, several of the minor committees were retained simply because no one believed they could be eliminated. Although Sarbanes insisted that a two-track alternative be prepared for the members, the basic model that went to the full committee on November 14 was a modified one-track plan:

Major Committees	Minor Committees
Appropriations	Budget
Rules	District of Columbia
Ways and Means	House Administration
Agriculture [and Consumer Affairs]	Merchant Marine
Armed Services	Standards of Official Conduct
Banking, Currency and Housing	Veterans Affairs
Commerce and Health	
Foreign Affairs	
Government Operations	
Judiciary	
Natural Resources and Environment	
Public Works and Transportation	
Education and Labor	
Science, Technology and Energy	

OR

Education
Labor
Science and Technology
Energy

Two committees were to be disbanded: Internal Security, whose jurisdiction would go to Judiciary; and Post Office, most of whose responsibilities would be in the hands of Government Operations. Ways and Means would yield health financing (among other things) to lend a new focus to Commerce. Several major committees—notably Agriculture, Foreign Affairs, Interior, Public Works, and Science and Astronautics—were deliberately broadened to attract a wider spectrum of members. Sarbanes and Steiger were careful, however, to identify unresolved issues and options. Realizing the sensitivity of the Education and Labor issue, for example, they outlined plans both for retaining and for splitting the committee. With an eye to Bolling's preference for a special energy committee, they included it along with the one they preferred—combining energy with other matters.

On November 14, the Sarbanes-Steiger "dog and pony show," as Steiger called it, went to the Select Committee. Issues had by no means been finally resolved, but for the first time the committee had before it a reasonably complete committee plan. Concrete alternatives were identified and stated. In the favored Washington jargon of the moment, the committee would have to "bite the bullet" on the issues.

A Trial Balloon is Floated

Before a closed meeting of the full committee—as usual, a working majority of six was present—Sarbanes and Steiger presented their reorganization package. On several basic principles they had reached a firm agreement: regardless of how jurisdictions were apportioned, it would be imperative to have a mechanism for resolving jurisdictional disputes and adjusting work loads; oversight was woefully inadequate and had to be strengthened; and changes in rules relating to committees would determine recommendations for committee structure.

By this time there was considerable agreement on the complicated matter of committee jurisdictions. In the modified one-track plan presented as the central alternative, no major committees were eliminated but significant jurisdictional shifts were proposed. "We want to be able to say to the country," Sarbanes explained, "where it is that environment, health, energy, and transportation are handled in the House—not fragmented as they are today." The plan, Steiger elaborated, was designed, though not altogether successfully, to render every major committee attractive to congressmen from varied areas and ideologies, and to stimulate constructive conflict within these committees. Even this plan, however, retained six of the so-called minor committees, thus assuring that at least some members would have multiple assignments.

The nub of the controversy was the degree to which the House should move toward the norm of single assignments to the major committees. Steiger stated the rationale for the one-track goal:

> The present system of multiple assignments diminishes the ability of members to do their legislative job in their committees. There are problems of time and scheduling. The present overlap in jurisdiction, moreover, decreases the capability of the institution to respond. It is fragmented, duplicative.

Sarbanes conceded that a one-track system would be preferable, but he was plagued by the practical barriers. "The one-track plan," he argued, "not only has the disadvantage of forcing members to choose which committee they will keep, but raises the possibility that members will be bumped off committees against their wishes." If size limitations on committees were adopted, he pointed out, perhaps fifty younger members, who would normally be expected to support reform, would be bumped from their current committees. Steiger replied that any reorganization would disrupt members. "You simply have to make judgments—some political, some intellectual." As for the two-track alternative, he claimed it "completely disintegrated" on the issue of scheduling. "It will break down before the first month is up," he said.

The members seemed agreeable to the modified one-track alternative. Frelinghuysen stated that such a system was "not an unreasonable development to move toward. Let's set a goal toward which members can work." Although he had argued consistently against large committees (in the 1947–1973 period his own Foreign Affairs had grown from twenty-five to thirty-nine), he suggested that flexibility in committee size could be built into the one-track system. Vice Chairman Martin, author of a one-track plan, thought that Sarbanes was overemphasizing his fears. Committee vacancies would soon resolve the problem, he said. Meeds said little during the discussion but expressed concern over displacing members from committees in order to pare down their size. Bolling, who praised his two young colleagues for "a remarkable job of clarifying alternatives," was clearly interested in moving forward to a tentative committee plan.

Bolling summarized the session by asking, "Aren't we at the point where we all sort of believe in a one-track plan with reservations? Do the six of us agree how to proceed?" Bolling fretted that only six members were present to make such a key decision. "If there were ever an argument for a one-track system, this is it," he observed ruefully. Yet the Select Committee had been fortunate in its attendance; at this meeting, the more faithful were present (except for Culver). Bolling said, "In the end, people who show up make the decisions." By this time Bolling was worried about the committee's timetable. Events had not erased his intuition that 1974 would be a bitter political year, and he was now calling for a tentative draft before the Christmas recess. "Unless we've given some alternatives to the public, we're going to be criticized for 'popping something out'," he reasoned. Yet less than a month remained, and Congress had scheduled a ten-day recess until November 26. When Congress returned, the members agreed they would "push like hell," calling evening sessions if needed, to produce a preliminary committee plan. Meanwhile, Sarbanes and Steiger urged their colleagues to study their report carefully.

Moreover, the shortness of time created a procedural dilemma that at one point threatened to disrupt the Select Committee's progress. Bolling had discovered that in order to assure publication of a preliminary report before the session closed, it was necessary that a draft copy be forwarded to the Government Printing Office immediately—even before the committee had gone over the Sarbanes-Steiger document. The copy could be revised as much as necessary before printing; but unless the work was begun, GPO would not guarantee publication. To get the publication process started, Bolling accordingly authorized printing of the Sarbanes-Steiger report. The move was innocent enough, but Vice Chairman Martin was incensed. Already suspicious of the Sarbanes-Steiger task force and unhappy about some of their recommendations, he suspected Bolling was trying to put something over on him. At this point no one, including Martin himself, knew what would happen next.

Bolling decided to force the issue. At the committee's second meeting on the Sarbanes-Steiger report, he began by observing that he was stymied. He recounted the course of the committee's work, especially his appointment of a drafting task force that happened to be composed of the committee's two youngest members. The task force report had uncovered underlying complexities, and perhaps he had been mistaken in delegating the task to it, he said. Explaining the GPO deadline, which he said might have fed "suspicions that I was railroading things," he went so far as to declare that "we've gotten so far off the track that perhaps we'd better back off." When Wiggins protested that further delays would serve no purpose, Bolling turned to his vice chairman. "I really need to know how Mr. Martin feels," he said pointedly. "I'd vote to proceed, and without judgment," replied Martin, and after a pause asked whether the votes they had taken the previous day had been final. Bolling quickly assured him they had not been. Frelinghuysen commented a bit tartly that he hoped the group would reach some decisions. "I don't know the significance of that earlier exchange," he said, "but I hope it's not a rift." "It's been papered over," Bolling replied. When queried again, this time by Steiger, for his views on the procedural problem, Martin agreed that the committee publish its preliminary findings as soon as agreement could be reached. "But yesterday we didn't agree on anything," he said.

The committee now turned to the numerous issues to be considered. Some members were casual about the impending committee report: the bolder the proposals were, the easier it would be to compromise later. The prevailing view, however, was that credibility would be lost if the committee report was too radical. Some issues were disposed of handily. A section of the draft detailing the ways in which the plan might strengthen the leadership was eliminated, with Bolling ripping the page out of his notebook for emphasis. Rotation of committee members was also deleted, though it was agreed to include in an appendix a staff discussion of voluntary rotation. Other nonjurisdictional items received favorable action but little discussion; these included the jurisdictional review mechanism, the proposed study commissions, and a Steiger proposal for an Office of Law Revision Counsel.

The nonjurisdictional issue that provoked the most debate was the proposal to require each committee (with certain exceptions) to create a separate subcommittee to conduct oversight on programs and agencies within the committee's purview. This was one of Martin's and Culver's favorite proposals, and because the draft document was equivocal Martin pressed for a vote, arguing that special subcommittees would emphasize oversight responsibilities. Frelinghuysen and Steiger thought it was an artificial solution. "We can't legislate oversight," Steiger contended. He argued that such subcommittees would be unpopular and would falsely differentiate between legislative and oversight functions. Both Martin and Culver held strong views, and most of their colleagues were willing to put aside reservations and accede to their wishes. The proposal for oversight subcommittees won eight to two with Steiger and Frelinghuysen dissenting.

The committee then turned its attention to the jurisdictional tangle. The pivotal jurisdictional choices revolved around the notion, developed by the drafters and taken up enthusiastically by Bolling, of "one-stop" committee handling of key policy issues. "There ought to be a single place in the House," Bolling stated, "where people should go who are interested in such issues as energy, health, transportation, and the environment. Then we can accept some messiness in other areas." To effect this design, a series of delicate shifts was made, involving several key committees—notably Ways and Means, Commerce, Banking and Currency, and Foreign Affairs. The plan was perfected with an eye to political realities as well as to logical policy clusters; and Bolling himself assumed an active role in shaping the committee's choices. "One's view of pressing domestic problems conditions how one puts together these building blocks," he explained.

Unquestionably, Ways and Means was the linchpin. Its power, even in the absence of its ailing chairman, Wilbur Mills, was admittedly impressive. Its vast revenue jurisdiction spilled over into so many key topics—like health, employment security, pensions, and revenue sharing—that it had neglected to give thoroughgoing review to the tax code itself, its central responsibility. Ways and Means Democrats also wielded influence by virtue of their committee assignment function, though observers disagreed about the impact of that activity upon the committee. Junior House members were naturally awed by this power; others, however, were inclined to believe that it had weakened the committee by distracting its Democratic members from their legislative tasks.

Bolling had devoted considerable thought to the Ways and Means problem and had developed a novel strategy. Despite his criticisms of the committee and its chairman, he was prepared to move cautiously. Divestiture of the Democratic committee assignment function was of course essential but solely the province of the Democratic caucus. Bolling had concluded that tariffs and trade—historically a keystone of Ways and Means' influence, but less important today—should be shifted to Foreign Affairs, in order to give that committee a "muscular domestic constituency" and reduce its dependence on State Department initiatives.[17] This move would in turn blunt Foreign Affairs' designs upon international financial institutions, responsibility for which was shared with Banking and Currency. Bolling reasoned that he needed to pacify Banking and Currency (more particularly, Robert Stephens, a member of the Select Committee who was also a member of Banking and Currency) in order to keep his reorganization effort alive. The Commerce Committee could be pared down and rationalized by pulling out energy and perhaps consumer legislation and perhaps adding to its transportation assignment by shifting highways and transit from Public Works. And of course, there was Bolling's prescription for a special committee to cope with the energy crisis.

This formula received a mixed reception from Bolling's colleagues. After repeated arguments on the need to strengthen Foreign Affairs, Bolling won agreement for his proposal to remove trade from Ways and Means. Not everyone was enthusiastic; but Foreign Affairs members Culver and Frelinghuysen were pleased at any additions to their committee, and other members were willing to yield to Bolling. The chairman was, however, unsuccessful in frustrating an assault on Ways and Means from another front. Sarbanes and Steiger urged that health jurisdiction be drawn together in the Commerce Committee. This would entail shifting health financing (Medicare, Medicaid) from Ways and Means; but to protect that committee's historic tax prerogatives they proposed to divide authority. As with highway and airport trust funds, the policy matters would be determined in the subject-matter committee, while the actual mechanics of financing would remain in Ways and Means. The plan was vigorously argued and finally won six to two with Bolling and Martin opposed. Martin had decided that health costs would increase without the protective custody of Ways and Means. Bolling would have preferred to move health but felt that it would be hard to extract it as well as trade from the taxing committee. He cautioned that the joint arrangement should not be made too explicit, and that Ways and Means' retention of taxing authority should be stressed. He wanted to make that committee's authority more manageable, but at the same time he hoped to contain opposition to reorganization. Moreover, he was reluctant to isolate Martin on the issue and thus voted with his vice chairman.

Bolling was overridden on the energy issue. Committee members discussed this problem for some time before resolving it. The problem was especially acute because of the many committees involved: Commerce, Interior, Science and Astronautics, Joint Atomic Energy, and Ways and Means. Basically, the problem was how to allocate responsibility in the three fields of natural resources, energy regulation and conservation, and research and development. The drafting task force contemplated a resources and environment body (the members coming largely from Interior), with energy either linked to research and development or housed in a separate committee. Bolling's solution was characteristically cautious: a separate energy committee with planning and research and development oversight authority. Abandoning his earlier notion of a special energy body to study and make recommendations on future jurisdictional allocations, he now saw this body as a major standing committee whose long-range responsibilities would not threaten such would be energy czars as Teague and Holifield. Others argued for a bolder approach. "If we're going to have a full reorganization plan," contended Sarbanes, "we ought to try to solve this problem." It was Charles Wiggins, though, who advanced the concept that unlocked the problem. He insisted that energy resources and regulation be combined in order to encourage trade-offs between producer and environmental concerns within the committee. Presumably Interior, as the Sunday Plan specified, would form the base of this jurisdiction, with ancillary functions removed to compensate for the broad scope of its new mission. Energy research and development, with its promise of long-range solutions to the energy problem, would be awarded to Science and Astronautics, whose responsibilities (especially since the curtailment of the space program) were in need of augmenting. This solution had the indirect blessing of Ralph Nader's Congress Watch, which issued a statement urging that energy and environmental concerns be linked. (Later the Nader group was to renege on this position.) Wiggins's argument carried the day; even the chairman agreed. "Floor fights can be handled if this committee is fairly well together," Bolling conceded. "With this apparent agreement, we might be able to win it."

A subsidiary issue was what to do with the Agriculture Committee, the classic example of a clientele-oriented body—"an unholy alliance between farmers and the food-stamp people," as one legislator said. Throughout the deliberations, members and staff had pondered strategies for broadening the committee's scope; natural resources, community development, and health were mentioned. Steiger had suggested consumer affairs because it would link the Department of Agriculture to consumers, thereby stressing the tie between what is produced in the field and what is packaged and distributed. Producer interests would still dominate the committee, Sarbanes argued, and besides, consumer affairs would have to be drawn from Commerce, already slated to lose several key portions of its jurisdiction. After a vigorous exchange of views and lobbying by groups like Nader's, the committee leaned toward Sarbanes's position. There remained significant aspects of resource policy left over from the massive energy and environment cluster, and it was decided to award those to Agriculture. The draft report thus contemplated enlarging Agriculture to embrace public lands, parks, and forestry (all from Interior), and wildlife and fisheries (from Merchant Marine).

Important shifts were made between Commerce and Public Works to turn the latter into a transportation panel. Once it had been decided to leave Commerce's consumer responsibilities alone and add new health responsibilities, its center of gravity became obvious. Then it was logical to take away Commerce's transportation jurisdiction (mainly air and rail regulation) and to add merchant marine affairs (from Merchant Marine) that, along with highway and mass transit legislation, would constitute a broadened Public Works and Transportation Committee. There were those who thought that air and rail transport ought to have been left in Commerce, but the prevailing sentiment held that transportation had to be put in one committee. It was not the formula Bolling would have preferred. He cautioned especially against abolishing Merchant Marine, with its insistent clientele support. Nevertheless, he acceded to the scheme, citing the nation's past failure to develop a rational transportation policy.

Banking and Currency was left virtually untouched, in line with Bolling's strategy. His obvious desire to retain that body's oversight of international financial institutions, a sentiment supported by Stephens, prevented Foreign Affairs' advocates from tampering with that important policy field. With Stephens's concurrence, mass transit was moved with other transportation items to Public Works. Other shifts were insignificant, except for the recommendation for folding in the Select Small Business Committee, thus removing a potential competitor. Originally created as a vehicle for Representative Wright Patman, it had since 1971 been in the anomalous position of a "permanent select" committee without legislative jurisdiction. Bills relating to small business were handled by the Banking and Currency Committee, to whose chairmanship Patman had ascended in 1964 after thirty-five years in the House. Yet, the committee served as a reference point for many members, who found it convenient in dealing with small businesses in their districts. As one legislator said, "It ought to be eliminated, but is it important enough to fight for? It's a major matter to many members, and it does very little harm." Stephens, chairman of Banking and Currency's

Small Business Subcommittee, professed not to care what was recommended. Either way, however, he said that the legislative and oversight jurisdiction should go together. It was agreed unanimously to combine the select body's functions with Banking and Currency.

Disposing of those central issues nevertheless left difficult choices. What, for example, should be done with Merchant Marine, whose chairwoman Leonor Sullivan had expressed anger over tampering with that committee. Not only was Sullivan known as a scrappy combatant, but she was the only woman to head a House standing committee. More significantly, her committee was an access point for one of the nation's most heavily subsidized lobbies, the maritime industry and the potent seamen's unions. The drafting subcommittee had tactfully ducked the issue in what Sarbanes, who sat on Merchant Marine and represented a major port, called "pragmatic judgment." Several Republicans (all from inland constituencies) urged abolition of the body because of its constricted mission. "We ought to clean it up or get rid of it," asserted Wiggins. "If we're going to talk about institutions and not personalities, we ought at least to recommend abolition." Sarbanes reacted with humor, nonetheless objecting. Bolling professed a feeling of foreboding at such a move but did not object strenuously. Late in its sessions, the Select Committee adopted a motion distributing Merchant Marine's responsibilities to several committees with related jurisdiction. More would be heard on this issue; indeed, this action, logical though it may have seemed, proved to be something of a self-inflicted wound.

When the Select Committee turned to the question of dividing Education and Labor, the debate became more partisan. Because of their differences on the matter, Sarbanes and Steiger presented their colleagues with a set of alternatives. Steiger, an expert on manpower training programs, believed that a more comprehensive manpower policy would emanate from a new committee built around education, training, and manpower. Besides, he noted, if a bill were reported that failed to split Education and Labor, many GOP members would move to do so on the House floor. Sarbanes, ever the pragmatist, pointed out that keeping the committee together would minimize members' dislocations. Moreover, he argued that Education and Labor already had a coherent jurisdiction, with its two major topics linked together by manpower concerns. "The move to split the committee isn't related to rational needs for change," he commented. The Republicans would not hear of retaining the committee; once they were satisfied that the resulting labor committee would have a broad, attractive jurisdiction, they pressed for the split. The vote was virtually unanimous. However, Steiger lost his personal fight to keep manpower programs with the education segment. The vote

was a tie broken by the chairman, who said he had always favored combining manpower and labor.

The locus for election regulation, including controversial campaign
financing measures, occasioned scattered debate. The drafting subcommittee, following earlier discussions, had moved this topic from Wayne
Hays's House Administration Committee to the bipartisan Committee
on Standards of Official Conduct. But that move was controversial. Although Hays was thought to be hostile to election reform legislation, the
latter committee was equally suspect. Created in 1966 in response to
several scandals involving House members, the Committee on Standards
of Official Conduct was apparently intended by Speaker John Mc-
Cormack to be noncontroversial. As one Select Committee member said,
"My impression is that the committee's function is to sweep things under
the rug and not make waves. It's made up of senior men—compatible
and isolated." Lobbyists working for election reform, like Ralph Nader's
Congress Watch, were upset at the prospects of entrusting their bills to
the Standards Committee. Bolling and Culver argued, however, that
the move would help strengthen the committee by directing public attention to it. Bolling viewed the issue in nonpartisan terms. Sarbanes
objected, holding that election reform was a partisan issue and should
not be assigned to a bipartisan panel, but the members agreed with
Bolling.

A few decisions were reached with comparative ease. Two committees—Internal Security and Post Office—were dropped without discussion. After a brief exchange it was agreed to retain the District of Columbia Committee. Although most members seemed to feel that the District
Committee had little claim to permanence, it was conceded that congressional attention would be demanded for some time after home rule
was achieved.[18] Besides, the committee was headed by Charles Diggs,
the House's only Black chairman. A more thorny problem was Veterans
Affairs. Created as a result of the Reorganization Act of 1946, the committee was a prime focus for the powerful veterans lobby, which in 1970
succeeded in persuading the Senate to form a separate committee. Consequently, the Select Committee realized that it would be a political
mistake to threaten Veterans Affairs.

In view of the extensive changes contemplated in committee structures, several members were bothered that the Rules Committee was virtually untouched; indeed, the proposed jurisdictional review procedure
would give it additional powers. Moreover, Bolling's and Martin's senior
positions on Rules could be used to discredit the Select Committee's
plan. Sarbanes and Steiger repeatedly implored Bolling and Martin to
consider recommending some reduction of Rules' authority—perhaps its

power to report "rules" waiving points of order or its power to consider legislation initially. Young vainly pursued his more radical proposal that Rules be divested of its agenda-setting role. Each time the Rules issue came up, Bolling or Martin would launch into a prolonged exposition of Rules' activity, implying that the issue was logical rather than political. Finally, Sarbanes put the proposition directly: "I still beseech the two of you at the head of the table to think of something that looks like a diminution of power." Nothing came of the suggestion.

Despite its bold amalgam of jurisdictional transfers, the Select Committee could not agree on the proper treatment of members whose committees would be abolished or whose jurisdictions had been moved to another committee. According to the more extreme view, the committee system could only be revived by the radical surgery of eliminating overlapping memberships. As one member said:

> We've been through this before—and we'll end up doing nothing. My committee isn't worth the powder to blow it up with, because of schedule conflicts. We could only barely get a quorum for [the cabinet member responsible for policy in the committee's jurisdiction]. The problem is multiple committee and subcommittee assignments.

Others, like Vice Chairman Martin, argued that normal turnover rates would soon obviate the problem. Still others, however, continued to worry about the impact of changes on individual members. Several members advocated methods of minimizing the transitional dislocations— perhaps "grandfathering" (exempting) existing committee assignments, or allowing one-time transfers between committees without loss of seniority. Someone suggested that party caucuses be urged to give special consideration to senior members losing jurisdiction; others protested that even that mild action could threaten members holding posts on existing committees. Bolling appeared to believe the problem could be contained if care were exercised in recommending changes. In the end, the committee report, except for an appendix on voluntary rotation, made no recommendation.

The committee report was, by congressional standards, a curious document.[19] It was a workbook, a rough outline of the Select Committee's concerns and tentative conclusions. No doubt many inside and outside of the House did not know how to react to the document. Because the draft contained no supplemental or additional views, it tended to obscure some of the critical points that still divided the committee; moreover, the report led legislators and outside groups to assume that the committee had already fixed on certain alternatives. Despite the high risk involved, Bolling had insisted that the committee raise a warning flag to its constituents in the House in order to attract their attention and prepare them for the final report that was to come. Nevertheless, the changes embedded in the document were controversial.

DECEMBER SEVENTH: THE COMMITTEE "GOES PUBLIC"

On the afternoon of December 7, 1973, members of the congressional press corps crowded into a small committee chamber, just around the corner from the Capitol's souvenir stand. Led by Bolling and Martin, the Select Committee unveiled the interim draft plan for reorganizing the House. No press releases were handed out—simply copies of the 119-page committee report and a press statement issued by Martin. Bolling wanted some, but not too much, publicity: his primary audience on Capitol Hill would, he assumed, read the document carefully; but outside pressure groups, on the other hand, need not be nudged into action.

Bolling outlined the Select Committee's approach to House organization. He praised his colleagues' participation. "It was a real group effort," he said. "I have never served on a committee like this." He explained that the report was only a tentative document; an onerous schedule of deliberations and mark-ups faced the Select Committee when Congress reconvened in January. There would be an open "rule" to permit amendments on the floor, he assured the reporters. "We want to begin an educational process," Frelinghuysen explained. "There is a general recognition of the need for change, but we felt we must surface our plans at an early point, and let the reactions come in." The legislators assumed a firm position, however, and Bolling challenged critics to suggest a total plan rather than offer unproductive criticism.

The report may have been a bit puzzling to the reporters, but they sensed its potential for inciting internecine House warfare. One asked whether the affected committee chairmen had been consulted. Bolling responded that "perhaps fifty members and one outraged chairman" had spoken to him before the document was released. He added that he had informed Speaker Albert that the report was a trial balloon that would inspire rumor. Bolling also said that he had informed Albert that the sole addition recommended for the Rules Committee would invade the Speaker's prerogatives. When a reporter wondered aloud how Wayne Hays would react to the proposed mixed commission on Administrative Services, Bolling said blandly that the question was not what was good for a particular committee but for the whole House. "We didn't try to be spiteful to anyone," Frelinghuysen observed. "We would hope that the interests of particular fiefdoms will be outweighed by the interest of getting the House's work done." Bolling and the others were optimistic. "I think this kind of product can be sold to the House in the next year," the chairman concluded.

Even if these prognostications were accurate, the Select Committee faced a prodigious task. During one of the deliberative sessions, a member of the Select Committee had been observed scribbling a list of "people I have to worry about" because of the Select Committee's decisions. At the head of the list he wrote, "every member of the House"—because, as he noted, "everybody loses something."

SIX

Committee Work:
The Fine Tuning

THE FIRST wave of response to the December 7 draft was gratifying almost to the point of mystification. Chairman Bolling, who had just piloted the budget reform bill through the House, was reaping the harvest of his success. No doubt some members, reasoning that he was likely to get his way in House reorganization, had simply concluded for the time being that it would be futile to complain. A remarkably conciliatory statement from Representative Thaddeus Dulski, whose Post Office Committee was slated for extinction, conveyed a similar impression. Bolling himself was surprised and encouraged by the initial reactions to the reorganization package. He worried, in fact, that the comments were too laudatory to be true.

If Bolling had, as he claimed, aimed at a limited public response to the draft plan, that too seemed to have occurred. Initially, few newspapers gave the plan much attention. As time passed, it gained mention in specialized and trade publications, and more analytical stories on the committee's work appeared in newspapers around the country. Leading papers like the *Los Angeles Times* and the *New York Times* bestowed their blessing on the committee. The *New York Times* called attention to the "growing paralysis of the House because jurisdiction, work load and power are distributed among its baronies with little regard for balance, coherence or capacity...." The *Times's* editorialists were especially intrigued by the jurisdictional plan because its provisions for balancing work load and limiting members' assignments gave promise of "imposing rationality on an institution that has lost too much of its effectiveness for lack of it."[1] The logjam in the Ways and Means Committee was frequently cited in editorials, as was the need for consolidating such fields as energy and transportation. Scant attention was paid to the key nonjurisdictional proposals dealing with oversight, bill referral, and jurisdictional review.

When the new session convened in early January, House members and their staffs scrutinized the proposals in earnest, and the momentum of the response quickened. All legislators had received copies of the preliminary document and had been asked to comment; on February 1 another letter was issued to stimulate reactions. Younger members praised the proposals. Many of them had campaigned on the theme of making Congress more responsive; almost all of them found House procedures slow and inefficient. Moreover, they had fewer stakes in the status quo than their senior colleagues. Freshman Representative William Lehman probably speaking for a majority of younger members said: "I don't have much to lose if the committee organization is changed, but I might have something to gain."[2] Support also came from committee leaders who would gain if the proposals were implemented. Perhaps because no one wanted to appear too intent upon gaining at others' expense, such expressions tended to be muted. Many of the beneficiaries, moreover, had specific reservations: Public Works was pleased to gain transportation but worried about keeping flood control; Foreign Affairs was interested in trade and tariffs but still coveted international finance; Interior, one of the greatest gainers, was upset about losing parks and recreation. And so it went.

From those individuals and groups that would lose in the reshuffle, the reaction was more intense and explicit. Newspaper speculation centered about Wilbur Mills's Ways and Means Committee; but surprisingly little was heard from that quarter. Mills himself was absent from Washington much of the time; without his leadership, his committee was divided and indecisive. Instantaneous and shrill complaints came from the maritime lobby over the proposed demise of the Merchant Marine Committee. Environmentalists were angered by the prospect of losing a sympathetic Merchant Marine subcommittee, and by the proposed move of parks and recreation to the Agriculture Committee. Increasingly recognized as the most disturbing sign, however, was the restiveness of mid-career Democratic liberals, many of them subcommittee chairmen who were the chief beneficiaries of the caucus subcommittee reforms of 1971 and 1973. Some of them were on the Education and Labor Committee, slated to be split in the reorganization; others were on Interior, Merchant Marine, House Administration, and other panels. A variety of rationalizations were advanced, but their primary concern seemed to be the future of their hard-won subcommittee posts. Bolling was genuinely shocked at their reaction. Bitterly, he referred to them as "dunghill liberals" because, as he put it, "sitting on their dunghills they can't see the horizon."

A large number of adjustments were made before the plan was reported to the House. For this purpose the Select Committee held a series of open markup sessions between February 4 and March 13, 1974. These were detailed negotiations during which the reorganization plan was worked over—literally, "marked up"—as errors were rectified, political bargains struck, and technical provisions forged. Congressional committees commonly schedule markup sessions to perfect legislative proposals before sending them to the House floor. Opening such sessions to the public was a relatively new development, and committee staff members wondered whether the legislators would be sufficiently at ease in such a setting. However, the Select Committee's rules specified, and Bolling insisted, that the meetings be open to the public unless members explicitly voted otherwise. Needless to say, not all the crucial decisions were reached in public. During the previous fall the committee had conducted numerous informal discussions that were neither announced nor open to visitors. Once the markups were under way, a significant portion of the bargaining was done outside the committee chamber. Nevertheless, all the committee's official actions were taken in public. Hence, the markups constituted a revealing and remarkably candid record of the committee's deliberation. As the members delved into their assignment, their confidence grew and they seemed willing to express their views on sensitive topics. Each day, audiences of from twenty to fifty people— often including other committees' staff aides and lobbyists dispatched to follow the proceedings—crowded into the committee's tiny room in the Cannon Building to learn for themselves the intricacies of reorganization. The sessions fascinated close observers of the House, who had witnessed nothing like them before.

During the sessions Bolling displayed his mastery of the proceedings, shifting his role from moderator to purposeful chairman as the occasion demanded. In the delicate balancing of interests, he was a potent yet unobtrusive force. "I'm pretty good at figuring out the moods of the House," he reminded staff members. "That's my specialty in this place."

The outlines of the Select Committee's plan were not fundamentally altered during the markups. The objective of a limited number of broad, single-assignment committees was retained, although for political reasons the number of minor, nonexclusive committees was increased. As Bolling described his committee's viewpoint:

We were going to lean very hard in the report on the notion that [the one-track system] was a basic underpinning of the plan . . . but that we also recognize that we had some difficulties in implementing that because we didn't control the method and detail of the method of transition.[3]

Scheduling of committee sessions received extended attention, mainly because information requested from the House Information Systems indicated that schedule conflicts were more widespread than anyone had realized. The jurisdictional review mechanism, so critical to the contemplated centralization of the Speaker's power, remained important in the group's thinking, though the idea became procedurally cumbersome, consuming much of the committee's time. Oversight, too, received great attention, although an intricate and problematic proposal for "oversight agendas" (another device for centralizing power) was finally deleted from the language of the proposed rule and relegated to the report.[4] Steiger still argued against mandating oversight subcommittees, but he gained no allies. Thus, oversight subcommittees remained a part of the resolution. As Bolling explained, "I can see the possibility of some good coming out of this, and I can see no possibility of any harm coming from it."[5] Otherwise, the group declined to specify the number or jurisdiction of subcommittees, regarding such a move as an improper intrusion into the committees' internal affairs.

The Select Committee did nothing to alter its "deliberate tacit decision" to finesse the prime issue raised by reorganization: what to do about members adversely affected by the committee plan. Bolling confessed that he was "looking for ways to grandfather," but he had no plan in mind. The members concentrated on the question, and detailed staff studies were presented on the impact of changes on individual members. Ultimately the committee suggested a "sense of the House" resolution providing that members serving on committees that were abolished, or a significant portion of whose jurisdiction was transferred, be allowed to choose the committee assignment they wished to retain, and that:

The length of such member's service on the former committee as well as in the House, and any chairmanship or status as a ranking member, should be meaningfully recognized in his or her placement on such committee.[6]

That was as far as the committee deemed it could go without invading the prerogatives of the party caucuses; it was something less than a House rule, yet something more than a mere report. To those who claimed that it was meaningless, Bolling responded that such language would make it easier for party leaders to negotiate the transition. "I suspect," he said:

if the Speaker and minority leader and two or three more said those are the things that ought to be considered it might ease the pain. We couldn't figure out in our discussion any way to ease the pain except by public relations.[7]

That was all the committee could do to allay members' fears. It became a subsequent stumbling block, however, for those who saw themselves as losers in the reorganization spoke as if their losses were irreparable.

As in the earlier discussions, the committee devoted the major portion of its time to the complexities of jurisdictional politics. Few if any of the members, however, thought that jurisdictional manipulations were the most important aspect of reorganization. Nonetheless, jurisdictional questions were demanding, both intellectually and politically. The members sensed, too, that outsiders would judge their product primarily by its packaging. Had not the Legislative Reorganization Act of 1946 been sold primarily to "streamline" the committees, even though such effects were mainly cosmetic? Certainly the jurisdictional features of the December 7 document drew the most press attention, and virtually all of the comments from fellow congressmen. Legislators were adding up their gains and losses with uncommon solicitude (indeed, most of them read only those recommendations that affected them personally); and, thus, the committee was lobbied with growing intensity. The dexterity with which the committee treated these allocations might spell the difference between acceptance or rejection of the plan. "The real test," Lloyd Meeds observed, "is going to be whether or not we have been successful in making these committees as nearly as possible equal in power and the weight they will wield in the House."[8]

REFLOATING THE MERCHANT MARINE COMMITTEE

The tentative decision to scuttle the Merchant Marine and Fisheries Committee, reached deliberately but without extended debate, caused more vehement protest than any other proposal the Select Committee made. Shortly after Congress reconvened for its second session, Merchant Marine's resourceful Chairwoman Leonor Sullivan accosted Bolling, her fellow Missourian, on the House floor and employed pungent terms to threaten retaliation. Sullivan—who, as one observer said, "never gave up anything willingly"—was not the sole cause of the explosion that greeted the plan to abolish Merchant Marine. The causes, in fact, lay in the role played by the House Merchant Marine Committee, which straddled three powerful constituent interests: the maritime industry, commercial and sport fishing, and environmental protection. The last-mentioned topic, acquired almost accidentally in the late 1960s out of jurisdictional disputes with the Interior Committee, had attracted the support of environmentalists for John Dingell's Subcommittee on Fisheries and Wildlife Conservation. Merchant Marine had become a high-payoff "second committee" for many congressmen. The panel's work load was undemanding and its staff relatively small. But its popularity as an assignment was attested by the fact that it had grown from twenty-five members in 1947 to thirty-nine in the 93rd Congress. Maritime interests regarded the committee as their strongest voice in the nation's capital. Its clientelism was admitted by friends and foes alike. "Unfortunately, although what is good for the American shipping industry or certain elements of it may not always be good for America," wrote the *Baltimore Sun* maritime editor, "the merchant marine committee has earned something of a reputation for acting as though that kind of thought rarely occurs."[9]

The plan to abolish the Merchant Marine Committee elicited an immediate reaction from the committee's constituency. Within a week after the preliminary reorganization plan was unveiled, maritime lobbyists were promising "one hell of a fight" to save their committee. Soon after the first of the year, Sullivan's staff called lobbyists together to enlist formal support and provide ammunition for a concerted campaign aimed especially at House leaders. At the same time they telephoned Select Committee staff members and promised that maritime labor and management would be solidly against the proposal. For example, a newsletter published by the Propeller Club of the United States termed the matter an "emergency" and urged that telegrams be sent to a list of Select Committee members and House leaders. On January 31, Sullivan wrote Speaker Albert to protest the plan and "the consequent downgrading of maritime affairs to subcommittee level."

> Such an extreme recommendation as the total elimination of a Committee which has existed and functioned well since 1887 [she wrote] is, of course, unacceptable to the Committee itself and to the various industries and constituent entities coming under the jurisdiction of the Committee. . . . Anyone at all acquainted with these subject matters knows that they are inextricably bound together, must function together, and cannot possibly function one in one committee and another in another committee.[10]

Referring to the decline in u.s. seapower and describing her committee as "the legislative entity supporting our maritime industry," she argued that the committee's demise would further erode seapower and harm defense efforts. A subsequent letter to Chairman Bolling delineated the committee's work load and even suggested that the body be given added responsibilities and be renamed "the Committee on Marine and Ocean Industries and Resources, Wildlife, and the Environment."[11]

Eighteen congressmen wrote during the Select Committee's markup sessions to corroborate Sullivan's position. Subcommittee Chairman Dingell defended his stewardship on environmental matters and attacked the "one member, one committee" aspects of the Select Committee's draft plan. The December 7 document was, he wrote:

> . . . inconclusive, obscure, and wholly unpersuasive. I am, in fact, persuaded that the kindest thing that we can do is to vote it down quickly, and to resume consideration of the needs and mechanics of congressional reform at another time, and by another Committee.[12]

Later he sought to determine the backgrounds of Select Committee staff members, presumably to use in attacking the reorganization plan; Bolling ignored the request. Dingell remained a noisy, obstreperous foe throughout the fight over committee reorganization. Others were more restrained in their opposition. Representative James Grover, ranking minority member on Merchant Marine, penned a thoughtful defense of his committee, arguing that the proposed reorganization was "a mixture of apples and oranges,"[13] while Democrat Parren J. Mitchell—like Sarbanes a representative of the port city of Baltimore—cited political reasons for retaining the committee, for "*no* other committee [has] the jurisdiction and the time and personnel resources to guard the interest of port cities."[14]

As the Merchant Marine staff member had promised, a highly organized letter-writing campaign was launched on behalf of the committee. A total of 175 separate communications was logged by the Select Committee—the largest on any aspect of committee realignment, and a reflection of many hundreds of duplicate letters to legislators. The sources of the communications are listed in table 2. Unquestionably the most

TABLE 2   *Maritime Lobby Communications Supporting the Merchant Marine Committee*

Category	Number
Shipping firms	36
Miscellaneous maritime firms	23
Local labor organizations	22
Trade associations	18
Members of Congress	18
Maritime clubs, organizations	15
Animal welfare groups	15
Educational institutions, groups	9
Port associations	7
National labor organizations	6
Federal and state agencies	6
TOTAL	175

startling source was an agency of the federal government, the Federal Maritime Commission (FMC), which unanimously passed a resolution urging that the Merchant Marine Committee be retained "in its present form." The resolution itself was such an unvarnished brief that it raised suspicions that it had actually originated in the committee rooms. Reciting the history of the merchant marine and referring to the Soviet threat on the high seas, the FMC employed colorful language in making its case:

> The presence of the American flag on the high seas is not a matter to be taken lightly. From the birth of our Republic, through its years of growth, to our rise to international leadership one form of commerce has formed the lifeblood to our economic greatness—the American merchant marine. . . .
> . . . [It] has been the . . . Committee which has sounded the warning to the American people that we must have an adequate and growing merchant marine and developed this vital aspect of sea power . . .
> Submersion of the House . . . Committee into a "super" committee will obscure this vision and crush the awareness and expertise sharpened by the Committee over the last near century of growth for American merchant shipping.[15]

The singular circumstance of a federal agency advising the House on its internal organization was not lost on the legislators, and left observers to draw their own conclusions about whether the FMC had or had not been "captured" by its constituency. In view of the FMC's regulatory functions, its intrusion in the internal affairs of the House was, to say the least, highly irregular.

Most of the other communications paled beside the FMC's colorful prose, although several state agencies were also heard from. There were appeals from shipping companies, ranging from well-known names—like the United States Lines and New York City's tourist-oriented Circle Line—to obscure firms, some of which emanated from the same address and may have been paper companies. Apparently many were mobilized by the American Maritime Association, whose resolution "to be opposed unalterably to the abolishment of the Merchant Marine Committee or reduction of its functions . . ."[16] produced a flurry of identical letters from its forty-five member firms. Allied enterprises—such as shipyards, suppliers, and insurors—were also heard from. Among the unions expressing their support for the committee were the Seafarers' International Union, the National Maritime Union, and the International Longshoremen's Union, with many local labor councils forwarding telegrams of support.

What made the maritime lobby so fearful was not its size but rather its strategic position. Not only was the industry one of the most heavily subsidized in the nation; it was also highly concentrated geographically, which assured the loyalty of legislators from those areas. The maritime unions—principally the Seafarers' International Union, the National Maritime Union, and the Marine Engineers Beneficial Association—underwrote this loyalty by generous campaign contributions to friendly legislators. In 1974 maritime unions spent some $617,000 in contributions and loans to more than 175 senators and congressmen.[17] Among the recipients was House Majority Leader Thomas P. "Tip" O'Neill, who received $16,000 though he faced no opposition (he distributed most of the money to needier candidates) and who expressed private but vigorous opposition to eliminating the Merchant Marine panel. Maritime unions accrued influence in other ways. It was reputed that they supplied large numbers of picketers for other unions conducting strikes, thus enhancing their leverage in the labor movement. No doubt this helped them in turning the AFL-CIO Executive Council against the Select Committee's report. Political clout, when combined with such emotional appeals as patriotism and national defense, lent the maritime interests an influence far outrunning their numbers or economic importance.

As unlikely bedfellows the committee had recruited some of the major environmental groups who were grateful for Representative Dingell's patronage and apprehensive of the proposed Energy and Environment panel, an unknown quantity. A Sierra Club newsletter foresaw new terrors from the reorganization plan:

> NEPA could be in new jeopardy. The Merchant Marine and Fisheries Committee, its present protector, would be abolished and jurisdiction over NEPA would be transferred to the Energy and Environment Committee, where fresh assaults could be expected.[18]

Compared with their suspicions over proposed Agriculture Committee jurisdiction, the environmentalists' objections to shifting NEPA were nebulous and little more than scare tactics. Yet the comments indicated that Chairwoman Sullivan, Dingell, and Merchant Marine staff members had done a thorough job of mobilizing their clienteles, and fostered doubts over the reorganization proposals. Animal lovers rushed also to defend Dingell's domain. One correspondent from Cats and Cat Owners Aid, Incorporated, of Upper Montclair, New Jersey, even castigated Bolling for wanting to "scupple" (*sic*) the Endangered Species Act, one of Dingell's responsibilities.[19]

The organized campaign weighed heavily in the minds of Select Committee members as they met to perfect their reorganization plan. Vice Chairman Martin, whose third district of Nebraska boasted no waterway larger than the Platte River, tended to dismiss the campaign as a lobbyists' ploy:

> . . . [I]t certainly is an organized campaign. There is no question about that. These people are prolific letter writers. They are a little bit like those who belong to the National Rifle Association. They all write the same person three or four times.[20]

Although conceding the desirability of consolidating transportation jurisdiction, Bolling did not take the opposition so lightly. Privately he conceded the earlier decision (which he had opposed) had been unwise. At the first markup session he reviewed reactions to the preliminary plan, referring to the Merchant Marine Committee as a key dilemma:

> To be frank about it, you have a coalition interest there, groups that are, in essence, quite disparate yet agreeing on one thing and that is that that Committee should have a jurisdiction of its own.
> I think the environmentalists are particularly interested in the Dingell subcommittee and are very concerned that they might lose the kind of people that they have because it is a second committee assignment. I think a variety of other people perhaps have the same concern in other areas.[21]

Frelinghuysen, who for years had held a seat on but one committee and was an inveterate advocate of "one member, one committee," saw the problem of special interest committees quite differently. "We want to be a large fish in a small pond rather than a little fish in a big pond," he commented. "This is saying basically we like things as they are because the jurisdictions are defined even though they are not fairly defined."[22] However, Bolling would willingly concede points to clientele interests as long as it would not endanger the central features of the committee design. "I would suspect that we are pretty well committed to the one-track system with exceptions," he said, "and I think probably what we are talking about now is how many exceptions."[23]

Bolling faced the tactical problem of staging a retreat on the issue. Sarbanes, who both represented a port city and served on Merchant Marine, felt keenly about retaining the committee but hesitated to lobby vigorously for fear of appearing too self-serving. Thus, Bolling arranged for Lloyd Meeds to speak on the matter, linking it to the emerging problem of distributing environmental responsibilities between Agriculture and the proposed Energy and Environment Committee—a matter of concern to Meeds as an environmentalist. The proposed Energy and Environment Committee seemed too heavily burdened, while the proposed shift to Agriculture of parks and natural resources left environmental groups in a dither. A separate committee was needed to resolve the situation. During the February 21 evening session Meeds made an explicit proposal: a minor (or "B") committee "which would be called Maritime Fisheries and Wildlife, or something like that, which would contain merchant marine, Coast Guard, fishing, and fisheries and wildlife, those four major headings."[24]

Revival of a maritime committee was attacked as thwarting the goal of combining transportation jurisdiction into a single committee for the first time in the nation's history. "I think it is worth taking that issue to the floor in spite of what I know might happen," Steiger asserted, "and I would like to see us keep the Public Works and Transportation Committee together."[25] Sarbanes argued that to sever maritime matters would not do violence to the general committee scheme. He held that the merchant marine was sufficiently distinct to be considered apart from such mass transit modes as roads, rails, and air. "It can be argued," he said:

> that this is something very different, that it is not tied into the national transportation network in the same way and is not as directly related with other forms of transportation either through competition or coordination.[26]

Besides, he stated, maritime lobbies consider themselves overwhelmed in the Senate Commerce Committee by competing transportation modes and look to the House body to gain fair representation. Bolling quickly seconded the Meeds-Sarbanes proposal, which he said could be adopted "with some logic and make a significant political gain. We could get some of the heat off of us."[27] After the discussion had proceeded awhile he turned to Robert Stephens for support. Stephens's reply was direct:

> As to whether to create or to leave a Maritime and Fisheries Committee? I think that from a political standpoint it would be very helpful to leave it. When I say political standpoint, I mean for passage of the bill.[28]

Vice Chairman Martin, while discounting the maritime lobbying campaign, was amenable to the solution because, as he said, the proposed Public Works and Transportation panel had been overloaded with jurisdiction. However, he wanted assurances that transportation would not be further fragmented:

> Frankly, I believe the merchant marine is more closely connected to the other forms of transportation than some would say, but I don't think it is as much a part of the package as are the ones that operate in this country.
>
> If I had my preference they would all be together, but I would hate to see us go beyond that and start ripping out rail, air, mass transit and so on, because I think we have a completely asinine, hopeless situation in this country unless we rationalize it.[29]

Sarbanes replied that if the transportation question were unraveled any further, "we really would no longer have a package which we could defend as a package." Though adamantly opposed, Steiger conceded that the other six members in attendance comprised enough votes to revive the maritime committee. "One fierce protest and six acquiescences," Bolling concluded. "I think this is the way we are going to go."[30]

Subsequent discussions refined the details of the reconstituted maritime panel. In the end, the panel was given much of its former jurisdiction, though it was focused more narrowly on maritime affairs and commercial fishing. The committee's environmental jurisdiction—including NEPA, wildlife and wildlife refuges, deepwater ports, and coastal zone management—was to go to the new Energy and Environment panel. Oceanography was awarded the broadened Science and Technology Committee, while Panama Canal matters would be in Foreign Affairs. The maritime body's only gain was oversight over international fishing agreements, brought from Foreign Affairs. Finally it was decided to retain the original name, Merchant Marine and Fisheries. "Why make them change their stationery?" Bolling asked.[31]

In justifying retention of the Merchant Marine Committee, the Select Committee's report mixed candor and rationalization. "Maritime affairs," the committee stated:

> are sufficiently unique to warrant the attentions of a separate committee. Moreover, the select committee recognizes that a strong merchant marine is necessary for both economic growth and national defense. These concerns might not receive the attention they deserve if merchant marine matters were shifted to a committee concerned with other modes of transportation.[32]

The reduced scope of the proposed panel would, the report stated, allow the committee to "better concentrate its efforts in two key related areas requiring special attention: maritime matters and fisheries." If this halfhearted solution was designed to neutralize the opposition of the key maritime interests, it failed. Sullivan and her fellow members were able to convince their supportive clienteles that any reduction in the committee's attractiveness and influence could jeopardize maritime interests. The Select Committee's compromise thus proved fruitless, but it was noteworthy as the most conspicuous change effected during the markups.

Public Employees Defend their Committee

The proposed abolition of the Committee on Post Office and Civil Service produced defensive countermoves similar, though milder and slower, to those mounted in the maritime industry. Like Merchant Marine, Post Office was essentially a clientele-oriented committee whose members were attracted to it for constituency reasons and whose decision premises could be summarized as "support maximum pay increases and improvements in benefits for employee groups and to oppose all rate increases for mail users."[33] Most members failed to sustain an interest in the committee's constricted domain, many of them eventually transferring to more prestigious committees. Those who remained on the committee quickly climbed the seniority ladder, developing a stake in perpetuating the body. A blow was dealt to the committee in 1970 with passage of the Postal Reorganization Act which shifted authority over postal rates and employee salaries to a newly created government corporation, the u.s. Postal Service.[34] The postal reforms, stimulated by public unrest over the postal system, forced the committee to relinquish its most valuable resources, control over postal salaries and rates. Its legislative work load was concomitantly reduced, from 1,182 bills introduced in the 90th Congress to 729 bills in the 92nd.

It seemed, then, that there would be only token resistance to eliminating the postal committee. During the hearings Chairman Thaddeus J. Dulski, a modest man soon to announce his retirement from Congress, defended his committee but conceded some adjustments might be made: "So it may appear that there is little legislation but that does not mean little work or a lack of things to do," he said candidly. "Now, my suggestion would be perhaps to cut this committee down to fifteen members."[35] The very same day that the Select Committee's draft report appeared, Dulski issued a statement praising the committee for "their tireless—and sometimes thankless—efforts during these past few months in handling this overdue review of the committee pattern in the House." Alluding to the proposed abolition of his own committee, Dulski promised to discuss the tentative reorganization plans with his committee colleagues. "I am not surprised at the Select Committee's initial recommendations for changes," he stated:

> After twenty-seven years under the present committee alignment, it is essential to consider the major changes in legislative emphasis which have developed. I urged changes in my own testimony. . . .
>
> If the House of Representatives eventually should decide to abolish or merge any committees, my one strong recommendation would be that preference on new committee assignments be given to members displaced.[36]

It was a generous and circumspect sentiment, exceedingly rare among chairmen jealous of their domains. Later, however, Dulski was to have more to say on the subject.

Alerted by Hill staff members, federal employee and postal workers' unions began to voice their opposition. A few days after the December 7 document surfaced, a Washington, D.C., newspaper reported that government employee unions would fight the proposed reorganization; later they were described as "working frantically behind the scenes" to defeat it.[37] While the response was subdued compared to the outburst from the maritime organizations, a number of organizations were heard from, including the National Federation of Federal Employees, the National Alliance of Postal and Federal Employees, and locals of the American Postal Workers Union, the National Association of Retired Federal Employees, the American Federation of Government Employees, and such specialized groups as air traffic controllers and customs officers. Union lobbying helped persuade the AFL-CIO Executive Committee that "it would be a mistake to eliminate the knowledge of problems peculiar to federal employees which the committee has accumulated."[38] A few bulk mailing firms argued that in a revised structure "the interests of business mailers will be low in priority and effective congressional monitoring of the postal system will suffer greatly."[39] Moreover, Postmaster General E. T. Klassen wrote a restrained letter noting that "there is a valid argument in favor of retaining a separate committee" to exercise oversight over the Postal Service.[40]

It was not long before the Post Office Committee's members expressed their own views. In a measured statement, Chairman Dulski urged that the panel's role be expanded to include all federal employee matters, including the Hatch Act (political activities of government employees) and travel and transportation regulations.[41] As an alternative, he repeated his suggestion of paring the committee down to fifteen members. Vice Chairman David N. Henderson, next in line to chair the committee, supported Dulski's position, as did subcommittee heads James Hanley and Charles H. Wilson and second-ranking GOP member Edward Derwinski. They stressed the continuing need for overseeing the Postal Service. As Wilson said:

> What are we to say when (and I deliberately use the word "when" and not "if") postal service, without stringent oversight, deteriorates to the point that there is a public outcry and our critics charge that we thought so little of it that we downgraded postal oversight to one committee?[42]

Overt defense of the committee emanated mainly from that minority of its members who had, as Fenno put it, "made a big investment in their clientele group relations."[43] Other than these individuals, primarily subcommittee chairmen, few legislators defended the committee. As for the external clienteles themselves, they could hardly contend that the proposed labor panel would be in the slightest degree hostile to federal employee and postal unions. Nor was it likely that their interests would be jeopardized under the aegis of a broader and presumably more influential House body. Rather, it was contended that such issues would be "submerged" in a broader committee—much as the maritime lobby had complained it would be overwhelmed in a "super committee." The reporters of federal employee affairs for the two Washington, D.C., newspapers—certainly no enemies of these clienteles—identified what were unquestionably the underlying motivations for defending the status quo. Union leaders, one wrote, "pointed out that the friendship and rapport which they have built up over the years among ... committee members would vanish overnight."[44] His colleague was more direct. "The changes," he explained:

> would upset long-established (and generally successful) lobbying practices of the unions and the special understandings they have now with most members of the committee which deals exclusively with civil service and postal matters.[45]

Though posing no substantive threat to the clientele interests, elimination of the committee would confront them with the task of establishing relations with a new congressional body. Like most human beings, lobbyists are reluctant to incur the costs associated with changing their mode of operation. No doubt these considerations were strongly urged on them by the committee's staff of thirty-three people, to whom the reorganization represented at best uncertainty and at worst loss of their jobs.

Within the Select Committee, there was little debate on the basic question either before or after the draft report. Bolling observed that objections to eliminating the committee had originally been *pro forma* but that by February some agitation had developed. "My guess is that it comes primarily from the staff," he said.[46] The fate of the committee itself never again was broached; but there was a lively debate over whether its jurisdiction should go to Government Operations or to the proposed labor committee. The December 7 draft, more because of politics than logic, had awarded civil service to Labor and the postal service to Government Operations. The head of the latter body, Chet Holifield, countered that his committee could not handle additional legislative tasks.[47] Holifield's contention was not without merit: although it was desirable to buttress Government Operations, too heavy a legislative burden might detract from its oversight responsibilities. The concerns of the postal unions, not to mention mounting pressures from labor Democrats in the House, pointed to the alternative strategy of strengthening the labor committee by awarding it postal and federal employee matters. The issue evoked a partisan split. Bolling and his Democratic colleagues favored the labor committee. Civil service and postal affairs belonged together, they contended, and logically fell in the labor category. Moreover, as Meeds explained:

> I think it will enhance . . . the labor committee which I think needs some additional jurisdiction. If it would be an equal committee with all of the other committees in the Congress, I think it needs additional jurisdiction which will attract members to that committee.[48]

The Republicans feared labor dominance of postal affairs. "The Postal Service has lots of problems," Steiger said, "some of them labor, some of them building, some of them management, some of them equipment, all kinds of problems."[49] He was vigorously supported by Martin and Frelinghuysen. Two motions—Sarbanes's to put civil service and postal affairs under labor, Martin's to transfer both to Government Operations —lost in tie party-line votes. Bolling abstained to counterbalance the absent Wiggins. At that moment the group recessed to allow members to participate in a vote on the House floor. When the committee reconvened a few moments later another Republican member was missing. When Steiger moved to reconsider, the vote was again along party lines but this time the labor committee won out by a four to three margin.[50] Vice Chairman Martin switched his vote to "aye" so that he could move to reconsider at a later date, but he did not make good the threat. Both logic and politics argued for placing postal affairs in the proposed labor panel. "The proposed shift is based on the fact that public and private employment are fundamentally similar, particularly because personnel management in the public sector increasingly involves labor-management relations," the committee's final report explained. "The Labor Committee has undeniable experience and expertise in these areas."[51]

THE EDUCATION-LABOR CONNECTION

Splitting the Education and Labor Committee induced a reaction that was fierce though slow to materialize. As we have noted, a strong presumption in favor of realigning Education and Labor's functions prevailed during the Select Committee's deliberations. Such a change had been proposed in 1966 by the Joint Committee on the Organization of the Congress (the Monroney-Madden Committee); it was renewed in the hearings by Minority Leader Ford, Albert Quie, the committee's ranking minority member, and Ways and Means Democrat Phil Landrum.

Although it was expected that some liberals on Education and Labor, especially the subcommittee chairmen, would be unhappy with the realignment, there was reason for believing the time was propitious for such a change. The second-ranking Democrat, Edith Green—over the years an ever-more-frequent critic of federal aid programs—had resigned from the committee to serve on Appropriations (at the close of the 93rd Congress she retired from Congress). The new second-ranking Democrat, Frank Thompson, a friend to both labor and education establishments, was considered interested in chairing the proposed labor component. Aside from Chairman Carl Perkins, none of the committee's Democrats had testified or in any way conveyed public opposition to a partition. Moreover, when AFL-CIO chief lobbyist Andrew Biemiller expressed no inherent reservations about the proposal, observers could be forgiven if they concluded that the old committee's days were numbered.

Initial reactions to the Select Committee's handling of Education and Labor were favorable, although one or two specific jurisdictional allocations were to cause trouble. Following the December 7 report, the Select Committee staff made routine checks with labor union representatives and received no indication of any difficulty. Everyone was waiting for Thompson, a chief beneficiary of the change, to express his views, and Thompson was taking his time. If Thompson decided in favor of the labor committee, some of the other subcommittee chairmen—John Dent of General Labor and Dominick Daniels of Select Labor, for example— were likely to follow. Other committee Democrats, including Chairman Perkins, would tend to defer to the popular Thompson. A founder of the liberal Democratic Study Group in the late 1950s, Thompson had once favored severing Education and Labor (so he explained later); but he had grown comfortable chairing his small Special Labor Subcommittee, whose responsibilities since the battle in the 1950s over the Taft-Hartley Act had been relatively undemanding. In fact, Thompson had won his reputation in the field of education and was currently engrossed in arts and humanities programs. "I think he'd like to just hide behind the arts portion of the education jurisdiction," one of his aides confessed. A committee chairmanship would also eliminate Thompson's main power base in the House: his chairmanship of the House Administration Committee's Subcommittee on Accounts. That position enabled him to review requests for funds from other standing committees. If he assumed leadership of the proposed labor body, Thompson would have been required by caucus rules to relinquish the Accounts chairmanship. In the end, therefore, Thompson decided he was not interested in the new post; he would join Perkins in opposing the separation.

Thompson's dilemma was accentuated by his own interests and life style, but it was indicative of the reactions of many of his fellow Education and Labor Democrats. The panel's most powerful clientele was organized labor, who informally passed on the assignment of Democrats to the committee, and who rewarded their loyalty with campaign endorsements and contributions. Nevertheless, the committee's prime growth areas lay elsewhere—in elementary and secondary education, higher education, manpower training, vocational education, vocational rehabilitation, and antipoverty programs. To liberal activists those topics were more glamorous and promised greater visibility than traditional labor-management conflicts. It is fair, however, to say that at least some of the committee's Democrats bought freedom to pursue education and welfare issues by "paying their dues" in the labor-management area. Thompson's own district (the New Jersey 4th) embraced the college community of Princeton as well as the blue-collar city of Trenton, and his committee assignment helped him gain support from both sectors. Other members, too, found the committee's two subject-matter areas useful in advancing their careers: education and welfare for publicity, labor for campaign support. Nor were these subjects precisely delineated. Manpower training and vocational education programs, growth fields in the 1960s, marked the substantive juncture of education and labor, where the interests of the labor movement and the educational establishment merged. In view of the committee's decentralized character, strong subcommittees, and open procedures, it was not surprising that the members roamed freely among the disparate legislative subject matter.

Deciding to fight for the retention of the combined committee, Chairman Perkins and his seven subcommittee chairmen issued a letter on February 6 asserting they were "unanimously, vigorously, and unalterably opposed to the division of the Committee on Education and Labor into two segments."[52] Citing the committee's "productive record of constructive legislation," the signers intimated that much of the impetus for separation came from people who hoped for "*less* legislation and *less* productivity." The same day, ranking GOP member Quie wrote Bolling to "reiterate my strong support for a separate Committee on Education."[53]

Organized labor soon withdrew its earlier support for dividing the committee. Meeting late in February at Bal Harbour, Florida, the AFL-CIO's Executive Council adopted a statement charging that the reorganization plan "destroys some old relationships between established committees and legislative functions vital to our membership."[54] Among their objections was separating Education and Labor, which they termed impossible "because the two functions are so intertwined." They also criticized the abolition of the Merchant Marine and Post Office Committees, and objected to the transfer of railway labor legislation from Commerce to Public Works and Transportation. Activated by friendly congressmen and committee staff members, union representatives for public employees, postal workers, and the maritime industry had succeeded in overturning Biemiller's earlier statement and putting the AFL-

CIO on record against key segments of the reorganization. Severance of Education and Labor was only one of labor's concerns; but a combination of unhappy union clienteles delivered a rebuke to Biemiller, the AFL-CIO's veteran chief lobbyist.

At the same time, a related jurisdictional issue brought immediate complaints to the Select Committee. In agreeing to separate education and labor, Select Committee members had voted to place "manpower programs" with the labor segment. However, this was a hotly contested issue, and Steiger, an expert in manpower training programs, argued vigorously that such programs had affinity to education and were usually administered by local educational agencies. In the federal bureaucracy, "manpower program" is an umbrella term covering a wide variety of services administered by a number of agencies, primarily the Labor and the Health, Education, and Welfare (HEW) departments. Discussion had not focused on detailed types of manpower programs, and in the draft document they all appeared in the labor column, in conformity with the recommendations of AFL-CIO's Biemiller. (The staff member responsible for preparing the list deliberately wrote in several categories of manpower programs by name, to dramatize the issue of their locus.) When vocational education and rehabilitation—HEW programs administered by state and local educational agencies—were discovered in the proposed Labor Committee, administrators of these programs were horrified. Groups like the American Vocational Association, the Community College Association, and the Council of State Administrators of Vocational Rehabilitation, not to mention numerous state agencies, wrote to insist that these programs "be considered within the educational mainstream."[55]

Because they perceived little threat to their programs, educational groups seemed scarcely interested in the Select Committee's proposed Education Committee. The *American School Board Journal,* among other periodicals, wrote a favorable editorial on the Bolling report;[56] and distinguished congressional observer Dr. Stephen K. Bailey, a vice president of the American Council on Education, told Bolling that "a separate committee on education would focus the attention and expertise of members and staff on educational matters in a manner not presently possible."[57] Later, during floor consideration of H. Res. 988, President Albert Shanker of the American Federation of Teachers expressed opposition to splitting the committee on the inexplicable ground that a proposed education panel would be dominated by antieducation members. If the educational community perceived the potential impact from the proposed reshuffling, however, they entirely failed to articulate their views.

Opposition to severing Education and Labor posed an insoluble dilemma for the Select Committee. Although Bolling was aware of agitation by maritime, public employee, and postal unions over the reorganization scheme, he tended to view Education and Labor Democrats as the chief instigators of antagonism. "The indications are," he said, "that the real key question underneath everything else is the question of splitting Education and Labor."[58] But with a majority on the Select Committee favoring the move, and with an assumption that the House supported it, the chairman did not retreat:

> I am not suggesting we make any adjustments to meet this problem because I don't know how to do it. I can't conceive of a rational proposal that would involve keeping the Labor and Education Committee together because I am sure it would be defeated, regardless of its merits.
>
> So we are between a rock and a hard place. It always seems to me when we get into this kind of trouble to do the reverse of what is the politically classical thing to do, and that is to say nothing.[59]

"Say nothing" was what the Select Committee did. Although devoting extended attention to ancillary issues, the members declined to review their basic decision. Instead, their final report reiterated the rationale for the proposed division: the subjects were sufficiently independent to justify two committees; the existing committee's work load was excessive and would have to be reduced for a balanced committee system; educational issues had expanded in number and importance since the Second World War; and separation was implied by the committee's current subcommittee structure. Formal division into two panels, it was contended, would "foster the goal of balancing and realigning workloads ... and ... providing each member with an opportunity to participate meaningfully on a committee concerned with a major national problem."[60]

Nonetheless, numerous adjustments were made to perfect the plan. Vocational education was easy: acknowledging that a "mistake" had been made in the draft document, the members assigned it, along with vocational rehabilitation, to the education panel. Because it was manifestly impossible to consolidate responsibility for all the 300 programs administered by some forty federal departments and agencies that pertained to education, the committee developed a rule of thumb for allocating these programs: if they affected overall educational policies and practices (for example, educational technology, libraries, or housing) they were assigned to the proposed educational panel; if their impact was primarily in a specialized professional field (for example, maritime education or science scholarships), they were awarded to the committees handling those topics. Thus, agricultural colleges (from the Agriculture Committee), Indian education (from Interior), and military dependents' education (from Armed Services) were considered general educational matters because they dealt with mainstream educational institutions. In contrast, mining schools (Interior), military academies (Armed Services) and maritime education (Merchant Marine) were deemed specialized enough to remain in other committees. The dexterity required for distributing such jurisdictions illustrated the arduous analytical task implied by reorganizing governmental functions.

A similar dilemma, with more serious political implications, surrounded the proposed labor committee. Were government programs dealing with railway labor, postal labor, and the Civil Service to be classed as labor matters, or were they matters of transportation, the Postal Service, and general government administration, respectively? Because labor's voice tended to be stronger than management's in these areas, the decision leaned toward the labor committee. Besides, in view of the restiveness of liberal Democrats with the proposed separation, the labor segment had to be made as attractive as possible. "You see," Meeds said, "I think the labor committee as it is composed has got to be a stronger committee. It has got to have more jurisdiction than it presently has."[61] Jurisdiction over Civil Service and the Postal Service was thus placed in the proposed labor committee, a move that also relieved the Government Operations Committee (slated in the draft document to receive those matters) of excess burdens. Railway labor matters, historically distinct from the main body of the labor movement, were coupled with rail transportation in the Public Works and Transportation Committee. A final major gain for the labor panel would be unemployment compensation from Ways and Means, but not without a fight within the Select Committee.

THUNDERCLOUDS FROM THE ENVIRONMENTALISTS

Allocating responsibilities in the vast and pressing topics of energy, natural resources, and environmental policy was the most intricate intellectual and political challenge faced by the Select Committee. The subjects themselves were broad yet tightly intertwined; potential claimants for the jurisdiction were numerous and, as we have seen, engaged in subtle lobbying throughout the hearings and deliberations. Resource policies were, and are, Exhibit A for the chaotic state of the congressional committee system. Some of the most basic instruments of environmental policy had found their way into a Merchant Marine subcommittee; natural resources were scattered among many committees, notably Interior, Agriculture, and Commerce. Concerted energy policy had for years been stymied, partly because of the byzantine profusion of committee claims. As Representative Wiggins described outer continental-shelf lands, the coveted prize of a half dozen House committees:

> Every committee of Congress has somebody worrying about energy, including the Judiciary Committee. We are holding great hearings, I understand, having people come down to tell us about oil production. That is public relations, that is not proper legislative jurisdiction.[62]

The committee's solution, as we have seen, was a multifaceted approach. A "super" Energy and Environment Committee was to be built upon the existing Interior panel with key segments added from Commerce, Merchant Marine, and Joint Atomic Energy; the Agriculture Committee was to be broadened with new natural resources responsibilities; research and development was to be placed in Science and Technology; and transportation was to be gathered together in Public Works. The allocations were staggeringly complicated. As Bolling observed:

> But the problem here is that we have four different committees in play on the table. It seems to me very important that we think about it. I don't know the answer. I really don't.
> WIGGINS: We want to throw them all up in the air and then we want to see where we can go so that when they come down none of them hits us.
> BOLLING: I don't care if a few of them hit me but I don't want all of them to hit me.[63]

The question had to be discussed in detail, for it appeared that some of the trial balloons were being shot down.

Repeated efforts to fashion a proposal that would broaden the appeal and representation of the Agriculture Committee were doomed, or so it seemed. At one time or another staff members had proposed community development, natural resources, or nutrition and health as potential subjects to counterbalance the Agriculture Committee's historic commodity orientation. The Sarbanes-Steiger draft nominated consumer affairs, but an instantaneous outcry from consumer lobbyists like Ralph Nader scuttled the suggestion. The December 7 draft proposed national parks, forests, and wilderness areas (from Interior) and wildlife, fisheries, and marine affairs (from Merchant Marine). The protest from Dingell and other Merchant Marine members was vitriolic; no less intense an aversion was expressed by environmental groups, who feared that their policies would be emasculated at the hands of producer-oriented Agriculture. "They just don't understand," the Sierra Club's Linda Billings complained. "They've thrown us to the wolves. If the committee is so foolish as to do that [adopt the draft plan], they will be buying a lot of trouble."[64] Privately, she said environmental groups could "lock the door and go out of business" if the report were adopted. Environmentalists began to pressure "public interest" groups like Common Cause and Ralph Nader's Congress Watch to oppose the reorganization plan. Most of the lobbying was directed toward friendly legislators, who immediately expressed their concerns. Representative Roy Taylor, chairman of Interior's Parks and Recreation Subcommittee, argued that the proposal ignored the historic link between this jurisdiction and environmental concerns. "What is to be gained by the transfer?" he asked.

> The Agriculture Committee has never had any interest in, or responsibility for, the nation's outdoor recreation program. . . . It is oriented toward rural America and maximum utilization of the land for agricultural purposes . . . rather than the preservation of land for its unique natural or historical purposes which are an increasing concern of the people of urban America.[65]

Other key members of Interior echoed this sentiment. About the only people to applaud the proposal were Agriculture Chairman W. R. Poage and his ranking minority member, William C. Wampler. Even the American Forestry Association, an industry group that favored Agriculture's control over forestry, thought it was going too far to award parks and recreation to the committee. "To transfer these traditional conservation programs to a commodity-oriented committee jurisdiction might be unwise," their representative stated.[66]

In all fairness, the imbroglio was quite involved, and both sides had some grounds for concern. Even after its "reform" in the 94th Congress, Agriculture remained the archetypical clientele-oriented body. Extending its jurisdiction into public lands had a certain logic. National forests, administered by the Agriculture Department's Forest Service, already fell mainly under the committee's aegis—a fact of which environmental lobbyists seemed unaware; and public lands policy embraced many agricultural usages, including grazing rights. And yet more was at stake than lumber, livestock, and recreation. The vast public domain also contained a preponderance of the nation's untapped energy resources in the form of coal, natural gas, oil, and oil shale—a fact with which future energy policy would have to cope. Select Committee members themselves differed over the feasibility of reforming Agriculture into a broad-gauged, multi-interest committee. Even Steiger, the most consistent proponent of the multi-interest concept, worried that "it is the one committee that is the most difficult to broaden in scope. . . . [W]e are not only discussing a theory, but a situation where interests inside and outside of Congress are not very happy with what we came up with. . . ."[67]

Others, like Sarbanes, were even more responsive to the environmentalists' fears:

> You have a dilemma: If you broaden its jurisdiction, will you attract to it
> a different kind of representation because it has a broader jurisdiction?
> Or will you, nevertheless, because the agriculture jurisdiction remains so
> paramount for many people, even if broadened, continue to attract those
> basically concerned with agricultural jurisdiction? I am inclined to think
> that the latter is what will happen.[68]

Almost no one outside the Agriculture Committee itself, it appeared, favored the proposed alternatives. While everyone conceded the need for reform, few were willing to offer their own favorite programs as the vehicle for its accomplishment.

The proposed supercommittee, Energy and Environment, also ran into difficulties. Its boundaries were arbitrary, it was true, but that was inevitable in such an extensive subject matter. The chief beneficiaries, the Interior Committee members, were naturally eager for the gains but were upset over compensatory losses in public lands, parks and recreation, and Indian affairs. (Chet Holifield, whose Government Operations Committee received responsibility over Indians, disparaged "the logic of your suggestion that my committee take over the noble red men."[69]) Originated as an alternative to the proposed energy committee Bolling had initially favored, the marriage of energy and environment was explicitly intended to counterbalance the influence of oil and gas companies, under the theory that optimal policies should embrace trade-offs between producer and conservationist interests. At first this notion was applauded. "We see disadvantages in the creation of a separate Energy Committee and generally favor creation of a combined Energy and Environment Committee," a Nader associate wrote during the Select Committee's earlier discussions.[70] But as time passed, the idea of intracommittee checks and balances lost its appeal. Environmental lobbyists, it seemed, feared direct confrontation with resource producers in the proposed committee, just as they fretted over commodity interests in Agriculture. The reasoning, as expressed by a coalition of environmental lobbyists, was indirect:

> The creation of a monolithic committee with jurisdiction over all
> energy and environment issues (except research and development) will
> not facilitate the rational consideration of national energy policy so much
> as it will enable the oil-coal-utility lobbies to capture one committee to
> serve their purposes. Public interest advocates, on the other hand, will be
> deprived of the opportunity of appealing to the broad-based constituency
> of Representatives who are now involved with energy issues.[71]

The premise of this argument, though a bit obscure, was that congressmen friendly to the environmental movement would shun such a committee as their sole assignment but would willingly involve themselves in environmental issues through secondary committees (Interior or Merchant Marine). Historically Interior had been treated as a nonexclusive committee, even though during the previous decade its duties had grown in national importance. Among Democrats on Interior, four (including the Select Committee's Meeds) also held seats on Education and Labor; two were on Foreign Affairs, two on Armed Services, and two on Judiciary, among others. A potent source of resistance to reorganization, Bolling told his colleagues, would come from

> the middle range—and it might as well be on the table—Democrats who serve on a number of committees, and from some of the groups with which they work closely.
>
> I think we might as well get it all out here. Some of these groups are fearful that if there isn't an opportunity for dual assignment on the Interior-connected type of thing, that they just simply are not going to have people make that a first choice.[72]

Such an argument was widely accepted though virtually impossible to appraise. It was, of course, entirely hypothetical. Nonetheless, it is difficult to imagine that the proposed Energy and Environment Committee would not have been one of the most attractive assignments on Capitol Hill for members representing every type of constituency. Indeed, the existing Interior Committee, upon which the proposed panel would be built, had gradually evolved from a regional, producer-oriented committee into a broadly representative body.

During markups the Select Committee again endeavored to adjust the jurisdictional components. First, the proposed Agriculture and National Resources Committee was cut back to Agriculture and Forestry. National parks and wilderness areas, recreation, wildlife, fisheries, and marine affairs were omitted, though in exchange Agriculture was reassigned small watershed programs (originally to be shifted to Energy and Environment) and oversight of the Commodity Credit Corporation (from Banking and Currency). Public lands management for farming, grazing and forestry was placed with Agriculture, along with the limited national forests jurisdiction they did not already possess. Some, including Steiger, claimed that the move negated the earlier efforts to bring diversity to Agriculture. "But so long as it retains its historic, almost total, sole focus on agriculture," he argued, "it would not achieve the kind of balance that every other committee can achieve."[73] Nevertheless, the political costs of this stratagem were too high for the Select Committee's Democrats, who contended that Agriculture was important enough to be classed as a major committee without substantial additions. In support of this viewpoint they repeatedly cited Vice Chairman Martin's reminders about the economic importance of agriculture. Meeds wanted to go still further and retain all public lands jurisdiction for Energy and Environment, but his motion failed. Thus the resulting Agriculture jurisdiction was only slightly enlarged.

The other adjustment aimed at balancing the Energy and Environment supercommittee. Because it had been awarded some of the resource responsibilities originally slated to go to Agriculture, some charged that the supercommittee would be overburdened. The solution lay in Meeds's proposal for a secondary committee containing residual environmental jurisdiction: the revived Merchant Marine and Fisheries Committee. Another "loss" for Energy and Environment was the Tennessee Valley Authority (TVA), which it was originally slated to receive (with other energy power administrations) from Public Works. However, the chairman of Public Works' Economic Development Subcommittee, which oversaw TVA, happened to be Robert E. Jones, whose north Alabama district also fell in the area served by the multistate authority. His committee, he said, had developed "an appreciation and understanding of this unique federal agency which would not readily be duplicated by a committee unfamiliar with the intricacies of the TVA Act."[74] Bolling regarded Jones a friend and a key southern ally. Whenever the matter of TVA came up, Bolling staged what can only be described as a filibuster on behalf of leaving it in Public Works. When members alluded to TVA's affinity with energy production, Bolling responded with prolonged lectures on TVA's origins and its unique multifunctional concept. "Why is it important to put TVA in the Public Works Committee?" Wiggins finally asked. Martin quickly replied, "Because Bob Jones will be chairman of Public Works and that is his district."[75] Therefore, TVA remained with Public Works.

The compromise that emerged out of the energy problem represented the Select Committee's most concentrated discussions and some of its most creative work. The centerpiece of the plan, the proposed Energy and Environment Committee, was an attractive application of the multi-interest concept. The easier solution—a special energy body with its threat of a single-purpose, "crash" energy program—had been resisted. However, at the moment few people seemed satisfied with the Select Committee's handiwork.

SEVERAL CONSERVATIVE ISSUES

The leading problem areas for the Select Committee seemed to emanate from middle-seniority Democratic liberals who held attractive multiple assignments and were unwilling to forfeit them to reorganization. Along with their staff aides and associated clientele groups, these members paradoxically became the most vocal spokesmen for the status quo, eventually forming the keystone of the antireorganization coalition in the House. Repeatedly during the markup sessions Bolling warned his committee of the danger signals he discerned from the Democratic left, pointing out that these forces might use the Democratic caucus to prevent the reorganization proposals from ever reaching the House floor. His Democratic colleagues, and eventually some of the Republicans, understood, and the major adjustments reached during the markups—Merchant Marine, the labor package, allocation of environmental responsibilities—flowed from that understanding. However, resistance was also appearing from conservative interests, and the Select Committee had to keep its collective eye trained on this problem as well. A great deal of discussion therefore focused on what might be called conservative issues.

Ways and Means. The Ways and Means Committee's excessive power had been from the beginning a major target of reorganization. Speaker Albert and Minority Leader Ford certainly had Wilbur Mills's domain in mind when they proposed the reform effort, and the subject frequently found its way into the committee's hearings. Bolling well understood that his solution to this problem would receive a careful appraisal from his most important constituency, the party leadership. His ingenious plan for shifting tariffs and trade would not only trim Mills's sails but would also help solve the equally vexing problem of bolstering Foreign Affairs. Urged on by his colleagues, Bolling had accepted additional curbs for Ways and Means in the fields of health (Medicare and Medicaid) and manpower (unemployment compensation). Opposition from Mills's committee was assumed; the challenge would be to isolate Mills and frustrate his search for allies.

Virtually every press account concerning the Select Committee leaned heavily on the "contest" between Bolling and Mills, often printing both men's pictures. It was true that the two were personally distant but, at least on Bolling's side, there was also grudging respect ("I am a dedicated Wilbur-watcher"). The reaction from Ways and Means was equally and characteristically low key. For the first time in his remarkable career, however, Mills was not firmly in command of his committee. Plagued by surgery on his back, he was in and out of a Little Rock hospital during the spring of 1974; his physical ailment may have well contributed to his alcoholism which, by the end of the year, was headline news. Meanwhile, the modest and competent Al Ullman cautiously put on the mantle of "acting chairman," and proceeded to decentralize intracommittee influence and to impress his colleagues with his democratic style. Nevertheless, Ullman's position was unsure, and many in Washington were asking, "What's the matter with Wilbur?"

Mills was not idle, however, and he planned a counteroffensive. The first overt move was a formal letter, cosigned by ranking GOP member Herman Schneebeli, on behalf of the Ways and Means members on both sides of the aisle. A curt document, it referred to "the heavy blow to sound organizational principles and sound public policy which would result should anything even approaching these initial recommendations be adopted."[76] The argument concentrated on tariffs and health care, which led to speculation that the document had been drafted by the staff aide specializing in those topics. Such topics as energy tax policies and tax expenditures were not mentioned. The proposed transfer of Medicare and Medicaid policy was criticized as "fragmentation" and an invitation to irresponsible raids on the Social Security trust funds, which finance medical delivery programs. Mills's argument on tariffs was less convincing. He suggested that transferring the House's constitutional privilege of originating revenue bills might be harmful:

> Jurisdiction on trade and tariffs legislation has evolved from the basic revenue jurisdiction, and is still legally based on the revenue function of the House. The results of transferring trade and tariffs to Foreign Affairs would be the loss of prerogative of the House . . . to initiate trade and tariffs legislation. It will be a signal that the House no longer considers it a revenue function and thus outside the purview of matters which must originate here.

Because the Constitution contains no requirement that revenue bills must originate from a particular committee, or any committee at all for that matter, Mills's argument was not taken seriously.

In any event, the Select Committee was in no mood to retreat on the issue of trade policy. Although historically the source of fierce sectional and partisan debates, trade policy had not played that role for more than forty years. The most common contemporary trade controls were not tariffs, but so-called nontariff barriers—for example, export and import controls, quotas, and packaging laws. Such control devices, and tariffs as well, were debated in terms of domestic economies or foreign policy, not in terms of the insignificant revenue they raised. The committee by now solidly supported Bolling on this issue where, as he put it, "the tail should not be allowed to wag the dog."[77] Support for the proposal also came from the Foreign Affairs Committee in a letter signed by Chairman Thomas Morgan and twenty-nine of his forty committee colleagues.[78]

The key controversy concerned the locus of responsibility for unemployment compensation. The division of labor had long been a night-mare for manpower analysts. The nation's federal-state employment security system, with its network of semi-autonomous state employment services, was created by the Wagner-Peyser Act of 1933 and adminis-tered through the Labor Department; yet unemployment insurance, administered by the system and the source of its operating costs, is a trust fund provided through Title III of the Social Security Act of 1935 —hence its locus under the aegis of Ways and Means. For years the em-ployment services were in the anomalous position of being the nation's largest dispenser of manpower services, while at the same time separated from every other federal manpower program by their mode of financing and congressional committee reference. The employment services—state agencies with total federal financing and hence answerable to neither level of government—had a reputation (though somewhat improved in recent years) for unresponsiveness. "So they just keep paying out the [unemployment] funds and they don't try to find the people jobs," Meeds explained. Within the Education and Labor Committee, Meeds and Steiger had backed attempts to amend the Wagner-Peyser Act to man-date closer cooperation between the employment security system and manpower training programs. "We were run over by a Mack truck called the Ways and Means Committee," recalled Meeds.[79] The two men now presented a powerful bipartisan front for shifting unemployment com-pensation to the new labor committee. While such a move would un-questionably make the proposed committee more attractive to labor Democrats, the argument was grounded primarily in policy considera-tions. "I don't think you can talk about any kind of a rational, comprehen-sive, cohesive manpower policy," Steiger said, "without at some point dealing with the Employment Service."[80]

Martin, in private life a retail businessman, worried that a liberal-leaning committee would sharply raise jobless benefits and jeopardize employer contributions to the trust fund. He fought hard to keep con-trol with the "safe" Ways and Means Committee. Labor interests, he asserted, would force a "drawdown" of the trust fund without consent from Ways and Means:

> Every employer in the United States outside of a few in the con-struction industry that have layoffs in the wintertime and so forth have built up millions and millions of dollars into these funds. It is their money, but they never get it back. It goes to employees that are laid off under the unemployment compensation program.
>
> That is what I am fearful of, that the Labor Committee is going to be somewhat unreasonable at times in some of the legislation that might be proposed and acted on by Congress.[81]

Martin's efforts were fruitless. His motion to leave unemployment compensation solely in Ways and Means lost, three to seven (only Frelinghuysen and Young joining him); a subsequent motion to give the labor committee oversight powers won only two votes (Martin's and Young's).[82] Moreover, the committee also declined to follow Meeds's suggestion to limit still further Ways and Means' review of unemployment compensation. "Let's understand," Steiger warned, "we have imposed a very, very real restriction" on Ways and Means.[83] Martin was not appeased, and when the committee's report was issued he appended a lengthy supplemental statement (the only public dissent expressed by a committee member) to the effect that dividing the unemployment program into tax and nontax segments was "like attempting to unscramble eggs." He announced his intention to introduce a floor amendment reversing the committee's recommendation.[84]

To soften the blow to Ways and Means, the members concentrated on a scheme, mentioned briefly in the draft document, for splitting tax and nontax responsibilities. On the model of the airport and highway trust funds, substantive committees would determine the broad policy outlines while Ways and Means would outline the financing. Meeds articulated the rationale:

> What kind of health program do you want? What kind of foreign trade policy do you want? What kind of unemployment compensation do you want?
> That is the policy question in each instance.
> The tax question is the same in each . . . situation. You call it tariff, call it whatever you want. The question is how do you implement this policy that you have decided on in tariffs, in health or in unemployment compensation via the tax method.

Retaining taxing authority in Ways and Means, he said, would assure that

> there remained that responsibility in the Congress and some substantive committee didn't just go off half-cocked and pass something that bore no relationship to what it was going to cost.[85]

The negotiators disagreed, of course, on the exact demarcation between the powers of Ways and Means and substantive committees. Martin and one or two of the Republicans preferred to tilt the balance toward the revenue committee, especially in unemployment compensation. Meeds, joined by Culver and Sarbanes, wanted to curb Ways and Means still further by prohibiting it from killing such legislation through delays. The majority, however, concluded that controls should be imposed through the Speaker's proposed joint bill referral powers. In this form the compromise was approved. As the report stated, Ways and Means would "retain its historic jurisdiction over taxes, tariffs and Social Security and relinquish direct control of other jurisdiction not directly related to those matters."[86]

Foreign Intelligence. One of Bolling's tactical objectives was to minimize expected opposition from the House's major conservative bastions. His underlying purpose was undoubtedly to isolate Ways and Means and prevent the redoubtable Mills from forging an antireform coalition with his natural allies. Central to this tactic were Appropriations Chairman George Mahon and Armed Services Chairman F. Edward Hébert. Accordingly, few inroads were made into either of those committees. As for Appropriations, the bold scheme for merging funding bills with authorizing committees was floated and conspicuously rejected; a milder proposal for realigning Appropriations' subcommittees—a desperately needed step that had eluded Mahon because of the subcommittee chairmen's increasing autonomy—was reluctantly shelved.[87] Mahon had no objections to the reorganization plan. Such was not the case with Hébert of Armed Services. Although few of his committee's vast responsibilities were challenged, Hébert voiced vigorous complaints, chiefly over foreign intelligence operations.

More serious was a flap over the tentative decision to share Armed Services' foreign intelligence jurisdiction with Foreign Affairs. Armed services committees on both sides of the Capitol supposedly held responsibility for legislation and oversight in the intelligence field, including operations of the Central Intelligence Agency (CIA), but their negligence was suggested by sporadic press accusations of CIA scandals. It was widely believed that the agency was out of control. Nor was the CIA the sole source of concern: the ten major federal agencies of the so-called intelligence community were duplicating efforts and spending several billions of dollars annually without accountability (because the funding was secret, no one knew exactly how much was being spent). Between 1947 and 1972, almost one hundred and fifty bills and resolutions for strengthening congressional oversight of intelligence activities had been introduced. In proposing shared jurisdiction, Select Committee members thought they had a solution that would preserve the military committee's claims but recognize the acute foreign policy implications of intelligence activities. It was expected that the two committees would set up a joint review panel to provide more vigorous oversight while maintaining control over classified information.

Soon, word reached the Select Committee that Hébert and his colleagues would not accept that solution. Hébert cryptically expressed "considerable concern" over unnamed issues and complained that his copy of the draft plan was blurry.[88] Through staff emissaries, it was relayed that a certain member (or members) of Foreign Affairs posed a "security risk" and could not be trusted to handle sensitive information. Bolling took the issue seriously, having earlier confided to a staff aide about certain members with "ties to foreign powers." Needless to say, such reports incensed Foreign Affairs members, who objected to withholding important policy information from any congressman and who protested that their security procedures were as reliable as Armed Services'. Foreign Affairs' second-ranking Democrat, Representative Clem Zablocki, author of several resolutions for a joint intelligence committee, gave a thoughtful endorsement of the coordinate jurisdiction proposal.[89]

A heated and at times acrimonious controversy ensued among the Select Committee's staff. As with most debates over the question prior to 1975, meaningful discussion was subdued by the smokescreen of "national security," which, along with vagueness about the intelligence function itself, cloaked such activities from review by outsiders. The term "intelligence" was itself a stumbling block. Critics of the CIA and its sister agencies had little quarrel with intelligence gathering per se, except perhaps that the agencies were duplicating each other's work. The real target was clandestine activities, like sabotage and assassination, which had serious repercussions upon the nation's international relations. Defenders of the agencies claimed that covert activities were an insignificant aspect of their work—though because the budgets remained secret the case could not be proved one way or the other. Defenders of the agencies assumed an attitude of "if-you-knew-what-I-knew" condescension. Eventually, revelations in late 1974 and 1975 of CIA's activities surpassed even the critics' most extravagant charges, and special intelligence review panels in both bodies began to exercise the oversight that the armed services committees had been unable or unwilling to do.

In view of his own predilections and the tactical need to placate influential conservatives, Bolling decided to soft-pedal the issue and engineer a compromise acceptable to Armed Services. "If it were to result in a decision by everybody in the Armed Services Committee to be against everything in this resolution," he told his colleagues, "I would be unhappy."[90]

With Bolling's encouragement, the Select Committee staff, in contact with Hébert's staff aides, drafted a revised plan retaining primary jurisdiction within Armed Services. This retreat incensed some staff members and was heatedly disputed by Meeds, who argued that foreign intelligence was an adjunct of foreign policy.[91] Defense of Armed Services was mounted by Representative C. W. Bill Young, who had recently transferred from that body to Appropriations and who contended that "the smaller the group of people with access to this information the better off we are."[92] Young's motion to leave the matter entirely within Armed Services was defeated, however, only himself and Stephens voting for it. The majority of the committee agreed with a compromise proposed by Steiger and approved by Bolling, giving Foreign Affairs special review powers in foreign intelligence in exchange for Armed Services' review over arms control and disarmament. Armed Services would retain control over authorizations for intelligence agencies, while Foreign Affairs would do the same for disarmament. Although Steiger noted that the compromise would ensure "equity of treatment" for the two committees, it appeared that Armed Services received the better deal. The matter was concluded when Frelinghuysen, Foreign Affairs' ranking Republican, agreed that "the oversight function is not an unreasonable role for us to play and let the Armed Services have the basic [responsibility]. . . ."[93] After prolonged discussion over the specific wording, the "mirror image" treatment of Armed Services and Foreign Affairs on arms control and foreign intelligence, respectively, was subsumed under the reform plan's provisions for "special oversight"—review over matters outside the committees' legislative jurisdiction.[94]

Small Business. The proposed elimination of the Permanent Select Committee on Small Business caused a stir on Capitol Hill. Created originally in 1941, the body was an investigatory agency with no legislative jurisdiction—although its functions had been written into certain provisions of the Small Business Act, whose jurisdictional home was actually Stephens's Banking and Currency Subcommittee on Small Business. As one member said, the body had "a hunting license everywhere but no gun." Whatever its formal legislative status, the panel found ready political support for its role of speaking up for the small businessman who, as one writer declared, "is being chivvied, harassed, ruined, and bankrupted by a political process that takes him for granted and is utterly indifferent to his problematic condition."[95] Many of its thirty-seven members found it a useful "second committee" from which to generate favorable publicity with a minimum of effort. Chairman Joe L. Evins flooded Bolling with a series of impassioned and flattering letters asking "what I can do to cause you" to reverse the tentative decision. "I hope my old Sewanee University friend will do this for me when you return to the Congress next year," he wrote on December 18.[96] Along with his ranking GOP counterpart, Silvio O. Conte, he noted that "the interests of small business would be 'lost' and downgraded in this large and diverse committee [Banking and Currency] at a time when small business especially needs strong representation in the Congress." Conte went so far as to intimate to Bolling and others that he would rather forfeit his seat on Appropriations than lose his place on Small Business. Moreover, a group of liberal Republicans, including Conte, who indicated support for the overall reorganization plan, termed retention of the panel "another gesture which can be made to attract support for the whole proposal."[97] Outside small business interests, often ignored by major business and producers' associations, were hardly heard from. The most conspicuous small business group, the National Federation of Independent Businessmen, was not enthusiastic about retaining the existing select body but wanted a standing committee with broad legislative jurisdiction.

The question was whether to fold small business oversight into Banking and Currency, which possessed legislative powers over the subject, or to reconstitute Small Business as a legislative committee with narrowly defined prerogatives. "The legislative politics of this is fairly simple," Bolling told his colleagues.

> Those who want an absolutely pure product from this committee feel if we back down on one or two of our eliminations of relatively lesser committees, then we are making ourselves vulnerable to a rollup of every group, inside and outside, that has a special interest.[98]

"I do not think it is critical," he added. "Frankly, I cannot figure out which way it will help us the most." The committee was divided but nobody felt strongly about the question. Steiger and Wiggins contended that because small business interests should be considered by every House committee, a separate committee was not warranted; but Wiggins wondered whether Banking and Currency, with its big business ties, was the best home for the jurisdiction. Stephens endorsed the notion of a separate committee with legislative jurisdiction, even though his own committee would lose in the exchange. He proposed a legislative committee with jurisdiction limited to the Small Business Act. "You don't disturb anything very much under that jurisdictional change and you obviate the necessity of claiming it is a major committee," he explained.[99] A straw vote on the motion found the members deadlocked, but a few days later when the matter came up for final resolution it was approved by voice vote.

Internal Security. Of all the House's committees, Internal Security (HISC) was probably the most consistently controversial, and it was to be expected that a proposal to abolish it would elicit both praise and anguish. Internal Security Chairman Richard Ichord preferred to see the committee awarded an expanded domain; failing that, he would acquiesce to combining it with Government Operations—or simply leaving it alone. The one unacceptable option was the one Bolling and his colleagues originally chose: transfer to the Judiciary Committee. "I think you will agree," he wrote, "that transferring this jurisdiction to the Judiciary Committee is the one way to ensure that the work will not be done."[100] Long-time enemies and defenders of HISC reacted predictably. Representative Robert Drinan, the liberal Catholic priest who when he was assigned to the committee vowed to abolish it, was understandably happy with the Bolling-Martin recommendation. "It should have been done years ago," he commented. "Of all the recommendations, it is the one that has the most chance of success." But one of the panel's conservative members, Roger Zion, promised to fight "abrogation by Congress of this vital investigative field."[101]

Although partly through Ichord's efforts HISC was less controversial than in the 1940s and 1950s, it had potent defenders among the nation's conservative writers and editorialists. These forces were slow to mobilize in defense of the committee, most of them surfacing after the Bolling report had been completed and sent to the House. On March 3, however, the seven Hearst newspapers printed a rambling editorial signed by editor-in-chief William Randolph Hearst, Jr., denouncing the "legislative ploy aimed at killing the HISC." Noting that a majority of the Democrats on Judiciary had previously opposed HISC, he charged the reorganization would "almost certainly finish the kind of vigorous continuing probe of subversive activity for which HUAC-HISC had been noted."[102] Columnist Holmes Alexander also voiced concern over abolishing HISC, and letters were received from groups like the Catholic War Veterans, the Non-Commissioned Officers Association, the National Sojourners, the Polish American Revival Movement Conference, the American Hungarian Federation, the Marine Corps League, and several medium-sized business firms.[103]

Although HISC's external constituency had not fully mobilized, it was obvious that tampering with the body would produce heated debate, and unquestionably a separate floor vote on that issue alone. Views within the Select Committee were as divided as in the general public. The committee's liberals wanted to see HISC extinguished and its files and functions turned over to Judiciary. "These people," Meeds said "... have a whole half a hall down there in the Cannon Building where people sit around and keep God knows how many files on whomever, and I just don't think it is that big in the total scheme of things today."[104] Only one conservative, Representative Young, wanted to keep HISC intact. The majority agreed with Wiggins, a Judiciary member, in supporting Ichord's suggestion for placing it in Government Operations:

... for the very pragmatic reasons that I do not believe that the Internal Security Committee has a future in the Committee on the Judiciary, and that the House of Representatives is going to insist that it have a real future.[105]

Sarbanes, also a Judiciary member, denied that Judiciary would stifle inquiries into internal security. "I think there is as good a chance as not that the work would be continued," he said.[106] Bolling sided with Wiggins. "My judgment is that it almost surely won't get to Judiciary," he declared. "I think that is about it. It is not an argument on justice, propriety, or anything else."[107] In the end this view prevailed (along with Bolling, votes came from Martin, Stephens, Frelinghuysen, and Steiger; Wiggins was absent); dissenting votes were cast by the three liberals, Meeds, Culver, and Sarbanes. Thus, under the reorganization plan, HISC went into Government Operations. As subsequent events were to demonstrate, the Select Committee's analysis was correct. The Hansen Committee's recommendation to transfer HISC to Judiciary was defeated on the House floor by a 246 to 164 vote: at least for the 93rd Congress HISC was granted a reprieve. The story for the 94th Congress, however, was to be quite different.

THE REPORT IS SENT TO THE HOUSE

Final ratification of the Select Committee reorganization plan came about three o'clock on the afternoon of March 13. In a real sense the action was anticlimactic. The meeting had been called primarily, in Bolling's words, "to clarify and make sure that what we are deciding upon is what we thought we had decided."[108] As the chairman called on his colleagues one by one, minor matters of detail and wording were raised and disposed of. There was a moment of tension when Representative Young was asked to raise any question he had. Young's attendance at committee sessions had been sporadic, and several of his proposals had been voted down resoundingly. "Mr. Chairman," he said amiably, "the only changes I would recommend have already been settled more than once and I think I will save the time of the committee and not bring them up the third time."[109] Without objection, the resolution was adopted. When Martin proposed that all ten members be listed as cosponsors of the resolution, everyone agreed.

What had the legislators approved? The question was not a simple one. At that moment staff members were feverishly drafting copy for the 460-page report that was to be published in only eight days, and much of the all-important "report language" was not available for the members to ratify. Bolling and Martin were granted authority to make technical changes and to give final approval to the copy, although every effort was made to send material to each member for review. What the legislators had ratified was primarily the text of a lengthy resolution, later numbered H. Res. 988. Title I dealt with committee jurisdictions, Title II with referral of bills and oversight, Title III with committee rules of procedure, and Title IV with miscellaneous matters like early organization, the administration and information commissions, the Legislative Classification Office, and the Office of Law Revision Counsel. Drafts of this language had been prepared by Lawrence Filson of the Legislative Counsel's Office in cooperation with lawyers on the committee's staff. The remainder of the product was prepared and edited by the staff as a whole, with Bolling and Martin retaining veto power.

To have come this far was no small achievement. The Select Committee members had transformed themselves from a study group to a decision-making body, had adapted from fascinating and quite pleasant seminars to tough bargaining sessions where theories and objectives clashed headlong into political realities both inside and outside of the House. Whether the task had been successfully done or not was yet to be answered. That the task had been done at all was remarkable in the history of Congress, and had been by no means a foregone conclusion. As they concluded their work, the committee members were, to use a popular phrase, "cautiously optimistic."

No one was unaware of the obstacles that still lay in the path of reorganization. The response to the Select Committee's trial balloon three months before had been ample proof that, whatever lip service was given to the idea of "reform," members and staff were loath to accept it if it affected them personally. Staff members with a vested interest in their jobs feared committee shifts, even though job opportunities as a whole would undoubtedly improve as a result of the changes. Outside of Capitol Hill, clientele groups were readily mobilized by Hill allies conjuring up visions of impaired treatment if committee shifts were made. Everyone, it seemed, suffered from a Hamlet complex, fearful of shifting current arrangements in favor of benefits that were, to their minds, theoretical. Bolling's objective was to get the reorganization package to the House floor so that it could be debated in the full light of publicity; but he knew that the effort could be stopped even before that time. To be successfully implemented, the plan must have the approval of the party caucuses; and thus Bolling and Martin were preparing to take their case to their party colleagues. The Republicans seemed to offer no problem, but Bolling saw trouble in the Democratic caucus. On February 13 he delivered a "tough" speech to the influential National Press Club, and that same day a letter enclosing copies of a favorable

New York Times editorial was forwarded to 350 influential journalists. In the speech he pointed his finger at some of his liberal colleagues:

> They are the ex-reformers, they're the middle-rank liberals who like their "pads." They are going to use any excuse to prevent change, simply because they like it where they are. Now they're not just time servers— some of them are pretty good men and women who feel strongly that their contribution to society through their particular little subcommittee is critical. They are going to devise a variety of techniques, and they'll join with any allies they need to. And they're very dangerous.

Only privately would he name names but it was clear that chief among them were individuals who had won reputations as "reformers" fighting the seniority system and who were comfortable with the niches they had carved for themselves now that subcommittee rule had come to the House. With enough allies, they might stop the proposals from ever reaching a floor vote. The Speaker's support would be crucial but, as Bolling warned, "Obviously no Democratic leader is going to be able to take to the floor a reorganization bill that is opposed by a majority of the Democrats."[110]

To forestall that type of ambush, Bolling and his colleagues hoped to build generalized proreform sentiment that, in the wake of the Watergate revelations, would coax members into voting for H. Res. 988, much as they were to be coaxed into voting for campaign finance reforms. Bolling spoke frequently of fashioning an "inside-outside" coalition to help sell the reforms; but several of his colleagues, sensing the need for public support, pushed him even further. It was Wiggins—enmeshed in Watergate as President Nixon's premier congressional defender—who urged that the word "reform" be attached to the resolution and who suggested the final title, "Committee Reform Amendments of 1974." Further, Culver, backed by Frelinghuysen and others, prodded Bolling and Martin to exploit their contacts with the press in winning publicity and editorial support.

Outside support was slow to appear, though it exerted a powerful influence later in the year when the committee's report was in trouble. Normal wire service stories went out on March 21, when the committee formally reported H. Res. 988 to the House. Interpretive reports soon appeared in *Congressional Quarterly, National Journal, Business Week, New Republic,* and *Commonweal.* To help journalists understand the intricacies of the reform proposal, Common Cause distributed an editorial memorandum explaining and supporting H. Res. 988.[111] With the exception of conservative complaints over the proposed demise of Internal Security, editorial comment was unanimously enthusiastic. The *Washington Post* called it "one of the most provocative and potentially valuable reforms in many years." "Whatever its imperfections," the *Post* editorialized,

> the select committee's plan is the most serious—and promising—attempt in a generation to inject coherence and vitality into a legislative scheme which is now burdened with overlaps, imbalances and incongruities.[112]

Other newspapers, ranging from the *New York Times, Des Moines Register, St. Louis Post-Dispatch,* and *Los Angeles Times* to the *Scranton* (Pennsylvania) *Times* and the *Lansing* (Michigan) *Journal,* strongly supported the measure. Public opinion of Congress was at an all-time low, according to surveys by Louis Harris and others, and when H. Res. 988 encountered organized hostility from the formidable House interests, the editorials sharply defended the Bolling report. Yet the internal organization of Congress is not, and perhaps never will be, a burning issue for the general public. No matter how many positive reviews it may command, no reorganization can be successful if it lacks the necessary votes within the chamber. "The issue now is whether the House will accept and implement this most important of reforms," observed political reporter David S. Broder, "and it is really a question of what the Democratic majority and its leaders will do."[113]

SEVEN

"King Caucus" and Committee Reform

ON MARCH 19, 1974, House Resolution 988, the Committee Reform Amendments, was introduced and referred to the House Calendar.[1] At that time, Chairman Bolling could have requested that the Rules Committee assign H. Res. 988 an open rule, permitting unlimited floor amendments, and it seemed likely that Rules would have acted favorably on such a request. Bolling, however, believed that neither meaningful nor lasting reforms could be achieved without the majority support of both parties. Therefore, Bolling first presented the reform plan to the Democratic caucus. He anticipated that party members would want to discuss the plan (especially because it affected so many of them), and he hoped that they would give the plan a majority endorsement. Bolling hoped that a majority in the Republican caucus would act in a similar manner.

Bolling's plans were not promptly or easily realized. Opponents to H. Res. 988 persuaded Speaker Albert and Caucus Chairman Olin Teague to postpone a scheduled caucus session in March and a tentatively scheduled session in April because they needed more time to consider the reform plan. Bolling accepted both postponements because those who sought delay, he said, "don't have the horses. They're thrashing around trying to figure out what to do to stop it."[2] At last, the Democratic leadership scheduled a caucus session for May 1 and 2.

These and any further delays, as the Select Committee knew well, had serious ramifications. With every passing week, it became more

likely that the House would soon be enmeshed in impeachment proceedings against President Nixon. Such a wrenching process would
dramatically direct attention away from the more mundane matter of
H. Res. 988. Further, if House consideration was delayed into the summer, the forthcoming fall elections might intensify partisan feelings to
the degree that they would upset the delicate bipartisan balance required for passage of H. Res. 988. More important, the delays gave the
opponents of H. Res. 988 time to organize a vigorous resistance.

CENTERS OF OPPOSITION

The opposition to H. Res. 988, most of which had already surfaced
following the appearance of the Select Committee's preliminary report,
escalated sharply in scope and intensity. Now the target was no mere
trial balloon, but a concrete reform plan that represented a palpable
threat to many centers of influence on Capitol Hill. Arguments first put
forward during markup of the reorganization plan continued to be
heard, along with some fresh objections. The opposition consisted mainly
of members who stood to lose committee assignments or chairmanships
under H. Res. 988; staff aides who faced the possibility of losing or
transferring jobs; and outside groups who did not want their established
ties with committees or individuals severed.

Member Opposition. A number of committee chairmen were hostile
toward H. Res. 988 because their committees were threatened with elimination or with reduced jurisdiction. Already known to be opposed were
Wilbur Mills of Ways and Means, Wayne Hays of House Administration, Leonor Sullivan of Merchant Marine and Fisheries, Harley Staggers of Interstate and Foreign Commerce, Carl Perkins of Education
and Labor, Thaddeus Dulski of Post Office and Civil Service, and Richard Ichord of Internal Security. Chet Holifield of Government Operations was also against the reorganization but for the opposite reason: he
claimed it would give his committee too much legislative and oversight
responsibility.

At the instigation of Chairman Mills, a dozen committee leaders met
on March 27, 1974, to plan the defeat of H. Res. 988. Five committee
chairmen attended: Mills, Staggers, Hays, Dulski, and Ichord. Also
present were several subcommittee chairmen, including Frank Thompson of Education and Labor, Frank Clark of Merchant Marine and
Fisheries, and David Henderson of Post Office. During the secret meeting (Mills later denied that it ever took place), it was agreed that "everybody against any part of H. Res. 988 must stand together and vote against

the rule." Notes taken at the session disclosed the senior legislators' strategy for wrecking the reform plan: "Vote against the rule when it comes to the floor on H. Res. 988 and defeat the whole thing right then and there in the first instance."[3]

Mills also acted quickly to counter the notion that Ways and Means was overloaded with work. Even before H. Res. 988 was introduced, Mills called a closed-door organizational session of his committee at which it was voted to request an additional $450,000 to augment Ways and Means' tiny staff. An elaborate plan submitted to the House revealed that the added staff would specialize in the very topics that the Select Committee proposed to shift elsewhere: trade and tariffs, health care, and unemployment compensation. Meanwhile, Mills cosponsored with Senator Edward Kennedy a comprehensive national health insurance proposal and promised to work on a major tax reform bill (later abandoned) before the end of the year. He was reportedly contacting his allies in the business community, warning that if reorganization occurred, employers would pay more money for inflated health programs and would suffer because of chaos in trade policies. The attempt at activating business groups was largely unsuccessful.

Many members had their own reasons for disliking the reform plan. A key opponent was Phillip Burton, an Education and Labor member and chairman of an Interior Subcommittee on Territorial and Insular Affairs whose duties involved pleasant travel. To charges of self-interest in not wishing to forfeit any of these seats, Burton had a characteristically blunt response: "Bolling has worked hard in the media to portray this [the reorganization plan] as reform—with the notion that everyone is just afraid of losing their accumulated power. But that is not the issue. ... It obscures the fact that this isn't really reform."[4]

While the Select Committee had selectively applied the "one-stop" and "multi-interest" concepts to jurisdictional shifts, opponents argued —equally selectively—that consolidating certain key functional areas like health, transportation, energy and environment into single committees would make them more susceptible to special interest pressures and eliminate a valuable flexibility from the committee system. Democrat John Dingell, an ardent foe of reorganization, said that "one damaging obvious result of setting up such one-interest committees will be that lobbyists will concentrate on one particular committee and devote great effort to persuading the members of that committee to suit their particular interests."[5]

Others argued that the Select Committee had left untouched or even strengthened such conservative bastions of power as Appropriations, Armed Services, and Rules. William Ford, a member of Education and Labor, complained that something should have been done to reform the Rules Committee. "Because of his position on the Rules Committee," Ford said, "Bolling might not be as sensitive as others of us to the inordinate power of that committee. The first way to start reforming the House is to make Rules into a traffic cop or abolish it."[6] Some legislators charged that Bolling was seeking to make himself czar of the House by giving the Rules Committee more power.

Other features of the Select Committee's plan aroused opposition. Among these were provisions limiting members to one major committee, banning proxy voting in committees, and providing the minority party with additional committee staff. Limiting members to one major committee assignment would, no doubt, have encouraged them to concentrate upon a subject field and contribute to policy formulation. Nevertheless, it ran counter to the political needs of many members, who liked to sit on numerous committees as a way of impressing constituents with their influence in the nation's capital.

Minority staffing and elimination of proxy voting were emotional issues for Democrats. As the majority party, Democrats argued, they shouldered many more responsibilities than the minority. Moreover, giving Republicans more committee staff would simply intensify partisanship on committees. Some Democrats even argued that if Republicans were granted one-third of the staff on a committee then Democrats should be entitled to one-third of the White House staff. Claiming to be spread more thinly on committees than Republicans, Democrats said they needed proxies to maintain control of committee policy making.

Staff Opposition. The staffs of committees that would be abolished or lose jurisdiction also objected to reorganization. Many of them were worried about losing their jobs if jurisdictions were juggled. "The staff has a bigger stake in this than the members," Bolling said, "and some lobbyists have more stake in the staff than they do in the members. It gets so triply incestuous as to be unbelievable."[7]

Key committee staff helped to mobilize and organize both member and interest group opposition to H. Res. 988. It was the Merchant Marine Committee staff that alerted the maritime unions and industry to the reform proposals and helped to coordinate their intense lobbying effort. They began soon after the Select Committee's preliminary report was issued. To outline possible strategy and tactics, the staff staged a meeting on January 25, 1974, in the committee's hearing room. The more than one hundred maritime lobbyists and nine committee members in attendance were given a summary of arguments to be used in lobbying members; to coordinate the lobbying efforts, a steering group representing the Merchant Marine and Fisheries Committee's major constituencies was established. Staff efforts also were crucial in activating postal and civil service unions. Much of the opposition to the Select Committee's plan was therefore provoked and orchestrated by the staffs of the committees adversely affected by H. Res. 988.

Group Opposition. Organized labor was the most potent opponent of the Committee Reform Amendments. As noted earlier, AFL-CIO's opposition was triggered by the Select Committee's preliminary proposal to abolish the Merchant Marine and Post Office Committees. Although the Select Committee retrenched on Merchant Marine, labor opposition could not be appeased. Big labor also opposed splitting the Education and Labor Committee. Illogically, they charged that a new labor committee, even if chaired as then expected by such a stalwart labor supporter as Frank Thompson, would attract many conservative "right-to-work" Republicans and only a few staunchly prolabor Democrats. More to the point, they foresaw that their political clout might be lessened if labor were separated from its mutually beneficial relationship with education groups. Labor opposition became even more intense when Thompson refused to chair a Labor Committee, which meant John Dent would become chairman. Although Dent was a strong labor supporter, he was regarded by union leaders as less predictable or less astute than Thompson.

After the AFL-CIO national executive council decided to oppose H. Res. 988, several of its member unions actively lobbied against it. Postal and government employee unions objected to eliminating the Post Office and Civil Service Committee; railroad unions opposed having their jurisdiction transferred from Interstate and Foreign Commerce, where they had the known support of a friendly chairman, to the Public Works and Transportation Committee. Railroaders thought the shift was undesirable because it would make their functional area a stepchild of other transportation matters. The maritime unions and industry fiercely opposed a diminished jurisdiction for the Merchant Marine and Fisheries Committee.

The unions, like other special interest groups, opposed the jurisdictional changes basically because they would destroy, as chief AFL-CIO lobbyist Andrew Biemiller phrased it, "some old relationships between established committees and legislative functions vital to our membership."[8] "Carefully nurtured contacts with key congressmen and their aides, as well as years of selective campaign contributions," one journalist wrote, "will all come loose when a new, unfamiliar committee takes jurisdiction."[9]

Environmental groups also criticized the Select Committee's plan, fearing that the proposed energy and environment committee would be controlled by the energy interests. Ecology lobbyists also contended that if members were limited to only one major committee as the Select Committee proposed, then many of their supporters would shun the energy and environment committee for other panels of more direct concern to their constituents. "For the first time," Ralph Nader explained, "there's a slim majority of environmentalists on Interior [the new Energy and Environment Committee under H. Res. 988]; industry will probably dominate the new committee. If the package can be modified, we're for it. It not, we may have problems."[10]

Members and staff threatened by the reorganization succeeded, therefore, in mobilizing key allies in their fight to protect their Capitol Hill domains. Most conspicuously active were groups in the maritime, postal, and environmental fields, and organied labor generally. Efforts to mobilize the business community, for example in defense of Ways and Means, were less successful. The Bolling reorganization might be said to have been the target of "reverse lobbying," in which legislators and staff members lobbied the lobbyists to come to their aid. The process underscored the closeness of some of the "subgovernment" relationships that link congressional subcommittees, executive agencies, and clientele groups in mutually beneficial relationships with the purpose of monopolizing policy making in given fields. Jurisdictional realignment appeared to threaten these relationships. When importuned by their congressional allies, some of the clientele groups fought aggressively to protect their established alliances, even at the risk of forgoing new alliances that might ultimately have proved fruitful.

The Select Committee Counterattacks

Realizing their resolution was controversial, members of the Select Committee were nonetheless optimistic about winning endorsement from both party caucuses. As Representative Culver said, "I don't see how, in a year of Watergate and a year when Congress' rating in the polls is at an all-time low, a member can vote against a plan to reform Congress. I'd love to run against a guy who voted against this."[11] The crucial contest, as everyone knew, would be in the Democratic caucus with its power, as David Cohen of Common Cause put it, to "torpedo the resolution."

Bolling, meanwhile, was busy refuting the charges made against H. Res. 988, speaking at numerous forums, organizing outside interests in support of reform, and planning countermeasures with members and staff. On April 1, 1974, speaking before the National Press Club, Bolling charged that the House was a shambles; its procedures and committee system were so unwieldy and archaic that it could not respond effectively to the national welfare. He also criticized certain liberal Democratic members as "dunghill" politicians, so enamored of their subcommittees that they would join with any allies to defeat committee reform.

Two days later, Bolling and three members of the Select Committee —Meeds, Sarbanes, and Culver—met with Gillis Long, a Rules Committee ally, and several staff strategists. They assessed the political situation and agreed on three counteroffensive moves. Meeds, Sarbanes, and Culver, it was determined, would meet the next day with Speaker Albert to ascertain his view of H. Res. 988 and the upcoming Democratic caucus. Those three should also see Al Barkan, key political strategist for the AFL-CIO. They would attempt to soften labor's opposition to reform, arguing that defeat of the reorganization would hand the Republicans a campaign issue for the upcoming campaign. They agreed, finally, to establish a whip system so the Select Committee could more accurately determine which members and groups were with them, which were against them, and which were undecided. Mrs. Bolling, a skilled legislative strategist, was assigned the task of keeping the tally in her husband's office.

On April 4, a larger group assembled in Room 321 of the Cannon Office Building. In addition to Bolling, Meeds, Sarbanes, and Culver, a dozen other Democrats who supported H. Res. 988 attended. Each member was assigned to contact certain colleagues and determine their position on H. Res. 988. With this more systematic information on House members, the Select Committee would be able to decide how best to strengthen Democratic support for reform. Bolling also shared questions of the committee's strategy with his friends in "the Group" (see chapter 3) during their weekly gatherings.

As a final effort to broaden support for committee reorganization, Bolling, Meeds, and Sarbanes met with the Executive Council of the Democratic Study Group (DSG) on April 23, 1974. Bolling and Meeds gave a general description of H. Res. 988, after which Sarbanes explained in detail several of its provisions. The Executive Council, however, was split. This meant that for the most part the DSG assumed a neutral position on committee reform. Some DSG members, like Phil Burton, James O'Hara, and John Brademas, worked actively to defeat the Select Committee's plan; others, like Bella Abzug, Jonathan Bingham, Donald Fraser, and Dante Fascell, supported the Select Committee.

The Parties Look at Reorganization

Both parties' caucuses convened in May to discuss H. Res. 988. Traditionally, party caucuses have four primary functions: discussing party and legislative policy, reviewing the committee assignments of party members, disciplining errant legislators, and electing party leaders and committees. For most of the twentieth century (except for the years 1911 to 1917), party caucuses were dormant institutions that simply functioned to elect party leaders. But in the late 1960s the Democratic caucus, and to a lesser extent the Republican conference, emerged as important instruments for making party policy. Many congressmen viewed the caucus as the forum where they could achieve more influence for themselves and better focus and direct the legislative energies of the House.

Within the Democratic party, the ever-more-numerous liberals, frustrated by conservative control of the House during the 1950s and most of the 1960s, looked to the caucus as a way to shift leadership influence to the liberal bloc of the House. It was in the caucus that they had the votes to win adoption of reforms that gave them a larger span of influence. Across the aisle, GOP defeats at the polls in 1958 and 1964 had decimated the ranks of senior members; in order to assure themselves adequate representation, younger members turned to the Republican conference (caucus) and reformed its structure. Beginning in 1965 for Republicans and 1969 for Democrats, therefore, caucuses began to discuss party policy in anticipation of floor debate on major measures.

The Democrats Meet May 1 and 2. Prior to the discussion on reform, Caucus Chairman Teague confided that he was not looking forward to presiding at the sessions because "there were so many people around here with blood in their eye."[12] Despite the split in party ranks, members of the Select Committee remained optimistic about the outcome. Paul Sarbanes predicted that "as more and more members come to take a look at the thing [H. Res. 988], they'll see its merits."[13]

When the secret caucus was called to order on May 1, Bolling and other committee members outlined the basic features of the plan.[14] Opponents quickly dominated the discussion. The first critic, Chairwoman Leonor Sullivan of Merchant Marine, expressed vociferous objection to the plan, observing that it gave too much power to the Rules Committee and reduced her own committee's jurisdiction. Chet Holifield reported that his Government Operations Committee lacked the needed expertise to cope with the substantial new legislative and oversight authority proposed by the reorganization. He also wondered why his committee had been granted responsibility for Indian affairs. "Congressional reform, as contemplated in this resolution, comes at a high price in concessions to Republicans and in a burgeoning congressional bureaucracy," he concluded. "Another price we pay for reform, when it comes in big packages, is turbulence and turmoil in the next Congress."[15] Representative Bob Eckhardt opposed the consolidation of jurisdictions into single committees. Thompson, ranking majority member on Education and Labor, said that although he had once favored splitting his committee, he now felt it would be disastrous for school children and working people. Education and labor were so tightly intertwined, he said, that they could not be separated. Phil Burton announced that he would offer a motion to refer the plan to the Caucus Committee on Organization, Study and Review (commonly called the Hansen Committee after its chairwoman, Julia Butler Hansen of Washington) with instructions to the Democrats on the Rules Committee not to report a "rule" until the caucus had examined the Hansen Committee's recommendations. He argued that committee reform should be delayed until the 94th Congress when there would be many more Democrats.

After two days of discussion, the caucus postponed until May 9 a vote on whether or not to endorse H. Res. 988. A majority vote for the resolution was uncertain, and would depend on how the undecided members voted. Bolling predicted that the May 9 caucus would bring on a "real blood-and-guts fight," the showdown vote coming on Burton's motion to refer the reform plan to the Hansen Committee.

Bolling and his Select Committee colleagues realized they were in trouble. The committee's five Democrats met with Speaker Albert and Majority Leader O'Neill on May 6. Albert promised to endorse H. Res. 988, and in the next few days telephoned numerous Democrats, urging them to vote for the reform plan. Send the proposal to the floor, Albert argued, and under an open rule any member could move to change features he did not like. However, if the caucus killed the resolution outright, the Republicans would be handed a campaign issue. Majority Leader O'Neill, on the other hand, was essentially a neutral observer. Some Democrats believed that O'Neill favored sending H. Res. 988 to the Hansen Committee as a way of diluting Bolling's influence in the House. O'Neill long had viewed Bolling as his principal political rival for the speakership. If Bolling succeeded in reforming the House's committee system, after his success as floor manager of the Congressional Budget and Impoundment Control Act, then his prestige would make him an important potential challenger for the top party post.

The Republicans Give Cautious Approval. When the committee reform package was considered by the Republicans, the result was more heartening but still not without its ominous signals. When the conference met on May 1, it discussed the provisions of H. Res. 988 and exchanged views, but did not vote. Unlike the fractious Democrats, House Republicans rarely if ever voted on taking positions.

The GOP conference opened as Martin outlined and explained the provisions of H. Res. 988. Frelinghuysen and Steiger followed with vigorous supporting statements. The report also received endorsements from three of the most respected House veterans—Minority Leader John Rhodes; Elford Cederberg, ranking Republican on Appropriations; and Albert Quie, ranking Republican on Education and Labor. This reflected a degree of high-level support not matched in the Democratic ranks.

The discussion was lively, however, and strong objections were raised. "It was no love feast," one observer remarked. Especially vigorous were the objections of ranking Republicans on the threatened committees—Herman Schneebeli of Ways and Means; Dan Kuykendall of the Commerce Committee's Transportation and Aeronautics Subcommittee; and Edward Derwinski, soon to become ranking member of Post Office and Civil Service. Minority Whip Les Arends suggested that an amendment be proposed specifying that committees be apportioned according to the party ratio in the full House (excepting Rules, Appropriations, Ways and Means, and Standards of Official Conduct). As in the Democratic caucus, concern was voiced that the powers granted to Government Operations would result in competition among oversight efforts. Even Bill Frenzel, one of the strongest supporters of H. Res. 988, admitted the Select Committee "may have gone too far" on that issue.

That afternoon the Republican Policy Committee met to agree on a formal position. A statement had been drafted for the occasion by a Policy Committee staff member, but Martin and his staff aide, Melvin M. Miller, thought it was insipid and not positive enough. Thus, Martin asked for a revised statement. By the following day the new draft was ready, and a second meeting went smoothly. The policy statement represented a general endorsement of committee reorganization, though more in terms of goals than of specific provisions of H. Res. 988. Arends's proposal concerning committee ratios was added, and the revised statement was adopted on a voice vote, with no dissenting votes heard. There was a distinct impression that the Policy Committee was more receptive to the Select Committee's report than the conference had been.

While sponsors of the reform package had received a friendlier reception from the Republicans than from the Democrats, they were by no means elated by the outcome. The candid exchange in the conference hinted that committee loyalties were essentially bipartisan and might outweigh other factors in influencing votes of legislators on the adversely affected committees. Martin himself complained that few members really knew what was in the proposal. "The only thing they did," he said, "was to open the report and see what would happen to their particular committee."

Prior to the GOP sessions, there was a general feeling that Republicans would support H. Res. 988, but this assumption was shattered when the Republicans embraced the proposal with less than undivided enthusiasm. Some time later, when the Select Committee met to assess the disaster in the Democratic caucus, one Democrat noted hopefully that only sixty-seven Democrats would be needed to pass H. Res. 988 if 150 Republican votes were available. "But we can't get 150 votes," Steiger retorted.

The May 9 Caucus. As soon as the Democratic caucus reconvened on May 9, the issue of reorganization was sharply joined. Recognized by Chairman Teague, Burton moved consideration of the following resolution:

> RESOLVED that the Committee on Organization, Study and Review is hereby directed to review H. Res. 988, Committee Reform Amendments of 1974, and report to the Caucus no later than the regularly scheduled July Democratic Caucus with any recommendations deemed appropriate.

> RESOLVED further that the Democratic members of the Rules Committee shall take no action with respect to H. Res. 988 until the Democratic Caucus has acted upon the report and recommendations of the Committee on Organization, Study and Review.

A key element of the resolution was the specified time for reporting back. Without it, Burton and his supporters realized the caucus would not have gone along, for it would have appeared as if they were killing H. Res. 988 outright.

In an action that caught many by surprise, William Clay, another foe of the reorganization, moved that the vote on the Burton proposal be by secret ballot. After a nonrecorded, stand-up vote of the members on the question of whether to have a secret ballot, Chairman Teague announced that the vote was ninety-eight to eighty-one for the Clay motion. Bolling immediately moved that there be a separate roll call vote on Clay's motion; but in the hullabaloo that ensued, Teague apparently misunderstood Bolling's motion, perfectly proper under parliamentary usage, and recessed the caucus for several minutes while he consulted a parliamentarian. Teague was apparently confused about the situation in talking with the parliamentarian, for he received advice that did not apply to the motion at hand. Upon returning to the chamber, Teague ruled Bolling's motion out of order, thereby causing another furor. Nevertheless, Burton and others insisted that the secret vote proceed, and it did. When the ballots were counted, the Democrats had agreed 111 to 95 to refer the Select Committee's plan to the Hansen Committee. Interestingly, a whip count conducted by the Select Committee prior to the session turned up a majority of Democrats who said they would vote to send H. Res. 988 to the floor.

Once the vote was complete, Culver and Meeds were ready to challenge the result and demand a recount. They were discouraged by Bolling, who discerned that even if the Select Committee won that tally, it would be a futile gain. The party was clearly split. If another vote overturned the 111 to 95 tally, it would only heighten bitterness among Democrats, even allowing reform opponents to complain that their victory had been stolen. Some supporters argued, moreover, that referral to the Hansen Committee could help defuse party sentiment against portions of H. Res. 988, and might even strengthen the reform package. Others claimed that the secret ballot had been necessary so that all members would feel free to express themselves.

The caucus vote was a victory for Burton and other Democrats opposing committee reorganization. Bolling acknowledged that the action wounded the chances for committee reform, but added that he was "stubborn" and had "no intention of this being the killing of it. We'll see what the Hansen Committee does and keep trying." He added that he hoped to cooperate with the Hansen Committee and would even make his own committee staff available to assist them, if so requested. Perhaps Majority Leader O'Neill best explained why the caucus voted the way it did: "The name of the game is power, and the boys don't want to give it up."[16]

Burning while the Caucus Fiddles

The caucus action drew sharp criticism. A representative of the liberal Americans for Democratic Action labeled the caucus action as a "cruel hoax" because more than half of the Hansen Committee publicly opposed the resolution. Common Cause charged that the caucus had killed the plan, describing the Hansen Committee as a "political graveyard." Common Cause soon organized a national campaign to ascertain how each Democrat had voted in caucus and who would continue to support committee reform, information that the Select Committee later used.

Chairwoman Hansen countered charges that her committee would bury reorganization in a statement on May 9. She said, "... [the] committee does not have a record of killing progress and is very sensitive to the many problems in the democratic process. While the referral was entirely unsought by me, the committee will attempt to fulfill the caucus' directive." Burton added that the Hansen Committee would not merely recommend a few procedural changes, "but how much more than that I don't know."

The "Lull" before the July Caucus. A day or so after the caucus, Bolling met with his committee staff and reflected on the defeat. Bolling blamed the loss on the committee's December 7, 1973, decision to abolish the Merchant Marine and Fisheries Committee, which had needlessly antagonized the labor unions. Moreover, he believed that he had relied too heavily on chief AFL-CIO lobbyist Andrew Biemiller to neutralize labor opposition. When Biemiller appeared before the Select Committee he agreed that no committee's jurisdiction was "sacred," including Education and Labor's. He laid down strict conditions for labor's acceptance of a split Education and Labor Committee. The Select Committee had essentially complied with Biemiller's request when they divided the Education and Labor Committee; and Bolling believed that Biemiller had enough influence within AFL-CIO councils either to neutralize opposition or win support for the committee's plan. However, it turned out that Bolling had overestimated Biemiller's influence with the union presidents.

Bolling then told his staff that the Select Committee still had some leverage, because it had sufficient votes in the Rules Committee to send H. Res. 988 to the floor. Knowing this, he said, the Hansen members would hesitate to kill the plan outright. Bolling urged the staff to remain alert for news and announced that there would be weekly meetings of Democratic staff and members to discuss political developments.

On May 13 two Select Committee staff members met with Representative Hansen and a staff aide, at Mrs. Hansen's request, to discuss H. Res. 988. Explaining that she had been unable to attend any of the caucuses on the issue, Hansen asked numerous questions about H. Res. 988. This meeting and a few more that Sheldon had with Hansen's aide and a staff member from Representative Barbara Jordan's office (Jordan was a Hansen Committee member) were the beginning and end of the Select Committee staff's cooperation with the Hansen group, for the staff was not asked for further assistance. For their part, Select Committee members preferred to avoid the impression that their staff had assisted in developing a counter proposal, lest it undercut the credibility of their own product. Bolling soon modified his earlier offer by forbidding staff from assisting the Hansen Committee unless his permission was secured beforehand.

The Democratic caucus action inevitably strained bipartisan comity within the Select Committee itself. Vice Chairman Martin was irrevocably embittered. The depth of his feeling surfaced when, on May 13, he called in the minority staff members and informed them that he had decided to dismiss them (except for the deputy staff director) as of July 1. Because H. Res. 988 had been killed by the Democrats, he explained, there was no need to spend any more taxpayers' money on staff. Needless to say, the staff members were stunned. The other Republicans on the committee, who were miffed at this unilateral action, tried to reverse the decision; but Martin would not be budged. Martin's feelings were perhaps understandable, but as many pointed out, it was politically unwise to pronounce H. Res. 988 dead at the very moment when efforts were being redoubled to get it to the House floor.

Partisan bitterness was evident a few days later, when the Select Committee met to assess the damage and regroup their forces. Bolling and his Democratic colleagues, on the defensive, tried to explain what had occurred, reiterated their determination to see the fight to the end, and urged their Republican colleagues not to give up. "We're sidetracked but not derailed," Meeds said. "The committee shouldn't give up." Culver delivered a rousing pep talk, and noted that Democrats' opposition was factionalized. "The Republicans shouldn't have stuffed down their throats something that was worked out in the back rooms of the Democratic party," he asserted. "Institutional reform must be bipartisan, and the opportunity [for committee reorganization] comes only every twenty-eight years."

Vice Chairman Martin bluntly countered that the reform plan was a "dead duck—water over the dam!" A bitter Frelinghuysen took up the theme: "I see no hope. You've done us in. You've destroyed it in the caucus." Other Republicans were more philosophical. Young worried about strategy, and Steiger took up the Democrats' theme that "we shouldn't totally abandon ship."

In attempting to mollify their colleagues, Bolling, Culver and Meeds outlined a strategy of bringing public pressure to bear on the caucus in order to assure that H. Res. 988 would reach the House floor. As Culver said, there should be "a drumbeat of public criticism of Congress in institutional terms, but especially of the caucus action." He continued:

> Let the Hansen Committee demonstrate the excellence of their work. They'll pick and choose things to keep the boys happy; they'll put a gloss of reform on it. But people in this age of Watergate are going to be looking at that vote, and we'll win by say 20 votes.

Thus, the leading strategy was to appeal to public opinion by exploiting press contacts and mobilizing outside groups. This would serve the dual function of keeping the Hansen group honest and, failing this, inducing the caucus to allow H. Res. 988 to be considered by the House.

The Democrats were willing to give the Republicans free rein in attacking the caucus action. Bolling remarked that he fully expected the Republicans "to do what comes naturally" as a result of the caucus vote, and Meeds openly invited the GOP to exploit the issue. "I hope you'll take advantage of it," he confided during a Select Committee session, "but don't give up." Thus, while proreform Democrats worked behind the scenes to mobilize pressure on their caucus, the brunt of the task fell on the Republicans. They set about this effort with grim determination.

Republican Noise-making. On May 16, a group of House Republicans held a press conference to denounce the Democratic caucus action. "All we want is a chance to consider this on the floor," Representative John Dellenback said. "It is a minority of the total Congress that has made this decision—the people are the losers."[17] As a followup to their meeting with the press, Representative Allan Steelman and more than fifty Republicans and a few Democrats cosponsored a resolution to bring H. Res. 988 to the floor under an open rule. No action was taken nor expected on the resolution, which was designed chiefly to put pressure on Democrats to bring H. Res. 988 to the floor.

In the following weeks, many Republicans and some Democrats regularly inserted statements into the *Congressional Record* criticizing the Democratic caucus. Select Committee Vice Chairman Martin led the critics with a series of short, pointed House speeches lambasting "King Caucus" and the Democrats' irresponsible actions. In one of his speeches, Martin referred to the "deep, dark secrecy in which the deed was done." H. Res. 988 was killed, he said, "in a secret caucus by a secret vote on whether to have a secret vote."[18] On June 19, Republicans organized a floor debate during which GOP members stressed the need for committee reform and the reprehensible behavior of the Democrats.

In a move that caught many by surprise, Republican Conference Chairman John Anderson sought to introduce a privileged resolution on the floor on June 27, 1974, and urged its immediate consideration. Anderson's resolution would have directed Select Committee Chairman Bolling to "forthwith seek a rule making in order for consideration by the House, House Resolution 988." Anderson contended that the "rights of the House and the integrity of its proceedings are being interfered with by the actions of the Democratic Caucus." Before he could offer his privileged resolution, Anderson—who fully expected to obtain the floor as soon as the House convened—was temporarily stymied by the majority leadership. An elaborate and unheralded farewell was staged for longtime House Parliamentarian Lewis Deschler, who had just submitted his resignation to Speaker Albert. Members of both parties heaped lengthy praises on Deschler, with Vice President Gerald Ford even offering his best wishes. When Anderson finally took the floor, Majority Leader O'Neill raised a point of order against the resolution; Speaker Albert, with Parliamentarian Deschler by his side whispering advice, then ruled the resolution out of order.[19] Anderson immediately appealed the ruling of the chair. Because no ruling of the chair had been overturned since 1931, excitement rose in the chamber and the galleries soon filled with Hill staff and newspaper correspondents.

With solid GOP backing and the support of at least half the Democrats, Anderson hoped he might carry the day. That was not to be the case. When the vote came, the Speaker's ruling was sustained 242 to 163, with only one Democrat, John Culver, voting with Anderson and the GOP. Representative William Randall spoke for most members of his party when he said the vote involved "purely a procedural matter" and not the issue of committee reform. Nevertheless, Anderson's major objectives—dramatizing the issue and embarrassing the Democrats—were achieved.

The Republican broadsides, though resented by some Democrats, probably helped keep the reorganization plan alive during the summer of 1974. To be sure, they manifested a tough partisanship that had been largely absent from the Select Committee's deliberations; yet they helped escalate the costs of the Democrats' caucus actions. With the Watergate affair in full bloom, nervous Republicans sorely needed a reform issue such as this one; for their part, Democrats were wary of assuming an antireform posture when they faced the voters in the fall. Thus the Watergate scandal, so feared by Bolling for its divisive potential within the House, turned out to benefit his committee's cause by making "reform" a popular word. If Hansen Committee members harbored any thoughts about killing committee reform altogether, the Republicans' sniping put an end to them. In this atmosphere, the Hansen group reluctantly began its work.

THE HANSEN COMMITTEE'S COUNTERPROPOSAL

While it had a record of success in internal party reorganization, the Hansen group was placed in an awkward position by its new assignment. Although it had become something of an institution since first created in March 1970 to study seniority, the committee lacked the continuous life that a full committee, or the Select Committee, enjoyed. Its members had lines of communication to virtually all segments of the caucus, for the Hansen group represented a broad spectrum of the party —ideologically, geographically, and in years of service. Not only were there recognized liberals like New Jersey's Thompson, but there were also conservatives like Georgia's Phil Landrum and moderates like Neal Smith of Iowa. The major regions of the country were represented, and its members ranged in House service from one to twelve terms. As a representative party committee whose past accomplishments included studies leading to seniority reform and the democratization of committee procedures, its recommendations would influence many Democrats.

As Thompson noted, "I think when the Hansen Committee recommends things, that puts them in a very strong position."[20]

The group's previous assignments, though requiring delicate political adjustments, had none of the scope or intellectual subtlety of the vast problem of the committee reorganization. With the possible exceptions of Burton and O'Hara, neither Hansen nor any of her colleagues had more than a vague notion of what was in the Select Committee's document—except for provisions affecting their respective committees. Moreover, the group had only one full-time staff person to assist them. Finally, as we shall see, members of the Hansen group were divided over whether to undertake a full-scale report, and what such a report might contain.

A majority of the Hansen members were clearly against reorganization and several of them had been outspoken during the caucus debate. Many would have been personally affected if the resolution were adopted. The most obvious example was the separation of Education and Labor, along with diminution of Merchant Marine's authority and abolition of Post Office and Civil Service. Organized labor preferred to retain those committees intact, and as a major component of the Democratic coalition they could expect a sympathetic hearing from the Hansen group. One of the moving forces on the Hansen body was Phillip Burton, whose stakes in the reorganization controversy have already been recounted. Joe D. Waggonner Jr. and Phillip Landrum served on Ways and Means, which would lose such jurisdiction as unemployment compensation, general revenue sharing, international trade, and the non-tax aspects of health care. Wayne Hays and Frank Thompson were chairman and ranking majority member, respectively, of the House Administration Committee, which would yield jurisdiction over Federal elections, the Hatch Act, and campaign financing; as ranking majority member on Education and Labor, Thompson had decided to oppose splitting that committee. O'Hara, also on Education and Labor, professed to be opposed to jurisdictional restructuring as a technique of reform, arguing rather for strengthening the central party leadership or, alternatively, making minor adjustments in the committee system.

As a bipartisan product, H. Res. 988 was viewed suspiciously by the Hansen members. Too much, they thought, was given away to the Republicans by augmenting minority staffing, splitting Education and Labor, and eliminating proxy voting. Some felt that the unanimous report of the Select Committee reflected its lowest common denominator. A few of the Hansen members distrusted Vice Chairman Martin and resented the notion that he should prescribe policies that the House might observe for the next twenty years.

The Hansen members quickly decided they could improve on certain provisions of H. Res. 988 which they thought might impair House efficiency—for example, the one hundred-word summary required before measures could be introduced. The committee also thought H. Res. 988 gave too much power to the Rules Committee, some terming it a power grab by Bolling. Beyond these specific items, however, the Hansen group was unsure how to proceed.

Groping for a Formula. At their first closed-door meeting on May 13, 1974, the Hansen members decided to send a "Dear Colleague" letter to all Democratic congressmen, requesting recommendations concerning the jurisdictional and nonjurisdictional aspects of H. Res. 988. As Hansen explained, her group needed to "know in detail the opinion of each member of the Caucus toward the recommendations of the Bolling Report." Between sixty and seventy Democrats responded to the questionnaire. Some were very brief—"Send H. Res. 988 to the floor with no amendments"; others ran to as much as fourteen pages of critical comment.

Before the next session, Thompson and O'Hara asked Education and Labor Chairman Perkins to permit his staff aide, William Cable, who had monitored all the open markup sessions of the Select Committee, to be assigned full-time to assist the Hansen Committee. Perkins agreed. When Cable attended the second meeting of the Hansen Committee on May 22, several members voiced their reluctance to have a staff aide participate in their deliberations. They feared leaks would result. But Thompson assured the group that Cable was reliable and would be an asset to the committee.

At this same May 22 session, the Hansen group split on a critical issue. Some members, like O'Hara, preferred a two-part report: one procedural and the other jurisdictional. Others, including Burton, argued that that was not a creditable position. Hansen agreed with Burton and insisted that to fulfill the caucus mandate the committee had to consider H. Res. 988 in its entirety. Her position was accepted by the group.

The Hansen Committee decided to concentrate on procedural matters first, simply because that was the easier task. They agreed quickly and unanimously to permit proxy voting, barred under H. Res. 988. Other procedural changes were adopted in the field of oversight, as the Hansen group generally followed the framework established by H. Res. 988. The committee met the next day and focused on subpena powers for committees. Then they adjourned until after the Memorial Day recess. In the meantime, Hansen directed Cable to telephone all committee chairmen and urged them to respond to the committee's May 13 questionnaire.

When the Hansen Committee reconvened on June 10, they resumed consideration of procedural issues but turned briefly to a jurisdictional matter. The group had received from Armed Services Chairman Edward Hébert a hand-delivered letter detailing why his committee should retain jurisdiction over Naval Petroleum Reserve #4, transferred to another committee under H. Res. 988. To secure Hébert's support, the Hansen Committee acquiesced to the request. For a time the Hansen group considered presenting a nonjurisdictional plan to the June caucus, or even having the House Administration Committee report another reform resolution. They also considered whether their jurisdictional changes could be debated under a "closed" rule, leaving nonjurisdictional matters open to amendment. All of those suggestions were rejected, mainly because Hansen had enough influence to persuade her colleagues that they were honor-bound to report a comprehensive assessment of H. Res. 988. The committee also pondered the procedural situation in the caucus when they reported—that is, who would control motions and debate, and what traps Bolling might be planning for them.

During the next two meetings (June 17 and 19), further procedural issues were discussed—for example, the conferee selection process, the minimum or maximum number of subcommittees per standing committee, and the Rules Committee "bypass" provision. The bypass provision was designed to emasculate the rule-granting authority of the Rules Committee by permitting the Speaker to recognize committee members to offer their own rules from the floor of the House. The Hansen group, realizing also that they were getting a bad press, developed several reforms designed to bring the news media on their side, for example, prohibiting "lame duck" members from traveling abroad after Congress had adjourned *sine die*.

Burton and O'Hara clashed over how their reform proposals should be presented. O'Hara favored dividing the committee's plan into procedural and jurisdictional parts. Burton countered that such a course would expose the committee to the charge of violating caucus instructions. They also disagreed on the scope of the jurisdictional changes. Burton favored developing their own jurisdictional scheme, while O'Hara preferred to make minimal changes. As late as June 25, the two were still at odds over the procedural versus jurisdictional issue. A strong-willed and persuasive leader, Hansen was able to persuade her colleagues that committee jurisdictions had to be dealt with. In order to get the discussion moving, she promised that all decisions on jurisdictions would be tentative. Other members followed Hansen's lead; O'Hara, lacking support for his alternative, went along as well.

The group began with the Education and Labor Committee, agreeing overwhelmingly in its first and only formal vote to keep the committee together. Even Landrum concurred, observing that he regretted having testified before the Select Committee that Education and Labor should be severed. Then the Hansen members agreed to leave Appropriations alone, and began to discuss the jurisdictions of the other standing committees.

The next day—June 26—the committee again discussed jurisdictions, focusing on the losses and gains of each committee under H. Res. 988. The proposed energy and environment panel, for example, was not to their liking. Burton had been meeting with various environmental groups and Nader's Congress Watch, all of whom were fearful of consolidating energy and environmental matters in the same committee. To gain their support, Burton and other Hansen members agreed that those two functional areas should remain dispersed among several committees. Burton was also talking with numerous Democrats about specific features of committee reform. His conversations were intended to gather their support and to build future political credits that could be used if he ran for the caucus chairmanship in the next Congress. (Burton was elected caucus chairman for the 94th Congress on December 2, 1974.) O'Hara, too, was meeting with outside groups, particularly labor, to solicit their support for the Hansen proposals.

Meanwhile, the Select Committee and its staff were attempting to follow the secret work of the Hansen group. Fortunately, several leaks lent some insight into the proceedings and provided the basis for our account here. Two days after the Hansen group's June 25 session, the Select Committee circulated a summary of procedural changes purportedly being considered by the group.

When the Hansen Committee met on July 9, there was an atmosphere of urgency. Time was running out, as everyone knew. The members considered asking Caucus Chairman Olin Teague for an extension of time, but Hansen persuaded her committee colleagues to redouble their efforts and try to meet the deadline. (Teague later revealed that he would have granted the extension had it been requested, for he endorsed the Hansen efforts.) After dealing with several minor matters, the committee agreed to a consolidation of transportation matters in a single committee, as H. Res. 988 had specified, and allocated health matters between the Commerce and Ways and Means committees.

Work on the plan was finally completed at a July 12 session. A final staffing plan was approved that gave ranking Republicans on subcommittees one staff person (a proposal designed to woo support among senior GOP members); the Rules bypass provision was accepted; and a proposal to require Appropriations' subcommittee jurisdictions to parallel the authorizing committees was dropped. The committee resolved to meet with party leaders as soon as their final plan was printed.

On July 15, all eleven members of the Hansen Committee met with Speaker Albert, Majority Leader O'Neill, and Majority Whip John

McFall. The Speaker was displeased with the Rules bypass provision. Most of the discussion, however, concerned energy research and development authority, which was to be assigned to the science committee. The Joint Committee on Atomic Energy, Albert protested, wanted to maintain control of nonmilitary nuclear energy research and development. The Hansen members agreed to make this change.

The next day the Hansen members briefed the standing committee chairmen. While most chairmen decided their interests had been taken care of by the Hansen group, others—especially Harley Staggers of the Interstate and Foreign Commerce Committee—were still not satisfied. In an emotional statement, Staggers urged that railroads remain with his committee rather than be assigned to Public Works and Transportation. Staggers's plea provoked sharp discussion among the Hansen members, who were split on the issue. Finally, however, the political argument won out: in order to gain acquiescence from Staggers and the railway interests, the Hansen members agreed to restore railroads to Staggers's committee. Meanwhile, the Hansen group cleared its proposals with appropriate outside interests before officially releasing it for public distribution. Two days before the report appeared, a staff member of Nader's Congress Watch supplied a letter, solicited by Burton, agreeing that the Hansen recommendations "would substantially improve upon significant contributions proposed earlier by the Select Committee on Committees."

Finally, on July 17, 1974, the Hansen Committee formally reported its recommendations in the form of a House resolution (H. Res. 1248). This was an unprecedented action. Not since the days of "King Caucus" had a party committee dared to take over a House committee's measure and completely rework it.

Comparison of the Hansen and Select Committee Plans. The Hansen Committee's resolution eliminated the largest portion of the jurisdictional changes proposed by H. Res. 988. In effect, the Hansen plan was a patchwork of provisions designed to mollify members and committees who lost jurisdiction under H. Res. 988, not to mention the outside interests associated with those committees. The Hansen group had "greased the squeaky wheels," by drafting a plan to achieve maximum political effect with individual legislators and factions. More specifically, the major changes were these:

Education and Labor, split by H. Res. 988, would be retained.

Post Office and Civil Service, abolished under H. Res. 988, would be retained and given additional new jurisdictional duties.

Merchant Marine and Fisheries would regain all that it lost under the Select Committee's plan and even be granted additional authority over international fishing agreements.

Ways and Means would lose very little under Hansen (general revenue sharing, work incentive programs, and renegotiation) compared to substantial losses under H. Res. 988, including foreign trade, nontax aspects of health, unemployment compensation, general revenue sharing, the work incentive program, and renegotiation.

House Administration would keep control of Federal elections and campaign financing, lost to the Standards of Official Conduct Committee under H. Res. 988.

Jurisdiction over five major policy areas, energy, health, environment, transportation, and trade, that were aggregated under H. Res. 988, would remain dispersed and fragmented under Hansen.

Rules, which would have a new jurisdictional arbitration role under H. Res. 988, had its authority to grant rules to measures substantially reduced by Hansen.

Under H. Res. 988, Foreign Affairs gained international trade and special oversight of foreign and military intelligence, both lost under the Hansen plan.

Government Operations, slated for major committee status with the addition of new legislative oversight duties by H. Res. 988, would be virtually unchanged except for the addition of general revenue sharing, the national archives, and a few more oversight duties.

From a liberal Democratic viewpoint, the major advantages of the Hansen document were the retention of the Education and Labor Committee, the transfer of the Committee on Internal Security to the Judiciary Committee (more liberal than Government Operations, where H. Res. 988 had proposed transferring it), and the diminution of the Rules Committee's authority. But there were costs to the Hansen plan which Democrats had to evaluate. Unlike H. Res. 988, which sought to equalize committee work loads and aggregate key policy areas, the Hansen plan left the conservative-dominated Ways and Means Committee with a disproportionate share of committee work—including all tax jurisdiction, health, trade, social security, unemployment compensation, and welfare. Energy provided an example of where the Hansen Committee failed to facilitate coherent policy making. Where H. Res. 988 concentrated most energy matters in a single committee, the Hansen group split energy among several different committees, in effect maintaining the status quo. This meant that the House would be no better off organizationally in dealing with energy issues than it had been before.

In the procedural realm, fewer disagreements existed between Hansen and the Select Committee, and in a few cases the Hansen group was bolder than the Select Committee. Substantial parallelism between the two plans was evident in such matters as joint referral of measures by the Speaker, early organization of the House, and the establishment of an Office of Law Revision Counsel. In these instances, the Hansen group simply borrowed provisions developed by the Select Committee.

Many changes contemplated by H. Res. 988 were absent from the Hansen resolution, among them a limitation of member committee assignments, size limitations on committees, and a jurisdictional arbitration role for the Rules Committee. Similarly, the Hansen group proposed several changes that were not in H. Res. 988. These included a requirement that at least four subcommittees be established within standing committees of more than fifteen members; authority for the Speaker to recognize committee members to bring measures to the floor without a rule from the Rules Committee (the bypass provision); and a requirement that select and joint committees adopt written rules to govern their proceedings.

Finally, there were numerous procedural issues on which the two plans differed. The Hansen report proposed a somewhat more restrictive use of proxies, whereas the Select Committee would abolish them outright. H. Res. 988 required that all committees except Appropriations establish oversight subcommittees, a matter that the Hansen resolution left to the discretion of each committee. H. Res. 988 tripled the size of professional and clerical committee staff while Hansen authorized each subcommittee chairman and ranking subcommittee member, up to six per committee, to be assigned a staff member who was to be paid no more than $27,000. The staffing provision of the Hansen resolution was designed to strengthen the autonomy of subcommittees and to appeal to senior Republicans on committees.

According to Burton, the Hansen Committee's recommendations were "clearly superior to the Bolling committee recommendations. They will facilitate consideration by the House of legislation and eliminate unjustified impediments to achieve that end contained in the Bolling recommendations."[21] Perhaps a more revealing assessment of the Hansen document was offered by a staff aide close to the group: "In every change they've [the Hansen Committee] made, they know whose ox is being gored and who is being assisted by the change."[22]

In summary, the Hansen product was essentially a patchwork of proposals fitted together from the Select Committee's plan and the members' own predilections. It was a political document, designed to gain the support of various House groups and factions, and more geared than the Bolling plan toward the subcommittee system where the strength of the caucus' liberal faction was more fully reflected. In truth, the Hansen group lacked the time and staff to undertake an in-depth analysis of H.

Res. 988. Pressure of time and circumstance therefore compelled them to rely heavily on the basic structural design of the Select Committee's resolution.

The July 17 and 23 Caucuses. The day before the July 17 Democratic caucus, Bolling sprang into action. He wrote to Rules Chairman Ray J. Madden requesting that he "schedule a meeting of the Committee on Rules to consider a request for an open rule on House Resolution 988." He also sent a "Dear Colleague" letter to every member announcing his request for an open rule. Finally, that morning he assembled the Democratic members and staff of the Select Committee, with whom he discussed his request for a hearing on a rule. Bolling was taking the steps to serve notice that the Select Committee had complied with the May 9 caucus directive and that the time for action on H. Res. 988 had come. Also on July 16, Bolling received a response to his letter to Chairman Madden from Rules Staff Director Laurie Battle who stated that the "Chairman and the Members of the House Committee on Rules look forward to your testimony at 10:30 A.M. next Tuesday, July 23, on House Resolution 988." That meeting never took place.

The Select Committee's Democrats reconvened on July 16 to discuss final plans for the next day's caucus. Bolling reported that he had been asked by Teague to meet with the Hansen group and negotiate differences between the two reform plans, but that he had refused. Subsequently Speaker Albert, at the behest of the Hansen group, phoned Bolling to reiterate the request; again Bolling refused, explaining that he did not want to be a party to any "backroom" deals. Bolling, too, felt strongly about his obligation under House Rule XI: "It shall be the duty of the chairman of each committee to report or cause to be reported promptly to the House any measure approved by his committee and to take or cause to be taken necessary steps to bring the matter to a vote." Under this rule, Bolling believed he was prohibited from undertaking political bargaining without the consent of his committee.

Lloyd Meeds arrived late for the meeting, having been at a DSG session where Burton, Hays, and other Hansen members were explaining their proposals. Meeds charged that the Hansen group had simply "caved in" to committee chairmen who wanted jurisdictional matters left as they were. After discussion, the Select Committee's Democrats determined that the prime objective for the following day's caucus was to keep H. Res. 988 intact and fend off weakening amendments that might be offered.

The Democrats convened on the morning of July 17 to hear Hansen and other members of her committee explain their report. Although the document was not available to members until that day, the DSG had managed to obtain copies (probably from their former chairman, Phillip Burton) and had sufficient time to prepare an analysis of the Hansen proposal. Of interest, too, was that the Hansen Committee had somehow commandeered funds to have numerous copies printed by the U.S. Government Printing Office. As an unofficial party committee, the Hansen group had no authority under the rules of the House to have their resolution and accompanying report printed by the GPO at public expense. It was rumored that the action had been authorized by Hansen member Wayne Hays, chairman of the Joint Committee on Printing and the Committee on House Administration, which has jurisdiction over "housekeeping" matters.

During the caucus discussion, Burton voiced his view that H. Res. 988 would impede the legislative process, citing such examples as the requirement that the Congressional Research Service prepare a one hundred-word summary of each bill or resolution *before* it could be introduced. (The Hansen group had altered that provision to require the one hundred-word summary as soon as possible *after* introduction of a bill or resolution.) Wayne Hays then attacked Bolling for developing a plan that favored Republicans. Bolling and other members of the Select Committee responded to these charges. When the caucus adjourned the debate had not concluded and no formal vote had been taken. The members agreed to reconvene on July 23, when it was expected that a final vote would be held.

Following this first caucus, Bolling declared that the Hansen Committee's product, though a worthy effort, was "highly inferior" to the Select Committee report. Bolling also said he thought the caucus had informally agreed to allow H. Res. 988 to go to the floor under an open rule, with the Hansen resolution to be in order as a substitute proposal. The Republican view of the July 17 caucus was perhaps best expressed by Conference Chairman John Anderson: "This attempt by the caucus to dilute and discredit the Bolling committee . . . was set in concert the moment this bipartisan product was referred to the stacked, partisan deck of a secret, anti-reform committee controlled by the Democratic power barons."

Nor was the Hansen product entirely successful in placating its would-be allies. Ralph Nader and various environmental groups who had been critical of H. Res. 988 now began to fault the Hansen report, charging that they had been sold out by last-minute changes. What irked them was retention of nonmilitary nuclear energy in the Joint Committee on Atomic Energy (JCAE). Under the Select Committee's plan, this subject would have been shifted to the proposed Energy and Environment Committee. As soon as the final report of the Hansen Committee was released, Nader heatedly wrote Mrs. Hansen that any proposal that did not reduce the power of the JCAE "is no reform at all." Ann Roosevelt, legislative director of the Friends of the Earth, called the last-minute changes "a political sellout."[23]

The day before the crucial second caucus a group of proreform Democrats—Jonathan Bingham, Dante Fascell, Donald Fraser, Thomas Rees, Patricia Schroeder, and Morris Udall—sent all party members a "Dear Colleague" letter opposing substitution of the Hansen report for H. Res. 988. The Hansen product, they charged, represented "an inadequate step towards meaningful reform." They concluded that "it would be tragic indeed if we are saddled with the inadequacies of the present Congress in the next session when we can accomplish so much if only our institutional arrangements are adequate to the task."

When the July 23 caucus convened, the initial debate centered on competing proposals dealing with the Rules Committee. Where the Select Committee had proposed strengthening Rules, the Hansen report recommended dilution of Rules' authority to clear legislation for floor debate. Despite the strong objections of Speaker Albert, who opposed the Rules bypass provision, a motion to delete that provision from the Hansen report was defeated 100 to 97. Caucus members received a surprise when Bolling and three other Select Committee members voted for the Hansen recommendation and against the Speaker. Bolling had long contended that the party leadership should have more control over the Rules Committee, and his vote reflected that viewpoint.

At last the caucus adopted, by voice vote, the following resolution introduced by Hansen Committee member O'Hara:

> Resolved, that the Democratic Members of the Committee on Rules be directed to report a resolution making in order the consideration of House Resolution 988 under an open rule providing for the reading of the resolution by section and making it in order to offer the Hansen Committee proposal . . . as an amendment in the nature of a substitute immediately following the reading of the first section of House Resolution 988.

Members of the Hansen Committee wanted the caucus to express its preference for one of the two plans but failed to establish who would offer such a motion. Indeed, at one point Burton thought Hansen was about to offer the motion when in reality she was simply rising to straighten her skirt. When in the final minutes of the caucus a motion was made to have the caucus express a preference for Hansen, it apparently lacked majority support and was tabled by voice vote. When some pro-Hansen Democrats complained that Chairman Teague had prevented a recorded preference vote, Teague angrily responded that he would entertain such a motion when the caucus reconvened later that day to consider the selection of members to the new Budget Committee. But when the caucus reconvened no member made that motion.

As soon as the caucus adjourned, the Hansen Committee members formally introduced their own reform resolution (H. Res. 1248), which was referred to the Rules Committee. Bolling and Albert expressed the hope that the House would consider the two reform plans before what then looked like an impending floor debate on the impeachment of President Nixon.

Conclusions

The struggle to gain party endorsement of H. Res. 988 illustrates several features common to most legislative reform efforts. Members perceive reorganization in different ways, often depending on whether a proposal promotes or hinders their advancement in the legislative process. In other words, self-interest often prevails over institutional welfare. While members were not particularly well-informed about the reorganization plan, they did know how specific provisions affected their own committees; and those who "lost" something tended to be more vocal against H. Res. 988 than those who gained new authority. Assets that were lost were somehow perceived as more tangible than expected gains. As a result there were relatively few vocal supporters of H. Res. 988 outside of the Select Committee itself.

In all fairness, it is often difficult to determine whether reorganization is really reform. In the absence of hard information anyone can make wild (and superficially plausible) predictions, often internally inconsistent or contradictory. But this creates a climate of doubt which can jeopardize the reorganization. This is compounded when there are competing reform resolutions. Members realize that today's reforms can become tomorrow's disasters, and are therefore reluctant to change established ways of conducting business. Even if members concede that their institution functions defectively, they may have long since adjusted to the defects or they may sense that the cure is worse than the malady. Put in cost-benefit terms, members who oppose change exaggerate the costs and minimize the benefits, while those who favor reform do the reverse.

Furthermore, legislative reforms are often assessed according to who is for them and who is opposed. Substantive issues become enmeshed with personalities. Some representatives, for example, distrusted Bolling. If he was for H. Res. 988, they thought, then the resolution was likely to be devious. On the other hand, many others distrusted the Hansen Committee and such members as Burton, whose reputation for political cunning rivaled Bolling's. Hence, legislators who sought the "high road" and focused on the issues often saw their arguments founder because of the personalities involved in developing the plan. Of course, it is more difficult to persuade members that what is good for the House will be good for them, rather than what is good for their committee or subcommittee is good for the House.

Finally, most major reform efforts require an "inside-outside" coalition. That is, members and interest groups who favor change must work together to overcome an institution's often natural reluctance to change. Conversely, mobilizing an inside-outside coalition is also the way to bring about defeat or modification of reform measures. Prevalent in our political landscape are political partnerships called "subgovernments," comprised of members of the bureaucracy, congressional committees, and various clientele groups. These triple alliances, which develop to control numerous policy areas, "strive to become self-sustaining in control of power in [their] own sphere."[24] Given that committees and subcommittees are vital partners in this triangular relationship, any revision of the committee system threatens this most powerful and durable phenomenon in American politics. In the fight over the Bolling report, there occurred "reverse lobbying," in which committee staff mobilized members to call in their political IOUs with interest groups pertinent to their coalition. Clientele groups would rather monopolize a committee or subcommittee than approach it as one of many rival interests competing for favorable policies. In this sense, interest groups tend to be conservative. They prefer to preserve and protect established relationships, even at the risk of forging new ones that might ultimately prove more fruitful for them.

Much depends on the size and resources of the inside-outside coalitions, but there is no linear relationship between size and success. Quite often, the intense commitment of a few can overcome that of the many. In this case, however, the groups traditionally associated with legislative reform were split, with H. Res. 988 supported by Common Cause, Americans for Democratic Action, and the League of Women Voters, while many labor and environmental groups opposed it. The split in the ranks of the "public interest" groups created doubt about the merits of H. Res. 988, and made it harder for Select Committee members to persuade their colleagues to support committee reorganization.

EIGHT

The House Accepts
Half a Loaf

THE DAY after the Democratic caucus, the House Judiciary Committee began its nationally televised deliberations on the impeachment of President Nixon. Also on July 24, the Supreme Court unanimously voted against President Nixon's claim of executive privilege regarding the release of certain Watergate tapes requested by Special Prosecutor Leon Jaworski. Six days later, the Judiciary Committee voted its third article in the bill of impeachment. All signs clearly pointed to an imminent and lengthy House debate on impeachment. Select Committee Chairman Richard Bolling wanted committee reform considered before debate began on impeachment; otherwise, the House might never consider H. Res. 988. On August 9, 1974, however, Richard Nixon resigned as President, thereby sparing the nation a prolonged battle and allowing the House to turn to other business.

After the July 23 Democratic caucus, the next major hurdle for H. Res. 988 was the Rules Committee. Although the Democrats on Rules were instructed to send both the Select Committee and the Hansen resolutions to the floor for debate, the Rules Committee is no mere "traffic cop." It can vote to deny rules, it can delay action, or it can ask that measures be amended as a condition for a rule being granted. In light of the heated controversy generated over H. Res. 988, there was no guarantee that the committee, even with Bolling and Dave Martin as members, would grant a rule at all—much less the one requested by the Democratic caucus.

CLIFF-HANGING IN THE RULES COMMITTEE

The tentatively scheduled July 23 Rules hearing on H. Res. 988 was, of course, canceled, because of the caucus session that day on reform. Bolling wanted the Rules Committee to act speedily on his request, however, and prodded Rules Chairman Ray J. Madden to set a definite date for a hearing on H. Res. 988. A break in the impasse came on August 13. First, Bolling had a disagreement with Speaker Carl Albert about the Speaker's apparent lack of commitment to committee reform. As a result, Albert agreed that H. Res. 988 would be scheduled for floor debate the week of September 16. Subsequently, the Rules Committee scheduled Bolling's appearance for August 20. Speaker Albert no doubt communicated with Madden about scheduling that meeting.

There were further ominous developments, however. One day Martin spoke with Bolling on the House floor, expressing strong displeasure with the Hansen product. Bipartisanship was over, he said. He was drafting his own "compromise" reform resolution, which he planned to offer as a substitute for H. Res. 988 and H. Res. 1248. Martin was secretive about the contents of the proposal, which was being written by his Select Committee staff aide Melvin M. Miller. Like everyone else, Bolling had to wait until Martin formally introduced his resolution (there were no cosponsors) on August 15 (H. Res. 1321). Martin viewed his plan, H. Res. 1321, as a "compromise" proposal. It incorporated several of the procedural innovations of the Hansen group, such as mandating subcommittees on almost all standing committees, but was not as far-reaching in its jurisdictional shifts as the Select Committee's plan. For example, Martin kept the nontax aspects of unemployment compensation in the Ways and Means Committee, unlike the Select Committee provision that shifted the matter to the proposed Labor Committee. The Martin plan, however, proposed more jurisdictional changes than the Hansen group's proposal.

It was ironic that for months Bolling had been subjected to verbal abuse from many of his Democratic colleagues for producing a bipartisan product. They charged that Bolling had sold out Democratic interests to gain the unanimous support of Select Committee Republicans. This was hardly bipartisanship, however. Now the Republican vice chairman had made an about-face and, in effect, jumped ship. Committee Democrats were furious with Martin, as were many of his GOP colleagues. William Steiger, for example, now had relatively little to do with Martin. Martin's action further complicated an already politically factionalized and acutely emotional issue.

On August 16, Bolling learned that Rules Chairman Madden had canceled the scheduled August 20 hearing on H. Res. 988 until September 12, when the House was to return from a four-week recess. Madden claimed the meeting had been canceled at the request of Representative Hansen, who would be away that day. The explanation was unsatisfactory to Bolling who—as he told Speaker Albert—had been assured by Hansen that she was unconcerned about Bolling's going to Rules. In truth, numerous Democrats who stood to lose jurisdiction and representatives of outside groups had talked with Madden and persuaded him to delay the hearing. Madden was also under some pressure to oppose H. Res. 988 from the AFL-CIO, who exercised considerable political clout in his Gary, Indiana, district.

Opponents and proponents of reform realized that if H. Res. 988 could be stalled in Rules, it could probably be killed then and there. The November general elections were only weeks away. Everyone connected with the Select Committee was convinced that action on committee reform had to occur before then, for it was assumed that a "lame duck" House would not be permitted to organize the new Congress.

On August 21, Bolling and the four other Democrats on the Select Committee issued the following statement:

> The postponement of the Rules Committee meeting until after the House recess could turn out to be the first of a series of steps designed to prevent action by the House this year on H. Res. 988. The opponents of H. Res. 988 having failed in all their previous efforts to kill it may now be attempting to bury it in the Rules Committee by stalling it to death. That is a tactic used in the past by opponents of the early civil rights laws who stalled such bills in Rules for weeks and even months.

> The original plan of those few in the labor movement who wish to prevent action on H. Res. 988 was to kill it outright in the Democratic Caucus. When they could not collect the votes for such an open and direct action, they turned to burying it by secret ballot in the Hansen Committee of the Caucus. That, too, failed and their motion in the Caucus as finally proposed provided for reference to the Hansen Committee but required a report back to the Caucus by a date certain. When the report was made to the Caucus, the membership of the Caucus by a nearly unanimous vote directed the Rules Committee to report out H. Res. 988 with an open rule making in order the provisions of the Hansen Committee proposal as a substitute. That is the rule which we have sought and which we would have requested at the meeting scheduled by Chairman Madden of the Rules Committee for . . . August 20. Chairman Madden abruptly cancelled that meeting.

> With apparently only about three weeks or a month of this session of Congress remaining after the House returns on September 11 from its recess, it is obvious that a strategy of delaying H. Res. 988 to death in the Rules Committee might succeed.

In fact, we fear that it will succeed unless the Speaker and the Majority Leader, who have been strong supporters of H. Res. 988 in the past, actively impress upon Chairman Madden and the Democratic members of the Committee on Rules the wisdom of their promptly reporting the rule the Committee has been directed by the Democratic Caucus to report.

To help ensure positive action by the Rules Committee, the members of the Select Committee mobilized their outside supporters. In succeeding weeks many newspapers carried editorials or articles urging House action on committee reform.[1] For example, in syndicated columnist Jack Anderson's August 24 "Reform Watch," a special column he established "to keep the public posted on what Congress is doing to put its own House in order," Anderson said he would report to the voters before November "on which of their elected representatives are still dragging their feet on overhauling the law-making machinery." The next day, *Newsday,* the Long Island, New York, paper, declared that Congress' ability to discharge its constitutional responsibilities "rests on efforts to overhaul the outmoded committee system." On September 3, the *Los Angeles Times* carried a hard-hitting editorial entitled "Lip Service to Reform," which said:

> It's up to Rep. Madden now. If he and the Democratic majority on Rules continue to stall, it will only confirm what is already apparent—the Democrats don't want reform, despite all their rhetoric that Watergate demonstrates the necessity for more open and responsive government.

That same day, an editorial in the Lansing, Michigan, *Journal* declared, "House Must Enact Full Reform Now." Scores of other newspapers also urged House action on committee reform.

Common Cause Chairman John Gardner mailed a letter on September 4, 1974, to all Rules members urging them to "act on September 12 and grant a rule for H. Res. 988." Six days later, Americans for Democratic Action (ADA) National Director Leon Shull wrote Speaker Albert and announced his organization's support for H. Res. 988, declaring that "it deserves the opportunity to be voted upon by the House of Representatives. Anything less would have to be viewed as a failure of House leadership." On September 10, two Select Committee staff members—Linda Kamm and Robert Ketcham—met with more than a dozen representatives of the League of Women Voters and helped to organize a lobbying strategy to get the reorganization plan to the floor. Representatives Culver and Sarbanes were instrumental in mobilizing the support of the League.

Meanwhile, the AFL-CIO mobilized union opposition to the Select Committee. Kenneth Young, assistant legislative director of the AFL-CIO, reportedly told union officials on September 9 that they would be in trouble if H. Res. 988 reached the floor, because President Gerald Ford allegedly supported it. The implication was that President Ford would be able to obtain solid GOP support for H. Res. 988 and probably influence some reluctant Democrats to support it too.

On September 11, the day before Bolling was to appear before the Rules Committee, the Select Committee met twice. Bolling first called a 10:30 A.M. meeting with the Democratic staff to discuss the prospects for reform. Bolling stated flatly that H. Res. 988 could not be killed. Even if no action occurred in 1974, he said, the groundwork had been laid for consideration of committee reform by the 94th Congress. Bolling then assessed the strategy of reorganization opponents which, he said, was either to prevent a quorum of the Rules Committee or to "filibuster" the resolution to death by having a long line of witnesses testify against H. Res. 988. Neither strategy would be successful, he declared, although the party leadership posed a problem. If Speaker Albert decided against the reform package, it would not get to the floor. Albert, however, had earlier told a delegation of freshmen members that the only way committee reform could be killed was if the caucus were to meet and instruct the Rules Committee not to grant a rule.

At a 4:30 P.M. session (attended by Bolling, Martin, Sarbanes, Meeds, Stephens, and Steiger), Bolling repeated what he had told staff members that morning about the opponents' tactics, indicating that ten members who opposed H. Res. 988 had already asked to testify the next day. Lloyd Meeds raised the issue of whether the Select Committee should recruit proponents of reform to testify before Rules. The members decided that such a tactic would simply prolong the "stalling" and play into the hands of the opponents. Bolling then stated that in his experience the best way to influence the Rules Committee was through member-to-member discussions, and he urged them to follow that course.

Finally, Bolling said the Select Committee had the votes on Rules to get an open rule on H. Res. 988. He calculated that there were at least three Democratic and five Republican votes. However, the Republicans could balk if Martin carried through on his plan to offer his own rule, which would send the Martin plan to the floor. In that event, the Select Committee might lose some GOP support for H. Res. 988. Martin said he was planning to offer his own rule at the Rules session, but if it was defeated, he would probably support the rule for H. Res. 988. All in all, the procedural hurdles faced by the reorganization plan were looking progressively more formidable.

"Filibustering" the Rules Committee. At 10:40 A.M. on September 12, Rules Chairman Ray Madden called his committee to order.[2] Thirteen of the fifteen members were present, and the hearing room was jammed with spectators, staff, other legislators, and reporters. Chairman Madden remarked facetiously that "we have a noncontroversial bill that shouldn't take too long." Little did members realize that it would take almost two weeks before the committee reached a decision. Bolling was the first witness, and ten other congressmen were scheduled to testify that day. Quite obviously, the opponents of H. Res. 988 decided to employ the "stalling" tactic rather than try to prevent a quorum of Rules members from attending the meetings. Under House rules, committee business cannot be conducted without a quorum.

Bolling explained how the Select Committee's plan evolved and outlined the effects it would have on members, committees, staffs, and outside interests. As Bolling noted, the Select Committee's plan "would affect the life of all the Members of the House and all the staffs of Members of the House and all the staffs of the committees and all those who seek to petition the Congress through lobbying. . . ." Then he asked for the rule suggested by the Democratic caucus: an "open" rule making the Hansen resolution a substitute for H. Res. 988. "I am not aware," Bolling said, "of any other committee which has been that considerate of the institution in giving it an opportunity to see what was coming at it." The time had come, he noted, for the House to consider H. Res. 988 without further delay.

Bolling went on to acknowledge that the Democratic party was divided on the issue. For one thing, he explained, many committee and subcommittee chairmen had a vested interest in the status quo and wanted nothing done that might jeopardize their positions. For another, the "great majority of Republicans who do not hold chairmanships support this bipartisan report," which aroused opposition within the majority party on the theory that if the GOP is for it then it must be bad for Democrats. In conclusion, Bolling argued that it would be a "catastrophic mistake" for the Rules Committee to prevent the House from considering H. Res. 988. "This is a matter of the public's business and it should be decided in public by the public's representatives."

Bolling then responded to numerous questions about the reform plan. Chairman Madden and other members were particularly concerned about which of the reform plans would transform the Rules Committee into a "sewing circle." Bolling assured them that the rules "bypass" provision (allowing the Speaker to recognize a committee member to offer a rule from the floor) was not part of his plan, but rather was a feature of the Hansen resolution. During the question period, Bolling stressed the importance of limiting members to one major committee assignment, which he stated was the "guts" of H. Res. 988. Bolling believed that if all committees could function like the Judiciary Committee did during its impeachment deliberations, the House would profit enormously. Judiciary members generally worked together as an integrated unit, attended committee deliberations, studied the issues, and conducted themselves excellently on a complex matter. However, would single committee assignments for legislators produce the same result or, as perhaps in Judiciary's case, was it really the "majesty" of the issue that compelled members to focus their energies on committee business? After more than two hours of discussion, the Rules Committee recessed.

When the committee reconvened at 2:10 P.M., Martin testified on his resolution. His was a compromise proposal, Martin told the Rules Committee, which included features from both H. Res. 988 and the Hansen proposal.[3] Martin then asked the Rules Committee to adopt his rule, which would make his resolution a substitute to the Hansen resolution. After some questions were addressed to Martin, Chairman Madden welcomed Hansen to the committee.

Hansen noted at the outset that she felt "like an early Christian coming into the lion's den"—no doubt because her committee had recommended curtailment of the Rules Committee's authority. Chairman Madden quickly reassured her that the committee "just had lunch."

During her statement, Hansen said that two concepts guided her committee: "One, we were not convinced that every change was necessarily beneficial to the workings of the House; and two, every change in the rules of the House had to meet the test that such a change would allow the House to work its will more efficiently, more openly and more expeditiously." Hansen conceded that her committee could not have developed its recommendations "on the magnitude to which we were commanded by the Caucus" without the foundation laid by the Select Committee. The basic procedural and jurisdictional differences between H. Res. 988 and her committee's resolution were explained. Hansen noted that other members of her committee would explain in detail various parts of H. Res. 1248. In conclusion, she assured the Rules members—particularly Republicans Martin and John Anderson who for months had been sharply critical of the Hansen Committee—that her group was "not trying to kill the bill."

Chairman Madden immediately questioned Hansen about the bypass provision. Like all other committee chairmen, Madden said, he had received an invitation to appear before the Hansen Committee to discuss the reform plan. On the day he was to appear, however, he had a Rules session and could not wait very long to testify. Because other chairmen were ahead of him, Madden had risen to leave when Hansen said, "Congressman, don't you worry, the Rules Committee is just not touched at all." Madden now repeated that the bypass provision would make his committee a "sewing circle" and wondered how that provision got into the resolution in light of her assurance. Hansen replied that Madden had misunderstood her. She had referred to the issue of membership on committees. "We were not discussing at that time," she said, "procedure in any way or manner." Madden quickly chimed in, "You finally got to it."

After other members questioned Hansen, Madden announced that the committee would meet a week later. This seemed agreeable to everyone. Bolling stated that he hoped the committee would come to some conclusion on that day or Friday at the latest, but Madden ignored Bolling's remark. Out of the ten members who had asked to testify, only three had been heard; even more legislators were asking to testify against H. Res. 988. Bolling was naturally worried about getting the measure to the floor at all.

Accordingly, Select Committee members Meeds and Culver worked to gather support for H. Res. 988. They sent a telegram to all new Democratic congressional candidates. The telegram said:

> House committee reform may be buried in Rules Committee giving GOP key campaign issue. Urge you contact Speaker Carl Albert, Majority Leader O'Neill and Rules Chairman Madden on the adverse effects for your campaign if Democrats kill reform.

Throughout the fall, Bolling and other Select Committee members kept in touch with a number of the new Democratic candidates for the House. The candidates were urged to support H. Res. 988 by "talking it up" with incumbent Democrats who might be supporting them in their campaigns. Moreover, the challengers could keep the "heat" on their Republican opponents (if they were incumbents seeking reelection) by making an issue of committee reform. For example, the Democratic challenger in New York's 25th congressional district, Nicholas Angell, told the constituents that incumbent Republican Hamilton Fish, Jr., should "actively demonstrate the desire for reform he has espoused by voting for the passage of [H. Res. 988]."[4]

When the Rules Committee reconvened a week later, ten members, including two committee chairmen, testified against H. Res. 988. The most caustic was John Dingell who charged that "reformers try to profit at the expense of their colleagues," and "never has the House of Representatives spent so much time and money and accomplished so little." He urged the Rules Committee to "summarily deny the rule" because H. Res. 988 was an "outrageous proposal." It will produce "fratricidal war," Dingell said, "and the most charitable thing to do is to inter it gracefully with some kind words for the author."

Three Hansen members, James O'Hara, Neal Smith, and Joe D. Waggonner, Jr., also testified. O'Hara argued that the reform plan would "not cure jurisdictional overlaps." O'Hara further suggested that the Rules Committee "consider reporting a bill that it would draft and report a clean bill." Because O'Hara was known as a strong supporter of the Democratic caucus, this came as a surprise to many members and staff. Would not this course of action, Bolling asked, "ignore the direction of the Democratic Caucus as to the kind of rule that should be reported?" O'Hara replied that if the Rules Committee "did a careful job . . ., they would certainly win the approval of the caucus for that sort of decision." Smith, on the other hand, said that many of the plan's provisions would make the House less efficient and effective. Waggonner observed that members of the Select Committee had ignored an important principle: "They have forgotten the art of gradualism and the art of gradualism is basic to good legislation." Moreover, he contended, H. Res. 988 would produce "severe ruptures in the legislative process."

Finally, Ways and Means member Sam Gibbons appeared to urge that the resolution be deferred indefinitely. Gibbons had a keen interest in international trade and did not want Ways and Means to lose that jurisdiction to the Foreign Affairs Committee (renamed International Relations in 1975), as the Select Committee proposed. Bolling countered by noting that six months had already elapsed; there was no need for further delay. Gibbons agreed that the resolution had been delayed, for "I have been doing the best I can to delay it." Bolling found the "gentleman's frankness refreshing," but pointed out that delay was unnecessary because the House "is hardly overwhelmed with current business on hand." The Rules Committee then adjourned until September 24, when nearly a dozen members were reportedly ready to testify.

It was apparent that the filibuster tactic was working. Labor lobbyists were scurrying around urging still more members to testify against H. Res. 988. At the same time, labor was lobbying several Democrats on Rules to vote against sending the reform resolution to the floor. Therefore, Bolling decided to end the hearing at the next Rules session.

The Issue is Brought to a Head. On September 24, at 2:15 P.M., the Rules Committee reconvened. A few minutes prior to the meeting, a letter to Speaker Albert was distributed to Rules members. Signed by representatives of six interest groups, including Ralph Nader's Congress Watch, Friends of the Earth, and the Consumer Federation of America, the letter expressed "deep concern" over the creation of a "monolithic" Energy and Environment Committee proposed by H. Res. 988. The signers suggested to Albert that there be "an opportunity for further study and accommodation on the energy issue . . . before bringing the issue of reform to the floor of the House." The letter (comparable to the earlier Nader letter opposing an Energy and Environment Committee) was designed to induce wavering Rules members to oppose sending H. Res. 988 to the floor and to create a "climate of doubt" about the reform plan.

The first witness was Government Operations Chairman Chet Holifield, who testified at great length on the demerits of H. Res. 988. Then Republican Edward Derwinski recommended that only the Hansen resolution be reported to the floor as the "lesser of two evils." At 4 P.M., when Derwinski concluded and the Rules Committee was preparing to adjourn for the day, Bolling made his critical move.

"This can go on forever," Bolling began. "There are new witnesses that want to be heard the next day and every day." He declared that it was the time for Rules Committee members to make a decision as to when they would vote to report H. Res. 988. Accordingly, Bolling moved that "the Committee meet and vote on this matter no later than 5 P.M. tomorrow." Meanwhile, Rules member Gillis Long, an ally of Bolling, had made a careful count and determined that the votes were available to carry Bolling's motion because several Rules opponents of H. Res. 988 were absent.

Spark M. Matsunaga said he would support Bolling's motion only if all witnesses who asked to testify were given that chance. Bolling explained that the Democratic leadership had scheduled H. Res. 988 for floor debate the following week (September 30), but it could take place only if the Rules Committee voted to report the measure. Timing was critical. If no action occurred, "then the Rules Committee as a whole," Bolling said, "will share the blame of not having filibustered it [H. Res. 988] to death, but delayed it to death."

Chairman Madden then tried to get the vote scheduled for Monday (September 30) to accommodate Rules member Clem Rogers McSpadden, who was running for the governorship of Oklahoma and would be absent the next day. Bolling kept repeating that the "Speaker would like to schedule [H. Res. 988] on Monday." Long pointed out that members already had had "eight months to be heard on this legislation." The time has come to "bring the matter to a head and vote on it tomorrow." Claude Pepper disagreed, remarking that the "stability of the universe" was not at stake if the Rules Committee debated Bolling's motion next week.

Then Bolling called for the question. Long followed suit. Both kept insisting that Madden put the motion to a vote, but Madden wanted to wait for the absent Rules members to return. Finally, Madden entertained the motion, and the roll was called. Bolling's motion was adopted six to five, and the committee recessed until the next day. Shortly after the vote, Rules member John Young entered the room, furious that he had not been notified of the vote. No one was there, except staff, to hear his complaint. Nevertheless, everyone realized that Young represented a tie vote, which would have defeated Bolling's motion.

Tension filled the air throughout the next day's meeting. Democratic opponents of H. Res. 988, the proponents learned, were planning a motion to reconsider the Bolling motion. If their strategy were successful, H. Res. 988 could not reach the floor the following Monday, probably ending once and for all any chance that the reorganization plan would be considered during that Congress. As the Rules members listened to the witnesses, each side carefully eyed the other. Neither the opponents or proponents of H. Res. 988 wanted to be caught short when the motion to reconsider was made. For example, when Republican John Anderson left the hearing room to testify in support of Nelson Rockefeller's nomination for Vice President, he was urged to return as quickly as possible because the motion to reconsider might be offered at any time.

All through the morning session, Select Committee members and staff were apprehensive. For the afternoon session, the first witness was Education and Labor Chairman Carl Perkins. Because a quorum (eight members) of the committee was not present when Chairman Madden reconvened the session at 2:15 P.M., Perkins refused to begin his testimony until a sufficient number of members was present. "I would like for the membership to hear what I have to say," Perkins said. After a recess of about fifteen minutes, a quorum appeared and Perkins began a lengthy presentation. In fact, he read several pages of testimony twice. During his ninety-minute-long testimony, Perkins urged the Rules Committee to defer action on H. Res. 988 until after the November elections. Following the statement, Republican Delbert L. Latta told Perkins that while he made a good statement, "It took you a long time to present it."

One other witness was heard, and by 4:45 P.M. no other members in the room wanted to testify. Bolling then asked Chairman Madden if he was ready to entertain his motion. "There are some other witnesses back here," Representative Young retorted. Bolling remarked sharply that "they are all favorable and they are not going to talk." Madden then announced that the hearing was officially closed.

Then Bolling offered his motion, asking for the rule suggested by the Democratic caucus with four hours of general debate on H. Res. 988. Young moved that "we defer action on this matter at this time." Before action occurred on Young's substitute motion, Republican Anderson announced that rather than offer a rule of his own he would reluctantly support Bolling's proposed rule. That clinched Republican support, for

Martin indicated he would not offer a rule of his own. Matsunaga, who had been on the floor handling some legislation, arrived late. Upon entering the room Matsunaga announced that he was "committed to the proposition that I will vote for deferment if any witness has been denied the right to testify." Madden assured him that "every witness who came in here has testified."

Madden declared that the vote was on the Young substitute. It was defeated by voice vote. Martin asked for a roll call vote on Young's motion, which was defeated by an eight to five vote. All five Republicans voted against Young's motion as did Democrats Bolling, Long, and Matsunaga. Those voting for deferral were Democrats Madden, James Delaney, Young, Morgan F. Murphy, and Pepper.

Several members asked how much time Hansen would have to discuss her resolution on the House floor. It was informally agreed by Bolling and Martin that each would give Hansen thirty minutes of their time (they controlled four hours to be divided equally between them). That was acceptable to all Rules members, whereupon the committee by voice vote adopted the Bolling rule. In a little noticed but critical request, Bolling asked Madden for control of the rule. Madden agreed, and the committee adjourned.

If the opponents of H. Res. 988 on the Rules Committee had been more alert, they could have delayed House consideration of committee reform for at least seven more days. Under the rules of the House, the report of any committee on a measure must be filed within seven calendar days. If Madden had kept control of the Rules report on H. Res. 988, he could have invoked that provision of the rules and prevented floor debate on reform the following Monday (September 30). That action, no doubt, would have effectively killed H. Res. 988. Instead, Bolling immediately filed the report of the committee, which is the act of placing it on the appropriate legislative calendar.

THE FLOOR DEBATE

Planning for the Floor. The next day Bolling met with committee members and staff to review the strategy for the next Monday's floor session. Bolling announced that he would make a general statement on H. Res. 988, and assigned Sarbanes and Meeds the task of "carrying the ball on details." Later, Sarbanes suggested that each member of the Select Committee be assigned specific topics to speak on during debate on committee reform. Bolling agreed. In Bolling's words, the political dilemma faced by the Select Committee was to overcome the "self-fulfilling death wish of our opponents who want to see the reform resolution killed no matter what." Martin, meanwhile, revealed little of his intentions, although members and staff expected that he would seek House approval of his committee reform resolution.

Culver mentioned the importance of obtaining an accurate count of members who would support the rule. Sarbanes agreed. Mondays, Culver reminded, are notable for the number of member absences. Moreover, labor lobbyists were putting the heat on numerous legislators to oppose the rule. Culver also asked if anyone knew why a special Democratic caucus had been called for Tuesday. No one had a clear idea, except to note that it was simply another attempt to kill H. Res. 988.

Under Democratic rules, the caucus chairman is obligated to call a party meeting "whenever requested in writing by fifty members of the Caucus." The opponents of H. Res. 988 who sought the special meeting had hoped to meet the following Monday morning, just hours prior to the scheduled start of House debate, and have the caucus vote to shelve floor consideration of committee reform. Barring that, the Tuesday caucus might instruct the Speaker to postpone further consideration of committee reform.

Some concern was expressed about the expected absences of Minority Leader John Rhodes and Conference Chairman John Anderson—both of whom had prior campaign commitments for Monday and would be out of town for the opening of the debate. Bolling and other committee members were concerned about soft spots developing in Republican ranks. Steiger responded that GOP support for the rule was solid, with the exception of Republicans on the Ways and Means and Post Office Committees. Meeds suggested that Rhodes and Anderson draft a "Dear Colleague" letter before they left town urging GOP legislators to support the rule on H. Res. 988; and Peter Frelinghuysen said he would see that something of that sort was done.

Yet another call for a renewed public campaign was made by Culver. Common Cause should be asked to alert its people throughout the country to urge their congressmen to support the rule; Americans for Democratic Action and the League of Women Voters should be encouraged to do likewise. In response, on September 26 League President Ruth Clusen mailed a three-page memorandum to all House members urging them to support the rule; reject the motion substituting H. Res. 1248 for H. Res. 988; amend H. Res. 988 to incorporate certain features of the Hansen plan; and adopt the amended Select Committee proposal. ADA National Director Leon Shull sent a letter on September 27 to all congressmen urging them to vote for the rule on H. Res. 988. The same day, Common Cause Chairman John Gardner mailed a similar letter to all House members. Culver also suggested that major newspapers should be contacted to write editorials on behalf of the Select Committee. On

September 30, for example, *The Washington Star* ran an editorial on the need to upset the "comfort zones" of senior House members.

Finally, Meeds raised the issue of whether Select Committee members should prepare a substitute resolution, embracing minor and conforming amendments but embodying the substance of H. Res. 988. If the committee had such a resolution, Meeds argued, it could be offered to the Hansen substitute and thus give H. Res. 988 priority consideration on the floor. Sarbanes and Steiger disagreed. They argued that the Select Committee should not offer a substitute to Hansen for two principal reasons: it would be perceived as a tricky move by many Democrats, in effect subverting the intent of the caucus; and it would increase confusion on the House floor. Bolling held that the Select Committee's policy should be to oppose the Hansen plan and dispose of it as quickly as possible so the House could then debate H. Res. 988. Meeds was concerned that Select Committee members should not be put in the position of "nay-saying" all amendments to the Hansen resolution, many of which could be worthwhile. The other members agreed that if the Hansen substitute was amended in such a fashion as to reflect the basic principles of H. Res. 988, they would support it.

The next day, Friday, September 27, the Select Committee staff, particularly Linda Kamm and Rob Ketcham, organized a count of members to determine who would be present on Monday to vote for the rule. Various outside groups, such as Common Cause and the League of Women Voters, joined in this effort, and staff in the offices of Steiger, Sarbanes, and Meeds were put to work telephoning members' offices to ascertain attendance. Interestingly, the Democratic leadership did not conduct a similar whip count of its own, perhaps because most Democratic whips opposed the Select Committee's plan. Hence Majority Leader O'Neill's office called Bolling's to ask how the Select Committee's count was coming along. However, a whip notice was issued to all GOP members from Minority Leader Rhodes's office. The notice stated that a "concerted action may be made to defeat the rule" and urged all Republicans "to support the rule so the House will have the opportunity to consider committee reform. The Leadership urges an 'aye' vote on the rule for H. Res. 988." In the face of the intense lobbying campaign, the efforts of Select Committee members and staff, and the legislators' growing uneasiness about quashing debate on reorganization altogether, opposition to the rule soon fell apart.

Meanwhile, the Hansen Committee called a strategy session for Monday morning, just prior to the scheduled start of debate. The basic floor strategy agreed upon by the Hansen group was to have the House spend so much time debating their resolution that members would not want to vote it down to debate the Select Committee's proposal. To accomplish that end meant creating a parliamentary situation in which members in effect could amend only the Hansen resolution. This could be arranged if another legislator—some "turkey," an aide to the Hansen group called him—offered a substitute to the Hansen substitute resolution. (Ironically, David Martin was the member who unwittingly accommodated the Hansen Committee.) Next, a Hansen supporter would offer an amendment to the new substitute, thereby foreclosing under House rules any further amendments to that substitute until the amendment was disposed of. This would then leave open to amendment only the Hansen resolution, because no effort would be made initially to dispose of the amendment to the second substitute. From then on, as soon as one amendment to the Hansen substitute resolution was disposed of, another would be offered, and so on.

In addition, the Hansen group agreed that certain amendments should be offered to their resolution in order to secure the support of various legislators. One member, Waggonner, announced his intention to offer an amendment deleting that part of the Hansen resolution that limited the rule-making authority of the Rules Committee. It was also agreed that a stronger amendment on minority staffing should be drafted to woo Republicans. (This could be repealed by the Democratic caucus before the start of the next Congress.) While the Select Committee and the Hansen group were preparing for floor debate, scores of members were sending "Dear Colleague" letters urging support for this or that viewpoint. Everyone was preparing for what was expected to be a monumental floor fight over the House committee system.

The Struggle on the Floor Begins. Unquestionably, most people who sit in the visitors' gallery above the House chamber view action on the floor as confusing and noisy. Often it is. Sometimes the floor is jammed to capacity as members debate controversial measures; at other times, there are only a few legislators present, with some of them reading newspapers or talking in groups at the rear of the chamber. The parliamentary procedures that are followed, moreover, are often quite complicated. Sometimes amendments to measures pile up one after the other with few members really knowing what is happening. Yet congressmen must usually vote on these occasions, lest they be accused in the next election of absenteeism or of "ducking" key issues. On issues with which they are not familiar, legislators rely on certain trusted "cue givers"—committee chairmen, subject-matter experts, party leaders, close friends, and so forth—to help them make informed judgments and steer them away from antagonizing either the "folks back home" or powerful House colleagues.[5] However, most members no doubt believed they were experts on committee organization, and were therefore less likely to solicit advice. For the same reason, members could be expected to have plenty to say during the debate.

The First Day (September 30). Shortly after the House convened at noon, it began to consider the "rule" (H. Res. 1395) from the Rules Committee.[6] The "rule" authorized four hours of general debate, directed the Hansen resolution to be in order as a substitute for H. Res. 988, and permitted the House to resolve itself into the Committee of the Whole. The Select Committee's whip count showed a clear majority of members committed to adoption of this "rule." Many Democrats did not want to oppose the rule authorized by their caucus, and, in general, legislators did not want to prevent by a procedural vote House consideration of committee reform. Members of the Select Committee realized, however, that if opponents of reform failed to prevent House consideration of H. Res. 988 by defeating the "rule," then they would try to kill the matter in a special Democratic caucus called for the next day. (That caucus never met because it lacked a quorum.)

Bolling and Martin explained the provisions of the rule on H. Res. 988. Six of the seven congressmen who spoke on the rule urged its adoption. Only Chairwoman Leonor Sullivan of the Merchant Marine Committee urged its defeat because she had "questions and misgivings concerning almost every change recommended by the Select Committee on Committees." Nevertheless, the House voted overwhelmingly, 326 to 25, to adopt the rule and proceed to the Committee of the Whole.

It is in Committee of the Whole, used ever since the First Congress, where measures are amended. Perhaps best conceived as a committee composed of the entire House membership, the Committee of the Whole's primary purpose is to expedite the consideration of legislation. That is accomplished in two ways. First, a quorum in the Committee of the Whole is only 100 members, as opposed to the normal quorum of 218 members (a majority of the membership). Second, the five-minute rule, rather than the hour rule, is in effect. Therefore, members in Committee of the Whole may speak only once on an amendment, either in support or in opposition, and for only five minutes. Of course, numerous *pro forma* amendments may be offered by members, usually by the artifice of "moving to strike the requisite number of words."

When Bolling proceeded to make the usual *pro forma* motion to have the House resolve into the Committee of the Whole, John Dingell jumped to his feet to raise a point of order. The Select Committee had violated the rules of the House, Dingell claimed, because it had not indicated in a comparative print (of the resolution) how H. Res. 988 had repealed or amended existing law (as required by the so-called Ramseyer rule). Dingell argued that H. Res. 988 changed the statute that created the Joint Committee on Atomic Energy by shifting the JCAE's responsibility for nonmilitary nuclear energy to the proposed Committee on Energy and Environment. In making that shift, the resolution failed to specify which provisions of the Atomic Energy Act had been amended or repealed and therefore was in violation of the rules of the House.

In response, Bolling simply read the rule cited by Dingell and pointed out that it applied to a bill or joint resolution. "What is before the House," Bolling said, "is a simple resolution, and therefore, the rule does not apply to it." Speaker Albert, who was presiding officer, overruled Dingell's point of order for the reason stated by Bolling. The motion to resolve into Committee of the Whole was then agreed to by voice vote.

William Natcher then took the chair as presiding officer (by precedent, the Speaker does not preside over the Committee of the Whole). A parliamentarian during his college years, Natcher was known as a strong and fair presiding officer. Moreover, he had some background in congressional reorganization matters, for he had presided during debate on the Legislative Reorganization Act of 1970. It would be Natcher's responsibility to keep order in the chamber and rule on various points of parliamentary procedure. Bolling made no effort to persuade Speaker Albert, who selected Natcher, to name a particular individual. This was the Speaker's decision, Bolling explained, and he did not believe it was his business to interfere. All factions, however, were satisfied with Albert's choice.

While debate on the floor may appear unstructured to spectators in the gallery, it is in fact closely regulated by convention and the managers of the legislation. Without someone determining during general debate who will speak and when, there would likely be chaos on the floor with members rising to speak at will. Hence, general debate time is controlled by the "managers" of the legislation; in this case, Bolling and Martin each controlled two hours of debate. Time during general debate is usually divided equally between the two committee members of the opposite party who represent the pro and con of a measure. Of course, if there are other major points of view regarding an issue, then other debate arrangements can be made, as occurred in this instance with Hansen.

Bolling immediately took the floor to clarify the informal debate arrangements agreed to in the Rules Committee. Hansen said that it seemed reasonable "since we are split three ways [Bolling, Hansen, and Martin] that there be approximately one-third of the time used for the presentation of House Resolution 1248." Bolling and Martin agreed. Accordingly, Bolling said he would make available fifty minutes from his two hours, and Martin agreed to thirty minutes. Hence, the four hours of general debate were divided as follows: Bolling, seventy minutes; Hansen, eighty minutes; and Martin, ninety minutes. Each of the members, of course, would sublet a certain portion of his time to other legislators supporting his position.

The major purpose of general debate is to discuss the substance of a measure. Most legislators concede that few votes are changed by debate. Nevertheless, there are several important functions of general debate. It compels members to come to grips with the issue at hand; constituents and groups can be alerted to a measure's purposes through the press; broad issues can be examined in an interrelated rather than piecemeal fashion; member sentiment for or against the proposition can be assessed; a public record is built; members can be alerted to the strategies of the proponents and opponents; solidarity can be reinforced among members who share the same viewpoint on the measure; and, occasionally, fence-sitters may be influenced one way or the other.

Each of the three managers was centrally located at long tables around the center of the chamber, with the main aisle separating the Democratic from the Republican side of the House. On the left of the Select Committee's table sat Hansen and her key floor strategists—Neal Smith, James O'Hara, Frank Thompson, Jr., and Phil Burton—while Martin, Steiger, and other Republicans, including GOP staff aide Melvin M. Miller, were on the right side of the chamber at their table. Assisting Bolling at the center table were Sarbanes, Meeds, and several committee staff members. Bolling wanted Sarbanes and Meeds to be the key floor advocates of H. Res. 988, supporting it when necessary and rebutting attacks. Stephens, meanwhile, was to work the floor, circulating among the members to line up support for H. Res. 988. Culver, locked in a close senatorial race in Iowa, could not devote his full attention to the committee reorganization issue. Moreover, Bolling was sensitive to his position, and did not want him speaking out on matters that might cause him trouble in Iowa. With Martin pushing his own reform plan, Steiger acted informally as the liaison between the GOP and Bolling.

Time, as usual, was a critical factor. Bolling wanted to conclude general debate that day because Speaker Albert had made it clear that he wanted committee reorganization to be concluded in about a week. Hence, it was important to reach the amending stage (the five-minute rule) as quickly as possible, rather than allowing general debate to extend over several days. For the next four hours, therefore, various members spoke for or against the three propositions. Seven of the ten Select Committee members either spoke for or submitted statements in behalf of H. Res. 988. Martin pushed his own reform resolution, while five of the ten Hansen Committee members spoke for their measure. As a "warm-up" session, the first day's debate offered little chance to judge the extent of support for any one of the three propositions. It did serve, however, to conclude the general debate phase of the proceedings.

The Second Day (October 1). After the opening ceremonies were completed, Bolling offered the standard motion to have the House resolve into the Committee of the Whole.[7] When the motion passed, Chairman Natcher announced that, as all time for general debate had expired, the next order of business was to have H. Res. 1248 (the Hansen substitute) offered as "an amendment in the nature of a substitute." This meant that the Hansen resolution would be substituted *in toto* for H. Res. 988, although the substitute resolution, if approved, would still carry the number H. Res. 988. Then David Martin made matters even more complicated by offering his resolution (H. Res. 1321) as a substitute to the Hansen amendment. Now, in effect, the House had before it three competing committee reform proposals, as illustrated in figure 1.

FIGURE 1

Offerings of Amendments to H.Res. 988

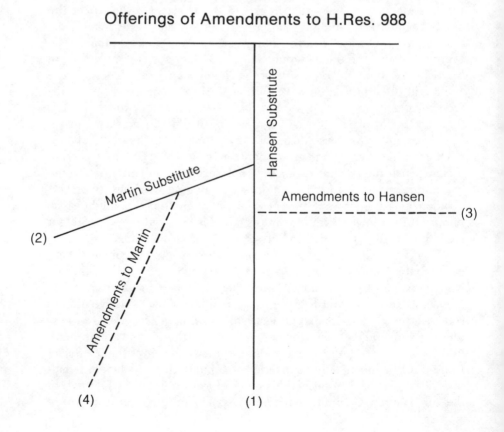

Strategically, perhaps, the Select Committee erred by not preempting Martin with a substitute amendment of its own, along the lines of the Meeds proposal. Under the rules of the House, only two substitute amendments can be offered to a measure—a limit reached with introduction of Martin's proposal. If a Select Committee amendment had been ready, it would have forestalled Martin, albeit temporarily, and simplified the parliamentary situation. Because it was clear that the battle was between the Bolling and Hansen resolutions, a substitute amendment sponsored by the Select Committee and offered before Martin's would have enabled members to concentrate on two rather than three resolutions.

Under House procedure, members could now offer and vote on amendments to either Martin or Hansen, switching back and forth at will. The original (Bolling) measure could not be amended directly until the substitutes had been disposed of. After all amendments to them had been considered, first Martin's and then Hansen's substitutes would be voted on. Only then would the House actually have a chance to consider and perfect the Select Committee's plan—assuming, of course, that the substitutes were defeated.

Bolling rose immediately in opposition to Martin's substitute, and then explained the basic strategy that Democrats on the Select Committee would pursue during the reform debate. He urged the House to vote down the Hansen and Martin substitutes and then proceed to amend H. Res. 988. Of course, he added, if either of the substitutes were amended "so as to be very like" H. Res. 988, then "all bets would be off."

Sullivan then moved to amend the Martin substitute by restoring everything the Merchant Marine and Fisheries Committee had lost under H. Res. 988 (both H. Res. 988 and the Martin substitute were identical in this respect). Sullivan's amendment was critical because, in effect, it was a "test" vote. The outcome would perhaps reveal whether the Hansen or Bolling forces would prevail. Its adoption would signal to all that further jurisdictional unravelings would be the order of the day.

After some discussion of the Sullivan amendment, Hansen committee member Frank Thompson, Jr., offered an amendment to his group's substitute. Thompson's staffing amendment conformed to the Select Committee's proposal (tripling the size of each committee's staff with one-third going to the minority party) with one major addition. The amendment would authorize each ranking minority subcommittee member one staff aide. Thompson's amendment was designed to attract Republican support for the Hansen substitute. As Bolling noted later, "I recognize a pot sweetener when I see one," but added he did not think Republicans "will be very enticed by this." Martin added that the amendment's primary purpose "is to stimulate or overstimulate support on the minority side for the Hansen plan."

There was plenty of confusion associated with Thompson's amendment. First, he obtained unanimous consent that the clerk not read his amendment. House rules require that amendments be read in full. Lloyd Meeds objected too late when he said, "Mr. Chairman, we have not had the amendment read. We do not know what it contains." Thompson, however, said he "would be glad to explain it." Another rule of the House requires that when amendments are offered in Committee of the Whole, five copies each are to be "transmitted promptly" to the majority and minority tables. In this case, Bolling and other committee Democrats received copies several minutes after Thompson was into his discussion. Moreover, they received the wrong copies. This caused some confusion as Bolling and the others tried to comprehend what Thompson was saying. Finally, the wrong amendment was even printed in the *Congressional Record*.

With the offering of the Thompson amendment, no other amendments were in order to either the Hansen or Martin substitutes. Either the Sullivan or Thompson proposal had to be disposed of. And with two amendments pending simultaneously, members could choose to speak to either one or the other. For awhile, several members discussed the Sullivan amendment. But then attention was concentrated on the staffing proposal, a super-charged emotional issue for both Democrats and Republicans.

Debate became heated. Many Democrats simply could not accept a proposal that would give Republicans additional committee staff. They argued that it would politicize the committees, undercut the majority party's ability to govern, give too much advantage to the Republicans, and waste the taxpayer's money. Some senior Democrats harkened back to the days when the Republicans controlled the House and retold old "war" stories about how the Democrats had been mistreated when the GOP ran the House. Don't give Republicans more committee staff, they said; if the GOP gained control again they would simply take away whatever additional staff was allocated to the minority party.

Nevertheless, 218 members voted in favor of the Thompson amendment, with 180 in opposition. Sixty-three Republicans voted for the proposal—not a good sign for backers of the Select Committee plan. As Thompson was quick to point out, his amendment "definitely" made the Hansen substitute more palatable to Republicans. "It puts more control in the hands of junior Republicans rather than concentrating it in the hands of one single Republican, the ranking member of the full committee."[8] Thompson's Hansen group colleague, Phil Burton, objected strongly to this provision. Burton was upset because Thompson's amendment changed House rules to guarantee staff assistance to the ranking GOP member of each subcommittee. However, Democratic subcommittee chairmen were not accorded similar rights under Thompson's amendment.

The day did not go well for the Select Committee, mainly because its strategists distrusted the "mood" of the House. While it might be difficult to quantitatively measure something as elusive as "mood," members and staff on the floor often sense whether things are going well or badly on an issue. Sometimes members are jovial; sometimes anxious to adjourn for the night; sometimes they exhibit anger; and sometimes they are impatient to move on to another issue. These and other attitudes of the body are fairly easy to sense, particularly when a sensitive issue is being debated. It is the task of the floor manager not only to guide the measure successfully through a parliamentary maze but also to sense when to advance, retreat, or stand fast in light of the House's general mood. On this day, however, many members were literally ranting and raving against the minority staffing provision. Rational debate was almost impossible. Agriculture Chairman W. R. Poage, for example, argued strenuously against increased committee staffing. As a colleague of his said, Poage "gets infuriated with the sound of his own voice. He starts out with a shout and works up from there."[9] Poage declared that additional staff would become "empire builders" and require the House to purchase several buildings to house them. Moreover, he kept shouting pointed questions and demanding answers:

> In the first place, for just how many new committee employees does this provide? Is it 150, as the gentleman from New Jersey suggested? Is it 300, as some other Member suggested? Is it over 500, or is it about 1,000, as I figure it will probably be?
>
> Have any of the advocates of change any suggestions? How many are we adding to the payroll? Let us not have everybody speak at once.[10]

Too many legislators had already made up their minds on this issue, and no amount of debate would change their viewpoint.

The issue was particularly divisive for Democrats. Speaker Albert, already jittery, came under pressure from opponents of committee reorganization to pull the whole package off the floor—scuttling H. Res. 988 for the 93rd Congress. At one point Albert came over to where Bolling was sitting and said that something needed to be done to stop the tirades. The Democratic party was being hurt. Bolling simply shrugged, for there was nothing he could do. The Select Committee was riding out the storm. When an ally of Bolling's heard about Albert's concern and the pressure being put on him, he immediately buttonholed Albert on the floor and reminded him that if the reform debate were cut off, the Speaker would be blamed by numerous members, outside groups, and the press. Reluctantly, Albert agreed.

The Third Day (October 2). When members came to the floor to debate committee reform on the third day, Government Operations Chairman Chet Holifield had numerous copies of a memorandum ready for them at the back of the chamber.[11] His prepared statement declared that junior legislators would lose their major committee assignment if H. Res. 988 was adopted. Holifield's purpose, of course, was to create a climate of doubt about the reform resolution among its probable supporters. Following agreement that the House resolve into Committee of the Whole, Bolling took the floor to explain how he hoped to proceed with the issue. Under the practices of the House (and the Senate), managers of legislation and party leaders are accorded priority when they seek recognition from the chair. This facilitates their control of activities on the floor. Recalling the near debacle of the previous day, Bolling said he wanted to establish an orderly procedure for considering all three resolutions. Moreover, time was running out, and the House could not consider reform indefinitely.

Even though the legislative work load was light that week, consideration of committee reorganization was often intermittent because privileged matters such as appropriation bills or conference reports took precedence on the floor. To complicate matters, numerous members, as was their prerogative under the House Rules, had indicated in the *Congressional Record* their intent to offer amendments to the various resolutions. An amendment printed in the *Congressional Record* in conformity with the appropriate House rule was automatically entitled to at least ten minutes of debate, five for and five against. Dingell, for example, surpassed everyone by publishing close to fifty amendments to the three resolutions. If Dingell insisted on offering each one, he would control more than eight hours of floor debate at the very least. Thus, Bolling decided, debate would have to be structured. Otherwise, opponents could kill reform by delaying final consideration of H. Res. 988.

Bolling moved to put the foes of reform on the defensive. He suggested that "those who would kill the bill should offer a motion to strike the resolving clause [an action equivalent to defeating H. Res. 988]. Then if it fails . . . it will be clear that we [the House] are going to proceed to the conclusion" of the debate on H. Res. 988. Once the motion to strike the resolving clause was disagreed to, an orderly procedure could be agreed upon for considering amendments to the Bolling, Hansen, and Martin resolutions.

Hansen committee member Waggonner objected to Bolling's suggestion, observing candidly that "one offers a motion to strike the resolving clause when one thinks he has the votes. At the present time, I do not think that such a motion would pass." Waggonner went on to say that if a motion to strike is made, it "will be at a point in time when we [the opponents of H. Res. 988] think there is a chance for it to succeed."

Smith, another Hansen proponent, then said that the key fight was between the Select Committee and Hansen resolutions. "Time spent debating the Martin proposal," he said, "is time lost." Thus far, of course, there had been little debate on the Martin substitute. Smith's suggestion angered Martin, who insisted that the regular order be followed, meaning that amendments could be offered to both the Hansen and Martin amendments. Perhaps in a moment of personal pique, Martin now announced that he would insist that all amendments be read in full. Normally, the reading of lengthy amendments by a clerk is dispensed with by unanimous consent.

Unfortunately, Martin was playing into the hands of the opponents of committee reorganization. Requiring all amendments to be read in full could only further delay the proceedings. Bolling urged Martin not to insist "rigidly" on this point, because a member could propose an "amendment that included the dictionary and we could be here until shortly before we adjourn." Nevertheless, Martin reiterated his position, "unless it is not completely reasonable."

After this preliminary and inconclusive skirmishing, the Committee of the Whole considered an amendment to the Hansen substitute offered by Republican Dan Kuykendall, a member of the Interstate and Foreign Commerce Committee. Kuykendall proposed that the status quo concerning transportation jurisdiction be maintained, that is, split among several committees. This would mean that the Commerce Committee (renamed Commerce and Health in all three resolutions) would retain jurisdiction over aviation, shifted to Public Works and Transportation under both the Select Committee and Hansen resolutions. Unlike the Select Committee's approach, the Hansen substitute would keep railroads in the Commerce Committee.

Members argued at great length about the merits of consolidating different modes of transportation in one committee. Gerry Studds emphasized the need for consolidation to facilitate a rational and coordinated approach to that fragmented policy area. Studds wondered aloud why the Hansen plan left railroads in the Commerce Committee. But then the answer came to him. The Hansen Committee "has placed railroads in the health committee, presumably because [the railroad industry] is sick." Phil Burton, however, revealed why the Hansen Committee had not moved the railroad jurisdiction. While the Hansen group agreed completely with the Select Committee's recommendation to consolidate transportation matters in Public Works, he said, they left railroads in the Commerce Committee "purely and solely out of love and affection for the beloved gentleman from West Virginia [Harley Staggers, chairman of the committee], and for no possible other reason." Burton went on to urge the defeat of the Kuykendall amendment because it would be "compounding an error with outrageous judgment if we further fracture the transportation system. . . ." Staggers, meanwhile, was scurrying about the floor trying to persuade his colleagues to support the Kuykendall amendment. The House, however, defeated the amendment by a 239 to 172 recorded vote.

The next amendment, offered to the Hansen substitute by Select Committee member C. W. Bill Young, would create a permanent Select Committee on Aging. Representing a congressional district with the largest concentration of elderly in the nation, Young was the logical person to offer such an amendment, although similar proposals had either been introduced or cosponsored by about two hundred members. There was some opposition from members of the Education and Labor Committee, which held legislative jurisdiction over aging; but in an election year the amendment was overwhelmingly adopted by a record vote of 323 to 84.

Finally, Chairman Richard Ichord of the Internal Security Committee proposed an amendment to the Hansen substitute that would retain his panel. All three reform resolutions had recommended the abolition of the Internal Security Committee. Long an issue of sharp contention between liberals and conservatives, the committee was retained, after strenuous debate, by a vote of 246 to 164.

The proposed abolition of the Internal Security Committee was strongly contested by numerous outside organizations and various legislators. Lobbying efforts to retain the committee were intense. In general, supporters of the panel argued that the Committee on Internal Security was the legislative unit that defended the United States against subversive activities. As one organization wrote to all members, "The only agency left in the House of Representatives to alert the public against subversion is the Richard Ichord committee on internal subversion." While many members viewed the committee as an anachronism and had tried unsuccessfully in previous years to terminate it, it simply could not be accomplished with the November elections only a few weeks away. (At the start of the 94th Congress, the committee was disbanded.)

The Fourth Day (October 3). Following opening ceremonies, members are recognized by the Speaker to make one-minute speeches on any topic. On this day, Dingell was recognized and he used the opportunity to place in the *Congressional Record* a Ralph Nader letter to Speaker Albert reiterating Nader's contention that the "Hansen Committee proposal will serve the public interest better than the Select Committee proposal" in energy and environmental matters.[12] Dingell, of course, was attempting to set the tone for the day's debate by demonstrating that a celebrated public figure opposed a principal feature of H. Res. 988.

After two other legislators made brief speeches, Bolling made the usual *pro forma* motion that the House resolve into the Committee of the Whole. However, Mendel Davis challenged the Speaker's decision that the "ayes appear to have it," and demanded a record vote on Bolling's motion. Of course, this was yet another tactic on the part of the opponents. "Oh, boy, we're going to keep it [the debate] going on for months," Davis was later overheard to say. "We may keep it going forever."[13] This time, however, the delay was longer than anyone expected as the electronic voting system broke down and the roll had to be called by the clerk. Under the electronic system, votes take fifteen minutes rather than forty-five minutes when tallied by the clerk. Even the electrical system, some reorganization proponents thought, seemed to be conspiring against them. In the end, Bolling's motion was adopted 384 to 2. Nevertheless, opponents of H. Res. 988 continued to exploit the malfunction by forcing time-consuming quorum calls and roll call votes.

Once in Committee of the Whole, Waggonner offered the previously announced amendment to the Hansen plan, restoring complete rule-making authority to the Committee on Rules. Hansen told Rules Chairman Madden that she was happy to "give you back your tatting society intact." Another amendment, creating a standing Committee on Small Business, was also accepted. Finally, Charles Bennett proposed that members could serve as committee chairmen for no more than three full terms. Most Democrats opposed the amendment not because it was unworthy of consideration but because it was considered a matter for the respective party caucuses to decide. Many legislators, too, disagreed on the merits of the proposal. No decision, however, was reached when the Committee of the Whole rose and the House adjourned until Monday.

Afterward, Bolling told news reporters that the House planned to recess for several weeks subsequent to the following week's close of business. He charged that opponents of H. Res. 988 were trying "to stall it off the map." What he proposed to do was "gradually, slowly exhaust not the interest but the proposals on the floor, so when we say it's time to get down to the voting, we'll seem reasonable."[14] After four days of debate, the House had adopted only six amendments, all to the Hansen plan, with scores of others to all three resolutions still pending.

The Fifth Day (October 7). Monday morning Bolling called a strategy session in his office. The Democratic members and staff of the Select Committee attended, as did Mrs. Bolling and Representative Gillis Long. A close friend of Bolling and a respected colleague on the Rules Committee, Long was known for his shrewd political judgments; he was active in support of the Select Committee during various stages of the legislative process. Everyone realized that debate had to be concluded that week because the House was racing to recess so members could campaign. Majority Counsel Linda Kamm suggested that the Select Committee offer another resolution, incorporating the amendments already agreed to, as a substitute for the Hansen package. This move, which would occur after the expected defeat of the Martin plan, would give the House a chance to have an up-or-down vote on the basic features of H. Res. 988. In essence, debate could be directed to the Select Committee's proposal rather than solely to the Hansen plan. Bolling rejected Kamm's proposal, however, on the grounds that it was inconsistent with what he was trying to have the House do: first vote down Martin, then Hansen, and then proceed to H. Res. 988.

Culver argued and everyone agreed that Bolling should seek to limit debate on both the Hansen and Martin substitutes. Long noted that members would appreciate knowing they were finishing with reform, which a time limitation would clearly signal. Culver added that Bolling should consult Speaker Albert to obtain the backing of party leaders for the move. Bolling agreed, emphasizing once more that, without Albert's strong support, H. Res. 988 would have been pulled off the floor long before. Albert, Bolling explained, was under pressure, particularly from the AFL-CIO, to kill committee reform. AFL-CIO President George Meany, for example, was urging Albert to postpone the whole matter.

Everyone was impatient for the debate to commence. It was conceivable, as some pointed out, that committee reorganization might not even come up that day. Monday was suspension day, and twelve measures were expected to be considered from the Suspension Calendar. Plus there was a joint resolution on aid to Turkey that was expected to be controversial. Concern was even voiced that Waggonner or Wayne Hays might move to strike the resolving clause of H. Res. 988 and kill it outright.

Committee reorganization was considered on the floor that day.[15] By the time Bolling was recognized, however, many members were anxious to adjourn for the day. They were simply not in the mood to spend much time on the bitterly disputed committee reform proposals. Realizing this, Bolling told his colleagues that he sought to go into Committee of the Whole "so that we might come to some kind of arrangement as to how, in a reasonable time tomorrow or perhaps the next day, we might conclude the matter."

Bolling proposed two alternatives. First, he asked unanimous consent to propose a reasonable amount of time to debate all three reform propositions. When Dingell objected, Bolling moved that all debate on perfecting amendments to the Hansen substitute be limited to five hours. The five-hour limit also included the Martin substitute because it technically was an amendment to the Hansen resolution. Any amendment already noticed in the *Congressional Record* could still be offered, notwithstanding the five-hour limit.

Bolling's motion infuriated Martin, ostensibly because he had not been informed about it beforehand. Of course, there was no reason for Bolling to have done so, because Martin was pushing his own reform package and not the Select Committee's. Martin then offered a privileged motion that surprised everyone. He moved to kill H. Res. 988 by striking the resolving clause. Martin charged that "fair consideration" would not be given to all resolutions (meaning his own) if the five-hour limit were accepted. Under those circumstances, he believed the whole reform effort should be shelved.

Bolling rose immediately to oppose Martin's motion. He said that thirty-five amendments to the Martin substitute had already been noticed in the *Congressional Record*, which meant more than five hours of debate on Martin alone. Martin would not budge. By voice vote, the House overwhelmingly rejected the motion. Martin then insisted on a recorded vote, which he lost 295 to 39. The vast majority of members of both parties, regardless of their stance on reform, simply did not want debate terminated that way. It would have been an embarrassment for both Democrats and Republicans. Martin, however, continued to oppose closing debate on committee reform through such dilatory devices as quorum calls and insistence that all amendments be read in full. In terms of parliamentary effect, he had joined the camp of the opponents of committee reform.

Bolling then asked Chairman Natcher whether there was anything "unparliamentary" in having his motion considered immediately. Natcher replied there was not. Nevertheless, before Bolling could request a vote, Dingell countered with a motion that took precedence over Bolling's. He moved that the Committee of the Whole rise—a move which, if adopted, would wipe out Bolling's proposal. By voice vote, however, Dingell's motion was defeated, and when he asked for a recorded vote— another delaying tactic—an insufficient number (20 are required) of members supported his request. The five-hour limitation was then adopted 274 to 56, and the Committee of the Whole rose. Thus, the strategy to limit debate, laid out at the Select Committee's morning session, had been successfully implemented on the floor of the House. By all accounts, this was a gain for the proponents of H. Res. 988.

The Sixth Day (October 8). Party leaders had reserved Tuesday for debate on committee reorganization, and as it turned out, it was all that was needed. The session was split in half, in effect, as the House and Senate recessed at 3 P.M. to assemble in joint session to hear President Gerald Ford speak on the state of the nation's economy.[16]

Before the recess, the Committee of the Whole rejected the pending seniority proposal sponsored by Bennett and three others. Four amendments to the Hansen resolution were adopted, however. Near the close of the first two hours of debate, Select Committee member Steiger informed his colleagues that henceforth he would object to all further unanimous consent requests for further time to speak on amendments. Although members are allotted only five minutes to speak for or against an amendment, very often they request unanimous consent to proceed for several additional minutes. Rarely do members object. However, Steiger was becoming concerned that, with numerous amendments still pending, far too much time was consumed debating each one. However, the rules of the House can be circumvented, as Steiger soon found out. The first time he objected was to Bob Eckhardt's request for more time. Dingell, however, raised a point of order that Steiger's objection came too late and was therefore out of order. The chair ruled against Dingell. However, when the next member was recognized, he simply yielded a portion of his five minutes to Eckhardt.

Following President Ford's economic message, the House resumed consideration of committee reform. By this time, many members were impatient to conclude the whole matter. Numerous amendments were still pending to all three resolutions. Once in Committee of the Whole, an amendment was adopted in response to President Ford's speech. Given the climate of concern about the national economy and Ford's request that Congress do something, the House adopted an amendment to require that all committee reports on measures contain a statement on their inflationary impact. Of course, no one knew how that proposition was to be implemented, but it was good politics for the House to respond so quickly to the battle against inflation.

Then the chair asked if there were further amendments to the Hansen substitute. No member sought recognition. Attention then focused on the Martin substitute and its pending Sullivan amendment to restore the Merchant Marine panel. At the time, Sullivan was absent from the floor (she was having dinner in the Capitol with several colleagues).

After waiting patiently for days just in case her amendment came up, the House in less than two minutes rejected her proposal by voice vote. Although one member requested a recorded vote, an insufficient number of legislators supported that request. As a result, the way was now clear for members to amend the Martin substitute. Sullivan was angry for a time because she lost an opportunity to win adoption of her proposal. Regardless of her alliance with the Hansen group, she had still been very interested in attaching her amendment to the Martin plan, just in case that substitute were adopted by the House.

Parliamentarily, the situation was as follows: When members had no further amendments to either the Hansen or Martin substitutes, the House would first proceed to vote on the Martin substitute, as amended. If that was rejected, then the House would vote on Hansen, and, finally, on the Select Committee's proposal. However, if either Martin or Hansen were adopted, the House would never have the chance to amend the substantive features of the Select Committee's plan.

Meanwhile, many members, Democrats and Republicans, approached Bolling on the floor, urging him to bring the whole matter to a close. Not only was it late in the day, but legislators were tired of the whole business. So Bolling took the floor and stated that many legislators would welcome a modification of the five-hour time limitation agreed to the day before. Two hours and nineteen minutes still remained of the five hours. Bolling asked unanimous consent to limit debate on the Hansen substitute to thirty minutes. Minority Whip Leslie Arends objected, however. Bolling explained that his request was designed to accommodate the House and "to see to it that there is reasonable time for the House to amend House Resolution 988, if it survives the test of the Martin and Hansen substitutes." Thus, Bolling renewed his unanimous consent request. This time Republican John Rousselot objected, and caustically noted that if H. Res. 988 was such "landmark" legislation, then the House should "consider all ramifications of the transfer of jurisdiction." Things looked grim for H. Res. 988.

However, there occurred an unexpected event that had the effect of moving the House a gigantic step closer to making a final decision on the whole matter. Chairman Natcher looked around the chamber to see if any member was seeking recognition. No one was, or at least no one moved quickly enough to catch his attention, and he immediately called the question on the adoption of the Martin substitute, which was overwhelmingly rejected by a 319 to 41 vote.

Martin then took the floor and urged his GOP colleagues to vote "no" on the Hansen substitute. Repeating his now-familiar arguments, he said that the Hansen plan was devised by a "partisan" body without anyone on the minority side having any say as to its composition. Hansen member Wayne Hays, notorious for his acidic comments, challenged this and asked sarcastically why Martin had offered a substitute resolution if he was so enamored of H. Res. 988. Martin did not answer. Hays explained how the Hansen substitute benefited Republicans, particularly stressing that ranking GOP subcommittee members would be entitled to one staff aide.

It was now late in the evening, about 10:50, and the chamber was crowded with over three hundred congressmen, most of whom were anxious to go home. Every time a member rose to propose an amendment to Hansen, the chamber echoed with a chorus of cat-calls, hoots, and groans. Members kept shouting "vote!" "vote!" Chairman Natcher tried to maintain order and repeatedly pounded his gavel to silence the chamber, but the sentiment of the House was to finish debate once and for all. Finally, after four amendments were quickly considered and rejected, no one rose to offer another. Dingell apparently had been prevailed upon by several Hansen members not to offer any of his pending amendments. By then, the Hansen group had calculated that they had the votes to win House approval of their plan.

The question, Chairman Natcher said, was now on the adoption of the Hansen substitute. Bolling demanded a roll call vote. As occurred on all key recorded votes, proponents and opponents rushed to and fro talking with their colleagues; they manned the doors leading into the chamber and grabbed members as they entered urging them to vote this way or that; and the respective floor managers offered advice on how to vote if asked by a colleague. As the allotted fifteen minutes for a recorded vote slipped by, with members following the tally on the electronic scoreboards on either side of the chamber, it became clear that the Hansen substitute would be adopted. Apparently the Hansen forces had won over a majority of members to their position. Bolling sat calmly throughout the vote, remarking to an aide that at this stage he simply wanted the democratic process to work. He refrained from soliciting votes among his colleagues, although he did respond to questions. The Hansen substitute was adopted by a vote of 203 to 165. The Committee of the Whole rose, and the House voted 359 to 7 to approve H. Res. 988, now the Hansen substitute. Martin was one of the seven who voted against final passage of the resolution. The debate on committee reform was over.

"Too Far, too Quick"

What the House approved when it adopted the Hansen substitute was a mild dose of committee reorganization. In effect, the House adopted the version of committee reorganization that made the fewest jurisdictional changes. No legislator would have to relinquish a committee, and no committee was abolished. Responsibility for major policy areas (energy, environment, and so forth) remained scattered among several standing committees. Some committees (Ways and Means) were still overworked and others underworked (Standards of Official Conduct). The jurisdictions of several major committees—Appropriations, Armed Services, and Rules—were basically left untouched. The reshuffling represented little change from the status quo, except in a few instances. For example, most transportation matters, except railroads, were shifted to the Public Works and Transportation Committee. In some cases, health care for example, jurisdictions were left more confused than before. On the procedural side, however, the changes appeared to infuse a measure of the needed flexibility into the committee system, particularly through the joint referral device.

Bolling professed not to be discouraged by the result, terming it "just the beginning." He accurately predicted that "there will almost surely be some follow-up" through the Democratic caucus. Hansen member Waggonner perhaps best explained why the Select Committee's plan lost: "It was too drastic, it went too far too quick." An analysis of the vote on the critical Hansen substitute clearly reveals that principal components of both parties opposed H. Res. 988. The vote on Hansen makes clear that the Select Committee either lost, or never had, the support of certain members—freshmen and the GOP, for example—who were assumed to be allies. Moreover, there was only a weak commitment of support from others—including the party leadership, whose alliances never materialized. On the key vote, 152 Democrats and 51 Republicans voted for Hansen; 64 Democrats and 101 Republicans supported Bolling.

The critical vote on the Hansen substitute (which precluded House consideration of H. Res. 988, as reported) can be analyzed in a number of ways, of which the following seem the most important: by the members' party affiliation and seniority in the House; by membership on the various committees; by full committee leadership status (chairmen and ranking minority members); by subcommittee leadership status (subcommittee chairmen and ranking minority members); by party leadership status; and by political ideology.

Perhaps the most conspicuous feature of the voting was its partisan division. On the key floor vote—the October 8 vote in favor of substituting the Hansen version for the Bolling proposal—fully 70 percent of the Democrats supported the Hansen committee while 66 percent of the Republicans opposed Hansen in favor of the original Bolling plan. Key Democrats had, it appeared, been successful in portraying the Select Committee's bipartisan product as favoring the minority Republicans. The charges were virtually impossible to prove or disprove, based as they were on speculation and inference. However, it is at least possible that Democrats, as the majority party, expected reorganization to benefit further the majority rather than having a neutral effect. More importantly, extensive reorganization is bound to affect the majority party more heavily than the minority, because the holders of formal positions of power are in the majority party. The holders of formal committee leadership positions in the House—committee and subcommittee chairmen—overwhelmingly opposed the Bolling reorganization.

Seniority status also affected a member's receptivity to committee reorganization. Support for the Bolling plan was highest among first-termers, steadily declining among members of higher seniority groupings. (See table 3.) This tendency was evident in both political parties.

TABLE 3   *Support for Committee Reorganization, By Party and Seniority*

| | SENIORITY STATUS | | | | | |
| | First Term | | Two to Seven Terms | | Eight or More Terms | |
	Dems	GOPs	Dems	GOPs	Dems	GOPs
For Bolling Plan	41%	77%	36%	64%	16%	56%
Against Bolling Plan	59	23	64	36	84	44
	100%	100%	100%	100%	100%	100%
n =	(29)	(39)	(113)	(96)	(75)	(16)

NOTE: The vote was on adoption of the Hansen substitute to H. Res. 988. *Congressional Record*, 120, 93rd Cong., 2nd sess., October 8, 1974, H10168-69.

Equally, the partisan variable appeared in all seniority groupings. While a majority of freshmen congressmen supported the Select Committee, a majority of freshmen Democrats (seventeen of twenty-nine) favored the Hansen substitute. Support for the Bolling plan was overwhelming among freshmen Republicans, thirty to nine. Members who had served from one to seven terms were split fairly evenly, with a slight majority favoring the Bolling plan. In that seniority grouping, however, Democrats voted heavily against the reorganization. Members with eight or more terms of service—mostly Democrats—overwhelmingly voted for the Hansen substitute, seventy to twenty-one. As Hansen was reported to have remarked, "Too many of us have put too many years into this institution to have it all torn apart and upset by so-called reformers."

Committee membership also seemed to have an impact upon a member's disposition to approve of the reorganization. The Bolling plan fared well with the members of many House committees (see table 4)—in-

TABLE 4   *Support for Committee*
Reorganization, Ranked by Committee Assignment

Committee	Percent	Number
Science and Astronautics	68	28
District of Columbia	68	19
Foreign Affairs	64	33
Veterans' Affairs	57	21
Judiciary	56	35
Banking and Currency	55	31
Government Operations	54	41
Education and Labor	52	31
Interior and Insular Affairs	52	33
Internal Security	50	8
Public Works	49	37
ALL VOTING HOUSE MEMBERS	45	368
Appropriations	43	47
Merchant Marine and Fisheries	38	32
Interstate and Foreign Commerce	38	40
House Administration	36	22
Rules	36	14
Armed Services	31	35
Agriculture	31	26
Budget	28	18
Standards of Official Conduct	25	8
Post Office and Civil Service	24	21
Ways and Means	5	21

NOTE: The figures are percentages of members from each group voting *against* the Hansen substitute to H. Res. 988. *Congressional Record*, 120, 93rd Cong., 2nd sess., October 8, 1975, H10168-69.

cluding such liberal bastions as District of Columbia, Foreign Affairs, Banking and Currency, Government Operations, and Science and Astronautics. As a general rule, it was supported by members from those committees that benefited from the Bolling plan: for example, Science, Foreign Affairs, Interior, and to some extent Public Works. Those committees that lost the most from the shifts favored the Hansen compromise: Ways and Means, Post Office, Commerce, Merchant Marine, and House Administration. There were a few anomalies. For example, the Bolling plan did surprisingly well with Education and Labor Committee members even though much of the protest about it came from its once-reform-minded subcommittee chairmen. However, the bulk of support for the reorganization came from the other side of the aisle where ranking minority member Albert Quie had given vocal support for the Bolling plan and its proposed severing of Education and Labor. Close to 90 percent of the Democrats on Education and Labor, in contrast, supported Hansen against Bolling.

Committee chairmen overwhelmingly disapproved the Select Committee's plan. Thirteen chairmen voted for the Hansen substitute, two voted against Hansen, and seven did not vote.[17] Of Democratic subcommittee chairmen, seventy-seven supported Hansen, twenty-five opposed it, and sixteen did not vote. No subcommittee chairmen on Agriculture, Education and Labor, House Administration, Interstate and Foreign Commerce, Merchant Marine and Fisheries, and Post Office and Civil Service supported the Bolling plan. The majority of subcommittee chairmen on only two committees voted with Bolling: Foreign Affairs and Science and Astronautics. Three subcommittee chairmen on the Banking Committee favored Hansen and three did not. Of the ranking minority subcommittee members, twenty-six supported the Hansen substitute, fifty-nine opposed it, and twenty did not vote. Every ranking minority subcommittee member on Education and Labor, Judiciary, and Veterans' Affairs opposed Hansen.

The leadership vote on the Hansen substitute clearly reveals the depth of Democratic division over the Select Committee's plan, which no doubt doomed H. Res. 988 almost from the start of floor debate (some might argue from the day the committee issued its December 7, 1973, preliminary report). Very few Democratic leaders supported Bolling, and some who did were indeed reluctant supporters. Of the three principal Democratic leaders, Majority Leader O'Neill and Majority Whip McFall both supported the Hansen position. Speaker Albert did not vote. Every deputy whip—John Brademas, James Fulton, Spark M. Matsunaga, and James Wright—supported Hansen. Of the Democratic geographic zone whips, sixteen supported Hansen, two opposed it, and two did not vote. Fourteen members of the Democratic Steering and Policy Committee supported Hansen, five opposed it, and four did not vote. The DSG Executive Committee divided five for Hansen, five against, and two did not vote. In other words, the Bolling report struck most heavily at the middle- and upper-level Democratic leadership, as any committee realignment necessarily would. Those leaders were essential to reorganization, but they were implacably opposed to any tampering with their domains (in some cases, newly won).

Of the three principal Republican leaders, Minority Whip Arends opposed Hansen, Conference Chairman Anderson opposed Hansen, and Minority Leader Rhodes did not vote. Rhodes was reported to be out of town attending a GOP campaign function. Conference Vice Chairman Samuel Devine supported Hansen. Thirteen members of the GOP Policy Committee opposed Hansen, nine supported Hansen, and four did not vote. Four members of the GOP Research Committee supported Hansen, ten opposed it, and two did not vote.

Political ideology also appeared to be related to members' predisposition toward congressional reorganization. The indicator we have employed is a liberalism score derived from *Congressional Quarterly's* "Opposition to Conservative Coalition" score.[18] In both political parties, members who voted for the Bolling plan (that is, who voted against the Hansen substitute) tended to score higher on the liberalism scale than did those who supported the milder reorganization scheme. While the average Bolling supporter fell significantly to the left of the mean scores in both parties, the average Hansen plan voter was somewhat to the right. Profiles for the two political parties (figures 2 and 3) illustrate this phenomenon in a somewhat different fashion. The magnitude of support for the Bolling reorganization was, of course, greater among Republicans than among Democrats. Nevertheless, in both parties the reorganization made its best showing among the more liberal groupings. Conversely, the Hansen plan received its heaviest support among the most conservative members of each party. Burton and several other vocal liberals had tried to portray the Bolling plan as a conservative plot in reformist clothing, but the pattern of support for the two plans suggests that, if anything, the opposite was more nearly the case. Within the Democratic ranks, for example, the Bolling plan just about broke even among the most liberal cadre but had virtually no support at the conservative end of the spectrum. No doubt this ideological phenomenon was closely related to other tendencies: for example, that senior members and those with committee posts to protect opposed the reorganization.

TABLE 5   *Support for Committee Reorganization, By Party and Ideology*

| | Average "Liberalism" Scores | |
	Democrats	Republicans
Bolling Plan Voters	74.8	29.1
Hansen Plan Voters	56.8	16.8
TOTALS	61.4	23.6
n =	(247)	(187)

NOTE: The vote was on adoption of the Hansen substitute to H. Res. 988. *Congressional Record*, 120, 93rd Cong., 2nd sess., October 8, 1974, H10168-69. "Liberalism" rankings for members were drawn from *Congressional Quarterly's* "Opposition to Conservative Coalition" scores, with the figures recomputed to eliminate the effect of absences from the House floor. *Congressional Quarterly Weekly Report* 33, January 25, 1975, pp. 189-194.

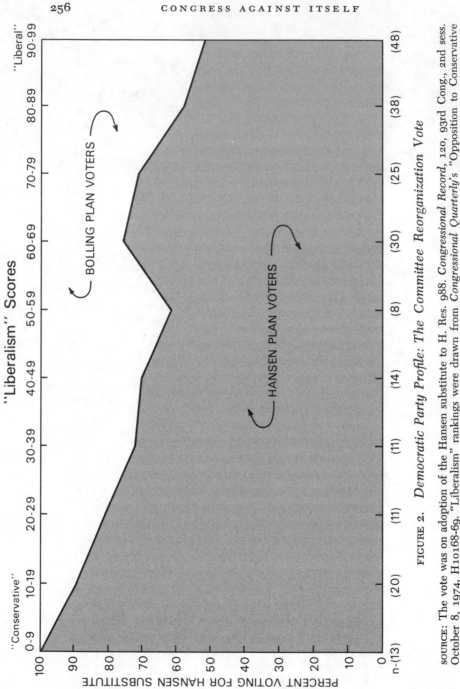

FIGURE 2. *Democratic Party Profile: The Committee Reorganization Vote*

SOURCE: The vote was on adoption of the Hansen substitute to H. Res. 988. *Congressional Record*, 120, 93rd Cong., 2nd sess. October 8, 1974, H10168-69. "Liberalism" rankings were drawn from *Congressional Quarterly's* "Opposition to Conservative Coalition" scores, with the figures recomputed to eliminate the effect of absences from the House floor. *Congressional Quarterly Weekly Report*, 33, January 25, 1975, pp. 189-194.

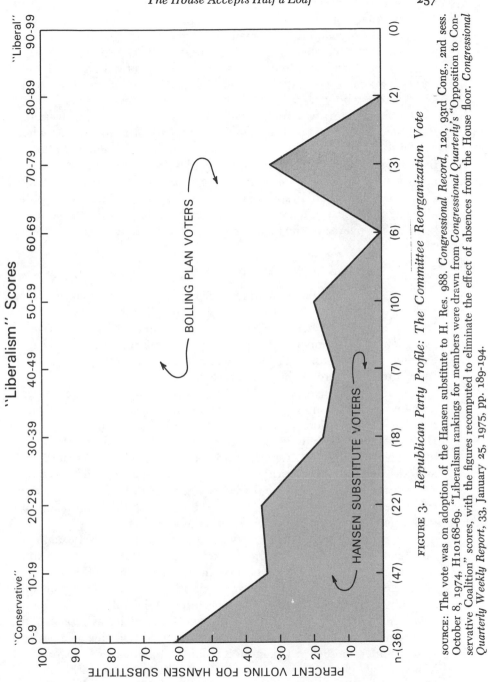

FIGURE 3. *Republican Party Profile: The Committee Reorganization Vote*

SOURCE: The vote was on adoption of the Hansen substitute to H. Res. 988. *Congressional Record*, 120, 93rd Cong., 2nd sess. October 8, 1974, H10168-69. "Liberalism" rankings for members were drawn from *Congressional Quarterly's* "Opposition to Conservative Coalition" scores, with the figures recomputed to eliminate the effect of absences from the House floor. *Congressional Quarterly Weekly Report*, 33, January 25, 1975, pp. 189-194.

Individual legislators' reasons for supporting Bolling or Hansen were, of course, complex and sometimes idiosyncratic. Nearly every major grouping of members split on the question. However, self-interest exerted a powerful force in determining members' votes. In general, the clash over committee reorganization pitted the "haves" against the "have nots." Those who were worried about immediate preservation of their committee domains had ample reason for resisting the reorganization; those who looked forward to gains, or who had little to lose, or who simply could afford to take the institutional "long view," tended to favor the reorganization. To induce power holders to accept changes, it is necessary to convince them that even greater evils will occur if they cling to the status quo. In spite of external pressures and internal turmoil affecting the House, it appeared that Bolling and his colleagues had not been able to overcome the inertia favoring the status quo.

THE SELECT COMMITTEE CLOSES ITS DOORS

Once the debate on committee reform concluded, the Select Committee had little more than two months before it, like the 93rd Congress, automatically terminated. In effect, the Select Committee became a staff operation as its members turned to more pressing matters, namely reelection. Chairman Bolling, of course, approved all staff projects and issued directives through his staff director.

During the final weeks, the three remaining professional staff aides prepared several committee prints for publication: a staff report explaining the provisions of H. Res. 988, as adopted; a monograph on House standing committees; and a compilation of letters and statements to the Select Committee from legislators, interest group representatives, and other individuals. Clerical staff packed the committee's files for storage, returned office supplies to the House, and generally closed down the committee's offices. In addition, the remaining professional and clerical staff began the process of looking for other jobs.

Two events occurred during this period that deserve closer examination. Each demonstrated that the passions unleashed by H. Res. 988 still stirred numerous members. The first involved the long effort by the Select Committee to have its hearings published as a House document. Normally a *pro forma* decision, this issue aroused the animosity of Democrats on the House Administration Committee, which has jurisdiction over printing resolutions. House Administration lost significant responsibility under the Select Committee's plan and gained little in return. Moreover, its chairman was Wayne Hays, who was a member of the Hansen Committee and an adversary of Bolling's. The second event was publication of a "red book" by the Hansen group. The "red book" was a brief summary of H. Res. 988, as adopted. However, its publication by the Democratic group aroused various Republicans, who used it for a short while as a political issue to lambast Democrats.

The Struggle to Reprint the Select Committee's Hearings. In the Select Committee's judgment, its hearings and panel sessions represented a valuable historical record on committee reform. Numerous citizens and scholars across the nation had written to the Select Committee requesting copies. Unfortunately, the Select Committee simply could not meet the demand. As early as April 1, 1974, Bolling wrote to John Brademas, chairman of the Printing Subcommittee of the Committee on House Administration, and requested that several thousand additional copies of the Select Committee's hearings be printed as a public document. As a House document it would be distributed to federal depository libraries throughout the United States, materially enhancing public access to the committee's hearing record.

Normally, printing resolutions are routinely approved by the House Administration Committee. Such was not the case in this instance. House Administration members were strongly opposed to the Select Committee's plan. Hence, no action was taken on Bolling's request despite repeated inquiries. After final House action on H. Res. 988, Bolling spoke with Hays and then wrote him, explaining the "continuing demand from Members and the public" for the indexed hearings. Pointing out that the "original printing of these hearings has been exhausted," he urged Hays to use his "good offices in bringing action on this matter when the Committee again meets."[19]

Then, at the request of House Administration members, Brademas inquired of the Select Committee how much it had spent on printing. Writing in reply, Bolling informed Brademas of the Select Committee's printing costs. He underscored that the Select Committee's "hearing record will represent for the next decade the greatest single treasure trove of thought on the needs and problems of the House," and repeated that "stocks are exhausted and if action can be taken now, at least the committee staff can mail out copies to those waiting in some cases for as much as a year for this material."

Brademas responded to Bolling on November 12, 1974. He candidly revealed the true reason for the delay in processing the printing resolutions:

> Of course, most printing resolutions are not at all controversial but I trust you understand that some members of the full Committee who did not enthusiastically support the recommendations of the Select Committee were equally unwilling to support H. Con. Res. 452 [the printing resolution]![20]

Brademas assured, however, that he would raise the issue again at the next House Administration Committee meeting. Later in the month, the Select Committee's staff director received a telephone call from a staff aide of the Printing Subcommittee who reported that the House Administration Committee had tabled Bolling's resolution.

Those incidents, petty in themselves, underscore the strong enmity generated by the Select Committee's plan, and the lengths to which certain legislators would go to block any proposal emanating from the committee. However, on March 6, 1975, the Committee on House Administration finally reported a resolution, which the House adopted, authorizing the printing of the Select Committee's hearings as a public document. Not until the Select Committee had gone out of existence did it win this skirmish over its public record.

"King Caucus" and the Red Book. Two days after H. Res. 988 was adopted, the Hansen Committee prepared a summary of the changes enacted on October 8.[21] The twenty-nine-page summary was printed by the Government Printing Office and had a bright red cover, but no congressional body was listed on the title sheet as authorized to publish it. Copies were distributed to all Democratic House members.

Two reasons help to explain why publication of the booklet was perceived by some as "scandalous." First, reports or prints of committees typically have white or beige covers. So far as is known, no panel had ever published a document with a bright cover. This was perceived by many legislators, particularly the losers on committee reform, as an affront to their viewpoint and a crass display. Moreover, many legislators were upset over the use of the taxpayers' money to produce a party document. Select Committee Democrats and staff were also irked by publication of the summary, because they had jurisdiction over H. Res. 988 and were preparing to publish their own detailed analysis.

No one seemed to match the anger of GOP Conference Chairman John Anderson, who was incensed by publication of the red book. In an October 16 statement for the *Congressional Record*, Anderson asked the Speaker who had authorized publication of 5,000 copies of the red book. "I can understand the caucus committee wanting to put the best face possible on its status quo power product," Anderson said, "but I simply cannot understand by what authority it can commandeer House funds, not caucus funds, and the Government Printing Office, for the purpose of peddling this partisan pap."[22] Anderson demanded that a full accounting be made regarding authorization of the Hansen Committee's publication. Following Anderson's criticism and complaints from other legislators, the Hansen Committee directed that the red covers be removed from their report.

While all this might be considered political maneuvering, the Hansen summary in fact contained numerous factual errors. For example, it stated that the Speaker was authorized to call early organizational caucus sessions. As a result, for some time Majority Leader O'Neill and his staff believed that O'Neill would have little to do with calling those party sessions and hence looked to the Speaker's office for direction. However, O'Neill's attention was soon focused on it as other staff and legislators pointed out that the language of H. Res. 988 specifically directs the majority leader to call the early organizational caucus. On November 25, 1974, the Select Committee published a detailed 219-page explanation of H. Res. 988, as adopted.

Conclusion

The House of Representatives rejected the widespread changes in its committee system proposed by the Select Committee. Instead, an alternative plan was adopted that did little to redistribute power or realign priorities. The committee system agreed to on October 8, 1974, was little different from that which has been in effect since the passage of the Legislative Reorganization Act of 1946. The struggle for committee reform, however, underscored the importance of the majority party. Democrats hold the key to institutional change. They control all committees and their chairmanships; they control the principal leadership posts; and they have the power to either revitalize the House or to preserve the status quo.

NINE

Epilogue

AFTER the October 8 vote, Richard Bolling attempted to explain why the House had blocked consideration of the Select Committee's resolution. Bolling indicated that adoption of the Hansen substitute resolved about 25 percent of the House's more acute jurisdictional problems. Two factors were paramount in preventing the House from facing up to the balance of its problems, he said. First, the "congressional reform [measure] received little attention in the formative stages" because the Watergate scandal dominated the news. As a result, adequate public support never developed for committee reform. Second, various groups, particularly labor, fought committee reorganization because they would "have lost their strongholds on committee leaders."[1] Other matters also contributed to the rejection of the Select Committee's plan.

THE LESSONS OF HINDSIGHT

First, in drawing up their committee reorganization plan, the Select Committee's members and staff perhaps made a fundamental conceptual miscalculation. They assumed they were dealing with a decision-making structure of standing committees, rather than one whose power had passed in large measure to the subcommittees. The focus on full committees was understandable, in view of their historic primacy in Congress and the attention paid them by the plethora of scholarly writing from Woodrow Wilson to the present. Yet, recent changes inaugurated by the

262

House Democratic caucus in 1971 and 1973 have accelerated a shift from committee government to subcommittee government. Subcommittees have assumed increasing authority and independence in legislative decision making at the expense of the standing committees and their chairmen. The dispersal of power bestowed upon more legislators a power base to nurture and protect. Thus, committee realignment is a more dangerous minefield than ever before. It must accommodate not only the committee chairmen but more than a hundred subcommittee leaders as well. Predictably, a majority of subcommittee chairmen opposed the reorganization proposals in H. Res. 988.

Second, the members and staff who were threatened by H. Res. 988 mobilized outside allies also interested in protecting their domains. Along with executive agencies and clientele groups, many congressional committees and subcommittees are enmeshed in "subgovernments" that monopolize specific policy through mutually beneficial relationships. Jurisdictional realignment threatened some of those relationships. When importuned by their congressional allies, these groups, especially elements of organized labor, fought aggressively to protect their established alliances. The Select Committee underestimated the tenacity of committee-clientele alliances and was unable to stimulate an effective "inside-outside" alliance of its own to overcome the opposition.

A third miscalculation concerned the composition of the Select Committee, particularly the Democratic side. While balanced in certain respects, the committee nevertheless did not adequately reflect the dynamics of the House. All the Democrats were allied closely with Bolling and, what was more important, virtually everyone knew it. That problem might have been alleviated by appointing additional Democrats to the committee, or at least Democrats not so closely associated with the chairman. In retrospect, it might have been prudent to include a member or two from the Hansen group. Doubtless that would have given the Select Committee greater awareness of the political resistance it would confront. Perhaps the Select Committee's final product would have been even less ambitious, but in any legislative struggle major trade-offs must be made. Of course, this reflects a common dilemma: should the work group be *compatible* or should it be *politically representative?* Either way, there are costs. In this instance, the blueprint for reform that emanated from a cohesive work group immediately encountered heavy odds.

If the Select Committee had not reached several other decisions, its chances for overcoming these odds might have been improved. Instead of presenting the Democratic caucus with a finished product in May 1974, it might have been more prudent to have offered a preliminary report. As it was, some Democrats were alienated by a reform plan handed to them as a fait accompli, believing that their input had been ignored by the Select Committee. The Select Committee also placed too much stress upon obtaining a unanimous report. Had the committee identified its internal disagreements on key issues, it might have had greater flexibility in accommodating the divergent viewpoints of legislators and committees. At a minimum, a committee report with dissenting views would have highlighted some of the critical points at issue as well as alternative approaches to resolving those issues.

The Select Committee perceived labor opposition to be monolithic. As a result, the committee did relatively little to take advantage of the weak links in AFL-CIO opposition and to win the strong support of independent unions such as the United Auto Workers. Moreover, the Select Committee did little to neutralize or accommodate the environmental, consumer, and other "good government" groups who opposed certain features of H. Res. 988, as reported. As a result, some reform-minded legislators developed second thoughts about supporting the Select Committee.

The Select Committee might also have presented a substitute resolution of its own during floor debate on committee reform. In this way, the House would at least have spent some time debating the Select Committee's plan rather than concentrating almost entirely on the hastily assembled Hansen product. Upsetting the strategy of the Hansen Committee might have built support for the Select Committee's objectives.

Two other factors were also important in the defeat of the bipartisan resolution: the uproar provoked by jurisdictional realignment and the partisan divisions provoked by the Select Committee's plan. The Select Committee's jurisdictional package threatened too many careers and political relationships to gain passage. So many legislators and staff people, especially Democrats, were adversely affected by the proposed changes that the plan immediately encountered bitter, personal opposition. While members were not particularly well informed about the reorganization plan as a whole, they quickly singled out those provisions affecting their own committee and subcommittee assignments. Those who were adversely affected tended to be more vocal concerning H. Res. 988 than those who stood to gain, whereas people expecting to gain were reticent about speaking out, perhaps fearing to appear self-serving to their colleagues. Thus H. Res. 988 split the Democrats, lost the support of most party leaders, and won few vocal supporters within the House. All too often, the Select Committee was preoccupied with defending its plan against criticisms rather than urging the merits of jurisdictional realignment.

Why did the Select Committee fail to deal effectively with this fundamental aspect of its plan—its effects upon the careers of members and staffs? Ironically, committee assignments and seniority were deliberately avoided because they were considered caucus matters outside the committee's purview. Hence, the Select Committee believed it could ameliorate transitional problems only by including in its resolution a policy statement urging each party to take account of members' jurisdictional losses in making committee assignments for the 94th Congress. Nor could staff members be provided for, although proposed increases in staffing levels made job losses unlikely. Following the principle that staff are directly responsible to committee members, it was decided that no assurances could be given that staff members could transfer along with the jurisdictional matters they had been handling. Nor did the Select Committee wish to guarantee job security to staff members whose committees were to be eliminated or modified. Reassuring language in the committee's report was all that was offered. Needless to say, such reassurances were wholly unsatisfactory to legislators and staff members whose careers might have been affected.

The Select Committee's bipartisan composition (five Democrats and five Republicans) doubtless hindered it from making the necessary adjustments to render the plan more palatable. Bipartisanship was based on the assumption that, to be adopted and implemented, committee reorganization would require the strong backing of both parties. Nevertheless, the bipartisan mode of operation inhibited the Select Committee's members, especially on the Democratic side, from initiating bilateral bargaining with affected members, perhaps calling on party leaders to mediate and offer incentives. Surprisingly, little such bargaining was attempted once the package was reported. The political adjustments were mainly left to the Hansen Committee, which, although experienced in such bargaining, nonetheless lacked the knowledge, resources, or inclination to consider wide-ranging reforms of committee jurisdiction. The Select Committee's bipartisanship also generated unnecessary criticism within the Democratic caucus. Many Democrats were suspicious of a unanimously reported committee plan that appeared to affect them so acutely. In trying to ensure Republican backing for committee reorganization, therefore, the Select Committee lost touch with the majority party whose support was essential for acceptance and ultimately implementation.

THE 94TH CONGRESS: GAINS AND LOSSES

If reform objectives were frustrated in the 93rd Congress, many of them were realized during the 94th Congress. Buoyed by their landslide victories in the fall 1974 elections, the majority Democrats began in the early organizational caucuses authorized by H. Res. 988 to approve a remarkable series of reforms. The objectives of the early party caucuses were to elect party leaders, name the committees on committees, and take whatever "steps necessary to achieve the prompt organization of the Members and Members-elect . . . for the ensuing Congress." The initial caucuses more than lived up to this charge. Several organizational concepts embodied in H. Res. 988 but rejected on the House floor were adopted by the Democratic caucus. Sweeping changes in committee assignment and chairmanship selection procedures were also effected. The early caucuses gained special impetus because the 1974 elections brought to the House ninety-two new members, seventy-five of them Democrats. Not only was the change felt more acutely in the Democratic caucus, but the Democrats controlled the 94th Congress by better than a two-to-one margin: 291 to only 144 Republicans. Again the legacy of Watergate was to shape the workings of Congress.

A major goal of the Select Committee—curbing the power of Ways and Means—was achieved when the Democratic caucus divested that body of its committee assignment function, transferring it to the Democratic Steering and Policy Committee, and when Ways and Means' size was increased from twenty-five to thirty-seven members, so new members could be appointed to alter its conservative complexion. With the influx of new Democrats, the desired reorganization of Ways and Means finally became feasible. The successful assault on the committee, however, was not jurisdictional but procedural.

Another Select Committee objective was realized when the caucus on January 13, 1975, voted to abolish the Committee on Internal Security, and transfer that function to the Judiciary Committee. In this instance, caucus action was quick and effective, with no public discussion or record. Some legislators who voted to retain the Internal Security Committee in October 1974 no doubt changed their vote in caucus. Neither constituents nor groups who wanted the Internal Security Committee left intact had any way of knowing how their congressman voted in caucus. The issue, too, caught many members by surprise, and prevented opponents from mobilizing opposition. And changes voted in caucus that require implementation through the rules of the House produce party-line votes. In this case, House rules for the 94th Congress (prepared by the majority party) made no reference to the Internal Security Committee.

The trend toward restoring the Rules Committee's role as an arm of the leadership, acknowledged by the Select Committee in its jurisdictional review proposal, was abetted in a somewhat different fashion by the early Democratic caucus. Over the years Bolling, third-ranking member of Rules, had contended that Rules should either be made an arm of the leadership or abolished, with its functions assumed by majority-party leaders. On December 3 the caucus adopted a Bolling resolution granting the Speaker authority to nominate, subject to caucus ratification, all Rules Committee Democrats. Another caucus action, introduced by Meeds with Bolling's support, was a resolution prohibiting a chairman of a major committee from serving at the same time as chairman of another standing, select, or joint committee. "It's an amendment that spreads the action and the burden," Meeds explained.[2] The resolution extended earlier caucus actions that opened leadership positions to larger numbers of members and, moreover, conformed with Select Committee recommendations about equalizing members' work loads.

Once the 94th Congress formally convened in January 1975, the Democratic caucus proceded to repeal two features of the Committee Reform Amendments: the minority staffing and proxy voting provisions. When the House adopted H. Res. 988, it increased to thirty per committee the number of professional and clerical committee staff. As the minority party, the Republicans were assured ten of these permanent staff members and a third of all investigatory staff members hired above that number. When the caucus met on January 15, 1975, it decided to alter that arrangement. The permanent staff level would be raised to forty-two, with the majority receiving twenty-six and the minority sixteen. Nevertheless, the minority party's guarantee of one-third of the investigatory staff was dropped. While Republicans were pleased with the sizable increase in permanent staff, they were "disappointed that once again, the minority has been deprived of its full entitlement to committee staff positions."[3] The Democrats had reneged on the one-third formula once before, in 1971 after passage of the Legislative Reorganization Act the year before; this time, the GOP justifiably felt betrayed because the formula had been recommended by the Select Committee and later embraced by Hansen Committee supporters in a bid to woo GOP support.

The argument over proxy voting was even more convoluted. As adopted by the House, H. Res. 988 banned proxy voting altogether in committees and subcommittees. It was widely believed (though never proved) that proxies were especially useful to Democrats, because of their alleged propensity to multiple committee and subcommittee assignments with their attendant schedule conflicts. Whatever the facts of the situation, the Democratic caucus voted to restore proxy voting in a limited fashion. Each committee was authorized to decide whether to permit proxies; if allowed, the proxies must be in writing, given to a specified committee colleague, and used only on specific amendments or on procedural matters. This restored things essentially to the status quo ante, because the 1970 Reorganization Act contained virtually identical language.

If the record of the Democratic caucus in these matters was mixed, its action in the selection of committee chairmen was a clear declaration that the seniority system, though still very much alive, was under caucus control. Under the new procedures adopted by the early caucus, the Steering and Policy Committee recommended that Wayne Hays and Wright Patman not be renominated as chairmen of the House Administration and Banking committees. By slim margins, W. R. Poage and Edward Hébert were renominated to their posts as chairmen of Agriculture and Armed Services. However, the full caucus was in no mood to accept these recommendations passively. It agreed to depose Poage and Hébert but failed to agree on replacements for Hays and Patman. The Steering Committee then recommended that second-ranking Democrats on Agriculture and Armed Services, Thomas Foley and Melvin Price, chair those committees. In addition, the Steering Committee voted to renominate both Hays and Patman to their chairmanships. Politicking was fast and furious. In the end, the caucus met on January 22 and in an historic action voted to replace three chairmen—Poage of Agriculture, Hébert of Armed Services, and Patman of Banking. In their place, the caucus elected Foley, Price, and Henry Reuss. All Appropriations subcommittee chairmen were ratified; but in response to a threatened challenge, one of them, the conservative Jamie Whitten, agreed to relinquish jurisdiction over environmental and consumer protection funding from his subcommittee.[4]

That climaxed a season of intensive structural and procedural change in the House of Representatives. Yet the 94th Congress, despite its new procedures and its outsized Democratic majorities, revealed that the problems of structure and coordination were far from resolved.

The 94th Congress did little to erase doubts concerning the health of its committee-based policy making. Some House committees strengthened by the Bolling-Hansen provisions—most notably, International Relations, Public Works and Transportation, and Science and Technology—demonstrated new vigor in implementing their broadened mandates. Nevertheless, in many cases, committee biases and clientelism, coupled with the pervasive decentralization of committee operations, yielded divided and incoherent responses to pressing issues. In the energy and environmental fields, jurisdictional disputes and procedural entanglements compounded tangible political controversies to the point that congressional Democrats were often compelled to concede that little or no action was possible. In the Senate, Majority Leader Mike Mansfield conceded that Congress was unlikely to grapple with the energy question until jurisdictions had been consolidated.[5] The House Ways and Means Committee originated the Energy Conservation and Conversion Act only because, as one committee member said, "we have some of the aspects of the President's program . . . dealing with quotas, imports, and all the rest of it."[6] At that very same moment, seven other House committees were advancing bills dealing with basic aspects of the energy problem.

The new joint referral device, authorized by H. Res. 988, was used extensively by Speaker Albert but with mixed results. During 1975, more than seven hundred bills and resolutions were referred to more than one standing committee, with one select ad hoc committee created.[7] However, some congressmen complained that instead of promoting cooperation and flexibility the procedure produced wasteful duplication of effort.

Such structural problems unquestionably contributed to the embarrassing difficulties that leaders encountered in performing their tasks. In a remarkable letter issued to all House committee chairmen only six months after Congress convened, Speaker Albert confessed that the 94th Congress would be unable to enact "programs and policies that will return us to full employment, economic prosperity and durable social peace and progress." He implored committee chairmen to devise "something practical—politically, economically, socially and psychologically feasible," for consideration by the next Congress.[8]

A natural reflex was to blame the leaders as individuals for what was happening. Speaker Albert was criticized, and at least one member suggested that he be replaced. However, it was questionable whether a change in leadership personnel would significantly affect the policy outputs of the House. A key ingredient in leadership is followership, which has been missing in the House at least since the days of Speaker Sam Rayburn, and, some would say, since Joseph Cannon. Electing another Speaker would no doubt produce a new leadership style and perhaps result in some peripheral changes in the functioning of the House. It is doubtful whether any significant change would occur in the House's capacity to handle complex issues.

Some members had second thoughts about the House's rejection of the Bolling plan's jurisdictional restructuring. At least in the energy field, the House's dilemma might have been ameliorated had jurisdiction been consolidated in an energy and environment committee as the Select Committee had proposed. "Let me say," remarked Bolling's colleague B. F. Sisk during a 1975 Rules Committee meeting:

> I am sitting here thinking to myself. I didn't support Mr. Bolling nearly as strongly as I should have on his reorganization proposal, and I am becoming more and more aware of it, and in public, Dick, I want to apologize.[9]

Bob Eckhardt, chairman of the Democratic Study Group during the 94th Congress, conceded that he "will now say publicly that I will have to revise it, my opposition to committee reform, considering what is happening here" on energy legislation.[10] Thomas Rees declared, "One reason [the House] made a disaster out of the energy field, both in the petroleum bill last year and the natural gas bill this year, is this problem of [over-lapping] jurisdiction."[11] As a result, junior and senior congressmen called for further jurisdictional reform. For example, Teno Roncalio recommended in 1976 that the House "take up a strong reorganization bill to reduce the number of committees" and to require members to "confine [themselves] to one committee."[12]

In all fairness, it must be pointed out that Congress' difficulties in grappling with such complex issues as energy involve more than committee structure or procedure. "Congress in order to be effective needs consensus," Thomas Foley observed, "and it is clear that on many issues there is no consensus."[13] Lacking clear cues as to how to proceed, legislators will do what comes naturally and delay action, even though their inaction may imperil the nation. Precipitous action in the absence of a consensus could bring even more acute peril. The energy imbroglio is indicative of a new generation of issues that cannot be resolved simply by spending more money or setting up another federal program. These are issues of resource constraints, which ultimately require legislators to ask citizens to give up things rather than to promise them more. The "distributive politics" of the future will involve scarcity rather than abundance—a perilous prospect for elected officials. Legislators are, after all, politicians as well as policy specialists. They are reluctant to take positions on difficult issues that might jeopardize their standing with their constituents. Many of the complex and intertwined issues of our day are volatile problems on which consensus has not coalesced—if indeed (considering the costs that will be involved) that will ever occur. Consequently, there is more to effective policy formulation than committee reorganization, or in fact any type of structural alterations.

What do these Changes Mean?

The 1970-1975 period was clearly an era of congressional change, perhaps not equalled at any time since the downfall of Speaker Cannon. House committee reform was part of a complex of changes designed to deal with external and internal challenges to congressional influence. What did all this change add up to? How will it alter the way in which Congress deals with public problems? There are no simple answers. We can only offer tentative insights. Moreover, it is realistic to speak in terms of possibilities or probabilities rather than certainties. Nevertheless, there are several generalizations that can be advanced about the recent struggles for structural and procedural change.

To those who minimize Congress' ability or capacity for structural innovation, the events of the 1970-1975 period offer at least partial refutation. In response to external pressures and internal factional shifts, Congress has undergone what can only be called major renovations.

First, Congress has become more democratic, more responsive, more accountable, and more open to public view. The emphasis on public committee hearings and markups, including conference sessions, and open party caucuses, has increased the visibility of the decision-making process. There are also proposals to televise House and Senate floor sessions. All this should strengthen the representative character of Congress. In addition, the changes should promote more public understanding, perhaps even trust, of Congress and lead to greater legislative accountability.

Second, power in the House has been further diffused ("spreading the action") by strengthening the autonomy of subcommittees and reducing that of committee chairmen. Greater dispersion means more member participation in policy making and greater citizen access to panels where important decisions are made. It also means the probable slowing down of the decision-making process. "Spreading the action" means that more congressmen will be consulted before anything approaching a coordinated or comprehensive policy or program develops.

Third, this diffusion of power has weakened such traditional House norms as apprenticeship and specialization. (Similar trends are even further advanced in the Senate.) Junior members are no longer expected to follow Speaker Sam Rayburn's advice: "To get along, go along." Freshmen have won privileges in recent years that few of their status enjoyed in earlier Congresses.

Fourth, caucuses have evolved as major instruments of party policy making. This occurred principally because there were congressmen who were receptive to change and organized to bring it about (the Democratic Study Group deserves much of the credit here), who saw in the caucus a way of achieving more influence for themselves, and who were challenged by aggressive Presidents to respond to exertions of executive authority. Liberal Democrats favored the caucus rather than the House floor as their forum of change because there they had the votes to adopt reforms benefiting their faction of the party. Members are now accountable and responsible to their caucus. Committee chairmen are elected by the caucus and may be removed if they abuse their prerogatives. No longer, then, should oligarchical chairmen forestall consideration of important legislation within their committee's jurisdiction. As Phil Burton, caucus chairman during the 94th Congress, stated, committee chairmen "now know that they cannot act independently of the will of a majority of the Democrats in the House, and bottle up key legislation."[14] Another viewpoint was articulated by Wilbur Mills, who said that no chairman "can perform looking back over his shoulder" at the Democratic caucus.[15]

Fifth, the custom of seniority has lost its rigidity, although it is still an important criterion for determining who will gain influence in the legislative process and indeed has been broadened to give regularity to subcommittee selection procedures. Ironically, seniority has become flexible regarding rank on the full committee but has become almost inviolable for subcommittees. Now seniority on the full committee is the criterion to determine which member will head what subcommittee.

Finally, and somewhat paradoxically, the Speaker gained significant new powers at a time of further diffusion. His chairmanship of the Steering and Policy Committee, his party's committee on committees, gives him a significant voice in determining who goes onto what committee; his authority to refer measures to more than one committee could inhibit committee "pigeonholing" of measures and facilitate the reporting of legislation he favors; and his ability to nominate all Democrats to the Rules Committee will enhance his control over the consideration of measures on the House floor. All in all, these new devices have the potential to strengthen significantly the Speaker's role in the legislative process, particularly his ability to coordinate the consideration of complex legislation.

Although these developments have eased certain inconsistencies that have plagued the House for the past generation or so, they have incurred —as all changes do—significant costs of their own. Just at a time when the majority party has nurtured the caucus as an instrument to curb some of the worst centrifugal tendencies of the seniority principle, it has taken decentralization to new lengths by creating and institutionalizing numerous independent subcommittees. "Spreading the action" to subcommittees may have further diffused power when many legislators believe centralization is needed. It is not extravagant to suggest that some day the caucus will have to deal with the fractionalized system it has nurtured, if the party is ever to sustain a serious policy-making role. Because so many legislators have a stake in decentralization, it may have the unexpected effect of inhibiting further significant reforms, particularly if the proposed changes are in the direction of strengthening party leaders at the expense of committee decentralization.

Moreover, no one has yet been able to control the caucus, or has assumed leadership of factions of the party. The caucus during the 94th Congress often seemed subject to direction by shifting coalitions and factions. It was "participatory democracy" run rampant. Whether the Speaker, the caucus chairman, or the Steering and Policy Committee has enough power to organize and to lead it over a sustained period is doubtful. Further, a few months after the heady reforms we have described, many Democrats were questioning the role of their caucus. Should it focus on procedural or substantive issues, or both?

A curious incongruity should be noted. Party institutions like the Democratic caucus have been revitalized when the two national parties appear to be on the decline. The long-run attachment of Americans to their parties, which undergirds the stability of the two-party system, seems to be loosening, as witness both the large increase in the number of independents and the rise in split-ticket voting. Members elected from a fragmented party environment are unlikely to have a strong commitment in Congress to either their party or party leaders. They are not willing to risk political defeat for the sake of party loyalty. Party institutions, on the other hand, have fulfilled several useful purposes. They have enhanced the legislative position of many members through adoption of various reforms. Equally important, they have facilitated the enactment of policies and programs favored by the majority.

Vigorous congressional leadership, therefore, is inhibited not only by the decentralized power points that jealously guard their prerogatives, but also by the lack of a firm base upon which to build leadership power. The political parties are flimsy foundations with which to erect a viable system of legislative leadership. The party has rarely been an overbearing force in the national legislature. For all the rhetoric about responsible parties, the recent Democratic caucus reforms have yet to prove themselves as something more than the instruments of factional advance by the liberal bloc. Moreover, as other entities have come to perform those functions historically monopolized by the parties, formal party structure is in a state of near collapse in many local areas of the country. Leadership with a partisan base is therefore highly problematic.

It is conceivable that a congressional leadership could develop that is more institutional than partisan in character. Although leaders will doubtless continue to be selected by the party caucuses, their base of influence need not be restricted to the caucus or conference. Enhanced control of internal institutional resources—including scheduling and the flow of information—could provide the springboard for a revitalized leadership on Capitol Hill. Such leaders could solidify their position by means of external visibility and media recognition as spokesmen for the congressional viewpoint. True, no congressional leader in modern times has fulfilled such a role, but the potentiality is there.

If such leadership is to succeed in restoring the visibility and prestige of Congress, it would have to coordinate the specialized committees without hampering their ability to provide "technical mastery" of the increasingly complex and interrelated issues of public society. Division of labor and committee specialization have been major ingredients in what success Congress has achieved in combating the antiparliamentary tendencies of our era. Thus, no leadership that seeks to strengthen Congress can cripple the committee system. As we have indicated, the committee system itself is nevertheless threatened by an excess of subcommittee proliferation, and there is need for coordination in assigning work load and scheduling business. It is there that vigorous leadership can make a contribution.

It appears, therefore, that procedural and structural reforms cannot guarantee improvements in the legislative branch. An equally important consideration is incentives for congressmen to take whatever actions are required to improve Congress' record and reputation. Without the will to formulate public policies, to hold Presidents accountable, or to keep pace with contemporary challenges, institutional reforms by themselves cannot ensure the continued vitality of Congress. As George Mahon, chairman of the House Appropriations Committee, once said, "We need more reform not of procedures and methods, we need more reform of the will."[16] And as seasoned observers of American politics will agree, this can only arise when citizens hold their elected officials strictly accountable not only for policy initiatives but for the institutional forms through which those policies can be processed. In this as in so many other ways, we get just about the kind of government we deserve.

SELECT BIBLIOGRAPHY

I. General Works on the Legislative Process

Bailey, Stephen K. *The New Congress.* New York: St. Martin's Press, 1966.

———. *Congress Makes A Law.* New York: Columbia University Press, 1960.

Bendiner, Robert. *Obstacle Course on Capitol Hill.* New York: McGraw-Hill, 1964.

Berman, Daniel M. *In Congress Assembled: The Legislative Process in the National Government.* New York: Macmillan, 1964.

Bibby, John and Davidson, Roger. *On Capitol Hill: Studies in the Legislative Process.* 2d ed. Hinsdale, Illinois: The Dryden Press, Inc., 1972.

De Grazia, Alfred, ed. *Congress: The First Branch of Government.* Washington: American Enterprise Institute for Public Policy Research, 1966.

Froman, Lew A., Jr. *The Congressional Process: Strategies, Rules, and Procedures.* Boston: Little, Brown and Co., 1967.

Galloway, George B. *The Legislative Process in Congress.* New York: Thomas Y. Crowell, 1953.

Griffith, Ernest and Valeo, Francis. *Congress: Its Contemporary Role.* 5th ed. New York: New York University Press, 1975.

Gross, Bertram M. *The Legislative Struggle.* New York: McGraw Hill, 1953.

Jewell, Malcolm and Patterson, Samuel. *The Legislative Process in the United States.* 2d ed. New York: Random House, 1973.

Keefe, William and Ogul, Morris. *The American Legislative Process: Congress and the States.* 3d ed. Englewood Cliffs, New Jersey: Prentice-Hall, 1973.

Mayhew, David. *Congress: The Electoral Connection*. New Haven: Yale University Press, 1974.

Ornstein, Norman, ed. *Congress in Change: Evolution and Reform*. New York: Praeger, 1975.

Rieselbach, LeRoy N. *Congressional Politics*. New York: McGraw-Hill, 1973.

Ripley, Randall B. *Congress: Process and Policy*. New York: W. W. Norton and Co., 1975.

Saloma, John. *Congress and the New Politics*. Boston: Little, Brown and Co., 1969.

Vogler, David. *The Politics of Congress*. Boston: Allyn and Bacon, 1974.

Wilson, Woodrow. *Congressional Government*. New York: Meridian Books edition, 1956.

II. THE COMMITTEE SYSTEM

General

Cooper, Joseph. "Jeffersonian Attitudes Toward Executive Leadership and Committee Development in the House of Representatives, 1789–1829." *Western Political Quarterly*. (March 1965), pp. 45–63.

_____. *The Origins of the Standing Committees and the Development of the Modern House*. Rice University Studies. (Summer 1970), Vol. 56, No. 3.

Eulau, Heinz. "The Committees in a Revitalized Congress." In Alfred de Grazia, ed., *Congress: The First Branch of Government*. Washington: American Enterprise Institute for Public Policy Research, 1966.

Fenno, Richard F., Jr. *Congressmen in Committees*. Boston: Little, Brown and Co., 1973.

Galloway, George B. "Development of the Committee System in the House of Representatives." *American Historical Review*. (October 1959), pp. 17–30.

Goodwin, George. *The Little Legislatures*. Amherst: University of Massachusetts Press, 1970.

Huitt, Ralph K. "The Congressional Committee: A Case Study." *American Political Science Review*. (June 1954), pp. 340–365.

McConachie, Lauros. *Congressional Committees*. New York: Thomas Y. Crowell, 1898.

Morrow, William L. *Congressional Committees*. New York: Charles Scribner's Sons, 1969.

Muskie, Edmund S. "Committees and Subcommittees in the Senate." In Nathaniel S. Preston, ed., *The Senate Institution*. New York: Van Nostrand Reinhold Co., 1969.

Nevins, Allan. "The Development of the Committee System in the American Congress." *Parliamentary Affairs*. (Winter 1949), pp. 136–146.

Robinson, George L. "The Development of the Senate Committee System." Unpublished Ph.D. dissertation. New York University, 1955.

Committee Assignments

Bullock, Charles. "Apprenticeship and Committee Assignments in the House of Representatives." *Journal of Politics*. (August 1970), pp. 717–720.

_____. "Freshmen Committee Assignments and Re-election in the United

States House of Representatives." *American Political Science Review.* (September 1972), pp. 996–1007.

Davidson, Roger H. "Representation and Congressional Committees." *The Annals.* (January 1974), pp. 48–62.

Gawthrop, Lewis C. "Changing Membership Patterns in House Committees." *American Political Science Review.* (June 1966), pp. 366–373.

Huitt, Ralph K. "The Morse Committee Assignment Controversy: A Study in Senate Norms." *American Political Science Review.* (June 1957), pp. 313–329.

Jewell, Malcolm and Chiu, Chi-Hung. "Membership Movement and Committee Attractiveness in the U.S. House of Representatives." *American Journal of Political Science.* (May 1974), pp. 433–441.

Malbin, Michael J. "Congress Report/New Democratic Procedures Affect Distribution of Power." *National Journal Reports,* December 14, 1974, pp. 1881–1890.

Masters, Nicholas. "Committee Assignments in the House of Representatives." *American Political Science Review.* (June 1961), pp. 345–357.

Rohde, David and Shepsle, Kenneth. "Democratic Committee Assignments in the House of Representatives: Strategic Aspects of a Social Choice Process." *American Political Science Review.* (September 1973), pp. 889–905.

Swanson, Wayne R. "Committee Assignments and the Nonconformist Legislator: Democrats in the U.S. Senate." *Midwest Journal of Political Science.* (February 1969), pp. 84–94.

III.   Studies of Individual Committees

The Agriculture Committees

Jones, Charles O. "Representation in Congress: The Case of the House Agriculture Committee." *American Political Science Review.* (June 1961), pp. 358–367.

A Brief History of the Committee on Agriculture and Forestry, United States Senate and Landmark Agricultural Legislation, 1825–1970. Senate Document No. 91–107, 91st Cong., 2nd sess. Washington: Government Printing Office, 1970.

The Appropriations Committees

Fenno, Richard F., Jr. *The Power of the Purse: Appropriations Politics in Congress.* Boston: Little, Brown and Co., 1966.

Horn, Stephen. *Unused Power: The Work of the Senate Committee on Appropriations.* Washington: The Brookings Institution, 1970.

Kirst, Michael. *Government without Passing Laws.* Chapel Hill: University of North Carolina Press, 1967.

Pressman, Jeffrey L. *House vs. Senate: Conflict in the Appropriations Process.* New Haven: Yale University Press, 1966.

The Armed Services Committees

Dawson, Raymond. "Congressional Innovation and Intervention in Defense Policy: Legislative Authorization of Weapons Systems." *American Political Science Review.* (March 1962), pp. 42–57.

Gordon, Bernard K. "The Military Budget: Congressional Phase." *Journal of Politics*. (November 1961), pp. 689–710.

Hersh, Seymour. "The Military Committees." *The Washington Monthly*. (April 1969), pp. 84–92.

Kolodziej, Edward A. *The Uncommon Defense and Congress, 1945–1963*. Columbus: Ohio State University Press, 1966.

Stephens, Herbert W. "The Role of the Legislative Committees in the Appropriations Process: A Study Focused on the Armed Services Committees." *Western Political Quarterly*. (March 1971), pp. 146–162.

The Banking Committees

Bibby, John and Davidson, Roger. *On Capitol Hill*. New York: Holt, Rinehart and Winston, 1967, chapter 5.

Norton, Bruce. "The Committee on Banking and Currency as a Legislative Subsystem of the House of Representatives." Unpublished Ph.D. dissertation. Syracuse University, 1970.

Salaman, Lester, director. *The Money Committees: A Study of the House Banking and Currency Committee and the Senate Banking, Housing and Urban Affairs Committee*. New York: Grossman Publishers, 1975.

The Budget Committees

Finley, James J. "The 1974 Congressional Initiative in Budget Making." *Public Administration Review*. (May/June 1975), pp. 270–278.

Havemann, Joel. "Budget Report/Committees Seek Stimulus but Call for Spending Curbs." *National Journal Reports*, April 5, 1975, pp. 495–508.

Schick, Allen. "The Battle of the Budget." *Proceedings of the Academy of Political Science*. Vol. 32, No. 1, 1975, pp. 51–70.

Wildavsky, Aaron. *The Politics of the Budgetary Process*. 2d ed. Boston: Little, Brown and Co., 1974.

The Commerce Committees

Price, David E., director. *The Commerce Committees: A Study of the House and Senate Commerce Committees*. New York: Grossman Publishers, 1975.

_____. *Who Makes the Laws?* Cambridge, Massachusetts: Schenkman Publishing Co., 1972.

The District Committees

O'Keefe, Dennis J. "Decision-Making in the House Committee on the District of Columbia." Unpublished Ph.D. dissertation. University of Maryland, 1969.

The Education Committees

Eidenberg, Eugene and Morey, Roy D. *An Act of Congress: The Legislative Process and the Making of Education Policy*. New York: W. W. Norton, 1969.

Fenno, Richard F., Jr. "The House of Representatives and Federal Aid to Education." In Robert L. Peabody and Nelson Polsby, eds., *New Perspectives on the House of Representatives*. Chicago: Rand McNally Co., 1963.

Committee on Labor and Public Welfare, 1869–1969. Senate Document No.

90–108, 90th Cong., 2nd sess. Washington: Government Printing Office, 1970.

Murray, Michael. "The House Education-Labor Committee and the 1967 Poverty Controversy: A Study of Congressional Avoidance." Unpublished Ph.D. dissertation. University of Illinois, 1969.

The Foreign Relations Committees

Acheson, Dean. "Arthur Vandenberg and the Senate." In Nelson Polsby, ed., *Congressional Behavior.* New York: Random House, 1971.

Dennison, Eleanor. *The Senate Foreign Relations Committee.* Palo Alto: Stanford University Press, 1942.

Farnsworth, David N. *The Senate Committee on Foreign Relations.* Urbana: University of Illinois Press, 1961.

Gould, James W. "The Origins of the Senate Committee on Foreign Relations." *Western Political Quarterly.* (September 1959), pp. 670–682.

Kalb, Marvin. "Doves, Hawks, and Flutterers in the Foreign Relations Committee." *New York Times Magazine,* November 19, 1967, pp. 56ff.

Maffre, John. "Congressional Report/New Leaders, Staff Changes Stimulate House Foreign Affairs Committee." *National Journal Reports,* June 19, 1971, pp. 1314–1322.

Robinson, James A. *Congress and Foreign Policy Making.* Homewood, Illinois: Dorsey Press, 1962.

Sparkman, John J. "The Role of the Senate in Determining Foreign Policy." In Nathaniel S. Preston, ed., *The Senate Institution.* New York: Van Nostrand Reinhold Co., 1969.

Westphal, Albert C. F. *The House Committee on Foreign Affairs.* New York: Columbia University Press, 1942.

The Government Operations Committees

Henderson, Thomas A. *Congressional Oversight of Executive Agencies: A Study of the House Committee on Government Operations.* Gainesville: University of Florida Press, 1970.

The Interior Committees

Magida, Arthur, director. *The Environment Committees: A Study of the House and Senate Interior, Agriculture and Science Committees.* New York: Grossman Publishers, 1975.

Wagner, James R. "Interior Subcommittees Move Slowly on Legislation to Reform Public Lands Policy." *National Journal Reports,* August 21, 1971, pp. 1768–1773.

The Internal Security Committee

Carr, Robert K. *The House Committee on Un-American Activities, 1949–1950.* Ithaca: Cornell University Press, 1952.

Goodman, Walter. *The Committee.* New York: Farrar, Strauss, and Giroux, 1968.

————. "The Committee Revisited." *The Washington Monthly.* (July 1969), pp. 50–54.

Kaplan, Lewis. "The House Un-American Activities Committee and Its Opponents: A Study in Congressional Dissonance." *Journal of Politics*. (August 1968), pp. 647–671.

The Judiciary Committees

Farrelly, David G. "The Senate Judiciary Committee: Qualifications of Members." *American Political Science Review*. (June 1943), pp. 469–475.

Lacy, Donald P. and Philip Martin, "Amending the Constitution: The Bottleneck in the Judiciary Committees." *Harvard Journal on Legislation*. (May 1972), pp. 666–693.

Schuck, Peter H., director. *A Study of the House and Senate Judiciary Committees*. New York: Grossman Publishers, 1975.

The Public Works Committees

Ferejohn, John A. *Pork Barrel Politics: Rivers and Harbors Legislation, 1947–1968*. Palo Alto: Stanford University Press, 1974.

Murphy, James T. "Political Parties and the Porkbarrel: Party Conflict and Cooperation in House Public Works Committee Decision Making." *American Political Science Review*. (March 1974), pp. 169–185.

The Committee on Rules

Fox, Douglas and Clapp, Charles H. "The House Rules Committee's Agenda-Setting Function, 1961–1968." *Journal of Politics*. (May 1970), pp. 440–443.

Jones, Charles O. "Joseph G. Cannon and Howard W. Smith: An Essay on the Limits of Leadership in the House of Representatives." *Journal of Politics*. (September 1968), pp. 617–646.

Peabody, Robert L. "The Enlarged Rules Committee." In Robert L. Peabody and Nelson W. Polsby, eds., *New Perspectives on the House of Representatives*. 2d ed. Chicago: Rand McNally, 1969.

Robinson, James A. *The House Rules Committee*. Indianapolis: Bobbs-Merrill Co., 1963.

Smith, Howard. "In Defense of the Rules Committee." In Joseph S. Clark, ed., *Congressional Reform: Problems and Prospects*. New York: Thomas Y. Crowell, 1965.

The Committee on Small Business

Vinyard, Dale. "The Congressional Committee on Small Business: Pattern of Legislative Committee-Executive Agency Relations." *Western Political Quarterly*. (September 1968), pp. 391–399.

The Committees on Space

Poke, Carl. "Congress and Outer Space." Unpublished Ph.D. dissertation. University of Pittsburgh, 1968.

The Committee on Revenue

Furlong, P. J. "Origins of the House Committee on Ways and Means." *William and Mary Quarterly*. (October 1968), pp. 587–604.

Manley, John F. *The Politics of Finance: The House Committee on Ways and Means*. Boston: Little, Brown and Co., 1970.

Spohn, Richard, director. *The Revenue Committees: A Study of the House*

Ways and Means and Senate Finance Committees and the House and Senate Appropriations Committees. New York: Grossman Publishers, 1975.

IV.   OTHER COMMITTEES

Conference Committees

Galloway, George B. "The Third House of Congress." *Congressional Record* 101, 84th Cong., 1st sess., March 8, 1955, A1552–A1557.

Gore, Albert. "The Conference Committee: Congress' Final Filter." *The Washington Monthly* (June 1971), pp. 43–48.

McCown, Ada C. *The Congressional Conference Committee.* New York: Columbia University Press, 1927.

Paletz, David L. "Influence in Congress: An Analysis of the Nature and Effects of Conference Committees Utilizing Case Studies of Poverty, Traffic Safety, and Congressional Redistricting Legislation." Unpublished Ph.D. dissertation. University of California, Los Angeles, 1970.

Pressman, Jeffrey L. *House vs. Senate: Conflict in the Appropriations Process.* New Haven, Connecticut: Yale University Press, 1966.

Rogers, Lindsay. "Conference Committee Legislation." *The North American Review.* (March 1922), pp. 300–307.

Steiner, Gilbert. *The Congressional Conference Committee.* Urbana: University of Illinois Press, 1951.

Vogler, David J. *The Third House: Conference Committees in the U.S. Congress.* Evanston: Northwestern University Press, 1971.

————. "Flexibility in the Congressional Seniority System." *Polity.* (Summer 1970), pp. 494–507.

————. "Patterns of One-House Dominance in Congressional Conference Committees." *Midwest Journal of Political Science.* (May 1970), pp. 303–320.

Joint Committees

Green, Harold and Rosenthal, Alan. *Government of the Atom: The Integration of Powers.* New York: Atherton, 1963.

Manley, John F. "Congressional Staff and Public Policy-Making: The Joint Committee on Internal Revenue Taxation." *Journal of Politics.* (November 1968), pp. 1046–1067.

Oleszek, Walter J. "House-Senate Relations: Comity and Conflict." *The Annals.* (January 1974), pp. 75–86.

Subcommittees

French, Burton L. "Sub-Committees of Congress." *American Political Science Review.* (February 1915), pp. 68–92.

Goodwin, George. "Subcommittees: The Miniature Legislatures of Congress." *American Political Science Review.* (September 1962), pp. 596–604.

"House Reforms Enhance Subcommittees' Power." *Congressional Quarterly Weekly Report,* November 8, 1975, pp. 2407–2412.

Select or Special Committees

Vardys, V. Stanley. "Select Committees of the House of Representatives."

Midwest Journal of Political Science. (August 1962), pp. 247–265.

Waters, Bertram. "The Politics of Hunger: Forming a Senate Select Committee." In Sven Groennings and Jonathan Hawley, eds., *To Be A Congressman: The Promise and the Power.* Washington: Acropolis Books, 1973, pp. 151–168.

Party Committees

Bone, Hugh A. *Party Committees and National Politics.* Seattle: University of Washington Press, 1958.

Humbert, W. H. "The Democratic Joint Policy Committee." *American Political Science Review.* (June 1932), pp. 552–554.

Jewell, Malcolm. "The Senate Republican Policy Committee and Foreign Policy." *Western Political Quarterly.* (December 1959), pp. 966–980.

Stewart, John G. "Central Policy Organs in Congress." *Proceedings of the Academy of Political Science.* Vol. 32, No. 1, 1975, pp. 20–33.

V. COMMITTEE STAFF

Cochrane, James D. "Partisan Aspects of Congressional Committee Staffing." *Western Political Quarterly.* (June 1964), pp. 338–348.

Fox, Harrison W. and Hammond, Susan Webb. "The Growth of Congressional Staffs." *Proceedings of the Academy of Political Science.* Vol. 32, No. 1, 1975, pp. 112–114.

Patterson, Samuel C. "The Professional Staffs of Congressional Committees." *Administrative Science Quarterly.* (March 1970), pp. 22–37.

Price, David E. "Professionals and 'Entrepreneurs': Staff Orientations and Policy Making on Three Senate Committees." *Journal of Politics.* (May 1971), pp. 316–336.

VI. SENIORITY

Celler, Emanuel. "The Seniority Rule in Congress." *Western Political Quarterly.* (March 1961), pp. 160–167.

Goodwin, George. "The Seniority System in Congress." *American Political Science Review.* (June 1959), pp. 412–436.

Hinckley, Barbara. *The Seniority System in Congress.* Bloomington: Indiana University Press, 1971.

Malbin, Michael J. "Congress Report/House Democrats Oust Senior Members from Power." *National Journal Reports,* January 25, 1975, pp. 129–134.

Polsby, Nelson, Gallagher, Miriam, and Rundquist, Barry Spencer. "The Growth of the Seniority System in the U.S. House of Representatives." *American Political Science Review.* (September 1969), pp. 787–807.

NOTES

Key to Documents of the
Select Committee on Committees

Several documents published by the Select Committee on Committees are
cited frequently in the foregoing chapters and are thus designated in the foot-
notes by brief titles. The titles and full citations are as follows:

Committee Monographs. U.S. House of Representatives, Select Committee on
Committees, *Monographs on the Committees of the House of Representatives* (93rd Congress, 2nd session, December 13, 1974), committee print.

Draft Report. U.S. House of Representatives, Select Committee on Committees, *Committee Structure and Procedures of the House of Representatives,*
Working Draft of Report (93rd Congress, 1st session, December 7, 1973),
committee print.

Final Report. U.S. House of Representatives, Select Committee on Committees, *Committee Reform Amendments of 1974,* H. Rept. 93–916 (93rd
Congress, 2nd session, March 21, 1974).

Hearings. U.S. House of Representatives, Select Committee on Committees,
Committee Organization in the House (93rd Congress, 1st session, 1973),
3 vols., committee print. Reprinted as H. Doc. 94–187 (94th Congress, 1st
session).

Letters and Statements. U.S. House of Representatives, Select Committee on
Committees, *Letters and Statements from Members, Groups, and Indi-
viduals regarding the Work of the Select Committee on Committees* (93rd
Congress, 2nd session, December 27, 1974), committee print.

Markups. U.S. House of Representatives, Select Committee on Committees, *Committee Reform Amendments of 1974,* Open Business Meetings (93rd Congress, 2nd session, 1974), committee print.

Staff Summary. U.S. House of Representatives, Select Committee on Committees, *Committee Reform Amendments of 1974,* Explanation of H. Res. 988 as Adopted by the House of Representatives, October 8, 1974 (93rd Congress, 2nd session, 1974).

CHAPTER 1

1. The historical concern over "congressional reform" is analyzed in Roger H. Davidson, David M. Kovenock, and Michael O'Leary, *Congress in Crisis: Politics and Congressional Reform* (Belmont, Calif.: Wadsworth Publishing Co., 1966), especially chapters 1–2. Since that volume was published systematic studies of the subject have become somewhat more numerous. An excellent recent collection is: Norman Ornstein, ed., *Congress in Change: Evolution and Reform* (New York: Praeger, 1975).

2. Louis Hartz, *The Liberal Tradition in America* (New York: Harcourt, Brace, 1955), especially chapter 1 and pp. 228–237.

3. James Q. Wilson, "Abolishing 'Reform'," *Washington Post,* April 14, 1975, p. A22.

4. Mary McInnis, ed., *We Propose: A Modern Congress* (New York: McGraw-Hill, 1966), p. xii.

5. Joseph S. Clark, *Congress: The Sapless Branch* (New York: Harper and Row, 1964)), p. xv.

6. Bruce R. Hopkins, "Congressional Reform: Toward a Modern Congress," *Notre Dame Lawyer* (February 1972), p. 443.

7. *Congressional Record,* 45, 61st Cong., 2nd sess., March 19, 1910, 3430.

8. *Washington Post,* March 3, 1963, p. E3.

9. *New York Times,* June 25, 1975, p. 36.

10. U.S. Congress, Joint Committee on Congressional Operations, *Congress and Mass Communications: An Institutional Perspective,* A Study Conducted by the Congressional Research Service, 93rd Cong., 2nd sess., 1974.

11. A. S. Mike Monroney et al., *The Strengthening of American Political Institutions* (Ithaca, N.Y.: Cornell University Press, 1949), p. 9.

12. U.S. Congress, Joint Committee on the Organization of Congress, *Organization of Congress, Hearings,* 79th Cong., 1st sess., 1945, p. 88.

13. Ibid., p. 96.

14. Ibid., p. 240.

15. Jerry Voorhis, "Congress and the Future," in U.S. Congress, Joint Committee on the Organization of Congress, *The Organization of Congress, Symposium on Congress,* 79th Cong., 1st. sess., August 1945, p. 287.

16. *Final Report,* p. 19.

17. *Congressional Record,* 92, 79th Cong., 2nd sess., July 25, 1946, 10040.

18. *Organization of Congress,* p. 288.

19. *Congressional Record,* 91, 79th Cong., 2nd sess., July 12, 1945, A3408.

20. *Hearings,* I, p. 357.

21. Hugh Bone, *Party Committees and National Politics* (Seattle: University of Washington Press, 1956), p. 168.

22. Madeline Wing Adler, "Congressional Reform: An Exploratory Case," unpublished Ph.D. dissertation, University of Wisconsin, 1969, p. 45.

23. Richard Bolling, *House Out of Order* (New York: E. P. Dutton, 1965), p. 233.

24. *Congressional Record,* 122, 94th Cong., 1st sess., June 19, 1975, E3317.

25. Gary Orfield, *Congressional Power: Congress and Social Change* (New York: Harcourt Brace Jovanovich, 1975), pp. 12, 18.

26. *The Reorganization of Congress,* A Report of the Committee on Congress of the American Political Science Association (Washington, D.C.: Public Affairs Press, 1945), p. 4.

27. *Congressional Record,* 116, 91st Cong., 2nd sess., September 15, 1970, 31842.

28. *Congressional Record,* 119, 93rd Cong., 1st sess., January 26, 1973, S1391.

CHAPTER 2

1. Woodrow Wilson, *Congressional Government* (New York: Meridian Books edition, 1956), p. 210.

2. Late in 1974 a long-awaited compilation was published: U.S. House of Representatives, *Deschler's Procedure: A Summary of the Modern Precedents and Practices of the U.S. House of Representatives, 86 Congress-93 Congress* (Washington, D.C.: Government Printing Office, 1974).

3. Max Farrand, ed., *The Records of the Federal Convention of 1787* (New Haven: Yale University Press, 1911), I, p. 49.

4. George B. Galloway, *History of the House of Representatives* (New York: Thomas Y. Crowell, 1961), p. 67. A complete listing of House committees appears in *Final Report,* Appendix A.

5. Testimony before the La Follette-Monroney Committee in 1945, cited in Galloway, p. 122.

6. Mary Parker Follett, *The Speaker of the House of Representatives* (New York: Longmans, Green, 1896), p. 246.

7. Neil MacNeil, *Forge of Democracy* (New York: David McKay, 1963), p. 68.

8. Joseph Cooper, "The Origins of the Standing Committees and the Development of the Modern House," *Rice University Studies* 56 (Summer 1970), p. 64.

9. Other students of the House tend to focus on individual Speakers, most notably Reed and Cannon. It is true the development of the office was uneven,

and decentralization often prevailed—especially in the years immediately preceding Reed's speakership. However, the trend was too broad to be attributed solely to a few forceful personalities; as we will indicate, deeper forces were at work. The strong speakership has been chronicled by a pioneering political scientist in one of the most remarkable and perceptive books ever written about Congress. See Follett.

10. Follett, p. 288.

11. Cited in Galloway, p. 133.

12. Wilson, p. 80.

13. Henry Cabot Lodge, "The Coming Congress," *North American Review* 149 (September 1889), p. 293.

14. L. White Busbey, *Uncle Joe Cannon: The Story of a Pioneer American* (New York: Henry Holt, 1927), p. 168.

15. Thomas B. Reed, "Obstruction in the National House," *North American Review* 149 (October 1889), p. 428.

16. *Congressional Record*, 21, 51st Cong., 1st sess., January 29, 1890, 949–950, and January 30, 1890, 21, 978ff.

17. Ibid., January 31, 1890, 21, 999.

18. William A. Robinson, *Thomas B. Reed: Parliamentarian* (New York: Dodd, Mead, 1930), pp. 233–234.

19. Chang-wei Chiu, *The Speaker of the House of Representatives since 1896* (New York: Columbia University Press, 1928), pp. 67, 70–71.

20. Nelson W. Polsby, Miriam Gallagher, and Barry S. Rundquist, "The Growth of the Seniority System in the U.S. House of Representatives," *American Political Science Review* 63 (September 1969), p. 794.

21. For a similar characterization of the situation, see Charles O. Jones, "Joseph G. Cannon and Howard W. Smith: An Essay on the Limits of Leadership in the House of Representatives," *Journal of Politics* 30 (August 1968), pp. 617–646.

22. Quoted in Booth Mooney, *Mr. Speaker* (Chicago: Follett Publishing Co., 1964), p. 104.

23. Kenneth Hechler, *Insurgency* (New York: Columbia University Press, 1940), pp. 49–65.

24. *Congressional Record*, 45, 61st Cong., 2nd sess., March 16, 1910, 3243.

25. Ibid., 3251.

26. Ibid., March 17, 1910, 3292.

27. Ibid., March 19, 1910, 3436.

28. Jones, "Cannon and Smith."

29. *Congressional Record*, 45, 61st Cong., 2nd sess., March 17, 1910, 3294.

30. Ibid., 3304.

31. Ibid., March 19, 1910, 3428.

32. Ibid., 3437; and see Busbey, pp. 265–266.

33. George Rothwell Brown, *The Leadership of Congress* (Indianapolis: Bobbs-Merrill, 1922), pp. 193, 202, 205.

34. Polsby et al., pp. 787–791.

35. Robert Luce, *Congress: An Explanation* (Cambridge, Mass.: Harvard University Press, 1926), p. 117.

36. Chiu, pp. 147, 163, and *passim*.

37. James A. Robinson, *The House Rules Committee* (Indianapolis: Bobbs-Merrill, 1963); and several unpublished papers by Walter Kravitz of the Congressional Research Service, Library of Congress.

38. Richard Bolling, *House Out of Order* (New York: E. P. Dutton, 1965), p. 220. A member of Rules since 1955, Bolling describes the committee's politics in detail in ibid., pp. 195–220.

39. *Congressional Record*, 45, 61st Cong., 2nd sess., March 19, 1910, 3321.

40. William Willoughby, *Principles of Legislative Organization and Administration* (Washington, D.C.: The Brookings Institution, 1934), p. 568.

41. Roland Young, *This Is Congress* (New York: Knopf, 1943), p. 95.

42. Busbey, p. 138.

43. Chiu, p. 316.

44. Galloway, p. 95.

45. Nelson W. Polsby, "The Institutionalization of the U.S. House of Representatives," *American Political Science Review* 62 (September 1968), p. 556.

46. Ibid.

47. The findings are summarized in Polsby et al., pp. 790–791.

48. Quoted in Richard F. Fenno, Jr., *Congressmen in Committees* (Boston: Little, Brown, 1973), p. 136.

49. For exposition of the "four-party" thesis, see James MacGregor Burns, *The Deadlock of Democracy* (Englewood Cliffs, N.J.: Prentice-Hall, 1963).

50. Barbara Hinckley, *The Seniority System in Congress* (Bloomington: Indiana University Press, 1971), p. 41. We are indebted to Hinckley for enhancing our understanding of the seniority system; however, as the reader will perceive, we are less sanguine than Hinckley about the effects of the system, at least in the 1937–1965 period.

51. Hinckley, pp. 75–76.

52. James MacGregor Burns, *Roosevelt: The Lion and the Fox* (New York: Harcourt, Brace, 1956), especially pp. 337–342.

53. Democratic Study Group, "Voting in the House" (March 10, 1969), reprinted in *Congressional Record*, 155, 91st Cong., 1st sess., March 18, 1969, E2108–2111.

54. Hinckley, p. 109.

55. Ibid., pp. 60–62.

56. Ibid., p. 32. Raymond E. Wolfinger and Joan Heifetz Hollinger, "Safe Seats, Seniority and Power in Congress," *American Political Science Review* 59 (June 1965), p. 343.

57. Hinckley, p. 40.

58. Ibid., p. 39; Wolfinger and Hollinger, p. 349.

59. Everett G. Burkhalter in *Congressional Quarterly Weekly Report* 22 (April 10, 1964), p. 690.

60. Fenno, p. 77.

61. Cited in ibid., p. 132.

62. Ibid., p. 136.

63. The close linkage between congressional reformism, liberalism, and the "responsible parties" doctrine was demonstrated in a survey of reform sentiment during the 88th Congress. See Roger H. Davidson, David M. Kovenock, and Michael K. O'Leary, *Congress in Crisis: Politics and Congressional Reform* (Belmont, Calif.: Wadsworth Publishing Co., 1966), pp. 72–73, 81–80, and *passim*.

64. Accounts of these Democratic caucus developments are found in: John F. Bibby and Roger H. Davidson, *On Capitol Hill: Studies in the Legislative Process* (New York: Holt, Rinehart & Winston, 1967), pp. 153–167; and (Hinsdale, Ill.: Dryden Press, 1972, 2nd edition), pp. 170–174.

65. In addition to the above sources, see Norman J. Ornstein, "Causes and Consequences of Congressional Change: Subcommittee Reforms in the House of Representatives, 1970–1973," in Ornstein, ed., *Congress in Change: Evolution and Reform* (New York: Praeger, 1975), pp. 88–114.

66. Ibid., p. 92.

67. The liberals were Phillip Burton (Calif.), James G. O'Hara (Mich.), Frank Thompson (N.J.), and Shirley Chisholm (N.Y.). The moderates were Mrs. Hansen, Wayne Hays (Ohio), Frank Annunzio (Ill.), and Neal Smith (Iowa). The southerners were Phil Landrum (Ga.), Olin Teague (Tex.), and Ed Jones (Tenn.).

68. Figures from H. Rept. 93–916, Appendix B.

69. See Ornstein, pp. 93–100, for an account of the origins of the subcommittee reforms.

70. An account of the "subcommittee bill of rights" is found in David W. Rohde, "Committee Reform in the House of Representatives and the Subcommittee Bill of Rights," *Annals of the American Academy of Political and Social Sciences* 411 (January 1974), pp. 43ff.

71. Ornstein, pp. 102–103.

72. John Maffre, "New Leaders, Staff Changes Stimulate House Foreign Affairs Committee," *National Journal* 3 (June 19, 1971), pp. 1314–1322.

73. *House Rules and Manual* (93rd Cong., 1st sess., 1973), Section 850.

74. George B. Galloway, *The Legislative Process in Congress* (New York: Thomas Y. Crowell, 1955), p. 591.

75. Joint Committee on the Organization of the Congress, *Organization of Congress*, Final Report, S. Rept. 89–1414 (89th Cong., 2nd sess., 1966).

76. *Final Report*, Appendix C.

77. S. Rept. 89–1414, p. 18.

78. *Final Report*, p. 247.

79. *Committee Monographs*, p. 77.

80. *Final Report*, pp. 247–255.

81. See, for example, *Committee Monographs*, pp. 8, 16, 55.

82. *Final Report*, p. 259.

83. See *Committee Monographs,* pp. 113–114.

84. *Final Report,* p. 263.

85. Ibid., pp. 265–266.

86. David W. Brady, *Congressional Voting in a Partisan Era* (Lawrence: University Press of Kansas, 1972), p. 190 and passim.

87. See Austin Ranney, *The Doctrine of Responsible Party Government* (Urbana: University of Illinois Press, 1962), p. 59.

88. Moisei Ostrogorski, *Democracy and the Party System in the United States* (New York: Macmillan, 1910), p. 292.

CHAPTER 3

1. *Hearings,* III, p. 373.

2. Woodrow Wilson, *Congressional Government* (New York: Meridian Books edition, 1956), p. 59.

3. Bertram M. Gross, *The Legislative Struggle* (New York: McGraw-Hill, 1953), p. 266.

4. U.S. Congress, Joint Committee on the Organization of Congress, *Organization of the Congress,* S. Rept. 1011 (79th Cong., 2nd sess., March 4, 1946), p. 2.

5. John Culver, "Dear Colleague" letter to all representatives (December 22, 1972).

6. *Hearings,* I, p. 533.

7. *Roll Call* (June 27, 1974), p. 2.

8. *Final Report,* p. 19.

9. *Hearings,* I, pp. 28–29.

10. Ibid., p. 154.

11. *Congressional Record,* 119, 93rd Cong., 1st sess., January 31, 1973, H602 (daily edition).

12. *Final Report,* 13.

13. *Congressional Record,* 119, 93rd Cong., 1st sess., June 19, 1973, H5321 (daily edition).

14. Ibid., March 12, 1973, E1476 (daily edition).

15. *New York Times* (October 3, 1974), p. 37.

16. *Washington Post* (November 26, 1972), p. B7.

17. *Los Angeles Times* (October 26, 1975), p. 17.

18. *Hearings,* I, p. 5.

19. Ibid., I, p. 42.

20. *Congressional Record,* 119, 93rd Cong., 1st sess., January 31, 1973, H597 (daily edition).

21. Ibid., H602.

22. Ibid., H592.

23. Ibid., H591.

24. Ibid.

25. Ibid., H595.

26. Ibid., H594.

27. "Liberalism" rankings are drawn from *Congressional Quarterly's* "Opposition to Conservative Coalition" scores, with the figures recomputed to eliminate the effect of absences from the House floor. *Congressional Quarterly Weekly Report* 30 (November 18, 1972), pp. 3022–3027.

28. *Congressional Record,* 119, 93rd Cong., 1st sess., January 31, 1973, H594 (daily edition).

29. Hearings before the House Committee on Rules on granting a "rule" to the Committee Reform Amendments of 1974 (H. Res. 988), September 19, 1974 (unpublished transcript).

CHAPTER 4

1. *Hearings,* I, pp. 3, 10.

2. Ibid., pp. 2–3.

3. Ibid., p. 10.

4. Ibid., pp. 4–5.

5. Ibid., pp. 26–27.

6. Ibid., p. 9.

7. Ibid., pp. 6, 15.

8. Ibid., pp. 28–29.

9. Memorandum, "Staff Recommendations concerning Hearings" (March 19, 1973), p. 1.

10. *Hearings,* III, p. 93.

11. Using a "liberalism" score (adapted from *Congressional Quarterly's* "Opposition to Conservative Coalition" score, with figures recomputed to eliminate the effect of absences from the House floor), Education and Labor ranked highest among all House committees for the 92nd Congress. The average member of Education and Labor had a "liberalism" score of 56 percent, compared to a 43 percent average for the House as a whole. For the raw score on which this comparison is based, see *Congressional Quarterly Weekly Report* 30 (November 18, 1972), pp. 3022–3027.

12. *Hearings,* I, p. 109.

13. Ibid., pp. 115–117.

14. Ibid., p. 614.

15. Ibid., p. 425.

16. Ibid., III, p. 103.

17. Ibid., p. 104.

18. Ibid., p. 111.

19. Ibid., pp. 112–113.

20. Ibid., I, p. 239.

21. Ibid., p. 269.

22. Ibid., p. 535.

23. Ibid., p. 331.

24. Ibid., pp. 383–390.

25. Ibid., p. 333.

26. Ibid., p. 589.

27. Ibid., pp. 291–321.

28. Ibid., p. 109.

29. Ibid., III, pp. 243, 273–274.

30. Ibid., p. 319.

31. Ibid., pp. 328–332.

32. Ibid., I, pp. 289–290, 393ff.; II, pp. 37–38; III, pp. 41–45, 207ff., 242ff., 271, 299–300.

33. Ibid., II, p. 271.

34. The concept of these cozy alliances is familiar to students of politics, and is in fact one of the most pervasive phenomena on the American political scene. They have been variously termed "policy whirlpools" (Ernest S. Griffith), "subgovernments" (Douglass Cater), and "cozy triangles" (Dorothy B. James). For the role these alliances play in the larger phenomenon of "interest-group liberalism," see Theodore J. Lowi, *The End of Liberalism* (New York: W. W. Norton, 1969).

35. *Hearings*, III, p. 211.

36. Morris S. Ogul, "Legislative Oversight of Bureaucracy," in *Hearings*, II, p. 701.

37. *Hearings*, I, p. 38.

38. See Roger H. Davidson, "Representation and Congressional Committees," *Annals of the American Academy of Political and Social Science* 411 (January 1974), pp. 48–62.

39. *Hearings*, I, p. 66.

40. Ibid., II, p. 21.

41. Ibid., III, p. 298.

42. Ibid., II, pp. 15–16.

43. Ibid., III, p. 320.

44. Ibid., p. 209.

45. Ibid., I, p. 361.

46. Ibid., p. 592.

47. Ibid., pp. 19–20.

48. Ibid., pp. 499–500.

49. Ibid., II, p. 506.

50. Ibid., III, p. 320.

51. Ibid., p. 325.

52. Telford Taylor, *Grand Inquest: The Story of Congressional Investigations* (New York: Simon and Schuster, 1955), pp. 21–22. Italics in the original.

53. Woodrow Wilson, *Congressional Government* (New York: Meridian Books edition, 1956), p. 198.

54. Hearings, II.

55. Richard F. Fenno, Jr., *Congressmen in Committees* (Boston: Little, Brown, 1973), pp. 289–291.

56. June 15 and 20, 1973. *Hearings*, II, pp. 83–183.

57. Ibid., p. 173.

58. Ibid., I, p. 316.

59. See Walter Shapiro, "Wilbur Mills: The Ways and Means of Conning the Press," *Washington Monthly* 6 (December 1974), pp. 4–13.

60. *Hearings*, I, p. 521.

61. Ibid., p. 524.

62. Ibid., pp. 522–523.

63. Ibid., p. 524.

64. Ibid., pp. 281–282.

65. Ibid., pp. 282–283.

66. Ibid., p. 349.

67. Ibid., p. 473.

68. Using the same "liberalism" score detailed earlier, Judiciary ranked second only to Education and Labor in "liberalism." Its members compiled a "liberalism" score of 55 percent in the 92nd Congress, compared to the House average of 43 percent. See note 11.

69. *Hearings*, I, p. 492.

70. Ibid., p. 500.

71. Ibid., p. 493.

72. Fenno, p. 31.

73. Ibid., p. 34.

74. *Hearings*, III, p. 223.

75. Ibid.

76. *Final Report*, pp. 40–42.

77. Letter dated March 26, 1973. *Hearings*, I, p. 644.

78. Ibid., p. 318.

79. Ibid., III, p. 119.

80. See ibid., I, pp. 334–340; III, pp. 17–24, 65–80, 127–163.

81. See ibid., II, pp. 525–875.

82. H. Rept. 93–916, pp. 211–366.

83. *Hearings*, III, pp. 413–578.

CHAPTER 5

1. *Committee Monographs*.

2. *Final Report*, Appendices A through N.

3. Select Committee on Committees, Staff Report (September 12, 1973), 2.

4. The "August study" is reprinted in *Hearings*, III, pp. 414–447.

5. Fraser's notion of committees as "mini-houses" is found in ibid., III, p. 42. The staff plan is reprinted in ibid., III, pp. 448–459.

6. Ibid., pp. 460–475.

7. Ibid., pp. 476–486.

8. Holbert N. Carroll, *The House of Representatives and Foreign Affairs,* rev. ed. (Boston: Little, Brown, 1966), p. 32.

9. *Final Report,* Appendix M.

10. The type of staff entrepreneurship described in Eric Redman's clever book, *The Dance of Legislation* (New York: Simon and Schuster, 1973), is as yet rarely duplicated on the House side of Capitol Hill. Redman expressed considerable impatience with House staff aides, with their innocuous titles and their limited authority. Part of the difference may be attributable to Redman's ingratiating combination of *chutzpah* and youthful exaggeration; but part unquestionably flows from the varying norms of the two bodies.

11. *Hearings,* II, pp. 488–501.

12. Ibid., III, pp. 482–486.

13. See *Committee Reform Amendments of 1974,* pp. 55–71.

14. Richard Bolling and Dave Martin, letter (September 20, 1973).

15. Much ink has been spilled about the politics of committee assignments, but relatively little is known of the mechanics of assignments. Traditional practices were described by Nicholas Masters in "Committee Assignments in the House of Representatives," *American Political Science Review* 55 (June 1961), pp. 345–357; an updated discussion is Robert Healy, "Committees and the Politics of Assignments," in Sven Groennings and Jonathan P. Hawley, eds., *To Be a Congressman: The Promise and the Power* (Washington, D.C.: Acropolis Books, 1973), pp. 99–120; and the perspectives of the assignees are probed in David W. Rohde and Kenneth A. Shepsle, "Democratic Committee Assignments in the House of Representatives," *American Political Science Review* 67 (September 1973), pp. 889–905. See also "Politics of House Committees: The Path to Power," in *Congressional Quarterly Weekly Report* 31 (February 10, 1973), pp. 279–283.

16. See Louis P. Westefield, "Majority Party Leadership and the Committee System in the House of Representatives," *American Political Science Review* 68 (December 1974), pp. 1593–1604.

17. Bolling's diagnosis of the Foreign Affairs Committee's needs closely paralleled scholarly findings. Richard F. Fenno, Jr., *Congressmen in Committees* (Boston: Little, Brown, 1973), pp. 69–73.

18. Limited home rule was granted the District of Columbia under P. L. 93–198, which cleared Congress in December 1973. In a referendum in May 1974, D.C. citizens approved the new form of government, which allowed them to select a mayor and a thirteen-member city council. But many powers were retained by Congress, including controls over spending.

19. *Draft Report.*

CHAPTER 6

1. "Rebuilding the House," *New York Times,* February 4, 1974. See also "High Time to Revamp the House," *Los Angeles Times,* December 31, 1973, p. II 4.

2. Quoted in Barbara Redding, "House Reform Shifts Lineup of Committees," *St. Petersburg Times,* March 10, 1974, p. 10-A.

3. *Markups,* II, p. 673.

4. *Final Report,* pp. 65–68.

5. *Markups,* I, p. 331.

6. H. Res. 988, Sec. 408 (a) (2).

7. *Markups,* II, p. 414.

8. Ibid., p. 594.

9. Richard Basoco, "Maritime Chiefs Seek to Rescue House Panel," *Baltimore Sun,* January 14, 1974.

10. *Letters and Statements,* pp. 106–108.

11. Ibid., pp. 132–133.

12. Ibid., p. 35.

13. Ibid., pp. 163–168.

14. Ibid., p. 123.

15. Ibid., pp. 259–267.

16. Ibid., p. 273.

17. Arthur Levine, "Getting to Know Your Congressman: The $500 Misunderstanding," *Washington Monthly* 6 (February 1975), pp. 56–59.

18. "Congressional Reform?" *Sierra Club National News Report* (February 15, 1974).

19. *Letters and Statements,* p. 309.

20. *Markups,* I, pp. 177–178.

21. Ibid., p. 9.

22. Ibid., p. 32.

23. Ibid., p. 9.

24. Ibid., p. 168.

25. Ibid., p. 174.

26. Ibid., p. 173.

27. Ibid.

28. Ibid., p. 175.

29. Ibid., p. 178.

30. Ibid., p. 179.

31. Ibid., II, p. 490.

32. *Final Report,* p. 49.

33. Richard F. Fenno, Jr., *Congressmen in Committees* (Boston: Little, Brown, 1973), p. 65.

34. Ibid., pp. 281–283.

35. *Hearings,* I, p. 136.

36. Statement by Chairman Thaddeus J. Dulski (December 7, 1973), mimeographed.

37. Joseph Young, "Young's Federal Spotlight," *Washington Star-News,* December 11, 1973, p. A2; Mike Causey, "The Federal Diary," *Washington Post,* March 20, 1974, p. G9.

38. *Letters and Statements,* p. 531.

39. Ibid., p. 492.

40. Ibid., p. 466.

41. Ibid., pp. 61–63.

42. Ibid., p. 186.

43. Fenno, p. 255.

44. Young, *Washington Star-News.*

45. Causey, *Washington Post.*

46. *Markups,* I, p. 169.

47. *Letters and Statements,* pp. 206–207.

48. *Markups,* II, pp. 576–577.

49. Ibid., p. 576.

50. Ibid., pp. 575–580. Careful readers may wonder why the interests of the absent Wiggins were protected while those of Young, absent a few moments later, were not. The answer lies both in the group's interpersonal dynamics and in the relative intensity of viewpoints on the two sides. Suffice it to say that members on both sides of the aisle understood that it would be useful for Democrats to win this issue, given the emerging intense resistance from union lobbyists and House labor Democrats.

51. *Final Report,* p. 41.

52. *Letters and Statements,* pp. 98–99.

53. Ibid., pp. 102–103.

54. Ibid., pp. 530–531.

55. Ibid., pp. 681–695.

56. "Washington Report," *American School Board Journal* (February 1974), p. 57.

57. *Letters and Statements,* p. 539.

58. *Markups,* I, p. 233.

59. Ibid., p. 234.

60. *Final Report,* pp. 34–35, 40–42.

61. *Markups,* 55, p. 486.

62. Ibid., I, p. 114.

63. Ibid., p. 111.

64. Shirley Elder, "Jealous House Powers Cool to Bolling Reform Plan," *Washington Star-News,* February 17, 1974, p. A4.

65. *Letters and Statements,* p. 173.

66. Ibid., p. 231.

67. *Markups,* I, pp. 33–34.

68. Ibid., p. 30.

69. *Letters and Statements,* p. 207.

70. Joan Claybrook and Nancy Chasen, Ralph Nader's Congress Watch, Memorandum to Members of the Select Committee on Committees (November 28, 1973), p. 1.

71. *Letters and Statements,* p. 604.

72. *Markups,* I, p. 94.

73. Ibid., p. 187.

74. *Letters and Statements,* p. 143.

75. *Markups,* I, p. 109.

76. *Letters and Statements,* pp. 40–42.
77. *Markups,* I, p. 117.
78. *Letters and Statements,* pp. 91–92.
79. *Markups,* I, p. 163.
80. Ibid., p. 236.
81. Ibid., p. 162.
82. Ibid., II, pp. 562–563.
83. Ibid., p. 567.
84. *Final Report,* p. 460.
85. *Markups,* II, p. 566.
86. *Final Report,* p. 46.
87. However, data on the problem were included as Appendix I of the Select Committee's report. See *Report,* pp. 293–301.
88. *Letters and Statements,* p. 31.
89. Ibid., pp. 129–131.
90. *Markups,* II, p. 456.
91. Ibid., p. 45.
92. Ibid., II, p. 542.
93. Ibid., p. 464.
94. *Final Report,* p. 70.
95. Irving Kristol, "The New Forgotten Man," *Wall Street Journal,* November 13, 1975, p. 12.
96. The series of letters is reprinted in *Letters and Statements,* pp. 10–24.
97. Ibid., p. 193.
98. *Markups,* II, p. 432.
99. Ibid., p. 433.
100. *Letters and Statements,* pp. 29, 64–65.
101. Quoted by Ed Zukerman, "U.S. House: Even That is Changing," *St. Paul* (Minn.) *Pioneer Press,* January 27, 1974, p. 10.
102. William Randolph Hearst, Jr., "Watchdog Committee," *Editor's Report* (Reprint from Hearst newspapers, March 3, 1974).
103. *Letters and Statements,* pp. 237–255.
104. *Markups,* II, pp. 480–481.
105. Ibid., p. 480.
106. Ibid., I, p. 143.
107. Ibid., II, p. 578.
108. Ibid., p. 663.
109. Ibid., p. 674.
110. Ibid., I, p. 175.
111. Common Cause, "Ten-Man Committee Seizes Prickly Pear, Challenges Committee Chairmen and Lobbyists," *Editorial Memorandum* (March 1974).
112. "Housecleaning in the House," *Washington Post,* April 30, 1974, p. A20.
113. David S. Broder, "House Reform and Leadership," ibid., April 28, 1974, p. C6.

CHAPTER 7

1. In an interesting use of parliamentary procedure, the Select Committee employed clause 2 of Rule XIII, wherein reports of committees on measures are referred to the appropriate calendar. In that way, the Select Committee ensured its control over H. Res. 988. If the committee had simply reported the resolution alone, H. Res. 988 would have been referred by the Parliamentarian to the Rules Committee, thus depriving the Select Committee of control over its own product.

2. *Washington Post,* April 30, 1974, p. A6.

3. Ibid., September 12, 1974, p. A7.

4. *Congressional Quarterly Weekly Report* 32 (April 27, 1974), p. 1026.

5. Ibid.

6. Ibid., p. 1027.

7. *Washington Post,* April 29, 1974, p. A21.

8. "Proposed Restructuring of Committees of the House of Representatives," Statement by the AFL-CIO Executive Council, Bal Harbour, Florida (February 25, 1974), p. 1.

9. *Washington Post,* April 29, 1974, p. A1.

10. Ibid., p. A2.

11. Ibid., April 30, 1974, p. A6.

12. *New York Times,* April 28, 1974, p. E19.

13. *Congressional Quarterly Weekly Report* 32 (April 27, 1974), p. 1028.

14. It should be noted that Democratic caucus sessions were held in secret at the time. The following material is derived from discussions with various Democratic members who attended the meetings. The Republican Conference also held its meetings in secret; but on April 29, 1975, the Conference voted 59 to 17 to open its meetings to the public. See *Congressional Record,* 121, 94th Cong., 1st sess., April 29, 1975, H3406 (daily edition). In March 1975, Democratic Representative Bill Chappell, Jr., proposed that party rules be changed to permit open caucus sessions. A large number of party members agreed with him—see *Congressional Quarterly Weekly Report* 33 (May 3, 1975), p. 914—and the sessions were opened to the public later in the year.

15. *Congressional Record,* 120, 93rd Cong., 2nd sess., May 1, 1974, H3465 (daily edition).

16. *New York Times,* May 10, 1974, p. 45.

17. *Congressional Quarterly Weekly Report,* 32 (May 18, 1974), p. 1308.

18. *Congressional Record,* 120, 93rd Cong., 2nd sess., May 15, 1974, E3008 (daily edition).

19. Ibid., June 27, 1974, H5841–H5844 (daily edition).

20. *Congressional Quarterly Weekly Report* 31 (January 20, 1973), pp. 70–71. Also see Norman J. Ornstein, "Causes and Consequences of Congressional Change: Subcommittee Reforms in the House of Representatives, 1970–1973," in Ornstein, ed., *Congress in Change: Evolution and Reform* (New York: Praeger, 1975), pp. 88–114; and David Rohde, "Committee Reform in

the House of Representatives and the Subcommittee Bill of Rights," *Annals of the American Academy of Political and Social Science* 411 (January 1974), pp. 39–47.

21. *Washington Post,* July 15, 1974, p. A2.

22. *Roll Call,* July 25, 1974, p. 1.

23. *Washington Post,* July 18, 1974, p. A19.

24. Douglass Cater, *Power in Washington* (New York: Random House, 1964), p. 17. Also see Theodore J. Lowi, *The End of Liberalism* (New York: Norton, 1969), and J. Leiper Freeman, *The Political Process: Executive Bureau-Legislative Committee Relations,* rev. ed. (New York: Random House, 1965).

Chapter 8

1. The items cited in this paragraph were just a few of the many that appeared in a similar vein: Jack Anderson and Les Whitten, "Congressional Reform in Trouble," *Miami* (Florida) *Herald,* August 24, 1974; Editorial, "Putting Congress Back in the Picture," *Newsday,* August 25, 1974; Editorial, "Lip Service to Reform," *Los Angeles Times,* September 3, 1974, II, p. 3; Editorial, "House Must Enact Full Reform Now," *Lansing* (Mich.) *Journal,* September 3, 1974.

2. Our account of the proceedings before the Rules Committee is based on personal observation and on the unpublished transcripts of the session, on file with the Rules Committee.

3. A detailed comparison of all three resolutions can be found in *Congressional Record,* 120, 93rd Cong., 2nd sess., September 30, 1974, H9606–H9610.

4. *Patent Trader* (Mt. Kisco, N.Y.), September 21, 1974, p. 12.

5. See, for example, Donald R. Matthews and James A. Stimson, "Decision-Making by U.S. Representatives: A Preliminary Model," in S. Sidney Ulmer, ed., *Political Decision Making* (New York: Van Nostrand Reinhold, 1970), pp. 14–43.

6. The first day's debate is recorded in *Congressional Record,* 120, 93rd Cong., 2nd sess., September 30, 1974, H9599–H9657.

7. The second day's debate is recorded in ibid., October 1, 1974, H9703–H9743.

8. *Washington Post,* October 2, 1974, p. A4.

9. *Congressional Quarterly Weekly Report* 33, February 22, 1975, p. 380.

10. *Congressional Record,* 120, 93rd Cong., 2nd sess., October 1, 1974, H9734.

11. The third day's proceedings are recorded in ibid., October 2, 1974, H9797–H9819.

12. The fourth day's proceedings are in ibid., October 3, 1974, H9890–H9903.

13. *Wall Street Journal,* October 4, 1974, p. 14.

14. *Washington Post*, October 4, 1974, p. A 4.

15. *Congressional Record*, 120, 93rd Cong., 2nd sess., October 7, 1974, H10009–H10013.

16. The final day's debate is recorded in ibid., October 8, 1974, H10105–H10120; H10146–H10169.

17. Committee chairmen who voted for the Hansen substitute included: Poage (Agriculture); Ullman (Ways and Means); Diggs (District of Columbia); Perkins (Education and Labor); Holifield (Government Operations); Hays (House Administration); Haley (Interior); Ichord (Internal Security); Staggers (Commerce); Rodino (Judiciary); Sullivan (Merchant Marine); Madden (Rules); and Price (Standards of Official Conduct). The two chairmen who supported the Select Committee were Mahon (Appropriations) and Morgan (Foreign Affairs). Seven chairmen did not vote: Hébert (Armed Services); Patman (Banking and Currency); Dulski (Post Office); Blatnik (Public Works); Teague (Science and Astronautics); Dorn (Veterans' Affairs); and Mills (Ways and Means). Ullman is included because he was serving as acting chairman of Ways and Means in Mills's absence.

18. The vote was on adoption of the Hansen substitute to H. Res. 988. *Congressional Record*, 120, 93rd Cong., 2nd sess., October 8, 1974, H10168–69. "Liberalism" rankings were drawn from *Congressional Quarterly's* "Opposition to Conservative Coalition" scores, with the figures recomputed to eliminate the effect of absences from the House floor. The vote, which was a test of the relative strength of the Bolling and Hansen plans, was not itself a "conservative coalition" vote. *Congressional Quarterly Weekly Report*, 33, January 25, 1975, pp. 189–194.

19. The entire correspondence between Bolling and Brademas was reprinted in *Congressional Record*, 120, 93rd Cong., 2nd sess., December 3, 1974, E6912–E6913.

20. Ibid., E6912.

21. Committee on Organization, Study and Review, *Summary of Major Changes in Rules X and XI of the Rules of the House of Representatives*, October 10, 1974.

22. *Congressional Record*, 120, 93rd Cong., 2nd sess., October 16, 1974, E6574–75.

Chapter 9

1. *St. Joseph* (Mo.) *News-Press*, October 28, 1974, p. 5.

2. *New York Times*, December 5, 1974, pp. 1, 42.

3. *Congressional Record*, 121, 94th Cong., 1st sess., March 10, 1975, H1492.

4. *Washington Post*, January 22, 1975, p. A2.

5. Quoted by David S. Broder, "Congress' Talk of Leadership: Well, What Happened to It?" *Los Angeles Times*, June 9, 1975, p. II7.

6. *Congressional Record*, 121, 9th Cong., 1st sess., June 11, 1975, H5279.

7. Ibid., April 22, 1975, H3072.

8. David E. Rosenbaum, "Albert Concedes Congress' Failure to Achieve Goals," *New York Times*, June 22, 1975, p. 1.

9. Hearings before the Rules Committee on H.R. 7108 (June 11, 1975), p. 37 (unpublished transcript).

10. Hearings before the Rules Committee on H.R. 6860 (June 3, 1975), p. 55 (unpublished transcript).

11. *Los Angeles Times*, February 13, 1976, p. 7.

12. *Congressional Record*, 122, 94th Cong., 2nd sess., February 17, 1976, H1078.

13. *Los Angeles Times*, February 1, 1976, p. 3.

14. *Roll Call*, December 18, 1975, p. 5.

15. *Congressional Quarterly Weekly Report* 34, January 17, 1976, p. 100.

16. Joint Committee on the Organization of the Congress, *Organization of Congress*, Hearings (89th Cong., 1st sess., 1965), p. 1630.

INDEX